I0729687

The Art and Life of
Francesca Alexander

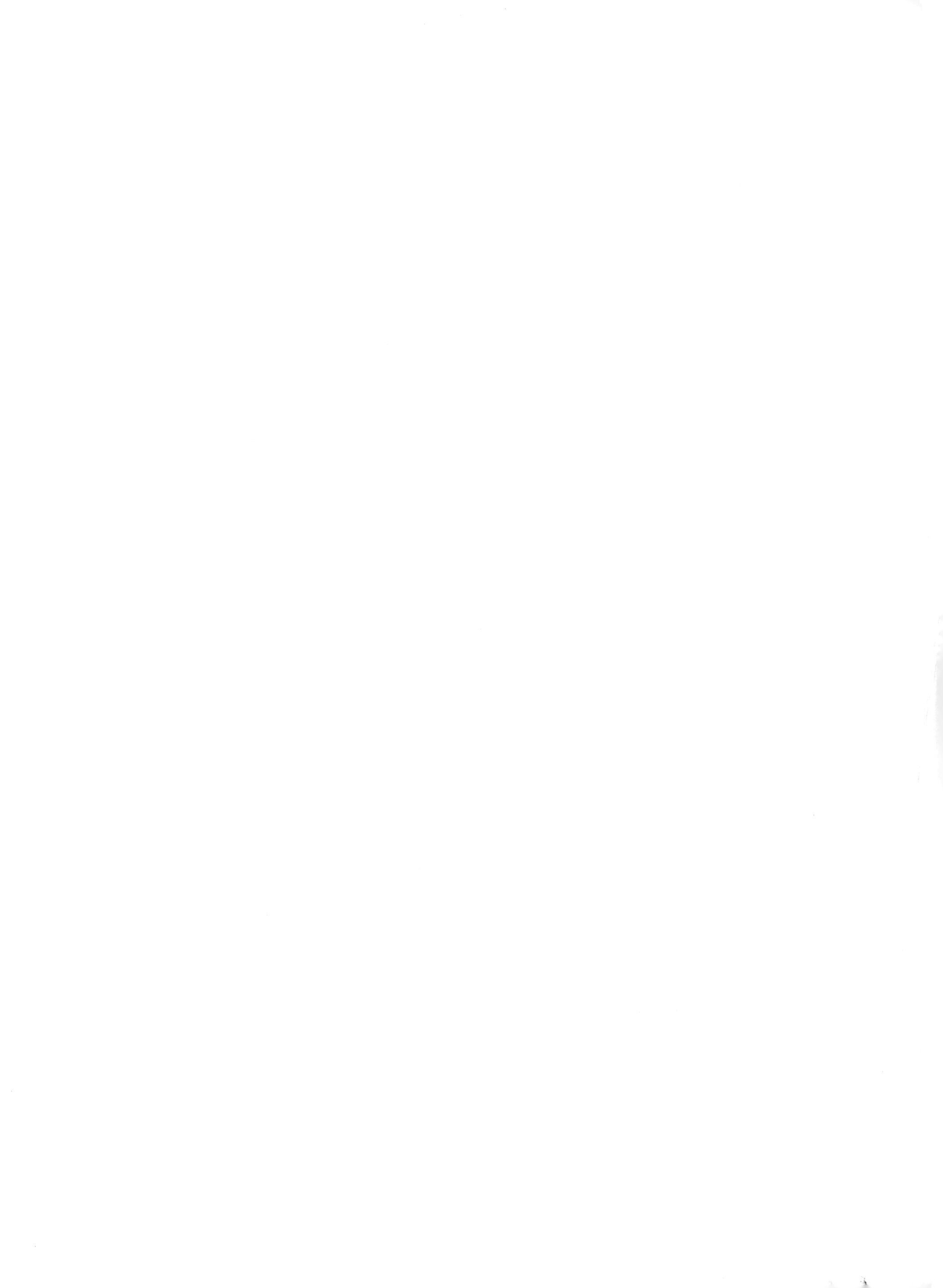

The Art and Life of Francesca Alexander
1837–1917

Jacqueline Marie Musacchio

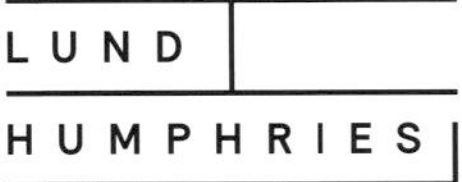

For Tony, Primo and Secondo

First published in 2025 by Lund Humphries

Lund Humphries
Huckletree Shoreditch
Alphabeta Building
18 Finsbury Square
London EC2A 1AH
UK

www.lundhumphries.com

The Art and Life of Francesca Alexander © Jacqueline Marie Musacchio, 2025

ISBN: 978-1-84822-636-4

A Cataloguing-in-Publication record for this book is available from the British Library.

Copy edited by Julie Gunz
Project managed and designed by Crow Books
Set in Adobe Caslon Pro
Printed in Bosnia and Herzegovina

With generous support from the Tavolozza Foundation

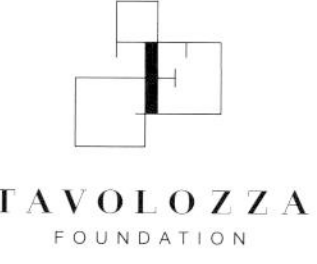

Front cover: Francesca Alexander, *Decorating a Shrine* (detail), 1865, oil on canvas, 125.2 × 93 cm (49 ¼ × 36 ⅝ in), Isabella Stewart Gardner Museum, Boston, MA
Back cover: Francesca Alexander, preface with view of Piazza Santa Maria Novella (detail), folio from 'Tuscan Songs', 1882, ink on paper, 37.8 × 27.6 cm (14 ⅞ × 10 ⅞ in), Collection of Deborah and Joseph Goldyne

Contents

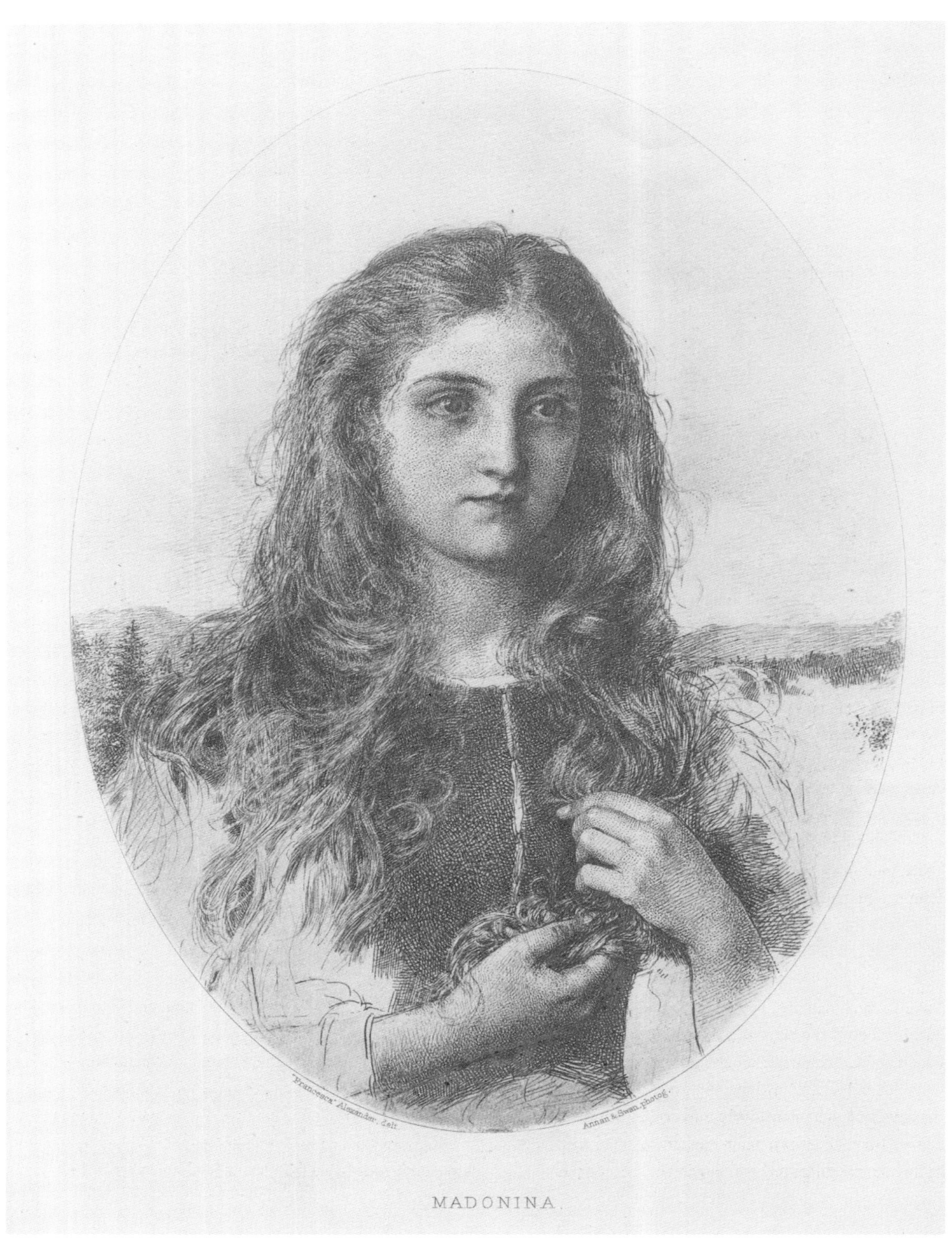

1 After Francesca Alexander, *Madonnina*, from *The Magazine of Art*, 1889, photogravure by Annan & Swan,
16.5 × 23 cm (6½ × 9 in), private collection

Prologue

And so this gentle lady – like a modern saint – has pursued her life, almost hermit-like to the outer world, among the glories, mediaeval and renaissance, of Florentine Italy. Her drawings, her plants, and her poor; her mother and her nurse; her religion and her poetry: these are all in all to her.

Marion H. Spielmann, 1895[1]

This 'modern saint' was the artist, author and philanthropist Esther Frances Alexander (1837–1917), better known as Francesca. Spielmann, an influential Victorian art critic, described her as inexorably linked to Italy's past and, with her charitable outreach to the Italians she referred to as 'her poor', its present, too, all while exemplifying devotion to art, nature, family and God. Spielmann exaggerated for dramatic effect, but he was not alone in bestowing this kind of praise. Although Francesca has largely disappeared from history, she was a celebrity during her lifetime. Her drawings, paintings and books were in great demand, her friendship with John Ruskin brought her wide recognition, her charity improved the lives of hundreds of Italians, and her home in Florence, and Francesca herself, were popular attractions for many Anglo-American travelers.

* * *

For much of the nineteenth century, Italy was not a unified country but instead a collection of states roiled by the Risorgimento, a protracted movement for unification and independence that resulted in massive political, economic and social upheaval. Some of this turmoil began years earlier when Europe's map was reconfigured following the end of the Napoleonic Wars in 1815, but it intensified as the century unfolded. Although this made life difficult for Italians, it meant that Italy was an affordable destination for Anglo-Americans like the Alexanders. Some went to take advantage of this financial respite, while others went for the supposed health benefits of the temperate climate, and still others for the prestige associated with an international experience during a period when transatlantic and transcontinental travel were still uncommon. Quite a few of these travelers were artists, and for them Italy provided contact with original works of art, training, materials and models, in quantities that were not available in the United States. It also provided a steady flow of compatriots who were eager to visit their studios and purchase their art while abroad.

But Francesca's experience was different from that of other Anglo-Americans in Italy, male or female, artist or not. She was 16 in 1853 when she left Boston with her father Francis Alexander (1800–80) and her mother Lucia Gray Swett (1814–1916). Funds from her father's painting career, and her mother's maritime family fortune, easily supported their Italian life. Although Francesca's family background and wealth would have made her a prime candidate for the marriage market, there is no evidence that her parents sought to find her a husband, either before they left Boston or after they arrived in Italy. Instead, Francesca lived her life as what was then defined as a spinster, as devoted to her parents as they were to her. While abroad they maintained their Boston relationships, through letters – which could take two weeks or more in transit – and in person when friends and acquaintances traveled to Italy. Moreover, although most Anglo-Americans stayed in Italy for a few weeks or months, the Alexanders lived there the rest of their lives, returning to the United States only once.

Like all transplanted Anglo-Americans, the Alexanders were viewed with curiosity and envy by travelers, who either plotted their own itineraries or were wrangled by the growing number of tour operators like Thomas Cook and S. Russell Forbes. The fictional Reverend Cuthbert Eager in E.M. Forster's novel *A Room with a View* (1908) was a stereotype of these residents, based on Forster's keen observations during a 1901 visit to Florence; Forster stayed briefly at the Hotel Bonciani, where the Alexanders lived for almost 50 years, before he switched to lodgings on the Arno for the much-desired view. He wrote that Reverend Eager and other residents were privy to experiences mere travelers could not access:

> [They] knew the people who never walked about with Baedekers, who had learnt to take a siesta after lunch, who took drives the pension tourists had never heard of, and saw by private influence galleries which were closed to them. Living in delicate seclusion, some in furnished flats, others in Renaissance villas on Fiesole's slope, they read, wrote, studied, and exchanged ideas, thus attaining to that intimate knowledge, or perception, of Florence which is denied to all who carry in their pockets the coupons of Cook.[2]

As part of this expatriate community, the Alexanders led a similarly charmed life. Francesca quickly grew to love everything about Florence and living there was vital to the development of her art. She drew under her father's tutelage before they moved abroad, but she never had formal lessons and as a result her rendering of anatomy and perspective were often problematic. She always preferred pen and ink, although she also painted and occasionally made prints. She was at her best when focused on the natural world – she was an amateur botanist – and portraits of the Italians she knew in Florence and in the more remote areas of the country where the family spent their summers.

One of those portraits is the *Madonnina*, rendered with her distinctive combination of fine lines and stippling and widely circulated through reproduction in a popular London arts journal (fig.1).[3] It represents her 14-year-old friend Emilia Pistolesi, a *contadina* or farm worker who was one of Francesca's 'poor' and for a time her favorite model for representations of the Virgin Mary, although Emilia confessed her greatest ambition in life was to marry a baker so she would always have bread.[4] Francesca portrayed her with an aura of solemnity and sanctity. Emilia wears a simple buttoned bodice over a tunic, and she twists the dark hair cascading in waves over her shoulders as she stares into the distance. Through her friendship with Italians like Emilia, Francesca learned their stories and songs, which she transcribed, translated, illustrated and eventually shared with an enthusiastic international audience.

The Alexanders' relationships with Italians like Emilia set them apart from most Anglo-Americans, whose interest in Italy was often at odds with their antipathy toward or their feelings of superiority over actual Italians. Many Protestant New Englanders, who comprised a significant percentage of Francesca's friends and patrons, were both anti-Italian and anti-Catholic, a prejudice acquired not only from their interactions with immigrants but also from their home pulpits. The Alexanders, though devout Evangelical Christians, occasionally attended Catholic services and were unusually sympathetic to the Italians they encountered. Several worked for them for decades, the most important being Eduvige, or Edwige, Gualtieri, the nurse Spielmann referenced. Edwige's life had been difficult; she had been forced to work a variety of debilitating jobs after she was widowed with five young daughters during the 1855 cholera epidemic. But her situation improved when the Alexanders employed her as a companion for Francesca in 1860, a position that turned into a combination housekeeper and family member until her death in 1899. When Edwige grew too infirm to manage household duties, her relatives stepped in to take her place.

But the Gualtieri were not the only Italians Francesca knew and loved. She focused much of her efforts on providing needy Italians with charity, using the money she made selling her art and books, as well as donations from her Anglo-American friends. Many of those friends donated not so much to help Italians but instead to support Francesca's efforts; her enthusiasm was infectious. Today her activities might be seen as indicative of a savior complex, but her empathy was genuine and her charity was essential for those who received it. She understood her work as a duty aligned with her religious faith, and hoped others would do the same. She emphasized this in a letter to William Dean Howells, an author and former United States consul in Venice, when praising the publication of his 11-year-old daughter's drawings in *A Little Girl Among the Old Masters* (1884): 'I do hope [Mildred] will go on and "follow her star", as the Italians say, and live to do much for the Lord's service; for I do believe that art may be used for his service, as well as all his other gifts to us.'[5]

The Alexanders' Italian friends also included members of the nobility and the cultural, religious and political elite, from Princess Luisa Rasponi Murat, the niece of Napoleon I and daughter of the former King and Queen of the Two Sicilies, to the poet Vittoria Aganoor, the Patriarch of Venice Domenico Cardinal Agostini, and General Giuseppe

Garibaldi. Some, like the patriot Giuseppe Barellai, wrote poems celebrating Francesca, as did American poets James Russell Lowell and John Greenleaf Whittier. The English Henry Edward Cardinal Manning commended her piety and even compared her writing to that of Saint Francis of Assisi. American artists, including Thomas Ball and Henry Roderick Newman, and British artists, including William Holman Hunt, Frederic Leighton and George Frederick Watts, praised her paintings and drawings. Although she rarely promoted her creative efforts, she never lacked patrons and admirers. And, like Spielmann, both friends and strangers regularly commented on her inherent innocence and saintly demeanor, qualities that aligned her with contemporary delight in a romanticized view of Italy's past.

Francis Alexander died in 1880, leaving his bereft wife and daughter questioning their future in Italy. But their lives were transformed in 1882 when they met the influential English aesthete John Ruskin during his last visit to Florence. Following this they carried on an intense correspondence that ended in the decade before Ruskin's death in 1900 only because he was too ill to continue.

Ruskin was fascinated by Francesca. Her great love of nature and her portrayal of Italian life in both art and text accorded well with his own interests, and he admired her charitable work and her piety. Although he tried to influence her art, he had no real impact; her style and subjects remained unchanged throughout her life. His influence, instead, was on her reputation; he shepherded her first three books to press – at times with a heavy editorial hand – and he praised her in his lectures and publications. The Alexanders were always popular with the Americans, and especially the Bostonians, who traveled to Florence. But following the meeting with Ruskin, Francesca became a celebrity on both sides of the Atlantic; according to fellow Florence resident and bibliophile Willard Fiske, she was 'Ruskined into fame'.[6] Her books were widely read, and travelers sought her out in the same way they sought out Florence's churches and museums. They climbed to her rooftop studio and garden to watch her work, and they left with a drawing or a flower, thrilled to have met the artist who so captivated Ruskin and exemplified his aesthetic and social ideals. She was known as Fanny from birth, although her Italian and Italophile friends called her by the Italianized Francesca. But once Ruskin published her first book under that name in 1883, everyone used it. I refer to her as Fanny up to that point in my narrative, but after it I use Francesca, too.

This fame did not last. By the early twentieth century, interest in Italy and its history was waning. The focus of the art community shifted to modernism – as far removed as possible from Francesca's painstakingly rendered flowers and figures – as the world shifted to new modes of technology, communication and of course war. Francesca continued her art and charity as long as she could, but her last decades were plagued by declining health and deteriorating vision that made creative efforts almost impossible. The Alexander women had always been inseparable, so it is no surprise that they died only eight months apart, Lucia in 1916 at age 102, and Francesca in 1917 at age 79.

Since then, knowledge of Francesca has faded. She created most of her work in Italy, outside of the market driven by galleries and exhibitions, so she appears only infrequently in scholarship and exhibitions on American art and Americans in Italy. She also appears infrequently in scholarship on Pre-Raphaelite women artists, more for her relationship with Ruskin rather than any affinity with that group. During her lifetime, her books about the Italians she knew and loved – *The Story of Ida* (1883), *Roadside Songs of Tuscany* (1885), *Christ's Folk in the Apennine* (1887), *Tuscan Songs* (1897), and *Hidden Servants* (1900) – went through multiple editions in the United States and England, and several of her stories were translated into Italian and published in cheaply printed booklets. These have all been long out of print, although scholars examining Italian folklore reference them occasionally.

Two biographies by Francesca's cousins provide uncritical and at times inaccurate narratives. The first of these is *Francesca Alexander. A 'Hidden Servant'* (1927) by Constance Grosvenor Alexander. She lived in Florence as a child in the 1870s while her father worked for the American Board of Foreign Missions and returned to visit the Alexander women several times as an adult. Her sympathetic portrayal was criticized by the book's designer as 'a foolish futile performance – all right perhaps for a private, family memorial, but of no earthly value to anyone else'.[7] The second biography is *John Ruskin's Letters to Francesca and Memoirs of the Alexanders* (1931) by Lucia Gray Swett (named after Francesca's mother), who incorporated lengthy quotes from the Ruskin correspondence into her account. Both biographies stress the image of Francesca as isolated from the wider world, dominated by a controlling mother and unable to function on her own, which was not entirely true; Francesca's life was much more complex, and much more connected to those around her. But these biographies have been cited extensively by later scholars with little nuance. To further complicate matters, many of the works of art reproduced in these biographies, and the documents cited, can no longer be located; in the case of the documents, when they can it is clear that they were heavily edited. So I use both accounts only sparingly.

Fortunately, there is a wealth of other evidence to reconstruct Francesca's world. Her drawings and paintings are held in various private and public collections, and her books, which are all autobiographical to some extent, provide additional insights. So does a cache of 11 large scrapbooks, many purchased from Edward Goodban's popular stationery shop off Florence's via Tornabuoni, full of art, letters, news clippings, photographs and other ephemera that

Francesca's mother Lucia assembled to document
and celebrate their lives. Letters and diaries from
travelers who describe meetings with the family, and
newspaper and magazine accounts, likewise recreate
Francesca's activities and fame. Much of the surviving
correspondence between Ruskin, his cousin Joan
Severn, his goddaughter Constance Oldham, and
the Alexander women is split between the Morgan
Library and the Boston Public Library. Additional
letters to and from them and other American, British
and Italian correspondents are pasted into Lucia's
scrapbooks and scattered in various repositories. There
are more letters from Francesca and Lucia, preserved
by friends and family, than to them, presumably
because much of the incoming correspondence was
destroyed by Francesca or discarded by relatives and
friends emptying the Alexander home following
her death.[8]

Francesca Alexander's life cannot be categorized
in simple terms. She had a successful artistic practice
and an engaged readership in the United States
and the United Kingdom. She enjoyed a large circle
of international friends and correspondents and
participated in Italian society, in company with the
destitute, the elite and everyone in between, in a way
that very few other Anglo-Americans even attempted.
And she truly made a difference in the lives of many
through her art, her writings and her charity. Her
biography demonstrates how an American woman
used her creativity, and her charitable inclinations,
to create both an impressive body of work and a
fulfilling life in Italy.

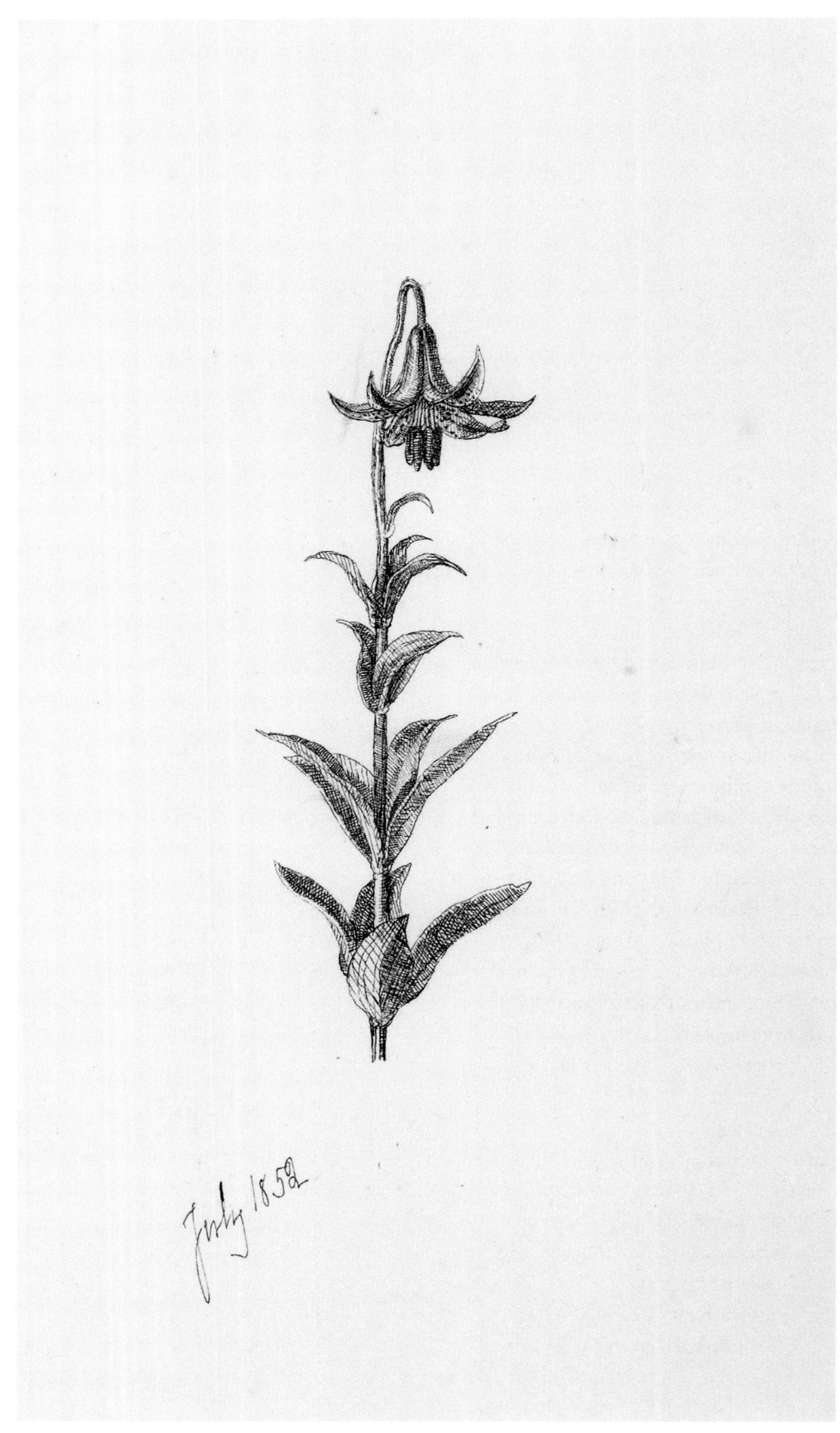

2 Francesca Alexander, *Lily*, July 1852, black ink on wove paper, 26.67 × 16.51 cm (10 ½ × 6 ½ in),
Munson Williams Proctor Arts Institute, Utica, NY

I

From Boston to Florence

Fanny Alexander would have had a very different life if her father had not been an artist. Francis demonstrated early ability as a painter and, although he was a Connecticut native, he moved around the east coast of the United States for training and commissions.[1] Americans were increasingly interested in art at this time but there were few original works to be seen in either private or public collections. Several institutions exhibited American art, often alongside copies or casts of famous sculptures or paintings and natural history, among them Charles Willson Peale's Philadelphia Museum (1784) and his son Rembrandt's Peale Museum in Baltimore (1814). The country's first public art museum was Hartford's Wadsworth Atheneum, which opened in 1844. Boston's Athenaeum, a private library popular with the city's intellectual elite, established an art gallery in 1827, but there was no public museum in the city until the Museum of Fine Arts opened in 1876. Nevertheless, Boston's rapidly expanding artist community included luminaries like Washington Allston and Gilbert Stuart, so it is no surprise that Francis settled there – indeed, he became friends with both men, and many other artists, too – and established himself as a portraitist.

His studio in Tremont Row became a gathering place for his peers and potential patrons. In 1825, the South Carolina artist John Stevens Cogdell described a visit to 'Mr Alexanders room a tall young gentleman with artist look and complexion – his portraits are said to be very strong resemblances to their originals [although] his like all young artists is not the good fortune to catch the best flesh colouring [yet] he is very agreeable + willing to oblige ($40 a portrait).[2] Francis found many patrons willing to pay that not insubstantial amount. In 1826, Mary Peabody (later Mary Peabody Mann) watched him paint author and activist Lydia Maria Francis (later Lydia Maria Child); artist and sitter enjoyed a flirtatious correspondence and she composed a poem inspired by the paintings in his studio, praising his skill as deserving of 'the wreath of fame'.[3] The following year, Francis sent a group of portraits to the Athenaeum's inaugural exhibition.[4] By 1829 his studio was described as a 'fashionable lounging place' and in 1830 an anonymous poem lauding his paintings appeared in *The American Monthly Magazine*.[5] His portrait of Mary Crowninshield Silsbee, the wife of later Harvard president Jared Sparks, with sloping shoulders, long neck and elegantly arranged hair, wearing a white satin dress, is typical of the flattering style that kept Francis in demand (fig.3).[6]

Despite his success, Francis wanted to travel to Europe, and especially Italy, for exposure to the

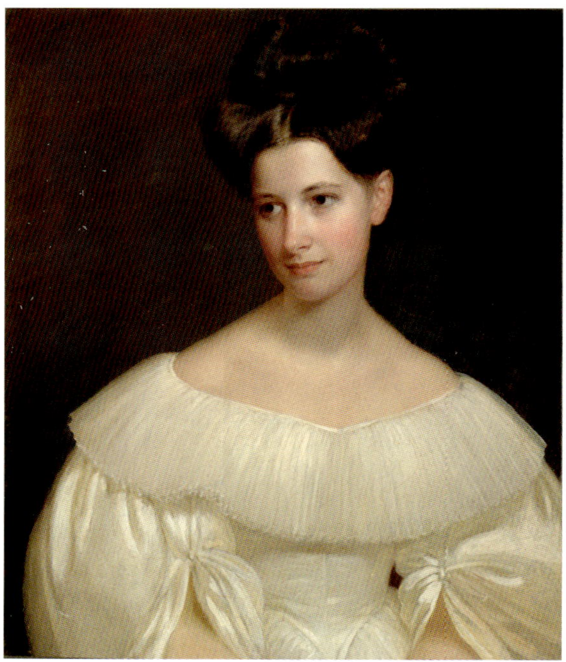

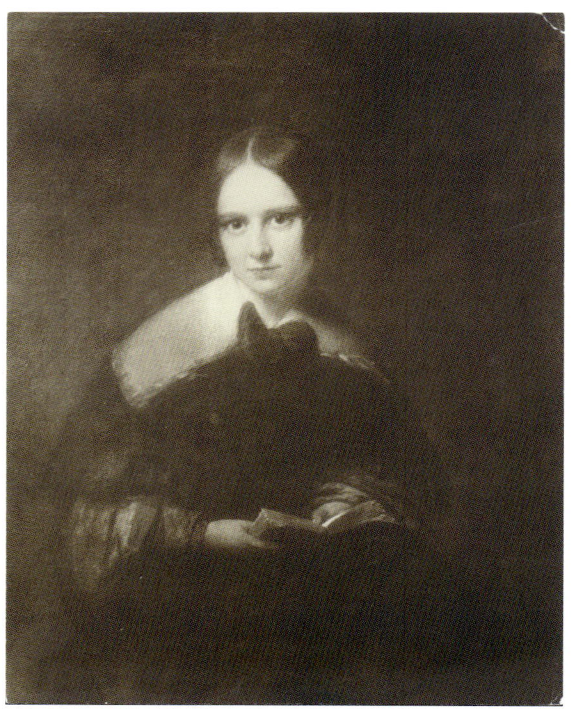

3 Francis Alexander, *Mary Crowninshield Silsbee Sparks (Mrs Jared Sparks)*, 1830, oil on canvas, 76.9 × 63.1 cm (30 ¼ × 24 ⅞ in), Harvard Art Museums, Cambridge, MA

4 Francis Alexander, *Lucia Gray Swett*, 1832, oil on canvas, dimensions unknown, location unknown

art he knew only from copies, casts and printed reproductions. This is hardly surprising; many American artists, and others interested in art and history at this time, admired Italy – its ancient past considered a model for the still nascent American democracy – and Italian art. Crossing the Atlantic was an arduous undertaking and travelers often remained abroad for extended periods to make the most of their efforts. Francis was no exception; he sailed in October 1831 and stayed in Europe, studying art and painting for almost two years.[7] His sketchbook from this trip is filled with unidentified portraits – some may be clients or models, and others the artists with whom he traveled – as well as landscapes and annotations recording stops in Florence, Turin, Livorno, Genoa, Mont Cenis, Chambéry and the Isle of Wight.

By early 1832 Francis was in Florence with sculptor Horatio Greenough, one of the first Boston artists to settle in the city.[8] While there, the Salem merchant Samuel Swett hired Francis to paint a portrait of his daughter Lucia Gray Swett, whose journey to Italy was likely intended to complete her education and give her the kind of experience desirable in a privileged young woman about to enter the marriage market (fig.4). This modest portrait, representing Lucia with a large bow on her dress and a book in her hand, gives no indication of her future role in Francis's life. After Florence he went to Rome with painters Thomas Cole and John H.W. Lane, where he worked in Claude Lorrain's former studio near the Spanish Steps and socialized with author Ralph Waldo Emerson.[9] There he painted a portrait of New York socialite Harriet Douglas, who brought

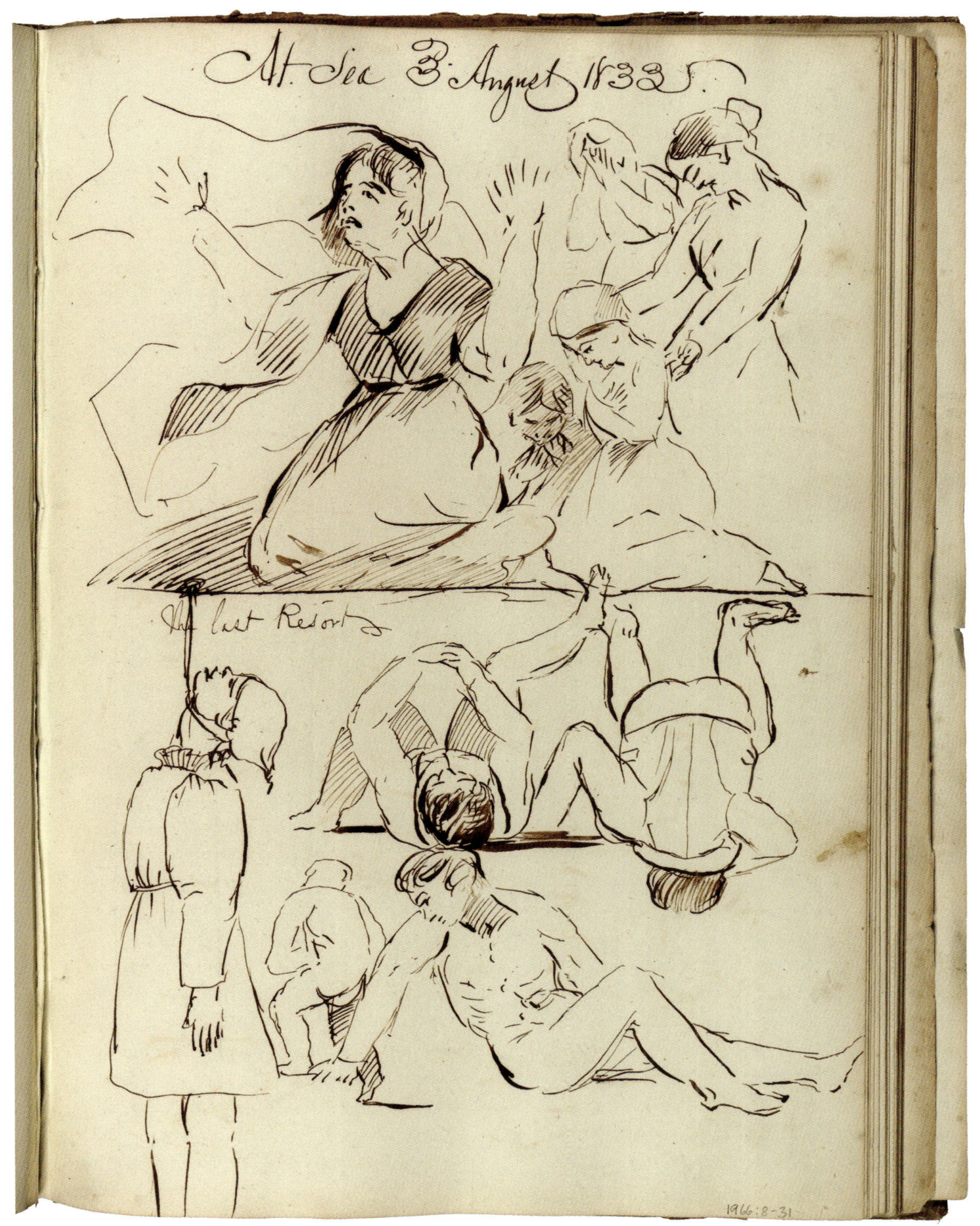

5 Francis Alexander, *At Sea*, 3 August 1833, pen and ink,
34.29 × 24.13 cm (13 ½ × 9 ½ in), Smith College Museum of Art, Northampton, MA

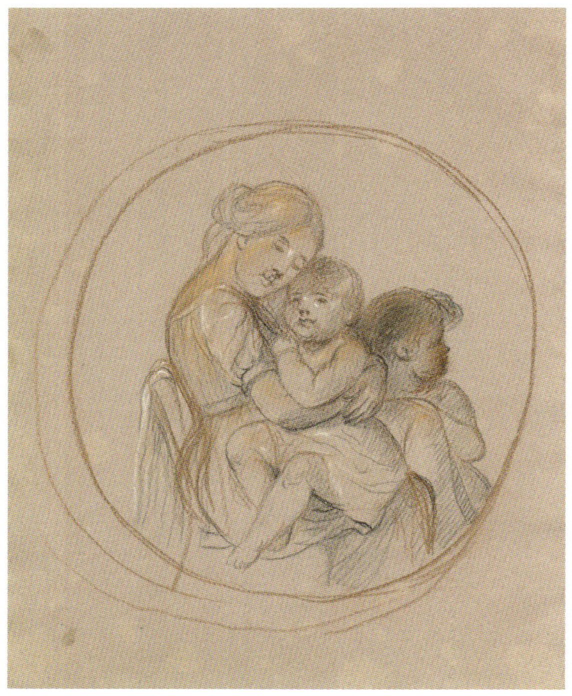

6 Francis Alexander, after Raphael's *Madonna della Seggiola*, late 1830s, crayon, 38 × 30 cm (15 × 11¾ in), Wellesley College Special Collections, Wellesley, MA

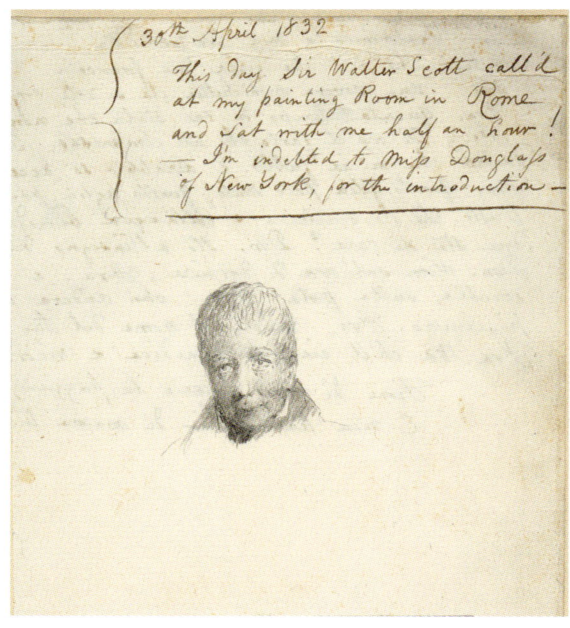

7 Francis Alexander, *Sir Walter Scott* (detail), 1832, pencil, 16 × 13.75 cm (6¼ × 5⅜ in), Manuscripts Division, Department of Special Collections, Princeton University Library, Princeton, NJ

the famed Scottish author Sir Walter Scott to his studio. Scott praised a sketch of the penitent Mary Magdalene, and the delighted Francis commemorated the visit with a quick portrait of Scott, annotated with the date and circumstances (fig.7).[10] Francis also traveled to southern Italy with Cole and painter Amasa Hewins, to Venice with painter John Cranch and author Nathaniel P. Willis, and to London with Emerson.[11]

The trip was transformative, but Francis always planned to return to his Boston life. He sailed home with painter William Allen Wall, docking in New York on 26 August 1833.[12] During the journey he sketched a group of passengers in distress, including one in a pose reminiscent of the famous *Dying Gaul* at Rome's Capitoline Museum and another hanging by the neck, labeled 'the last resort' (fig.5). That suicidal passenger was, presumably, an exaggeration of shipboard conditions, but in light of the difficulties of transatlantic travel it may have some connection to reality.

In addition to portraits, Francis made a number of copies of famous paintings on his journey, knowing these would find eager buyers. He purchased paintings, too, including what was described as a Guido Reni *Magdalene* and a Raphael *Madonna and Child*.[13] Many came to his Boston studio to see this collection. Sarah Freeman Clarke, the artist sister of minister James Freeman Clarke and an Italophile herself, described the Reni as 'very simple and very beautiful, I saw it about five minutes, and I yet have a more distinct idea of it than of any other picture I ever saw except those we saw last summer at the Athenaeum'.[14] She was

referring to the Athenaeum's annual exhibit, which in
1833 also included paintings attributed to Caravaggio,
Titian, Annibale Carracci, Carlo Dolci, Tintoretto,
Domenichino and Leonardo da Vinci, so Francis's
collection must have been impressive.[15]

Seeking broad exposure, and new patrons, Francis
regularly contributed his own paintings to the
Athenaeum's exhibitions.[16] He also displayed 42
portraits, Italianate scenes and Old Master copies
in May 1834 at Boston's Harding's Gallery, alongside
work by Hewins, Thomas Doughty, Alvan Fisher
and Chester Harding himself.[17] Portraits of elite
Bostonians continued to be his specialty, and his
prices went up; in 1834 he received $65 from William
Lloyd Garrison as partial payment for a portrait of
abolitionist Prudence Crandall.[18]

Despite the disparities in their social status, Francis's
success must have convinced Samuel Swett of his
suitability as a husband for Swett's daughter Lucia. In
September 1834 Thomas Cole wrote to congratulate
Francis on his engagement, though the couple did
not marry until May 1836.[19] Swett family connections
provided Francis with more potential sitters, including
Lucia's uncle, the art collector and politician Francis
Calley Gray.[20] Through a letter of introduction from
senator (and later Massachusetts governor) John Davis,
Francis met Hiram Powers when the sculptor arrived
in Boston in 1837.[21] Francis painted Powers's portrait,
and though he suggested Powers model him and
Lucia, there is no evidence this ever happened.[22]

Francis also acquired work by his contemporaries
and his collection grew rapidly; an indication of its
size comes from the fact that an 1884 sale of part of
it included 93 paintings by American and European
artists.[23] In 1835 Thomas Cole gifted Francis a now
lost version of his *Tornado in the Wilderness*, in part
to repay money Francis loaned him to purchase cork
models when they were in Italy.[24] His most expensive
acquisition, at $1500, was Washington Allston's *The
Sisters*.[25] Francis proudly wrote to Hiram Powers,
who had by then moved to Florence, about this

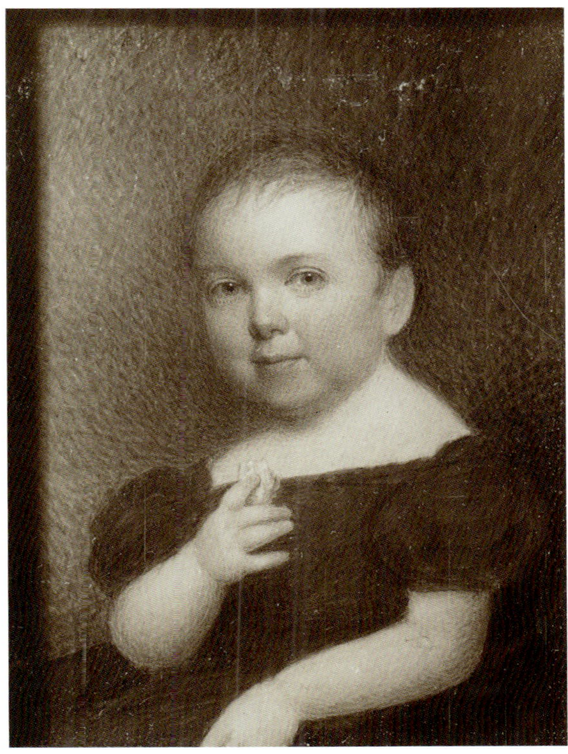

8 Alvan Clark, *Fanny Alexander*, c.1840, painting on ivory,
8.57 × 6.35 cm (3⅜ × 2½ in), location unknown

purchase: 'I mention the particulars that you may tell
the Italian Artists, how, in young America, American
Artists are paid for their works.'[26] Francis occasionally
put paintings in his collection on exhibition at the
Athenaeum in the hopes of selling them.[27] He also
brokered the sale of one of Gilbert Stuart's portraits
of George Washington from the Joy family of Boston
to Francis Calley Gray.[28]

With Francis's activities as an artist, collector
and dealer, the family was quite comfortable when
their only child, Esther Frances, known as Fanny or
Fan, was born on 27 February 1837. One of Francis's
sketchbooks contains repeated mother and child

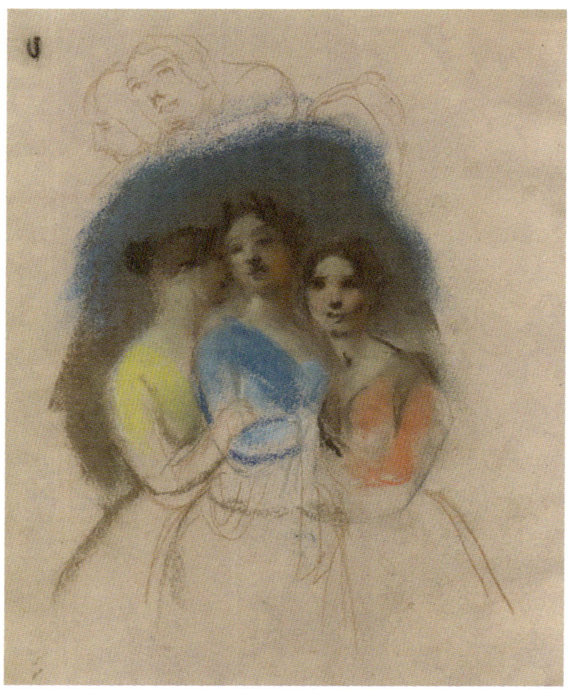

9 Francis Alexander, *Three Women*, late 1830s, crayon, 38 × 30 cm (15 × 11¾ in), Wellesley College Special Collections, Wellesley, MA

images, presumably representing his wife and daughter, including one in the pose of Raphael's *Madonna della Seggiola* from Florence's Palazzo Pitti (fig.6). This was a painting that Anglo-Americans admired for its focus on maternal love rather than obvious Catholic sentiment. Francis bought an old copy of it while he was abroad – those wanting to copy it *in situ* allegedly booked years in advance – and he must have known the versions by other American artists, including Benjamin West, who painted his own wife and son as the holy figures.[29]

Francis made several paintings of Fanny at different ages and, as an indication of his place in the artist community, he asked his friends to capture her, too. Horatio Greenough may have felt some obligation to carve Fanny's bust, based on drawings Francis sent him, because Francis had provided him with a copy of Gilbert Stuart's portrait of George Washington to help Greenough create his colossal statue for the United States Capitol.[30] But Greenough was more daunted by Fanny than Washington; he reported to his brother Henry, 'Had it been an old man's head, I should be sanguine; but these little milk sponges are so subtle in their forms, so difficult to copy under the most favorable circumstances, that I fear it will be labor lost.'[31] After further consideration, Greenough wrote to Francis,

> If you knew how difficult I find it to imitate infantine forms and expressions you would feel less sanguine even were the breathing little cherub before me ... the feeling of doubt paralyzes my hand and my work would be tame and poor. However I feel too lively a sympathy with your feelings toward your darling to refuse to try.[32]

If Greenough did try, the bust has not been identified. Francis turned to Hiram Powers next, writing, 'I wish you could model her. I'd give a great sum to have her best look transformed to the marble.'[33] But nothing came of this more subtle approach, either. Another sculptor, Shobal Vail Clevenger, modeled Fanny in 1839, but if he completed the portrait, it too is lost.[34] Only Alvan Clark's miniature of Fanny, seated in a chair and looking at the viewer with a cookie in her hand, can be associated with this period (fig.8).[35]

Fanny's childhood coincided with a productive period for Francis, who was named an honorary member of the National Academy of Design in 1840 and became a founding member of the Boston Artists' Association the following year.[36] He made numerous iterative chalk sketches of women, alone or in interwoven groups, with long graceful necks and carefully coiffed hair, similar to his painting of Mary Crowninshield Silsbee but with an expressiveness lacking in his formal portraits (fig.9). Those formal

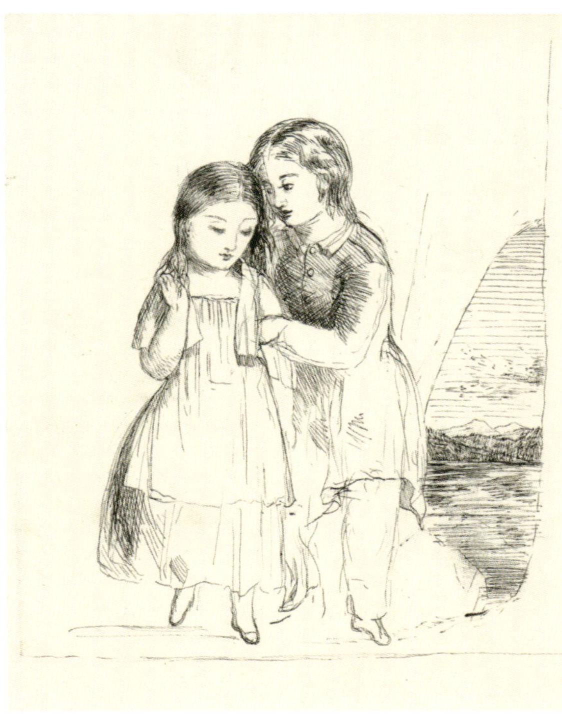

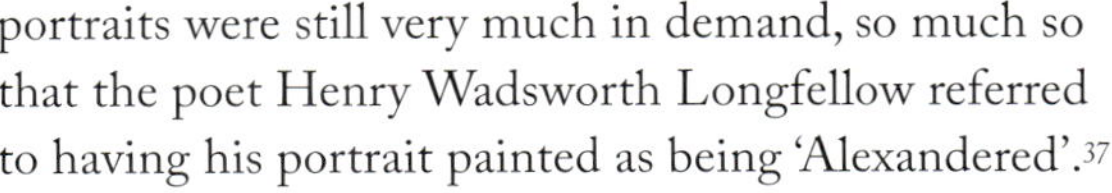

10 Francesca Alexander, *Evangeline and Gabriel*, *c.*1849, pen and ink, 12 × 17 cm (4¾ × 6¾ in), private collection

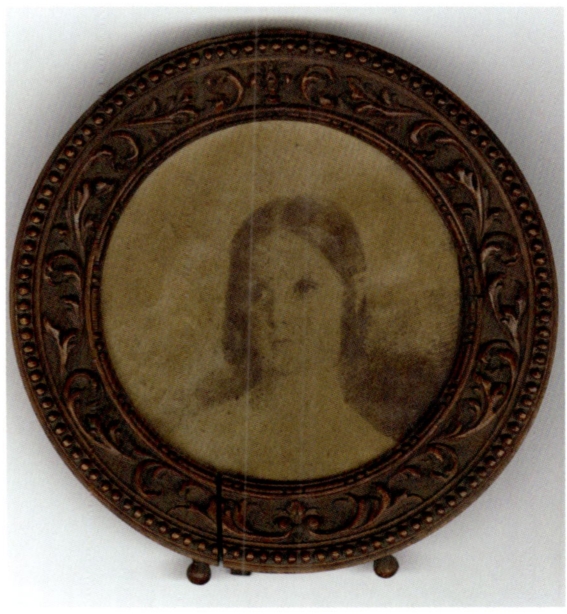

11 Photograph of Francis Alexander, *Fanny Alexander*, late 1840s, original painting now lost, frame diameter 16 cm (6¼ in), Longfellow House-Washington's Headquarters National Historic Site, Cambridge, MA

portraits were still very much in demand, so much so that the poet Henry Wadsworth Longfellow referred to having his portrait painted as being 'Alexandered'.[37]

Longfellow would know this, since Francis made his portrait, and the men and their families were close. In 1849 Francis invited him to their summer home in the coastal town of Lynn, north of Boston, emphasizing their shared appreciation of nature – an appreciation Fanny would later echo – when he wrote, 'I was already dreaming of pleasant rambles with you along the coast, where, + when, we might talk over + feel the poetry of nature together. For you, and for all who have their eyes open – there is a Book of poetry, illustrated wide open, not only here by the seaside but every-where.'[38] Francis mentioned Fanny's love of Longfellow's *Evangeline* (1847), a poem about the effects of the eighteenth-century expulsion

of Acadians from Nova Scotia on a fictional girl named Evangeline and her lover Gabriel, prompting Longfellow to gift her a signed copy.[39] One of Fanny's earliest drawings was probably prompted by this gift, illustrating the couple before their tragic separation with the idyllic landscape – Longfellow's 'forest primeval' – behind them (fig.10). The two figures, arms linked and heads close together, may be based in part on Francis's chalk sketches of women in similar poses. Friendly exchanges between the families continued, and decades later Lucia gave the poet's daughter Alice a photograph of a painting Francis made of Fanny around this time (fig.11).[40]

Francis's career peaked in 1842 when he painted a portrait of Charles Dickens, just arrived in Boston with his wife Catherine Hogarth for a much-anticipated tour of the United States.[41] In this case, too, the families were friendly. Later that winter Lucia

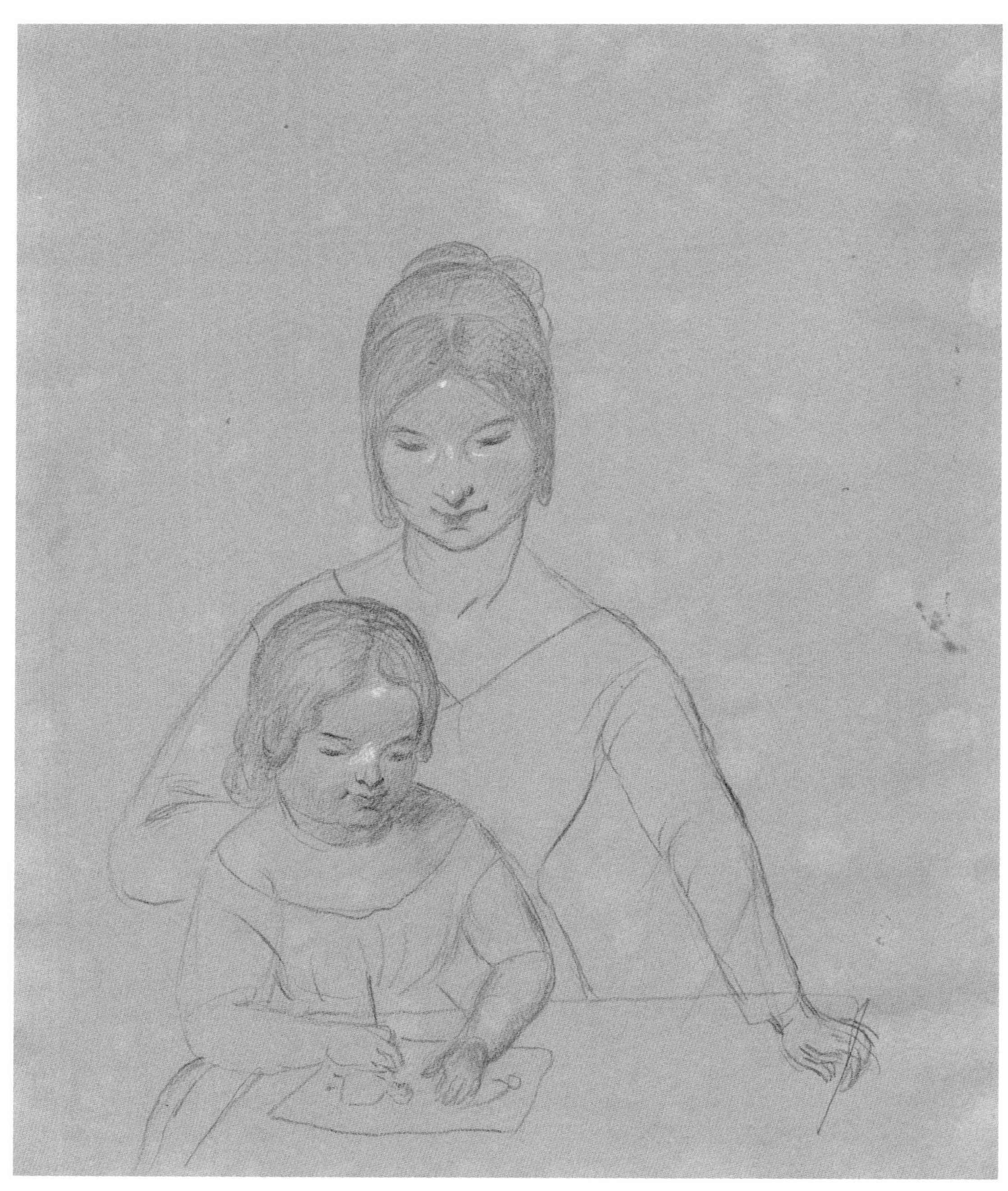

12 Francis Alexander, *Lucia and Fanny Alexander*, 1840s, crayon,
38 × 30 cm (15 × 11 ¾ in), Wellesley College Special Collections, Wellesley, MA

sent Dickens a volume of drawings, presumably by Francis, and in thanking her he playfully wrote, 'Mrs. Dickens . . . begs you to kiss "Fan" in her name. If you will ask Fan to kiss you in mine (when Mr Alexander is looking another way) I shall be even more indebted to you than I am already.'[42] Catherine continued to correspond with Lucia, sharing her grief following Dickens's death in 1870 – though they had been separated since 1858 – and promising to return the volume if she found it among his possessions.[43]

Francis certainly influenced Fanny's artistic path. Drawing and painting were acceptable activities for women, providing they remained amateur occupations. And most did remain amateurs; by mid-century there were several options in the United States for women to receive artistic training, but lasting professional success remained somewhat elusive.[44] The informal training provided by her artist father gave Fanny an advantage from an early age. Indeed, Francis's sketch of a woman watching a girl draw presumably represents Lucia and Fanny, the little girl awkwardly gripping a pen or pencil as she outlines figures on the paper in front of her under his instruction (fig.12).

Some of Fanny's early drawings – and some of her later work – were based on literary sources, like Longfellow's *Evangeline*, but she focused especially on the natural world. Her earliest dated drawing, executed on 2 August 1851 when she was 14 years old, is a view of the woods at Swampscott, near her summer home (fig.13). A year later, a drawing of a lily with its stalk bent by a heavy bloom, its volumes and shadows rendered in fine cross-hatching, is another indication of her keen interest in nature and botany (fig.2). Surely Francis provided her with the necessary guidance to create these and other related drawings.

Francis's example as a portraitist was also important. His quick sketches may have inspired Fanny's of a sleeping infant's head, the face in shadow against a pillow or the crook of a caregiver's arm (fig.14). And, like Francis, Fanny captured more detailed portraits from life, too. She drew two women of African ancestry, both identified by name: Julia Benson wears a striped top with a dark ribbon secured by a brooch around her neck and large hoop earrings (fig.15) while Deborah Dorsay wears a more humble madras headscarf and a dark top over a shirt with an embroidered or lace collar (fig.16).[45] There was a sizable free black population in Boston, many of whom were active in the abolition movement, and the Alexanders' home on West Cedar Street on Beacon Hill was near that community.[46] They knew prominent abolitionists like Francis's patrons Lydia Maria Child and William Lloyd Garrison, and Francis and Lucia were married at nearby Park Street Church, an important center for both Evangelicals and abolitionists, so it is likely that Fanny knew the women in these closely observed portraits quite well.

These drawings, and dozens more from this period demonstrating various stages of finish and skill, were later placed in a scrapbook, some apparently cut down from larger sheets to excise unsuccessful or unfinished sections and create an edited understanding of Fanny's youthful efforts. They seem to be studies, allowing Fanny to experiment with representing her world and the people in it. But she also made at least one much more complex drawing during this period, in which she combined portraits with a domestic setting. This drawing places the viewer at the end of a dining room, framed by architectural details like pointed arches and pendants, with three generations of a family around a table (fig.17). An older woman is at the head, with a couple and five children seated nearby while a nurse holds an infant, and two black men, presumably servants, carry food and drink in the background. The figures have a variety of poses and expressions, from the boy who looks out at us to the girls with their eyes cast down, from the father reaching for his glass to the infant reaching for the ties of the nurse's bonnet. Dinner is finished, and the family are about to start on the dessert course. The mother at left will use the spoon on the table in front of her to serve the impressive blancmange, a

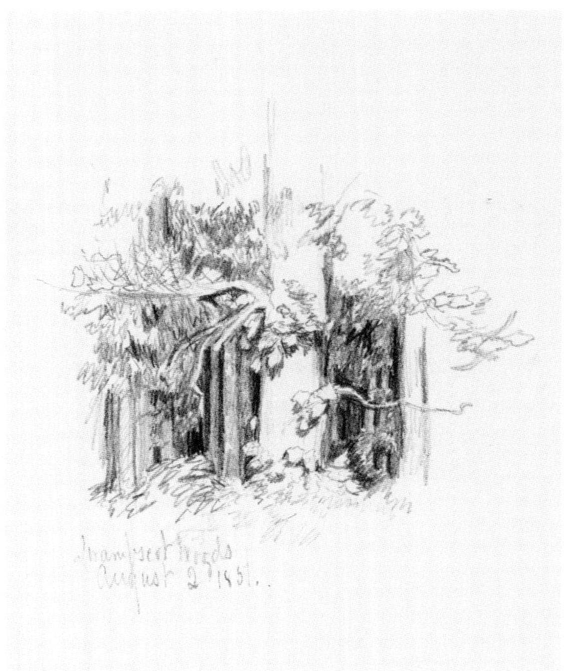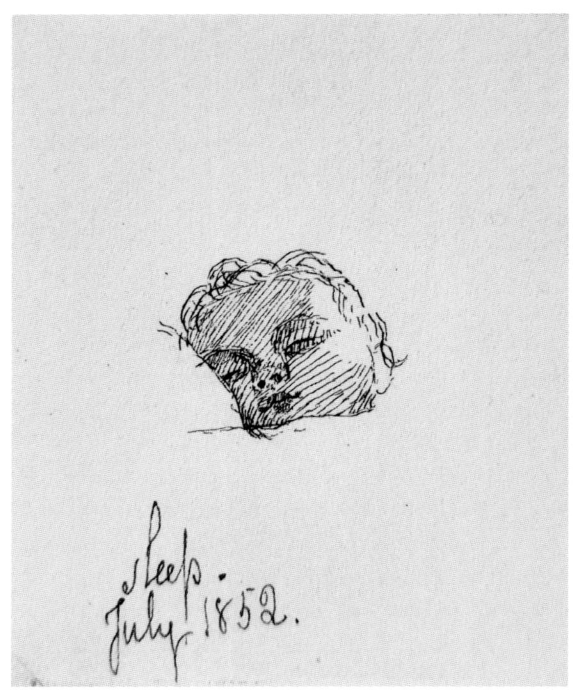

13 (left) Francesca Alexander, *Swampscott Woods*, 2 August 1851, graphite on paper, 11.4 × 9.2 cm (4 ½ × 3 ⅝ in),
Palmer Museum of Art at Penn State, University Park, PA

14 (right) Francesca Alexander, *Sleep*, July 1852, pen and ink, approx. 6 × 7 cm (2 ½ × 2 ¾ in), Paul Worman Fine Art,
Worcester, MA

17 (opposite) Francesca Alexander, *Family at Table*, c.1853, pen and ink, approx. 20.32 × 31.75 cm (8 × 12 ½ in), Paul Worman
Fine Art, Worcester, MA

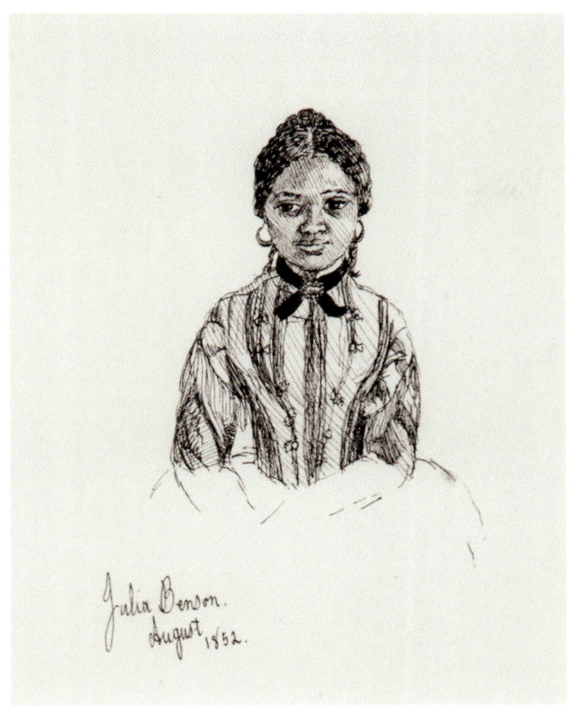

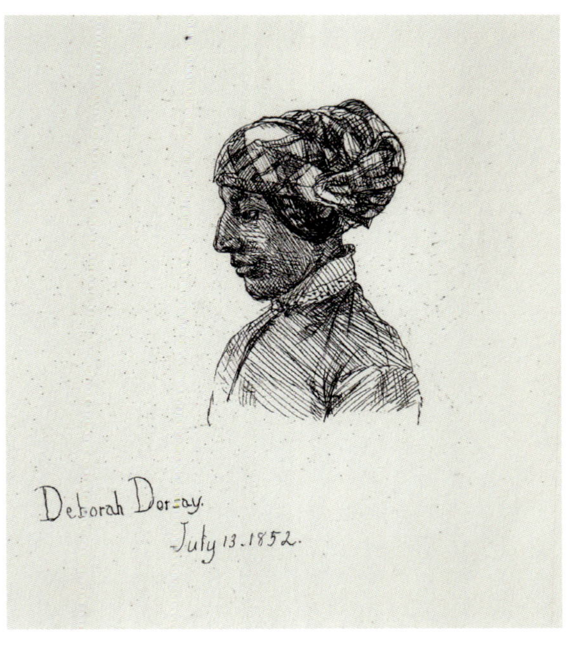

16 Francesca Alexander, *Deborah Dorsay*, 13 July 1852, pen and ink, approx. 16 × 12.5 cm (6 ½ × 5 ½ in), Paul Worman Fine Art, Worcester, MA

15 Francesca Alexander, *Julia Benson*, August 1852, black ink on paper, 19.4 × 16.4 cm (7 ⅝ × 6 ½ in), Memorial Art Gallery, University of Rochester, Rochester, NY

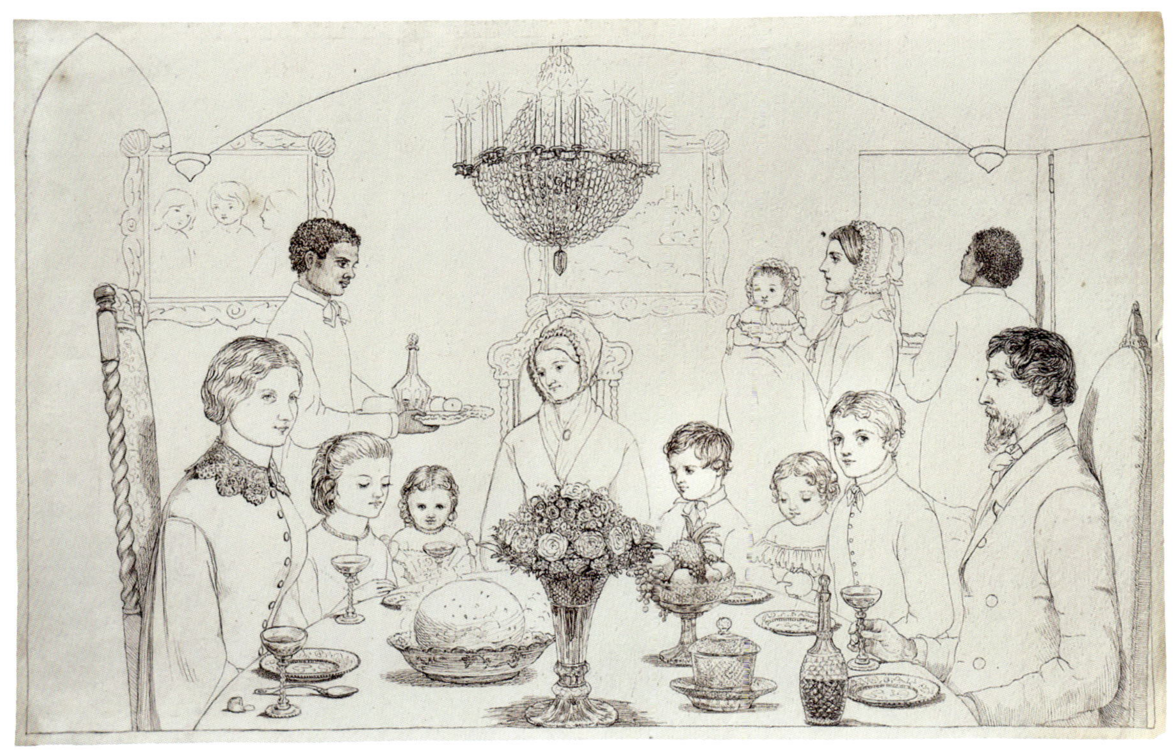

pudding made of milk and flavorings and thickened
with isinglass and, in this case, set in a spherical mold
and adorned with spun sugar.[47] The great precision
of the still-life details – the crystal chandelier with
its glowing candles, the cut-glass decanter, covered
compote, and bowls of flowers and fruit – and even
the mismatched chairs and the hinge on the open
door contrast the lightly sketched paintings in their
matching frames on the far wall. Such a complex
composition could not have been done *in situ*; Fanny
must have sketched each portrait, and the details
of foods and furnishings, and then combined them
in the finished drawing. Unfortunately, although
she inscribed many of her drawings with names
and dates, this one has no identifying details. But
the family must be one the Alexanders knew well,
allowing Fanny to take the necessary time to capture
the people and their comfortable setting.

This cache of drawings demonstrates that Fanny
practiced a distinct style, and preferred working from
life, from an early age. She was a literal artist, and
almost always represented what she saw in the world
around her. That was true during her childhood in the
Boston area and, after 1853, in Italy, too.

2

'Truly an Artist's Home'

Although the Alexanders were both financially secure and socially connected in Boston, they debated relocating to Italy as early as 1838, when Francis wrote to Hiram Powers to say they might join him in Florence in two years.[1] In reality, it took 15, and what finally precipitated their move is uncertain. They may have hoped to find musical instruction for Fanny, or health benefits for Francis, or perhaps Francis and Lucia simply wanted to be in Italy, where they first met and where so many of their contemporaries journeyed.[2] Whatever the reason, in 1853 they stored some of their possessions, packed others, and Francis obtained a passport. Although passports were not a requirement for international travel until the twentieth century, they did facilitate movement across borders and provide proof of identity. Since passports did not include photographs at this date, the document described Francis as 6 feet 1 ½ inches tall, with hazel eyes, a Roman nose and brown hair, and stated that he, his wife and daughter planned to sail from New York on 4 June.[3] Their voyage lasted several weeks, during which time Fanny and Francis occupied themselves by drawing some of the other passengers and the sights they saw.[4] The family disembarked in Le Havre and stopped in Paris before continuing south, arriving in Florence that October.

They took rooms at the Hotel Suisse, described in guidebooks as a second-rate but nevertheless popular accommodation for travelers on both long and short visits, including writers Fyodor Dostoevsky and George Eliot, with her lover George Lewes, and musicians Gaetano Donizetti, Gioachino Rossini and Giuseppe Verdi.[5] It was a few steps from the Duomo, at the corner of via della Vigna Nuova and via Tornabuoni and across from the west facade of the Palazzo Strozzi (fig.18). This central location provided the Alexanders with an ideal setting to experience the city, as well as an ever-changing view of Florentine life, with beggars, roasted chestnut sellers and assorted passersby outside their windows.

Francis and Lucia knew that Rome was dominated by the papacy and Naples was controlled by the Kingdom of the Two Sicilies, marking both of those cities as emphatically Catholic and giving Florence an advantage in their minds, and those of many Protestant travelers. However, when the Alexanders arrived, religious freedom was an issue in Florence, too. Prior to 1849, as part of the Grand Duchy of Tuscany under Grand Duke Leopoldo II, the last Habsburg-Lorraine ruler, Florence's Protestant population – comprised of residents and travelers of all nationalities as well as a growing number of Italians – had several places to worship. But that year,

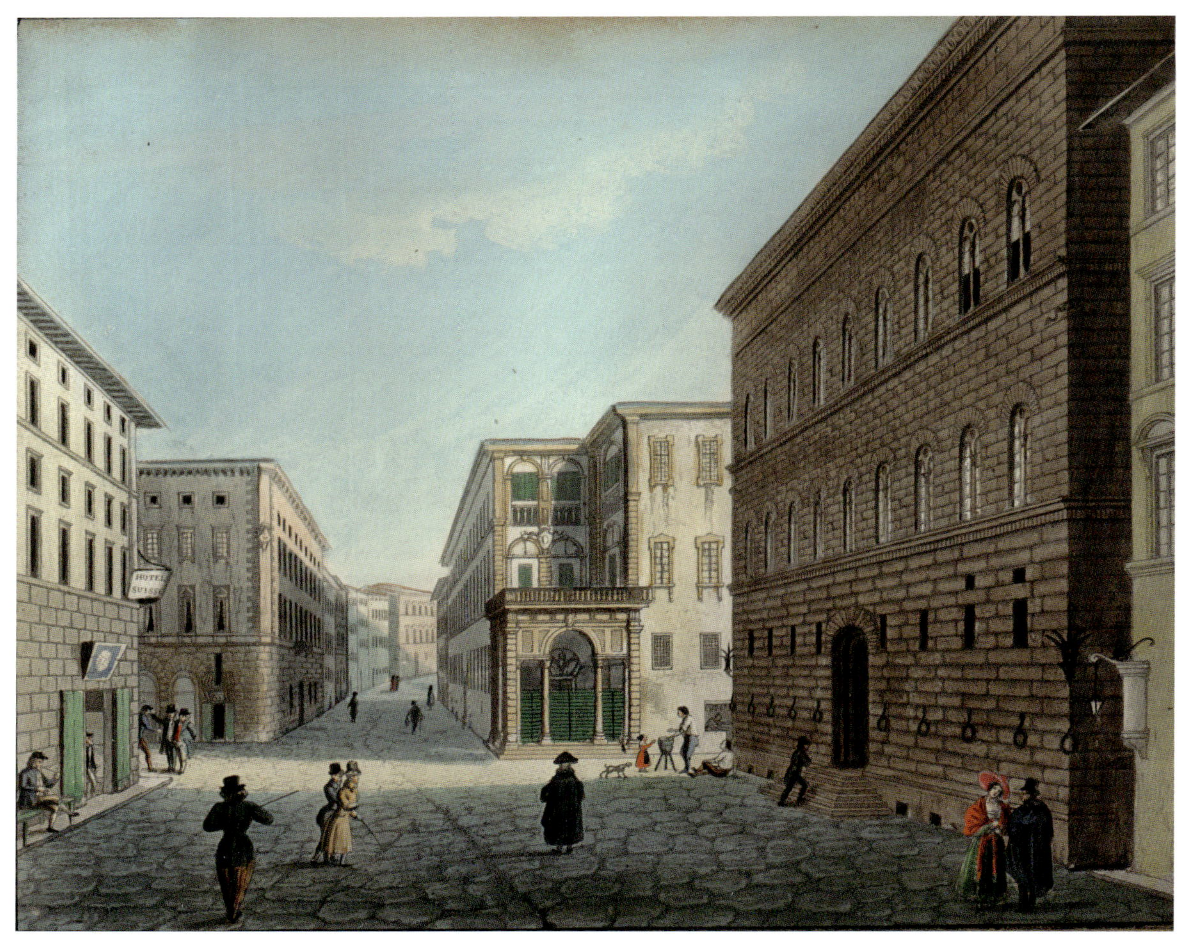

18 Emilio Burci, *View of the Palazzo Strozzi*, early nineteenth century, hand-colored etching,
25 × 27 cm (9 ⅞ × 10 ⅝ in), Antiquariat Clemens Paulusch, Berlin

the start of what became an almost five-year-long Austrian occupation weakened Leopoldo's control. In 1851, an agreement with the papacy removed the right to worship freely and banned the use of Italian Bibles, insisting that scripture come directly from priests on pulpits. Protestantism was increasingly viewed as allied with the anti-papal upheavals of the Risorgimento, and harsh penalties were exacted on transgressors, the most famous of whom were Francesco and Rosa Madiai. The couple was at the center of an international outcry in 1851 when, after Bibles were found in their Florence home, they were tried, jailed and exiled.[6] Foreign Protestants like the Alexanders, were not subject to the same harsh penalties as long as they did not proselytize; customs officials occasionally confiscated their Bibles at border crossings for that reason.[7] For Tuscans, religious freedom, and with it the free resumption of non-Catholic services – and the re-entry of the Madiai – was permitted again only after Leopoldo stepped

down in 1859.[8] But even then, Catholicism remained
the dominant religion and Italians who chose to
worship as Protestants encountered discrimination.

Religious tension was just one aspect of life
in Risorgimento Italy. Like most in the Anglo-
American community, the Alexanders were great
supporters of Giuseppe Garibaldi and the other
patriots who sought to unify the Italian states as one
secular nation. They joined Italians in celebrating
the events leading to the establishment of the
Kingdom of Italy in 1861 and the unification of the
peninsula ten years later. A key moment came in
1860, when Britain's Queen Victoria recognized
Vittorio Emanuele II of Savoy as the King of Italy,
a title he would not formally achieve for another
year. In a letter to her family, Boston author Annie
Adams Fields reported from Florence that as soon
as this news broke, 'the gay tri-color of Sardinia [the
green, white and red striped flag associated with
the Italian state] flamed in every street and almost
every house catching the rare rays of sun-light which
sometimes penetrate them reminding us that life was
still left in this heretofore unhappy people'.[9] Like so
many, Fields could not help being patronizing while
equating the Italian struggle with her own country's
revolution and civil war. A few months later, again
describing these events, she made the link more
unequivocal when she wrote, 'I hope you like to
hear about Italy because nothing ever can be more
interesting than the liberation of [Italy] except the
liberation of our slaves.'[10]

The Alexanders agreed with this sentiment. Soon
after they arrived in Florence, Fanny began collecting
cheaply printed broadsides with lyrics to popular
Italian songs, many of which were patriotic. In 1860,
a friend who visited Solferino, the site of a decisive
victory the year before, picked a flower and sent it
to Lucia as a memento.[11] In 1866, the Alexanders
organized the donation of three trunks of medical
supplies, alcohol, books and a spirit lamp designed
by Francis to the soldiers of the 61st regiment. One

of Lucia's scrapbooks contains a clipping from an
unidentified Italian newspaper praising this effort and
quoting Fanny's letter to the regiment's commander,
Pier Eleonoro Negri, written in perfect Italian,
claiming that it was the least her family could do 'for
those who do so much for us. I say for us, because I am
sure that my parents feel like me that whoever works
for Italy is for us; that we always have this Italy in our
hearts as if it were our homeland: may God grant us
to see it free soon!'[12] Lucia also worked with a group
of prominent Anglo-American and Italian women
in Florence to donate clothing for Italian troops and
visit them in hospitals.[13] When Garibaldi came to
Florence, the Alexanders lined up alongside his Italian
supporters, waving an American flag and distributing
refreshments to the enthusiastic crowd. Lucia joined
a deputation to meet Garibaldi and presented him
with photographs of President Abraham Lincoln and
Generals William T. Sherman and Ulysses S. Grant,
her choices emphasizing the connection between the
Risorgimento and the American Civil War; she later
acted as an intermediary between Garibaldi and John
Greenleaf Whittier.[14]

Anglo-Americans in Florence became even further
embedded in these events in 1865, when Italy's capital
moved to the city for five years. This resulted in an
influx of politicians, administrators and others who
understood the opportunities that came with this
new designation, as well as costly renovations to
the urban fabric. New buildings were erected, while
some historic buildings were repaired and others
were demolished. Under the direction of architect
Giuseppe Poggi, the medieval walls encircling the city
were destroyed, roads were widened and reoriented,
and the Piazzale Michelangelo was constructed below
the church of San Miniato in the Oltrarno, providing
an ideal vantage point to admire the city. These
renovations continued even after the capital moved
to Rome in 1870. But some found changes to the
city's historic fabric problematic. The long-unfinished
facades of Florence's Santa Croce and Duomo were

completed, partly according to Renaissance-era plans, in 1863 and 1887 respectively, largely with funds from a number of British residents. But later in the century another group of foreign residents led by journalist Helen Zimmern, author Vernon Lee and collector and art historian Herbert Horne, formed the Association for the Defence of Old Florence to voice concerns about modernization.[15] The Alexanders sympathized with this group, though they were not active members; in 1874 Fanny wrote to a friend, 'Florence is now sadly changed since I first knew it: modern ideas have arrived even here, with the usual modern antipathy to everything venerable and beautiful.'[16]

The financial strain that resulted from these changes to the city contributed to economic collapse by 1878, burdening the native population even further. Ironically, foreigners benefitted from this; they could enjoy a better lifestyle for less money than in their home countries, all while surrounded by the art and history that drew them to Florence in the first place. The thrill the city provided is exemplified by Constance Fenimore Woolson, an author like her great-uncle James Fenimore Cooper, who wrote to a friend in 1880,

> Here I have attained that old-world feeling I used to dream about, a sort of enthusiasm made up of history, mythology, old churches, pictures, statues, vineyards, the Italian sky, dark-eyed peasants, opera-music, Raphael and old Michael, 'Childe Harold', the 'Marble Faun', 'Romola', and ever so many more ingredients – the whole having I think taken me pretty well off my feet![17]

Florence's appeal to the Alexanders, and to other Bostonians, was also due in no small part to its perceived familiarity. In an 1847 letter, journalist Margaret Fuller wrote, 'Florence is more in its spirit like Boston, than like an Italian city.'[18] For some, like the sculptor William Wetmore Story, this was not an entirely positive feature, especially in comparison to larger and more cosmopolitan Rome.[19] But an overwhelming number appreciated Florence, and they came to the city in droves. In 1863 Lucia Alexander urged friends to visit, writing, 'You would feel at home here just at the moment, for it is full of Bostonians.'[20]

Like Francis, some of these Bostonians were artists, and they knew that travelers inclined to purchase art would be a boon to their practices. Many of these travelers sought out the sculptors Hiram Powers and Thomas Ball, whose ability to capture portraits put them in particular demand. When the Putnam family visited in 1866 they stopped at Ball's studio, prompting Sarah Gooll Putnam to write in her diary, 'He had a good many nice busts of people we knew.'[21] Sarah later became a portrait painter herself, so those busts naturally interested her.

But there was an enormous variety of both contemporary and historic art available in Florence, and taste fluctuated over the century. In 1847, the English antiquarian and long-time Florence resident William Blundell Spence lamented the poor market for contemporary art; instead, he claimed, collectors bought Old Masters in various stages of repair, and copies after them, as well as the diverse objects popularly known by the French term *bric-à-brac*.[22] However, a few years later, as comments by Sarah Gooll Putnam and others indicate, travelers were increasingly keen to purchase art by their countrymen, or occasionally countrywomen.

It is no wonder, then, that the artist community had grown since Francis's first trip. Horatio Greenough died in 1851, but Hiram Powers was still in Florence, and he would have been among the first people Francis sought out, not least because he brought the portrait he had painted of Powers to give to his friend.[23] During the Alexanders' time abroad other American sculptors in Florence included Horatio Greenough's brother Richard Saltonstall Greenough as well as Thomas Ball, William Couper,

Florence Freeman, Joel Tanner Hart, John Adams Jackson and Larkin Goldsmith Mead, while painters included Lizzie Adams, Lizzie Boott, Frank Duveneck and Thomas Buchanan Read. Many other artists passed through Florence for long or short visits, and even more settled in Rome.

A minimal grasp of Italian was helpful when living or traveling in Italy, and guidebooks provided the names of local instructors, as well as lists of key phrases and words. Some Anglo-Americans arrived with this knowledge from prior study. The presence of native speakers in Boston, including several Risorgimento patriots forced into exile for their activities, made it a good location to learn the language. The Alexanders knew at least rudimentary Italian before 1853 – either through such study or, in the case of Francis and Lucia, from their first experience abroad – and all three were bilingual within the first few years.

But many Anglo-Americans got by with no Italian at all, because they lived, shopped, ate and socialized in English-speaking enclaves that catered to their every need and kept them apart from the local population. In Rome, the area around the Spanish Steps constituted a well-defined Anglo-American quarter, but the Florence community was smaller and more scattered. Some residents and travelers lived in hotels, pensions and apartments around the center, where the Alexanders lived when they first arrived and again after 1869. Others rented villas at Bellosguardo, now about two miles from the center beyond the Porta Romano to the south-west, where the Alexanders moved in 1856, and around Fiesole, about five miles beyond the Porta San Gallo to the north-east.[24]

By the late nineteenth century, Florence's Anglo-American population was as high as 30,000 residents, and a seasonal influx of travelers enlarged this group every year.[25] Community connections were facilitated by the English-language newspapers and magazines that provided local and international news and gossip as well as advertisements, studio addresses and lists of residents and travelers.[26] Some publications, like *The Tuscan Athenaeum* (1847–8), *The Times* (1865), *The Fleur-de-Lys* (1868–9) and *The Anglo-American Gazette* (1869), lasted only a few months or years. Others, like *The Florence Gazette* (1890–94), which later became *The Italian Gazette* (1894–1915), *The Florence Herald* (1906–13), which later became *The Florence Herald and Italian Herald* (1913–17), and *The Florence Directory* (1908–13), had longer runs. Newspapers published elsewhere, particularly Paris-based *Galignani's Messenger* (1814–1904) and *American Register* (1868–1909), later *American Register and Anglo-Colonial World* (1909–14), and the various titles associated with British tour operator and archeologist S. Russell Forbes in Rome (1874–98), included Florence news alongside information about other popular destinations. Anglo-Americans accessed these newspapers and magazines by individual subscriptions or at their hotels, banks and stationers. In Florence they were also available at the Gabinetto Vieusseux, a subscription reading room and library with an international clientele whose founder, Giovanni Pietro Vieusseux, was a prominent Swiss Protestant and Risorgimento supporter.[27] In his novel *Indian Summer* (1886), William Dean Howells described the Vieusseux as 'a place where sooner or later you meet everyone you know among the foreign residents in Florence'.[28] It must be for this reason, as well as for reading material, that the Alexanders subscribed to the Vieusseux within days of their arrival in 1853 and repeatedly renewed their subscription over the years.[29]

In 1847 Margaret Fuller decried the isolation these foreign enclaves and their amenities promoted, believing they gave Anglo-Americans little sense of the real Italy.[30] But her experience was different from most. She lived in Italy in the late 1840s, and, as the first female foreign correspondent, she sent back dispatches to the *New-York Tribune*. While abroad she married the impoverished nobleman Giovanni Angelo Ossoli, and she gave birth to their son before

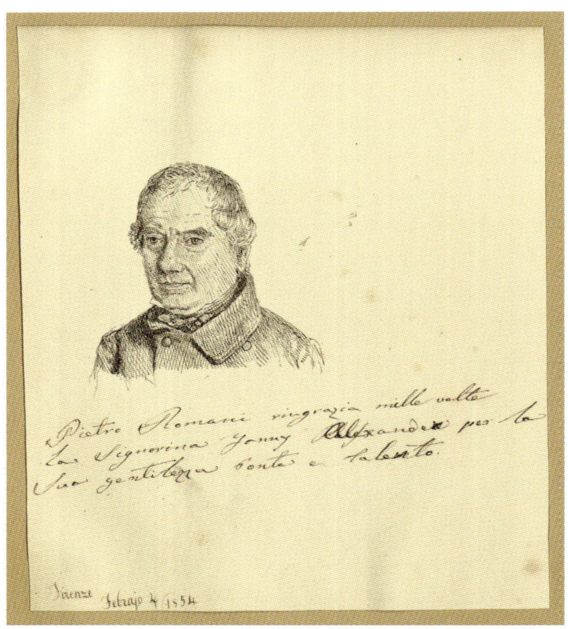

19 Francesca Alexander, *Pietro Romani*, 4 February 1854, pen and ink, 16 × 19 cm (6 ¼ × 7 ½ in), Wellesley College Special Collections, Wellesley, MA

former vice-consul Henry Greenough Huntington (a nephew of Horatio Greenough) cautioned,

> Too many unhappy examples of ruined lives in young unprotected girls . . . have been brought to my notice, for me not to caution persons in such positions, as to the intimacy they may form with men, whose ideas of conduct and propriety are utterly at variance with what they might have been accustomed to in their own countrymen.[32]

Henry James, who spent many years in Florence, made one such intimacy the plot of his novella *Daisy Miller* (1878). The Italian men Huntington described, like Daisy Miller's suitor Mr Giovanelli, were deemed opportunists by Americans. There were exceptions, of course. Fanny was close to Edith Story, the daughter of William Wetmore Story and, after 1875, the wife of the Florentine Marchese Simone Peruzzi de'Medici; she became a successful author and translator as well as a bridge between the Americans in Florence and the royal circle around the Peruzzi and other prominent Italian families.[33] And, occasionally, Anglo-American men married Italian women; the Alexanders must have known Larkin Goldsmith Mead and his wife Marietta di Benvenuti. But relatively few marriages between Anglo-Americans and Italians were considered acceptable by the community.

Despite this, encounters with Italians in the political, literary and artistic elite took place at the Gabinetto Vieusseux and in the homes of the more enlightened Anglo-American residents. At mid-century, the most coveted invitations were for the regular teas, seances and other events hosted by poets Elizabeth Barrett and Robert Browning at Casa Guidi in the Oltrarno, and by their friends, the authors Isa Blagden on Bellosguardo and Theodosia Garrow and her husband Thomas Trollope at their Villino Trollope in what is now Piazza dell'Independenza.[34] The Alexanders attended many

all three drowned sailing back to the United States in 1850. Few Anglo-Americans were willing to be so involved in Italian life.

Like Margaret Fuller, however, the Alexanders were not bothered by religious differences and social distinctions. Francis and Lucia were even unconcerned about Fanny's contact with Italian men. They certainly knew of Margaret's relationship as it was the subject of much gossip in Boston. More immediately, they knew another Bostonian, Elizabeth Doane Chapman, who arrived in Florence while they were there and rather scandalously fell in love with, and eventually married, her music instructor, the conductor Luigi Vannuccini.[31] These were not isolated incidents. In 1884, long-time Florence resident and of these events, and hosted their own, too.[35] Soon after arriving in Florence they befriended a number of prominent Italians; Fanny's correspondence and art, and Lucia's scrapbooks, provide much evidence for these relationships. Lucia was especially proud of her family's social circle; as she later wrote to a friend, 'I am delighted to see those who are really distinguished for anything good.'[36] One such person was the statesman and historian Gino Capponi, whose daughter, Marianna Capponi Farinola, Fanny considered a sister.[37] Capponi provided a cache of letters from Risorgimento patriots for one of Lucia's scrapbooks.[38] In fact, several Italians did this over the years; the politician Ettore Leopardi donated a scrap of paper written by his great grandfather, the celebrated poet Giacomo Leopardi, and the author Niccolò Tommaseo donated autographs from a number of eminent Italians.[39]

Tommaseo's expertise in popular traditions and songs would prove to be of particular interest to Fanny. Fanny and Lucia corresponded with the author, as well as with his wife Diamante, son Girolamo and daughter Caterina, and Lucia devoted an entire scrapbook to these letters and other documents about the family.[40] She dedicated another scrapbook to the Bonaparte family, with letters, photographs and ephemera gifted from Princess Luisa Rasponi Murat.[41] Two further scrapbooks were dedicated to Sigismondo Castromediano, the Duke of Morciano and Marchese of Cavallino, a Risorgimento patriot who had been imprisoned for more than a decade. In 1868 Lucia reached out to Castromediano for a memento; his reply was accompanied by a fragment of his prison clothing and a photograph. They continued to correspond until 1894, the year before he died, and his letters demonstrate not only his great affection for the Alexanders but also the outline of his activities during these years and his reflections on Italian politics.[42]

Another important friend was author Caterina Percoto, who like Tommaseo was engaged with folklore traditions; in 1866 she dedicated one of her short stories to Fanny.[43] Percoto's correspondence with the prominent Pisan chaplain Giovanni Lotti indicated that he too had great affection for the Alexanders.[44] But more important to Fanny were Percoto's female friends, among them the Italian-Armenian poet Vittoria Aganoor and the noblewomen Marina Sprea Baroni Semitecolo and her musician and poet daughter Silvia Pasolini-Zanelli. In one letter Aganoor referred to Lucia and Fanny as 'those excellent and holy creatures!'[45] Semitecolo and her family had been forced into exile in Florence for supporting the Risorgimento – her uncle was Pier Eleonoro Negri, whose regiment the Alexanders assisted – but after the 1866 annexation of the Veneto to the Kingdom of Italy they returned to their Villa Rezzonico in Bassano, where the Alexanders later passed many summers. The Alexanders also visited Venice and the monastic complex on the island of San Lazzaro, a community of Mekhitarist monks much celebrated by Lord Byron, Henry Wadsworth Longfellow and John Ruskin, among others. There they befriended Ghevont Alishan, an Armenian priest and leader of the community who, among his many accomplishments, translated Byron's *Childe Harold's Pilgrimage* into Armenian; Fanny sent him seeds to plant in the San Lazzaro gardens.[46]

The Alexanders knew many other Italian cultural figures. Several composed poems about Fanny, including the Risorgimento heroes Giuseppe Barellai and Francesco Rota and educational reformer Erminia Fuà Fusinato, praising her gentle spirit, her affinity with Saint Catherine of Siena and her charity work.[47] Fusinato and the painter Francesco Lojacono also dedicated poems to Lucia, and the politician Marcello Bruni dedicated two to Lucia, one to Fanny and another to the whole family.[48] In 1854 Fanny drew a portrait of the musician Pietro Romani (fig.19), who praised her character and talent, and Lucia's scrapbooks include art by Raffaello Morghen and Giovanni

Dupré.[49] Fanny was also close to the sculptor Pasquale Romanelli, his wife Elisa, who enlisted Fanny's aid in her charitable endeavors in support of Risorgimento causes, and their daughter Letizia.[50]

Fanny and her parents took part in some of Florence's celebrations of its past, including the 1898 commemoration of Paolo Toscanelli and Amerigo Vespucci and the 600th anniversary of Dante Alighieri's birth in 1865. They may have received tickets for these events from the American consul or their bankers – tickets were allotted to many Anglo-Americans in this manner – and Lucia pasted the programs into her scrapbooks.[51] Lucia wrote about the Dante events to Henry Wadsworth Longfellow – then in the midst of his translation of *The Divine Comedy* – and sent him several related photographs.[52] Dante's popularity with Bostonians like Longfellow and others was only surpassed by his popularity with Florentines, and of course the Alexanders were at the nexus of both communities.

Fanny, who described the final cantos of Dante's *Paradiso* as 'the grandest poetry I ever read',[53] also wrote about the celebrations, and the gift she received from the scholar Giambattista Giuliani, in a letter to a friend:

> The city was certainly more beautiful than I ever saw it; all the streets were hung with garlands and banners; the old red lily rather taking the lead, and the white cross not very conspicuous. The court and loggia of the Uffizi were fitted up for a ball room, with mirrors, flowers, evergreens and tapestries, and a fountain of wine in the centre . . . You know how Dante's remains were discovered just about that time, and how we all had just a little hope that Ravenna might be generous and give him back to us. But that was too much to expect, and after all I think Ravenna was right. With the bones were discovered a few withered bay leaves, which had once formed part of a garland, and it was suggested that one should be given to every Italian city, but that was also refused.

I knew one of the commissioners who were sent on from Florence to verify the remains and heard from him a most interesting account of all that took place. At my request he brought me a flower which had been touched to the bones which I keep as a most precious relic. I dare say you know who this gentleman was: Padre Giuliani, the commentator of Dante . . . I had quite a sympathy for him, as he told me about his visit to the remains. He was permitted, at his request, and as a particular favour, to kiss the forehead of the great Florentine: that he said in a solemn and tremulous voice, was the great moment of his life, a moment never to be forgotten.[54]

While the Alexanders met these many Italians, they settled into their Florentine life and filled their rooms in the Hotel Suisse with art. Some of this art, including Francis's portraits of the family and Thomas Cole's *Tornado in the Wilderness*, traveled with them across the ocean, a sign that they intended to remain abroad for an extended period and wanted their prized possessions around them. But these paintings were soon overwhelmed by a great quantity of Italian objects. Despite the Alexanders' Evangelical faith, these objects – most of them altarpieces and altarpiece fragments, representing Madonnas, saints and sacred narratives – grew into an extensive collection. Francis had apparently grown weary of catering to demanding sitters, and this prompted him to end his lucrative career as a portraitist in favor of collecting, restoring and dealing.

Florence's growing art market made this possible. The American critic James Jackson Jarves, who was building his own collection at this time and likely competed with Francis for certain acquisitions, described the city as 'a vast picture-shop' where collectors and dealers of all nationalities sought out the best objects.[55] But with so many families selling their possessions, the suppression of sacred institutions clearing out centuries of church furnishings, and the growing numbers of fakes and forgeries, there were plenty to be had.

According to Thomas Ball, who moved to Florence a year after the Alexanders, from the time Francis arrived he

> had spent most of his time repairing and touching up old paintings which he delighted to hunt up in every out-of-the-way corner . . . every morning there would be an array of 'old masters', in various stages of dilapidation, strung along in front of the [Palazzo Strozzi], their owners watching intently the house opposite, for Mr. Alexander to appear at the window, when if he saw anything promising he would descend and examine it. I asked him if he himself no longer painted; he answered modestly, in his bluff manner, 'No; what's the use, when I can buy a better picture for a dollar and a half than I can paint myself?'[56]

Many of those paintings, probably hung from the combination standard bearers and horse hitches known as *ferri* on the Strozzi facade, were gold ground panels from the early Renaissance; with their sacred iconography and often fragmentary or compromised condition they were of little interest to many Anglo-Americans and therefore quite affordable. Francis only had to look out the windows of the Hotel Suisse to see the sun glinting off the gold before running across the street to negotiate a purchase.

Fanny joined her father in this pursuit. One of her earliest acquisitions was a *Coronation of the Virgin* with saints and music-making angels that she attributed to Andrea Orcagna. She described it in enthusiastic detail to a friend, while acknowledging that it and some of her other purchases had condition issues: 'I am sometimes afraid that when you come to see my pictures you will be disappointed, for after all they have their faults. And yet, after I have written this, I cannot tell what their faults are. They are a good deal out of repair, but I do not think you can

help liking them.'[57] Fanny later described her studio as:

> a hospital for infirm pictures, for I have put there all the old broken worm-eaten boards that I bought when I was a very young girl, at which time I spent pretty much all my money for dilapidated saints and Madonnas. Some of them still appear beautiful to me, and the others are such old friends that I cannot bear to part from them.[58]

The Alexander collection was dispersed long ago. But Harriet Georgina Ellis Caetani, the English wife of renowned Dante scholar Michelangelo Caetani, took six photographs of the salon in their third Florence home, the Hotel Bonciani in Piazza Santa Maria Novella, which reveal a great many paintings and sculptures alongside antique furnishings, photographs of friends and family, maiolica, glass, armor, textiles, books and whatever else appealed to their eclectic taste (fig.20). The few paintings that can be identified through these photographs and other sources include a Saint Nicholas (fig.21), a Nativity (fig.22), a *Saint Biagio Visited in Prison by a Widow* (fig.23), and a Saint Onuphrius (fig.24), as well as five Madonnas, two associated with Sano di Pietro and one each with the Master of the Castello Nativity (fig.25), Biagio d'Antonio (fig.26) and Domenico di Zanobi di Piero (fig.27).[59] On occasion Fanny copied these paintings. She made at least two drawings of the Domenico di Zanobi di Piero panel; one has only a faint outline of rolling hills in place of the background landscape and simplifies the textiles and Christ's halo (while omitting the Madonna's halo entirely), but it captures the gestures, poses and expressions with considerable accuracy (fig.28).

During their years in Florence, descriptions of the Alexander homes mention additional paintings, including representations of a Transfiguration, a Crucifixion, and saints Catherine of Alexandria, Francis and Thomas, with ambitious attributions

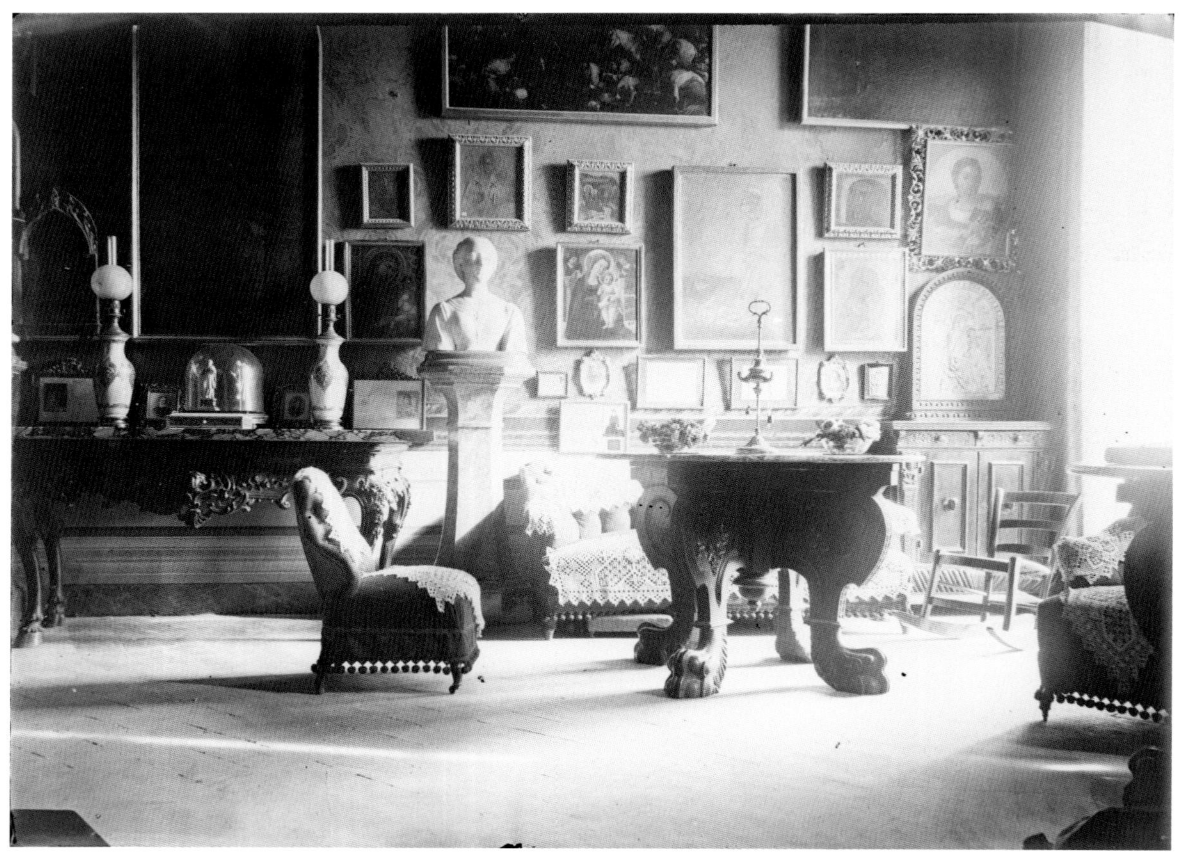

20 Harriet Georgina Ellis Caetani, *The Alexanders' Drawing Room at the Hotel Bonciani, Florence*, between 1869–84, photograph from a glass negative, New York University, Acton Photograph Archive, Villa La Pietra, Florence

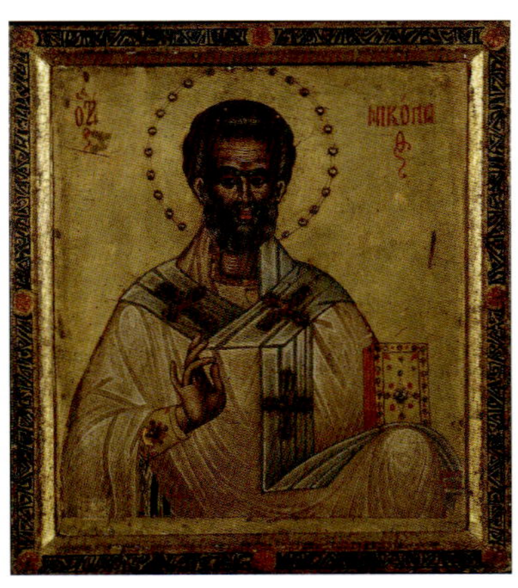 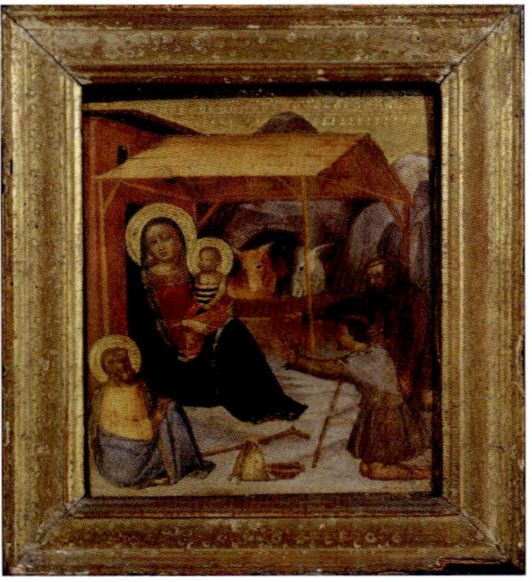 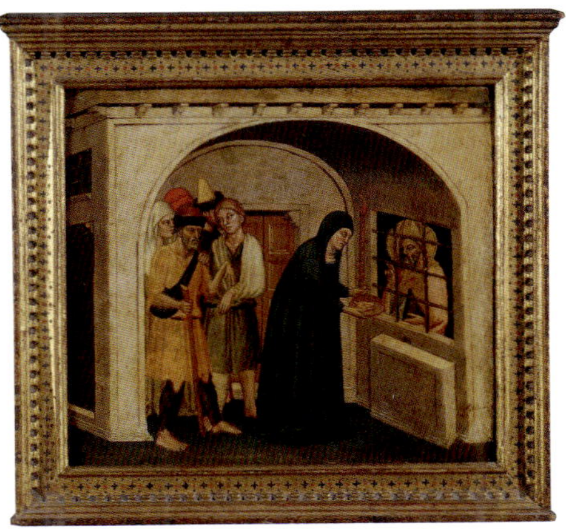

21 Cretan, *Saint Nicholas*, fifteenth or sixteenth century (?), tempera on panel, 41 × 36 cm (16⅛ × 14⅛ in), New York University, Acton Collection, Villa La Pietra, Florence

22 Close to the Master of the Misericordia, *Nativity*, c.1370, tempera on panel, 34.5 × 30.2 cm (13⅝ × 11⅞ in), New York University, Acton Collection, Villa La Pietra, Florence

23 Matteo di Pacino, *Saint Biagio Visited in Prison by a Widow*, c.1380, tempera on panel, 26.5 × 29.5 cm (10⅜ × 11⅝ in), New York University, Acton Collection, Villa La Pietra, Florence

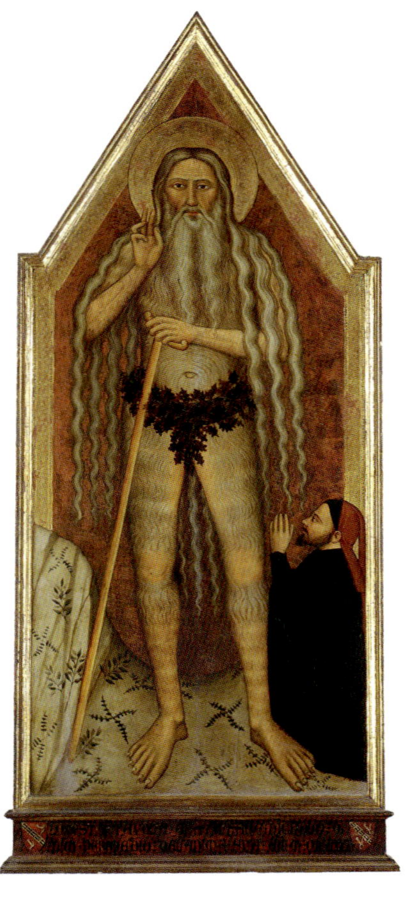 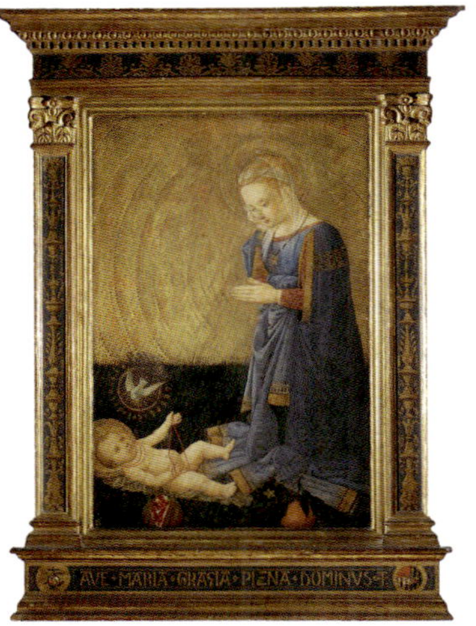 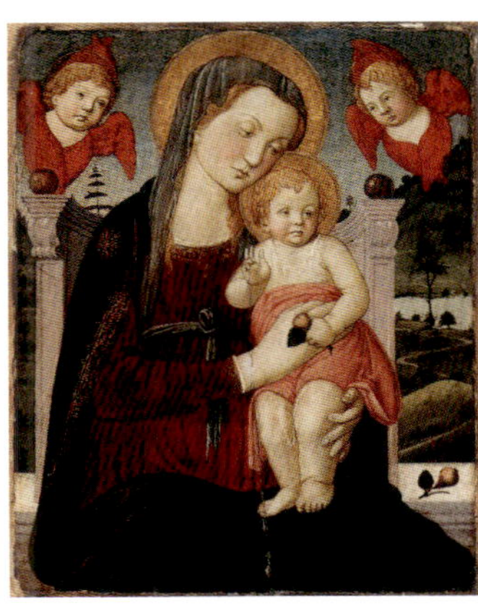

24 Giovanni del Biondo, *Saint Onuphrius with a Donor*, 1380, tempera on panel, 156.5 × 70.5 cm (61⅝ × 27¾ in), New York University, Acton Collection, Villa La Pietra, Florence

25 Master of the Castello Nativity, *Madonna and Child*, c.1450, tempera on panel, 123 × 92.5 cm (48⅜ × 36⅜ in), New York University, Acton Collection, Villa La Pietra, Florence

26 Workshop of Biagio d'Antonio da Firenze, *Madonna and Child*, late fifteenth century, oil on panel, 46.5 × 36.8 cm (18¼ × 14½ in), location unknown

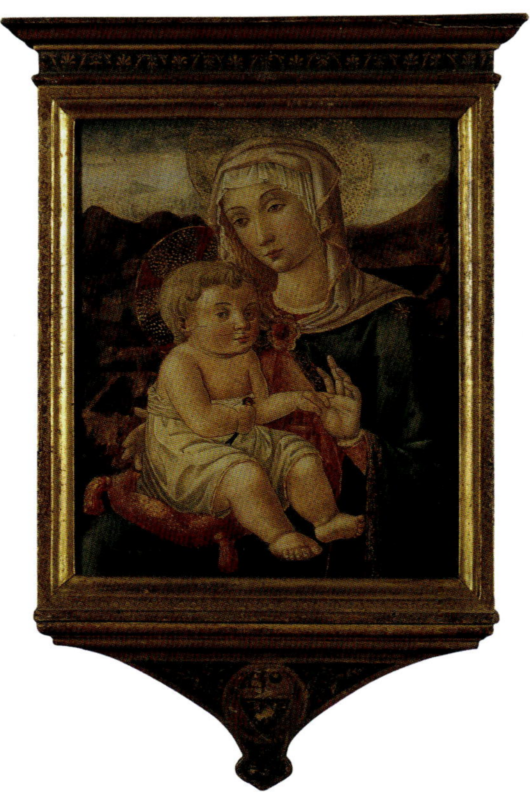

27 Domenico di Zanobi di Piero, *Madonna and Child*, *c.*1450, tempera on panel, 66.5 × 43 cm (26⅛ × 16⅞ in), New York University, Acton Collection, Villa La Pietra, Florence

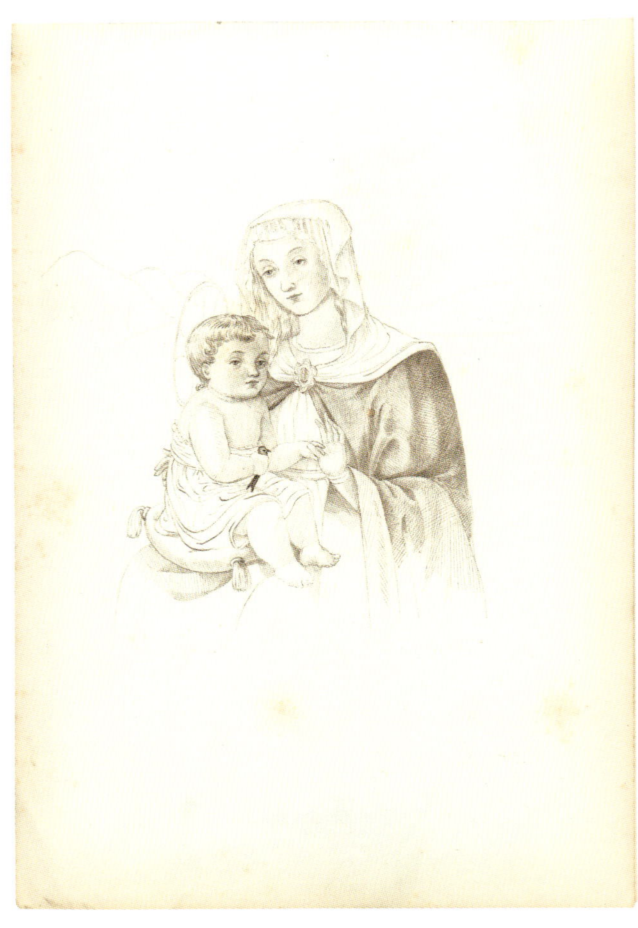

28 Francesca Alexander, after Domenico di Zanobi di Piero, *Madonna and Child*, 1850s, pen and ink, 21 × 30 cm (8¼ × 11¾ in), Wellesley College Special Collections, Wellesley, MA

to artists like Giotto, Ghirlandaio and Perugino.[60] Sculptures included a painfully thin ivory Christ hanging from a wooden cross, which Fanny's cousin Constance Grosvenor Alexander later donated to the Episcopal Chapel of St Anne in Arlington, Massachusetts; a second ivory crucifixion said to be by Giambologna can no longer be located.[61] Nor can sculptures of the Madonna associated with Luca della Robbia and Donatello – the Donatello allegedly purchased from a Lucca flower show – or a group of marble busts, including Giovanni Bastianini's so-called *Luisa* or *Aloysia Strozzi*, known today in several versions, though whether it was acquired as a work by Bastianini or as a Renaissance bust is unknown.[62] A cache of early modern drawings, among them landscapes, figure studies and a triumph over vices, further indicates the family's eclectic tastes and acquisitive habits (fig.29).

Many of Florence's foreign residents owned similar objects.[63] The French sculptor Félicie de Fauveau's drawing room was filled with carved furnishings, silver crucifixes, and paintings ranging from gold-ground panels to canvases by Sodoma and Jusepe de Ribera.[64] The Villino Trollope had maiolica, marriage chests, carved furniture and hundreds of other Renaissance objects.[65] And the American painter Henry Roderick Newman filled his home and studio with Renaissance paintings, rugs, textiles, tapestries, ceramics, rare books and other collectibles.[66] These spaces were described with awe by travelers, who saw in them the sort of charm obtainable only by those privileged to live in the city. The Alexanders' collection certainly contributed to the appeal so many felt in their presence; in 1860, Annie Adams Fields pronounced their residence, which she visited together with Harriet Beecher Stowe, to be 'truly an artist's home'.[67] Of course, at that time most visitors thought the artist was Francis, and despite Thomas Ball's later report he did occasionally continue to paint.[68] As late as 1878 he was still celebrated as a Boston portraitist, though he had neither been in Boston, nor taken on portrait commissions, for many years.[69]

Instead, the real artist in the Alexanders' home was Fanny. Several male artists were willing to take on female students, and women she knew took advantage of this. During their time in Florence, Sarah Gooll Putnam had instruction from Italian painter Ernesto Bensa while her sisters had lessons from Canadian copyist Antoine-Sébastien Falardeau, Lizzie Boott studied with Greek painter Giorgio Mignaty, and Florence Freeman worked with Hiram Powers.[70] Beginning in 1871, a Madame Frier (perhaps the Scottish painter Jessie Frier) ran an art school for women, and Fanny's Scottish friend Georgina Forbes studied there.[71] Fanny apparently had a few lessons in perspective from an unnamed household painter because, according to Lucia, Fanny could only learn from those who were not actual experts.[72] But guidance from Francis, and simply being in Italy, proved to be enough for her.

Many of her early Florence drawings were similar in subject matter to her Boston drawings. Some were based on literature: she sketched (and painted) Italian friends as Cinderella (fig.30) and as Hans Christian Andersen's 'Match Girl'.[73] She also sketched the landscape and animals she encountered during her walks in the countryside, including a pig with bristly hair and curly tail standing on its cloven hoofs (fig.31).[74] And she continued making portraits, whether of Anglo-American friends or Italians like members of the Martelli and Matteoni families, their facial features captured in minute detail (fig.32).

While the paintings in her home were influential, she was similarly stimulated by the art all around her. There is no evidence that Francis or Fanny requested permission to copy from paintings hanging in the Uffizi, but they did work together in Florence's churches.[75] The custodian at Santa Maria Novella opened the stained glass windows in the choir and provided them with chairs and a table so they could copy Ghirlandaio's frescoes in 1854.[76] Around the same time, Fanny copied the frescoed figures of Mary Magdalene and Dante in the

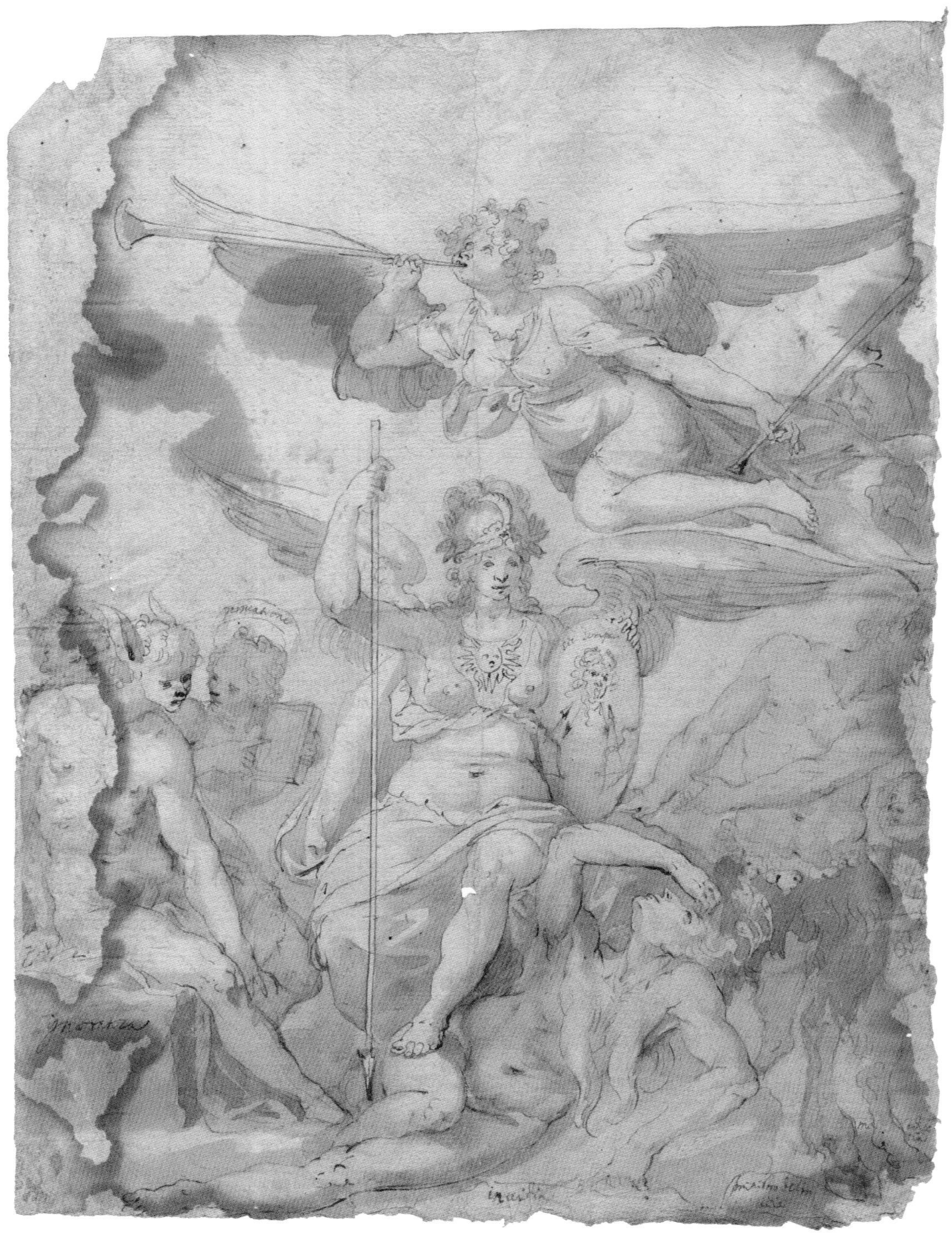

29 Florentine, *Triumph over Vices*, sixteenth century, pen, ink and wash, 20.49 × 27 cm (8 ⅛ × 10 ⅝ in), Wellesley College Special Collections, Wellesley, MA

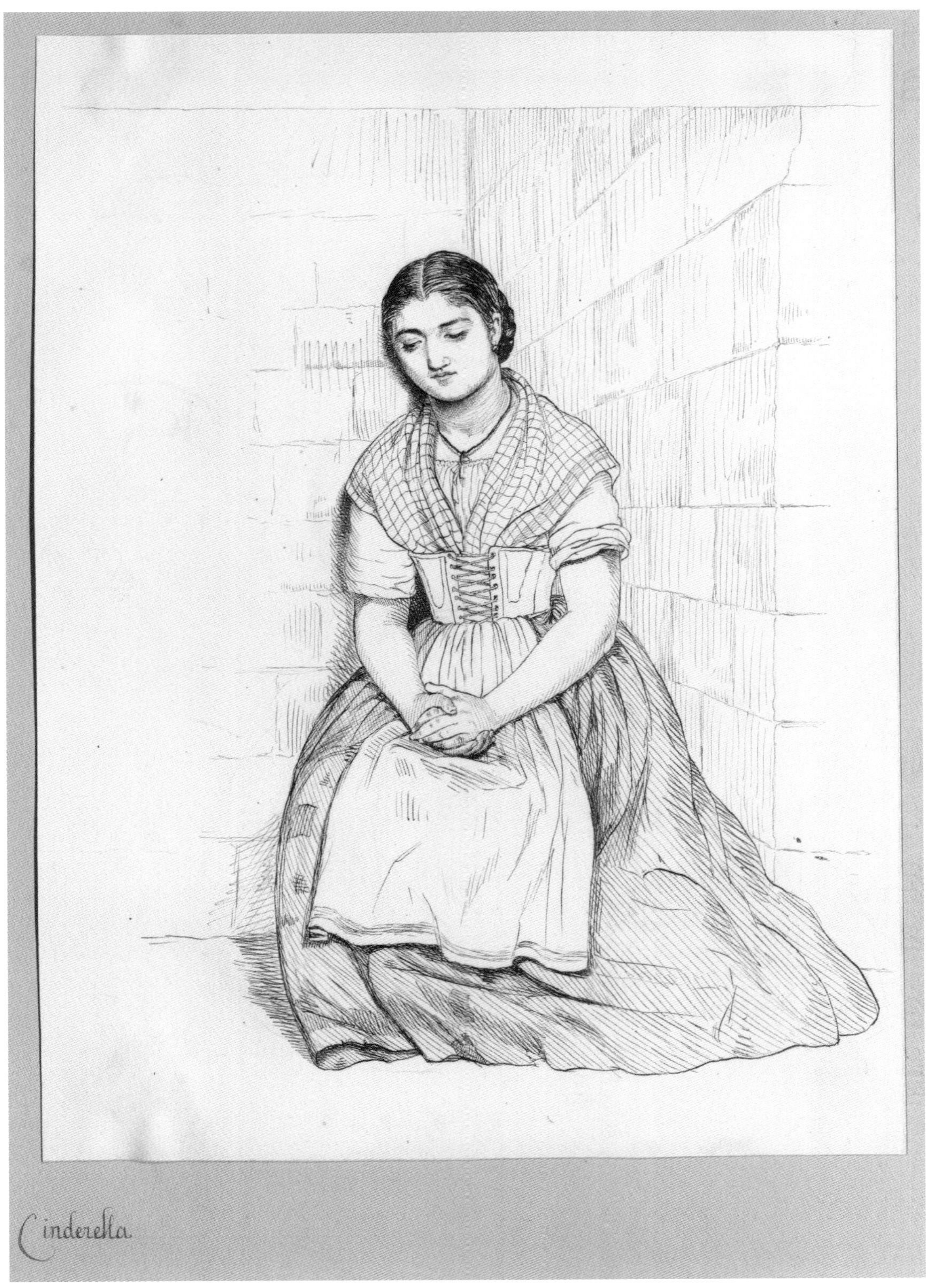

30 Francesca Alexander, *Cinderella*, 1850s, pen and ink, 16 × 22 cm (6 ¼ × 8 ⅝ in),
Wellesley College Special Collections, Wellesley, MA

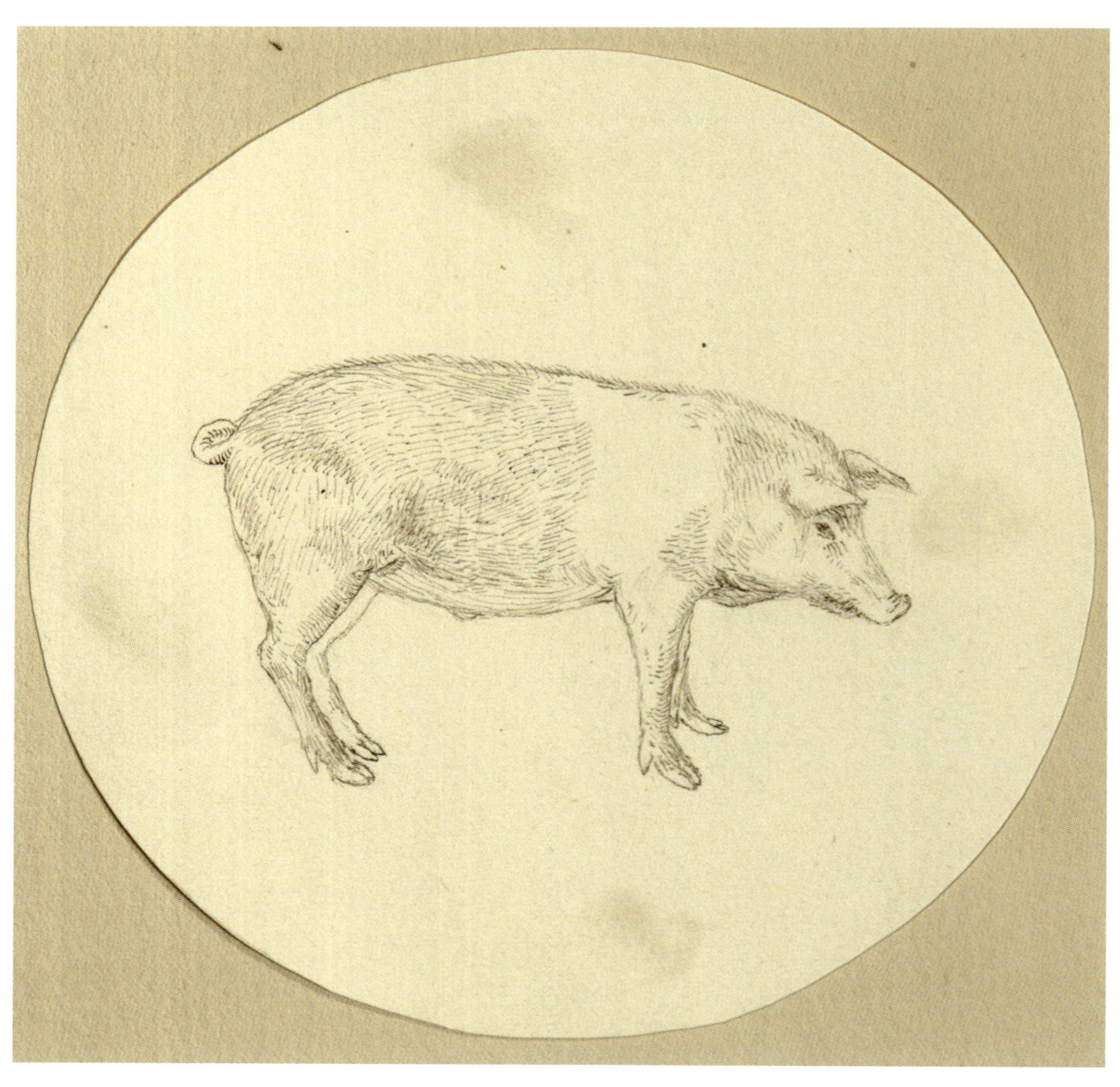

31 Francesca Alexander, *Pig*, 1850s, pen and ink, diameter 9.5 cm (3 ¾ in),
Wellesley College Special Collections, Wellesley, MA

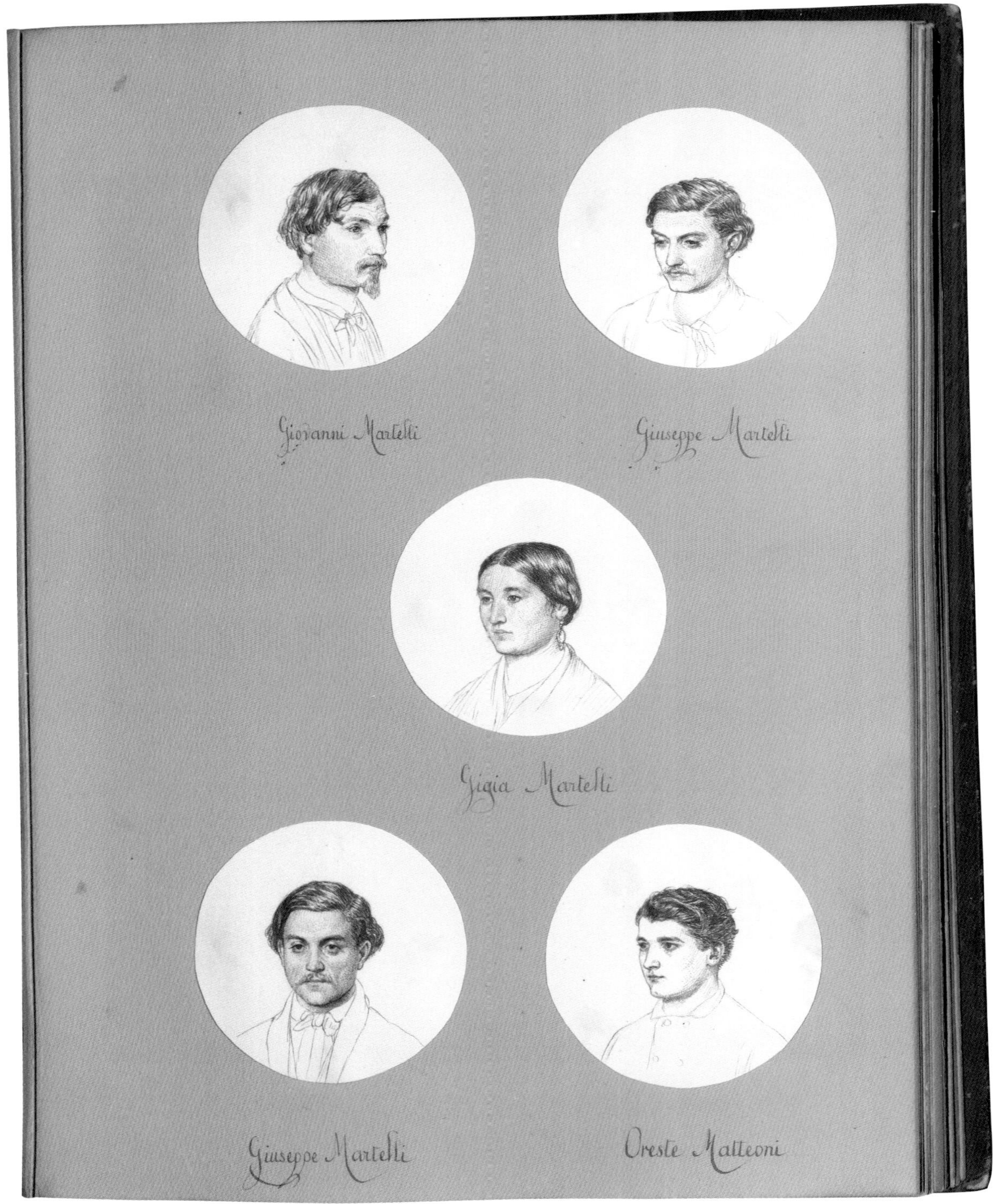

32 Francesca Alexander, *Martelli and Matteoni Family Portraits*, 1850s, pen and ink, 24 × 30 cm (9 ½ × 11 ¾ in), Wellesley College Special Collections, Wellesley, MA

Bargello's Magdalene Chapel.[77] Reflecting on this years later, Thomas Ball noted that Fanny 'drew exquisitely; working every day in the churches and cloisters under her father's guidance, she acquired a style as pure and simple as that of the old masters themselves'.[78]

She mentioned what she saw, and her enthusiasm for it, in her correspondence. In 1865 she was thrilled to have the opportunity to see frescoes by Fra Angelico in San Marco and Perugino in Santa Maria Maddalena de'Pazzi with sisters Georgina and Christina Forbes, who secured a papal dispensation that allowed them into spaces normally forbidden to women.[79] Fanny even missed Florence's art when she traveled. After returning from a summer in the Apennines, she wrote,

> One of the first friends whom I visited . . . was that very stately and quiet one, the marble Archbishop of San Francesco, whom I always find more companionable than most living people. It was a happy day for me when I found myself once again sitting by his side and looking at his kind and thoughtful saintly old face, always turned a little towards me as it lies on the rich pillow.[80]

That friend was Luca della Robbia's tomb for Bishop Benozzo Federighi in the church of San Francesco di Paola, and Fanny's confession of love for this sculpture, and her preference for its company over that of actual people, gives some insight into her relationship with the art around her.

Fanny appreciated what she saw beyond Florence, too. During an 1873 visit to Venice, she admired the thirteenth-century mosaic of *Christ Emmanuel* in the west arm of the basilica of San Marco, representing a youthful blessing Christ standing on a cushion set on a bejeweled base against a starry background (fig.33). Fanny sketched the mosaic, capturing the overall composition with a particular focus on the complex folds and gathers of the draperies and the tiny blooming plants springing from the ground, the

sort of precise details that accorded well with her style (fig.34). Two years later, the Alexanders were in Venice again and an outbreak of cholera emptied the city, but she even found joy in this, because they were able to see the early sixteenth-century Grimani Breviary, an extravagant Flemish manuscript held in the Biblioteca Marciana, 'quite by ourselves, there being no one else to look at it. What a wonder it is! . . . two hours spent in looking at it, without interruption, entirely recompensed me for the misery of those last days and nights at Venice.'[81]

In addition to copying what she saw in her home and elsewhere, Fanny made Renaissance-inspired compositions. She drew Thomas Ball's wife Ellen Louisa Wild in the guise of Saint Cecilia, in three-quarter view from the waist up; she holds the palm of martyrdom and wears a floral wreath, a simple halo around her head and a view of a landscape with a church and belltower behind her (fig.35).[82] In her usual style, Fanny only outlined the body but focused attention on her sitter's head with precisely rendered eyelashes, hair and wreath. She sometimes used shapes reminiscent of polyptych fragments, as she did in a drawing of Mary Magdalene holding her ointment jar (fig.36).

Fanny devoted much of her art to Italian themes, and particularly representations of her *contadini* friends. Francis painted similar themes during his first trip abroad; the list of paintings he exhibited at Harding's Gallery in 1834 includes scenes of Roman peasants and a Capuchin friar, among others.[83] In Fanny's case, however, the models for her art also became her friends, the recipients of her charitable efforts and, eventually, the subjects of her books. The author and diplomat John Lothrop Motley, who knew the Alexanders from Boston, was entranced by these drawings. He visited Florence in 1855 and wrote to tell his mother Anna of a gathering:

> we saw a large quantity of Fanny Alexander's drawings, and I assure you they are really wonderful. She draws

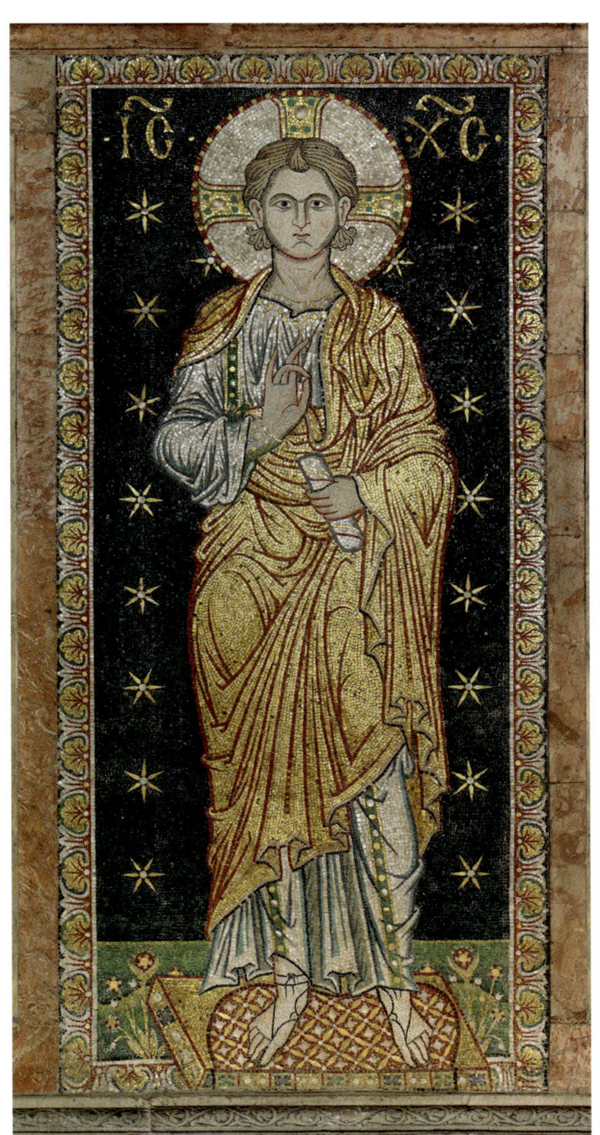 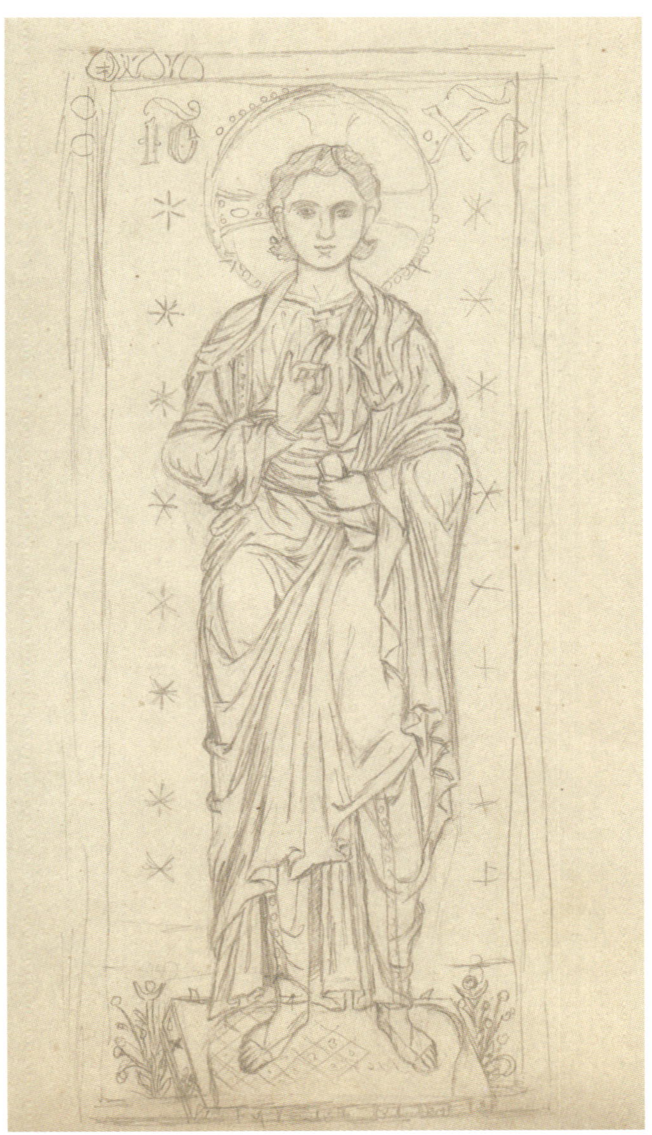

33 Venetian, *Christ Emmanuel*, thirteenth century, mosaic, 240 × 100 cm (94 ½ × 39 ⅜ in), San Marco, Venice

34 Francesca Alexander, after *Christ Emmanuel* (detail), 1873, pencil, 24.76 × 16.82 cm (9 ¾ × 6 ⅝ in),
Schlesinger Library on the History of Women in America, Harvard Radcliffe Institute, Cambridge, MA

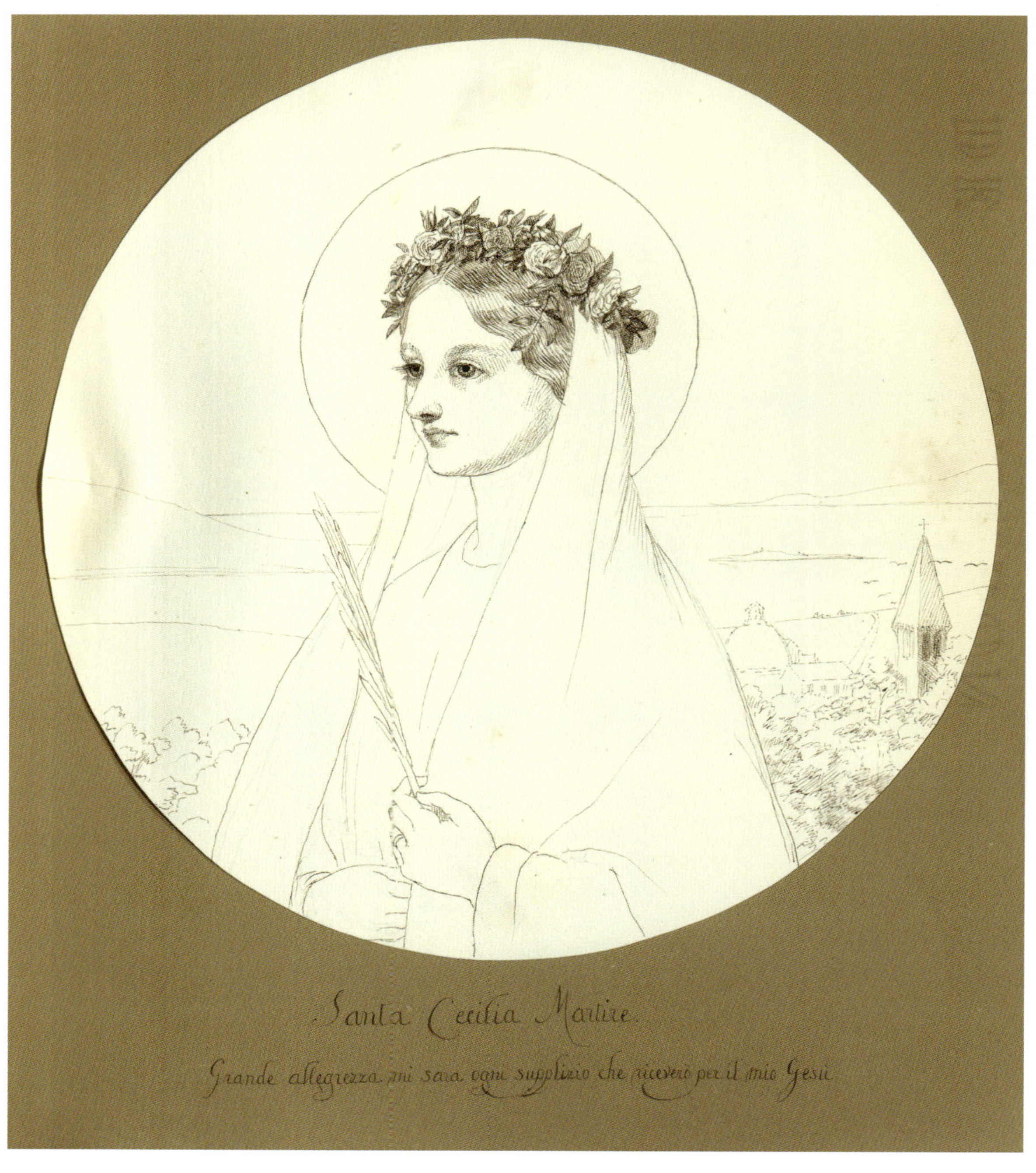

35 Francesca Alexander, *Saint Cecilia*, 1854, pen and ink, diameter 19 cm (7½ in),
Wellesley College Special Collections, Wellesley, MA

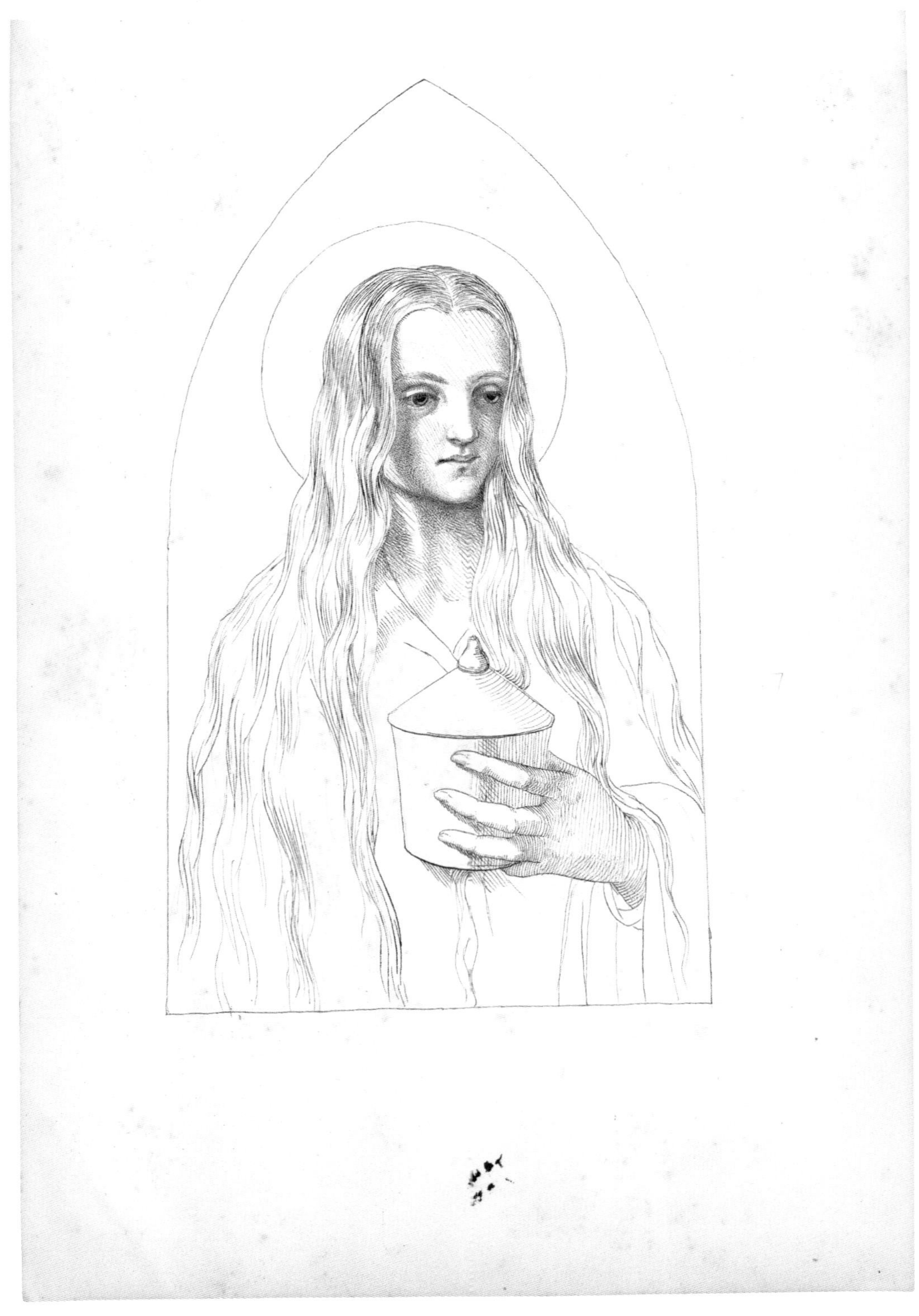

36 Francesca Alexander, *Mary Magdalene*, 1850s, pen and ink, 21 × 30 cm (8 ¼ × 11 ¾ in),
Wellesley College Special Collections, Wellesley, MA

entirely with pen and ink, composing out of her own imagination or from her recollection. But her facility and grace and purity of style are unequaled by any modern drawings which I ever saw. She has the good taste to form her artistic education in the school of the wonderful Quattro centisti of Florence – the painters, I mean, of the fifteenth century, whose works here spread each a halo of glory around this city, and which heralded the extraordinary effulgence which was to illumine the world in the early part of the fifteenth century. In these pre-Raphaelite productions Florence is very rich … She draws outlines, human figures, Madonnas, peasant girls, saints in endless variety, and illustrates old Italian songs, of which she furnishes herself, very pretty translations. She is a young person of unquestionable genius, and as simple and unaffected as she is clever.[84]

Motley's description was prophetic; many would echo his assessment of Fanny's talent and character over the years. His is also the earliest comment about her interest in these themes. This kind of praise probably encouraged Fanny to submit a drawing of Saint Agnes, with a young Lucchese woman named Carolina Pazienza as her model, for consideration in Florence's Esposizione Nazionale Italiana of 1861, the first exhibition held in the newly established Kingdom of Italy. That February she wrote to tell a friend, 'I am engaged now on my picture for the exhibition, which I think you will like to hear about. It represents a Sant'Agnese with her lamb, and I am doing it in pen and ink, for I do not paint well enough yet in colors.'[85] Fanny was excited by the prospect of sharing her work with a large audience; she continued, 'I can hardly realise it yet, myself, it is as if I could speak to all those thousands of people, for indeed I can speak through my pictures easier than in any other way.' But this drawing, with the saint sitting against an olive tree in a flowering field, an open prayer book in her lap and a lamb dozing at her side, was rejected by the exhibition jury (fig.37). This exhibition showcased

propagandistic work by established Italian artists like Saverio Altamura, Pietro Magni, and Stefano Ussi, so the rejection is hardly surprising. But Fanny was disappointed in herself, and wrote, 'I might have known that my works were not fit to put with those of professors and hope I shall be wiser another time.'[86] Although she occasionally exhibited her work in later years – or more accurately others exhibited it on her behalf – she never competed to do so again.

The Hotel Suisse was surely intended as a short-term residence while the Alexanders familiarized themselves with Florentine life. But Fanny's (and Francis's) love of nature, and the need for larger quarters for their growing art collection, made a move outside the city walls inevitable. It was also healthier, an important consideration following an especially deadly cholera outbreak in 1855, which decimated the population and killed several Anglo-Americans, including the daughter and pregnant wife of the painter Thomas Buchanan Read.[87] The Alexanders, to the surprise of other Americans, remained in the city throughout that summer.[88] But it was probably the memory of that experience that prompted them to relocate the following year to an apartment in the Villa Brichieri on Bellosguardo, where Francis's friend Horatio Greenough once lived. Fanny especially loved it there; when they left in 1868, she stated that 'all the happiest years of my life' took place at that villa.[89]

Constance Fenimore Woolson, who lived in the same apartment years later, claimed the Villa Brichieri had a better view of Florence and the surrounding countryside than others on the hilltop.[90] That view was important; Anglo-Americans celebrated Bellosguardo's location and the panorama of Florence and the surrounding countryside that gave it its name. The Alexanders must have known their friend Charles Dickens's description in his *Pictures from Italy* (1846), and they may have watched English artist John Brett – coincidentally, given Fanny's later life, a Ruskin follower – paint the view from the nearby Villa Fioravanti (fig.38).

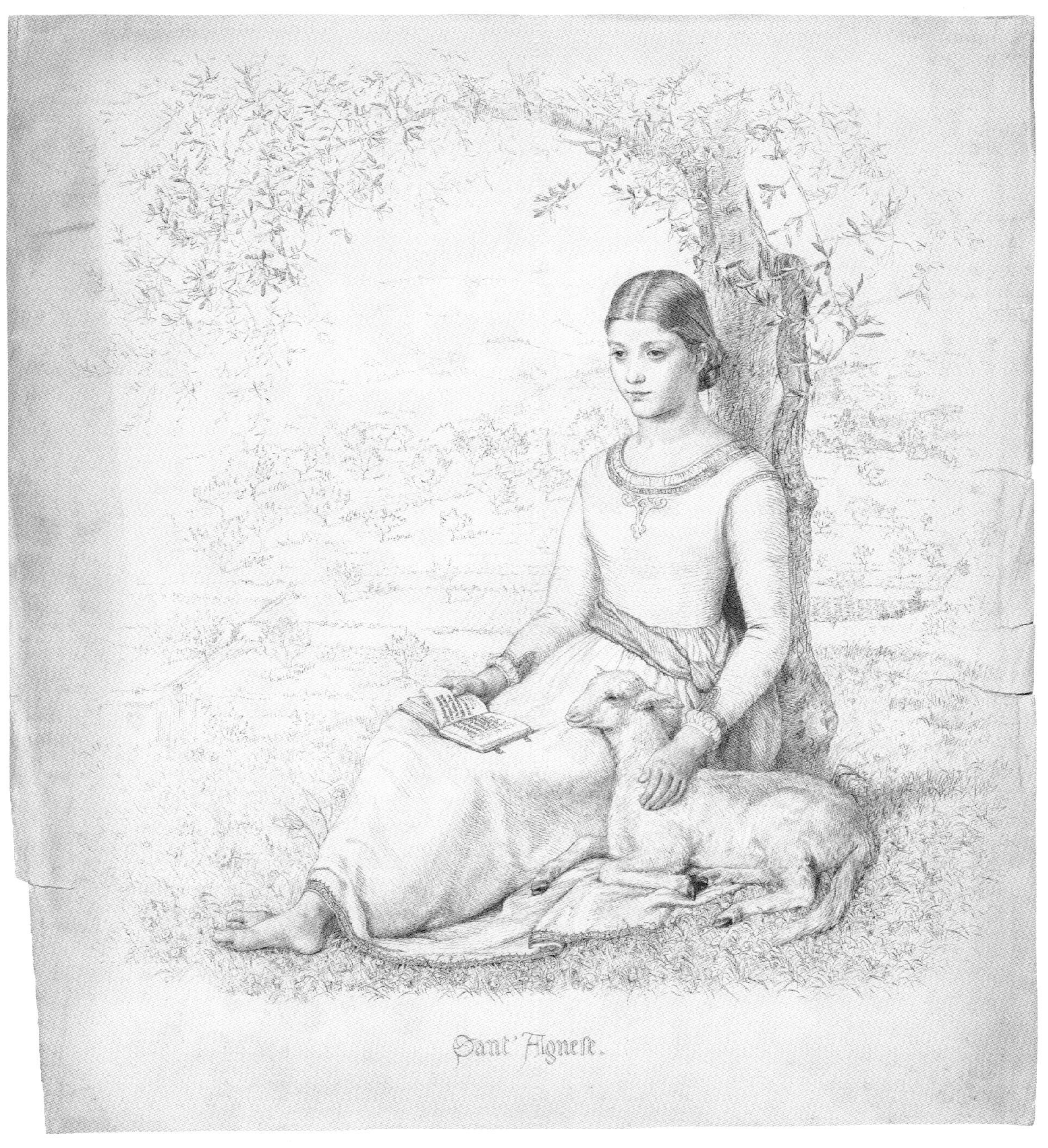

37 Francesca Alexander, *Saint Agnes*, 1861, ink on paper, 38.5 × 35 cm (15 ⅛ × 13 ¾ in),
Wellesley College Special Collections, Wellesley, MA

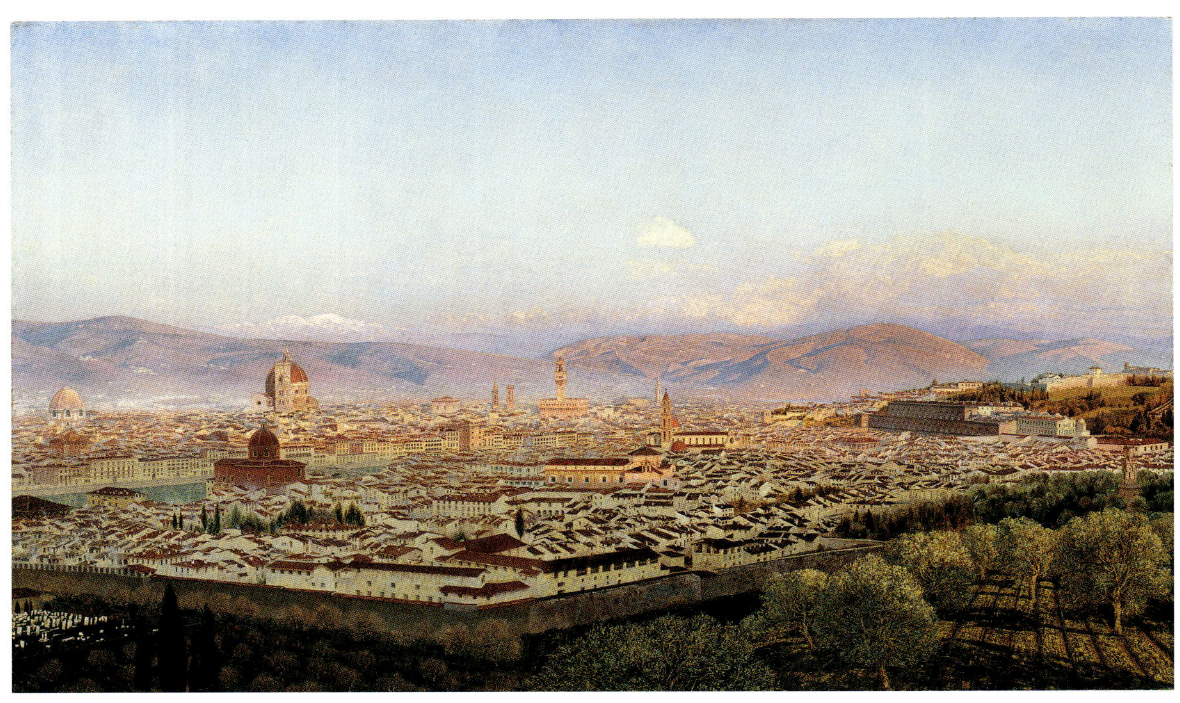

38 John Brett, *Florence from Bellosguardo*, 1863, oil on canvas, 60 × 101.3 cm (23 ⅝ × 39 ⅞ in), Tate, UK

But Elizabeth Barrett Browning did the most
to spread awareness of Bellosguardo, and the Villa
Brichieri view, in her evocative poem *Aurora Leigh*:

I found a house, at Florence, on the hill
Of Bellosguardo. 'Tis a tower that keeps
A post of double-observation o'er
The valley of Arno (holding as a hand
The outspread city) straight toward Fiesole
And Mount Morello and the setting sun, –
The Vallombrosan mountains to the right,
Which sunrise fills as full as crystal cups
Wine-filled, and red to the brim because it's red.
No sun could die, nor yet be born, unseen
By dwellers at my villa: morn and eve
Were magnified before us in the pure

Illimitable space and pause of sky,
Intense as angels' garments blanched with God,
Less blue than radiant. From the outer wall
Of the garden, dropped the mystic floating grey
Of olive-trees, (with interruptions green
From maize and vine) until 'twas caught and torn
On that abrupt black line of cypresses
Which signed the way to Florence. Beautiful
The city lay along the ample vale,
Cathedral, tower and palace, piazza and street;
The river trailing like a silver cord
Through all, and curling loosely, both before
And after, over the whole stretch of land
Sown whitely up and down its opposite slopes,
With farms and villas.[91]

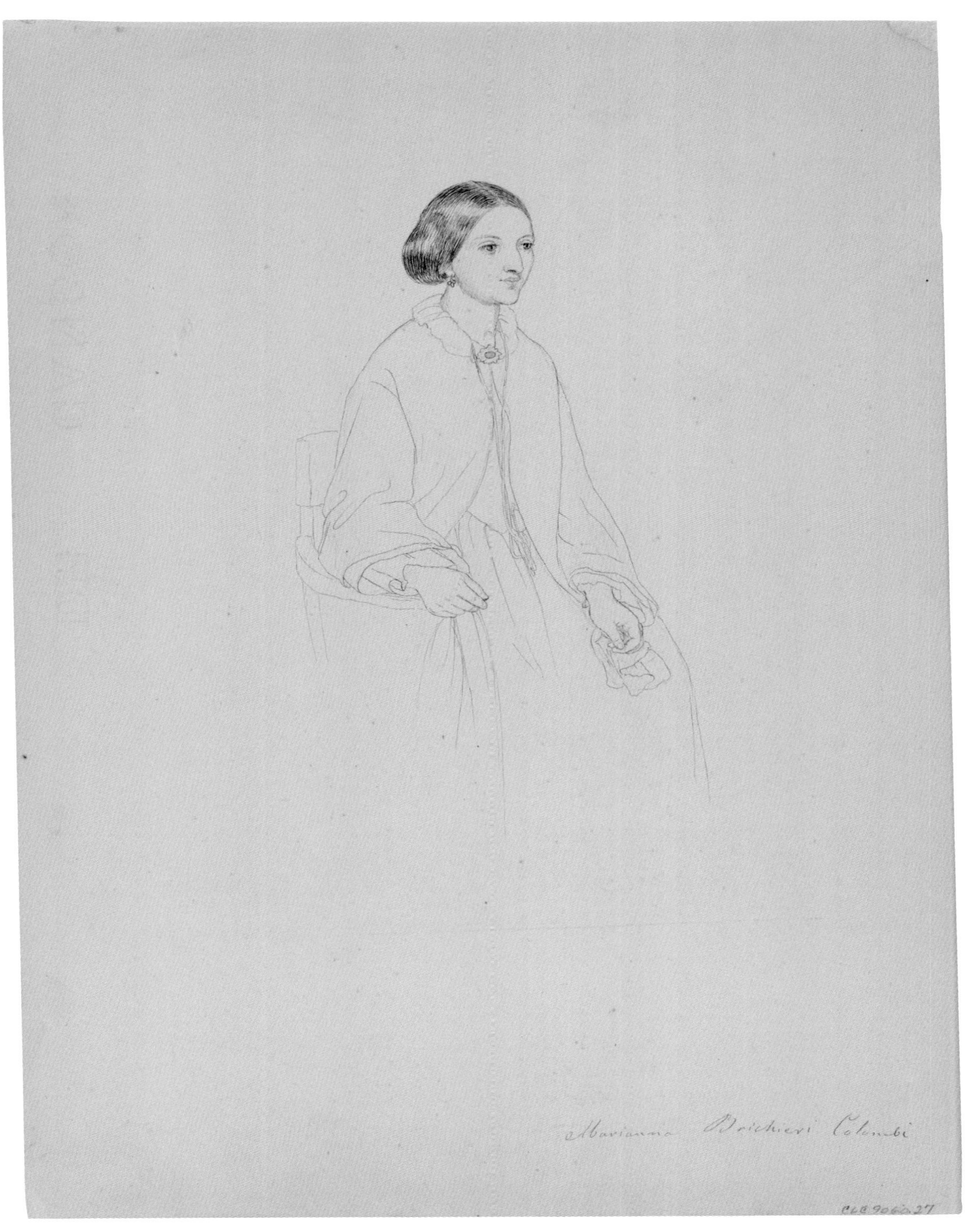

39 Francesca Alexander, *Marianna Brichieri-Colombi*, c.1856, pen and brown ink over pencil,
33.6 × 25.5 cm (13 ¼ × 10 in), Cantor Arts Center, Stanford University, Stanford, CA

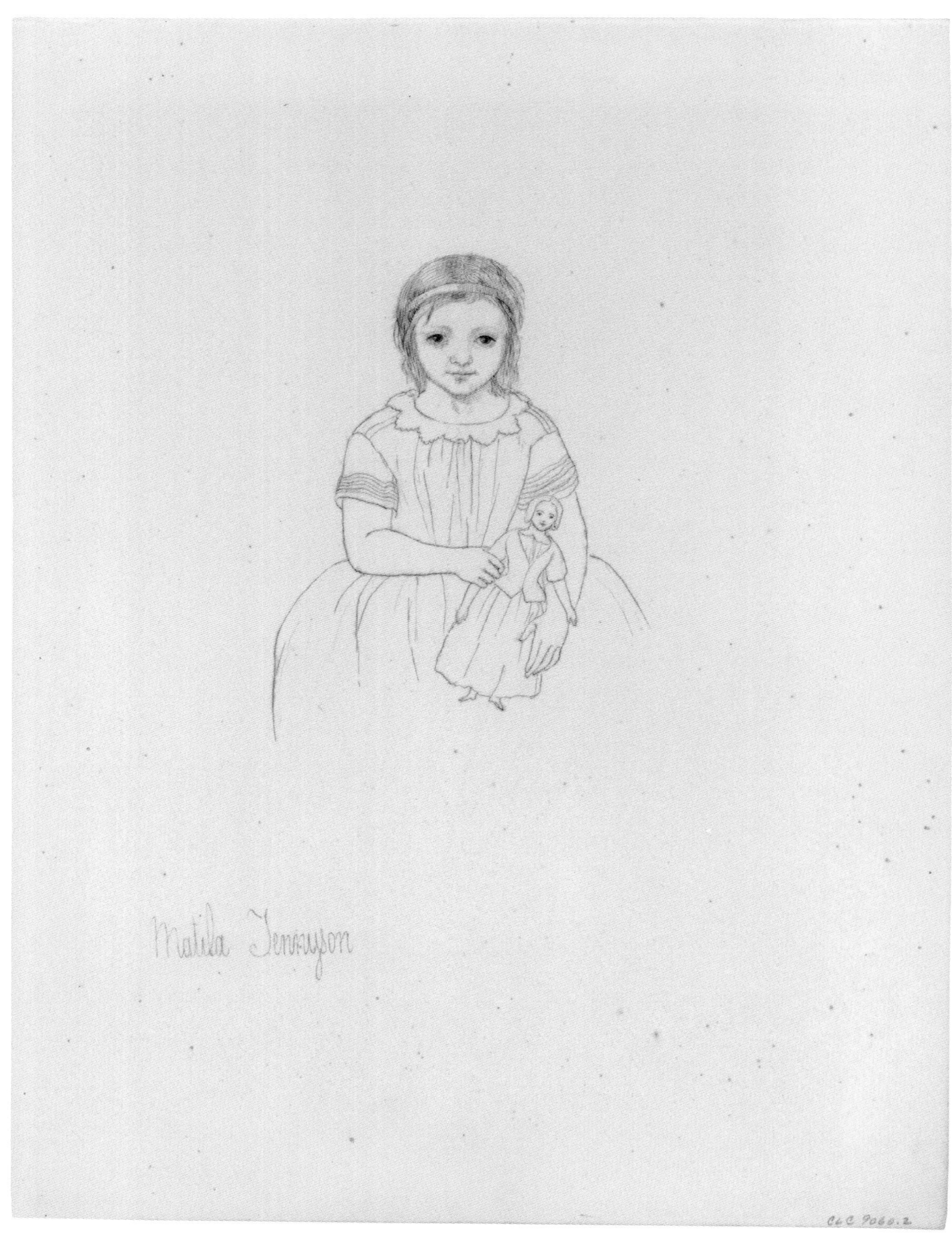

40 Francesca Alexander, *Matilda Tennyson*, c.1858, ink on paper,
33.81 × 25.56 cm (13 ¼ × 10 in), Columbus Museum, Columbus, GA

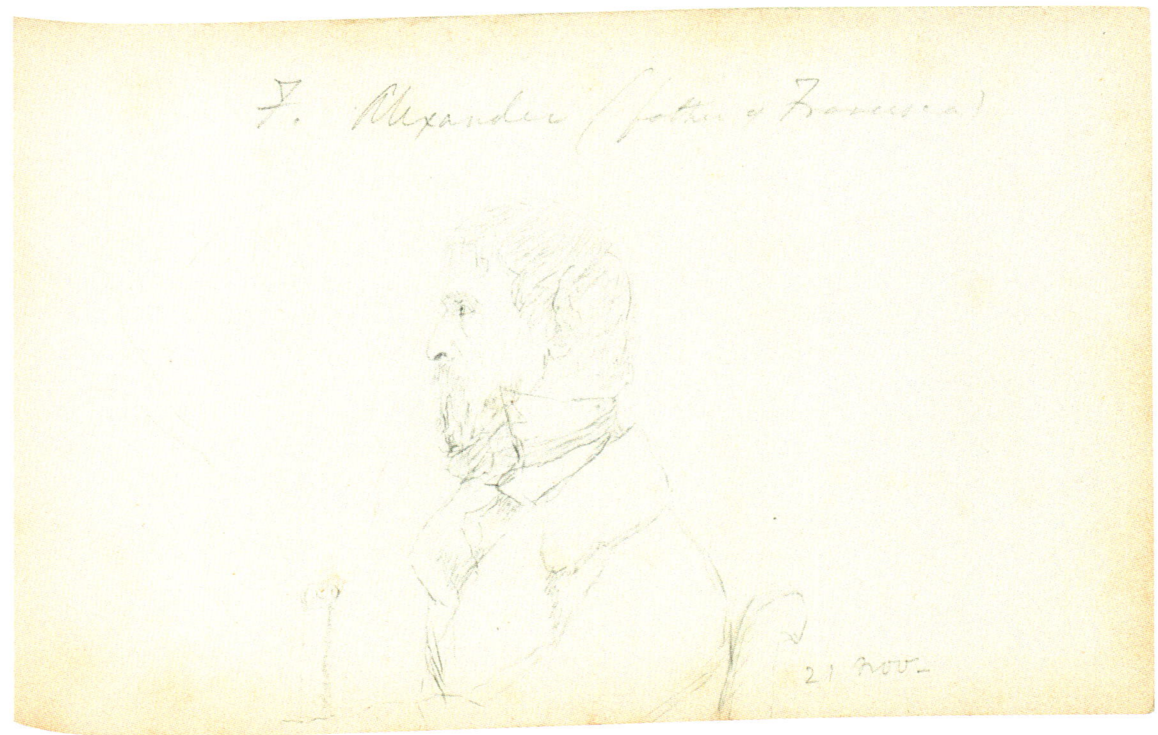

41 Elizabeth Boott Duveneck, *Francis Alexander*, 21 November 1856, pencil,
dimensions unknown, Archives of American Art, Smithsonian Institution, Washington, DC

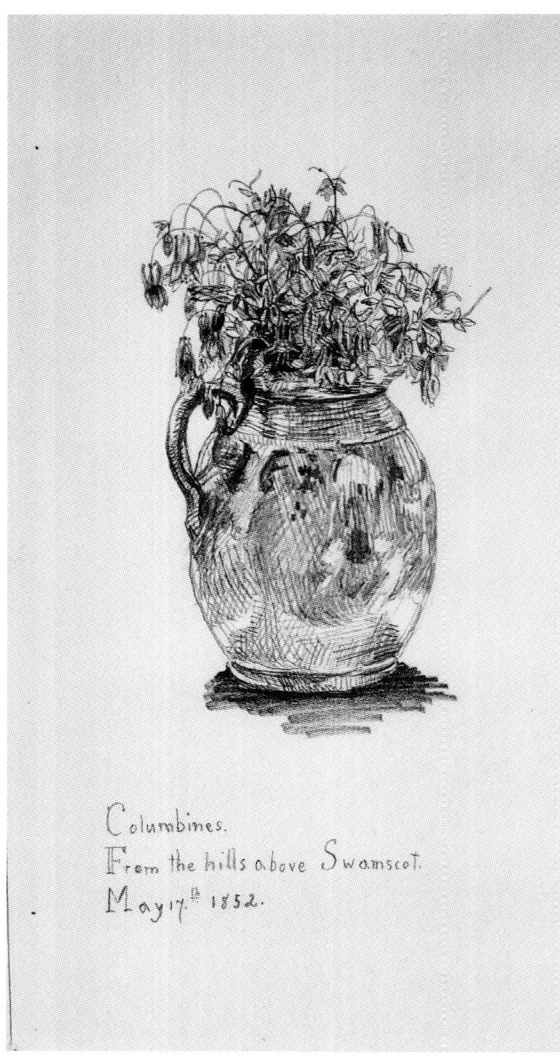

42 Francesca Alexander, *Vase of Columbines*, 17 May 1852, pen and ink, approx. 18 × 8.5 cm (7 × 3 ½ in), Paul Worman Fine Art, Worcester, MA

The Alexanders quickly made friends with the owners of the Villa Brichieri. One of Fanny's early Florentine drawings is a portrait of Marianna Brichieri-Colombi (fig.39) and it was through her husband that Fanny was presented to the celebrated statesman Bettino Ricasoli at a Palazzo Vecchio ball in 1861.[92] When they moved in, the villa also housed English authors Isa Blagden and Lord Tennyson's brother Frederick with his Italian wife Maria Carolina Giuliotti – derisively described by the poet Elizabeth Kinney as a *contadina* – and their five children, who sometimes served as Fanny's models (fig.40).[93] Americans elsewhere on the hilltop included the widowed Boston musician Francis Boott and his artist daughter Lizzie, who were in Florence intermittently starting in 1847, part of that time in the nearby Villa Castellani; Boott's sister Frances was the wife of Horatio Greenough's brother Henry. Soon after the Alexanders moved to Bellosguardo, ten-year-old Lizzie made a sketch of Francis (fig.41). Over the years Lizzie and Fanny painted together, exchanged gifts and letters, and had friends in common, making it possible that Fanny is one of the many unidentified young women in Lizzie's sketchbooks, too.[94]

Henry James lived occasionally on Bellosguardo and he used some of the people he knew there – including the Bootts – and some of the villas as characters and settings for his novels.[95] In 1878, with only slight exaggeration, he claimed that Anglo-Americans obsessively discussed these villas: 'This one has a story; that one has another; they all look as if they had stories. Most of them are offered to rent (many of them for sale) at prices unnaturally low; you may have a tower and a garden, a chapel and a stretch of thirty windows, for three or four hundred dollars a year.'[96] Reports of rental prices on Bellosguardo varied widely, but travelers and residents marveled at what they were able to afford. Despite their fantastic view, the Alexanders probably paid a relatively low rent, perhaps similar to the $28 a month Nathaniel Hawthorne and his family paid in 1858

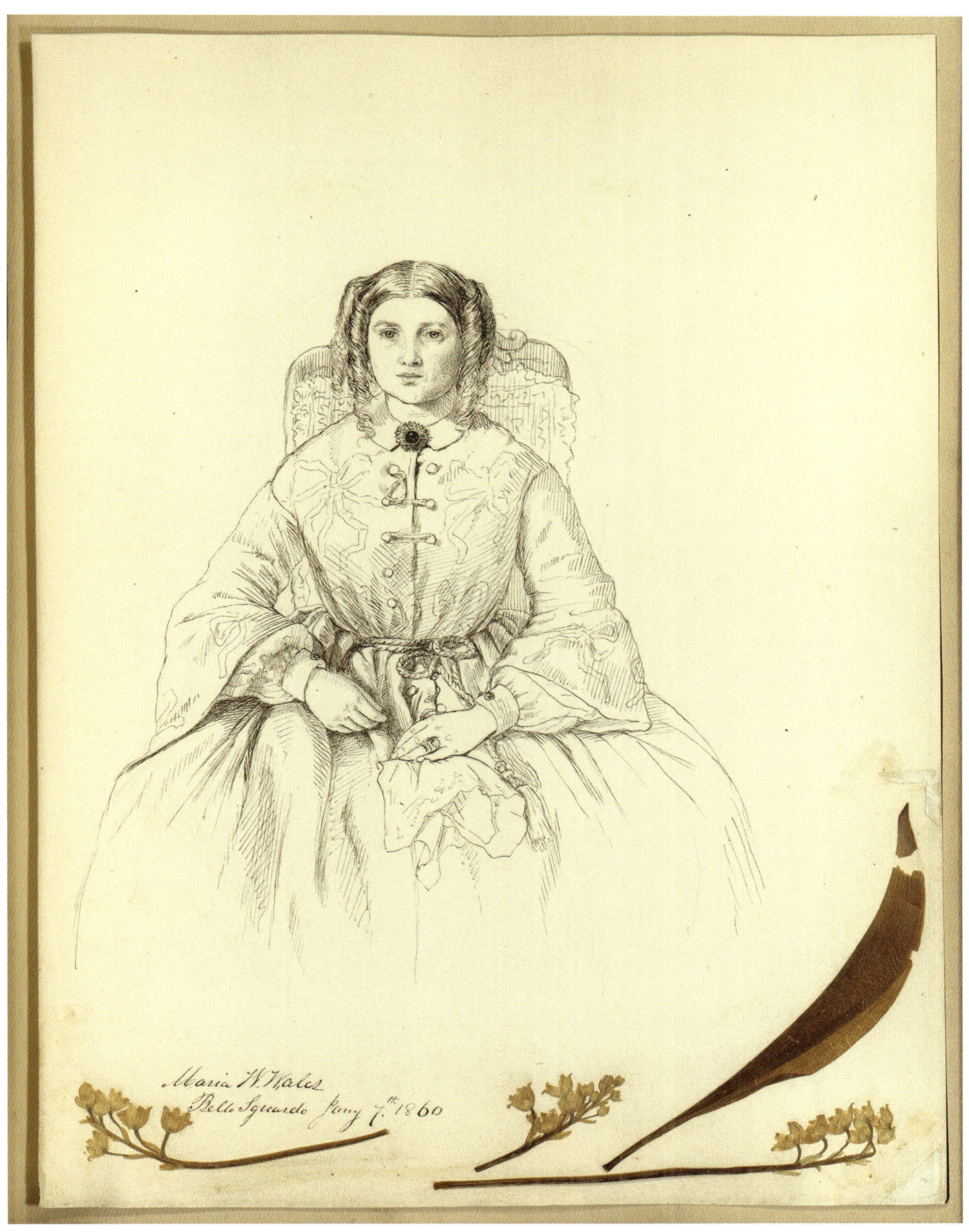

43 Francesca Alexander, *Maria W. Wales*, 7 January 1860, pen and ink with dried flowers,
20.5 × 28 cm (8⅛ × 11 in), Wellesley College Special Collections, Wellesley, MA

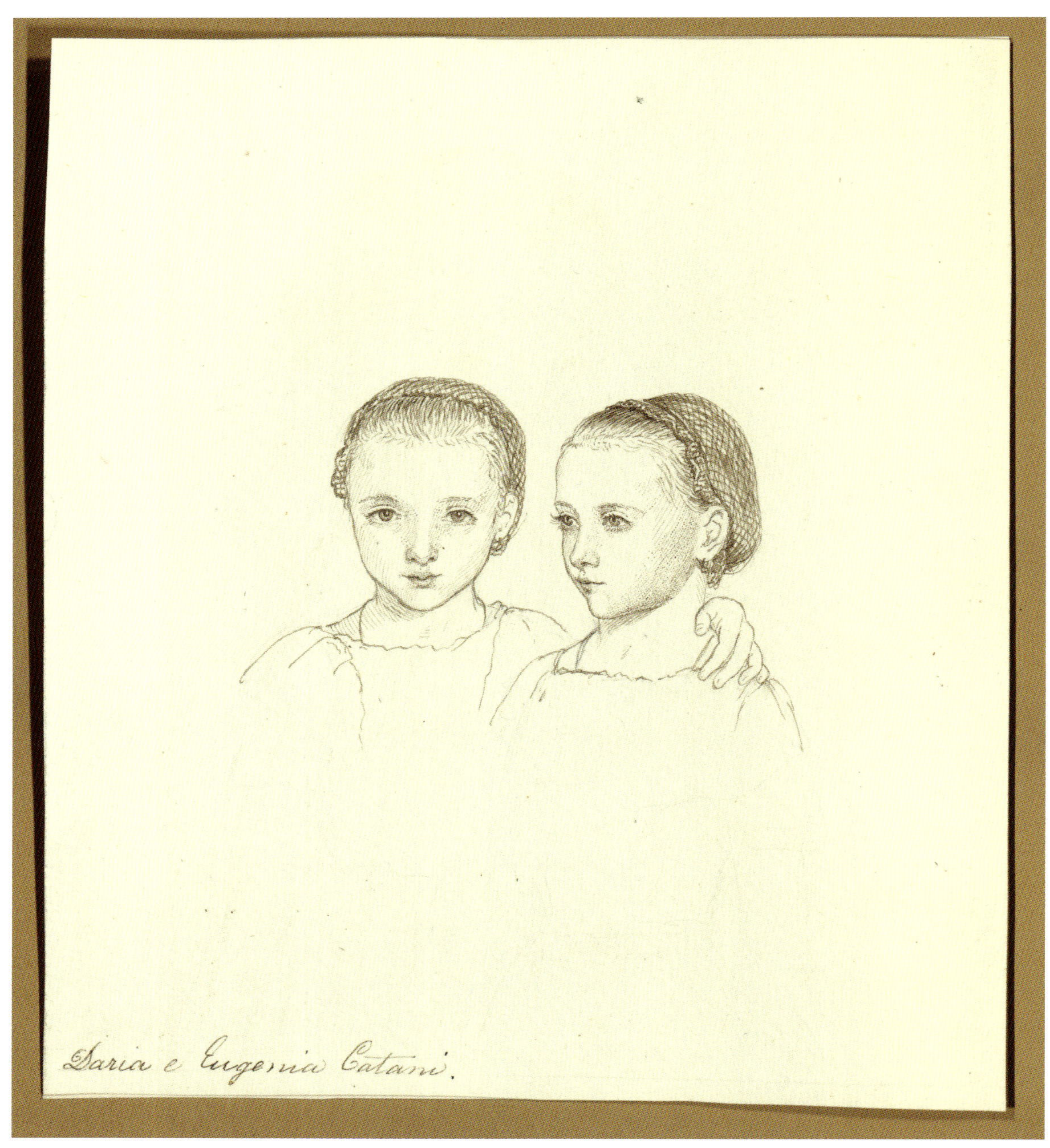

44 Francesca Alexander, *Daria and Eugenia Catani*, *c.*1856, pen and ink,
14 × 16 cm (5 ½ × 6 ¼ in), Wellesley College Special Collections, Wellesley, MA

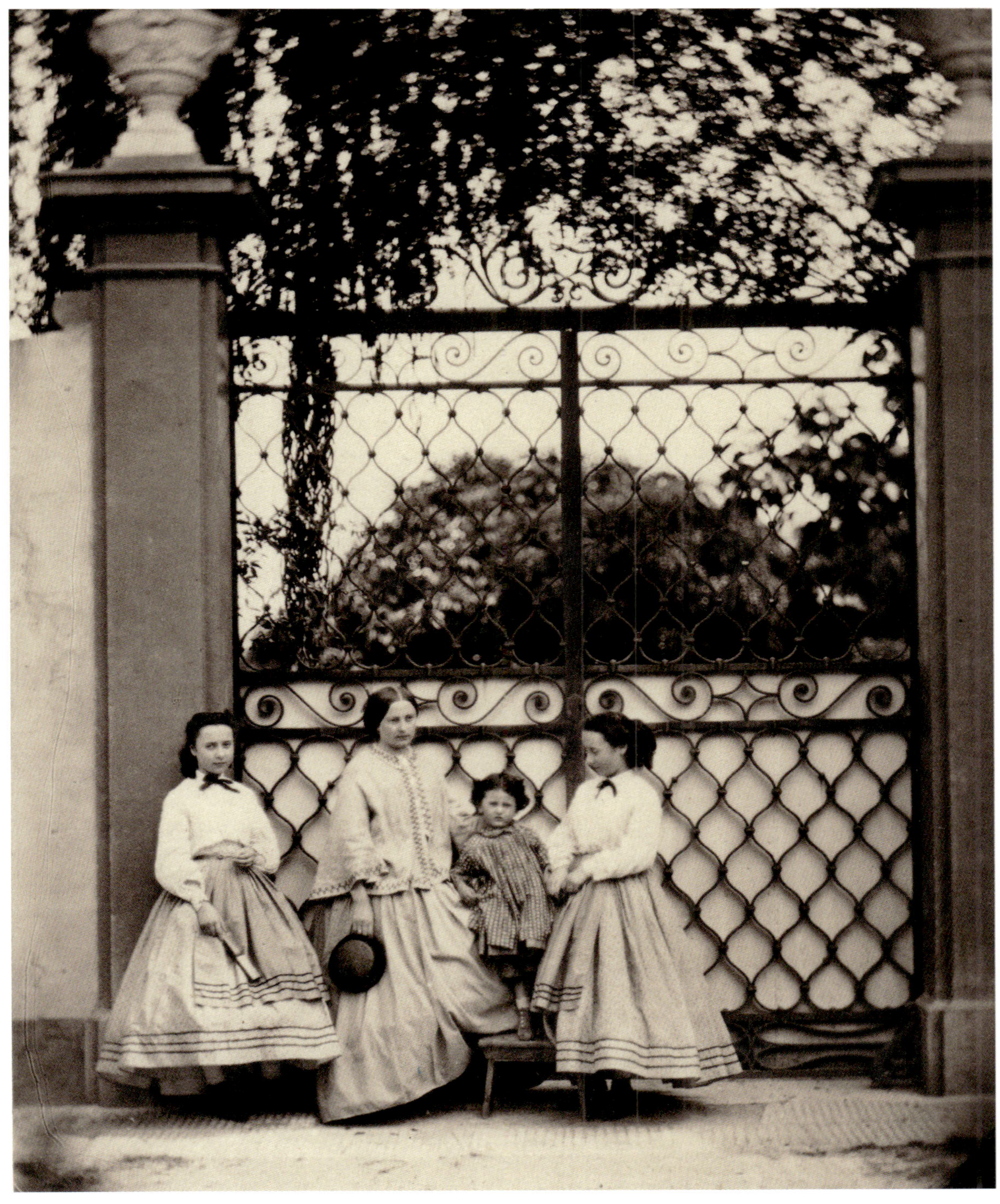

45 Longworth Powers, *Francesca Alexander and Three Friends*, 1860, albumen print, 10 × 8.1 cm (3 ⅞ × 3 ⅛ in), The Nelson-Atkins Museum of Art, Kansas City, MO

for a spacious set of rooms in the Villa Montauto, Hawthorne's model for the ancestral home of the character Donatello in his novel *The Marble Faun* (1860).[97] More extravagant was the £20 ($97) Isa Blagden and the Irish author Frances Power Cobbe paid in 1860 for a 14-room apartment on the floor above the Alexanders in the Villa Brichieri, complete with a maid and a manservant, a carriage, fire, candles and food.[98]

Bellosguardo's bucolic setting allowed Fanny to start a garden; she probably acquired her copy of Giovanni Battista Ferrari's treatise on gardening, *Flora overo cultura di fiori* (1638), around this time, and she proved to be an impressive amateur botanist.[99] Like Hiram Powers and Thomas Ball, and the Rome-based sculptor James Henry Haseltine, Fanny nurtured American plants alongside native Italian ones with the help of seeds sent by friends, some of which she shared with contacts at the botanical gardens at Florence, Bologna and Messina.[100] When Fanny lamented the absence of columbines in Italy – a favorite flower she sketched in a handled jug the year before leaving Boston (fig.42) – Annie Adams Fields sent her some seeds and Fanny wrote to thank her: 'I hope now that before long I shall be able to astonish all my Italian friends with a sight of them.'[101] In fact, it may have been through the efforts of Fanny and other Americans that plants like the persimmon (*Diospero americano*), indigenous to parts of the mid-Atlantic and south-eastern United States, and the magnolia (*Magnolia grandiflora*), also from the south-eastern United States, now thrive on Bellosguardo.[102]

While in Florence, the Alexanders continued their relationships with friends in the United States via correspondence, even arranging hotel rooms if needed.[103] Sometimes, at the request of Lucia or Fanny, these friends provided material for Lucia's scrapbooks, supplementing the letters and other ephemera provided by Italians.[104] The scrapbooks include poems by Louise Chandler Moulton and Harriet Beecher Stowe; letters from General William T. Sherman and inventor Samuel Colt; drawings by

Thomas Hoppin; and photographs of Longfellow's home in Cambridge.[105] Americans in Florence contributed, too. Knowing Lucia's interest in what would have been deemed curiosities, James Read Chadwick, who later loaned a drawing by Fanny to Boston's Museum of Fine Arts, gave her the calling card of Zhang Deyi, one of three Chinese students from a government-sponsored language school who traveled to Europe and the United States from 1866 to 1871.[106]

When Chadwick and others visited, they had no trouble finding the Alexanders. George Perkins Marsh, the United States Minister to the Kingdom of Italy from 1861–82, who resided in Florence for many years and assisted the American population both practically and socially, had entries for them in his address books.[107] The Alexanders were close to the Marshes; when Fanny and her parents returned to the United States in 1868, they offered to carry letters for them.[108] Many travelers sought out the Alexanders. When the Dorr family arrived in April 1859, they took a carriage to see the Alexanders even before they went to the Uffizi, and socialized with them several times.[109]

Fanny's art generated considerable interest from these travelers. Some, including Boston philanthropist George Washington Wales and his wife Maria Wharton Dow, became Fanny's patrons or sitters (or both) (fig.43). During a visit in 1866, Sarah Gooll Putnam marveled at the view from the Villa Brichieri and at Fanny's drawings, which she pronounced 'beautifully done, some almost as fine as engravings'.[110] The first letter the sculptor Florence Freeman wrote home after arriving in Florence in 1862 mentioned visiting the Alexanders with Annie Adams Fields's sister, the painter Lizzie Adams.[111] Florence admired Fanny's drawings, but she was also struck by her behavior, which others apparently gossiped about; Florence noted that Fanny was 'rather peculiar . . . her mother is as particular with her as if she were a child I hear; she never goes to the theatre or into society, nor is allowed to read a love story, so she appears in some respects as simple as a child, and yet one can see at once that her mind is bright and cultivated'.[112] Like so many others over the years, Florence Freeman seemed to consider Fanny Alexander one of the many sites worth seeing in Florence.

Florence Freeman remained in Italy for the rest of her life; though she moved to Rome, she did occasionally return to Florence and would have seen the Alexanders when she did. Among the artists in residence in Florence, however, the Powers family were among their closest friends.[113] Hiram's eldest son Longworth began a successful photography practice around 1860, both in the studio and, with the help of a pushcart, outside of it.[114] He probably used that pushcart to photograph Fanny with three companions – the two identically dressed girls likely the twins Daria and Eugenia Catani, subjects of an earlier drawing by Fanny (fig.44) – in front of the gate of Florence's Palazzo Le Monnier (fig.45). Fanny also socialized with Boston poet Sophia May Eckley, a cousin of Louisa May Alcott who had an intense friendship with Elizabeth Barrett Browning, much of it based on their shared interests in spiritualism, until a much gossiped-about falling out in 1859.[115]

One of Fanny's most cherished friends was Bostonian Elizabeth, or Lilly, Callahan Cleveland. Lilly first came to Europe in 1858 with her widowed mother Sarah Paine Perkins, as well as her uncle, aunt and grandmother. They arrived in Florence that fall and spent their time with the Alexanders as well as other prominent members of the Anglo-American community like the Brownings. They stayed at the Villa Capponi, some two miles west of the Villa Brichieri, with Lilly's other uncle Charles Callahan Perkins and his wife Fanny Bruen. Perkins, the great-nephew of Francis Alexander's early patron Thomas Handasyd Perkins, later became one of the founders of the Museum of Fine Arts in Boston. He lived in Florence and wrote about art from 1857 to 1869; he even taught Fanny about the Bishop Federighi tomb, which he included in his book *Tuscan Sculptors* (1864).[116]

Lilly captured her initial impressions of the Alexanders, and especially Fanny, in her diary, a perceptive description that accords well with that of others through the years:

As to sociabilities, there is Mr Alexander, the portrait painter, his wife + daughter, all of whom are the essence of kind-heartedness. Miss A. is a very queer person. Brought up entirely away from the world, the delight, + joy, + one object of her father + mother. She is very good natured + knows all the peasants about their villa. She has a passion for antiquities, + has picked up a collection of old missals, books written in the year one, + old pictures of the early painters. She has a great talent for drawing, especially for pen + ink, + in reading a ballad she sees in her mind the people she reads about, + then draws them. She is 21, + looks as if she was 30. She reads in Italian . . . She is altogether a curiosity, + I like her, being addicted to peculiar people, + she is so thoroughly good + so kind hearted. [We] are going out to their villa now to spend the day, + she is to take me to see a peasant beauty.[117]

Lilly's scrapbook contains three cuttings from Renaissance choral manuscripts, presumably gifted from Fanny's collection, and a print of that 'peasant beauty', a *contadina* named Carolina Nardi; Lilly surrounded the print with a few fronds, dated it 13 November 1858, and labeled it 'The Belle of Bello Sguardo etched on copper by Miss Alexander' (fig.46). Fanny would have needed special supplies and equipment to create etchings, presumably obtained through the assistance of other artists in Florence. According to the illustrator Joseph Pennell, in the early 1880s there was an 'old wooden press in an old shop behind the Uffizi' that was apparently used by many artists.[118] Perhaps with the help of this press, around this time Fanny created another etching, of the Madonna and Child appearing to a praying *contadina* (fig.47). An architectural pendant is suspended from the vault, an arched window, supported by a twisting colonette, has a view to the

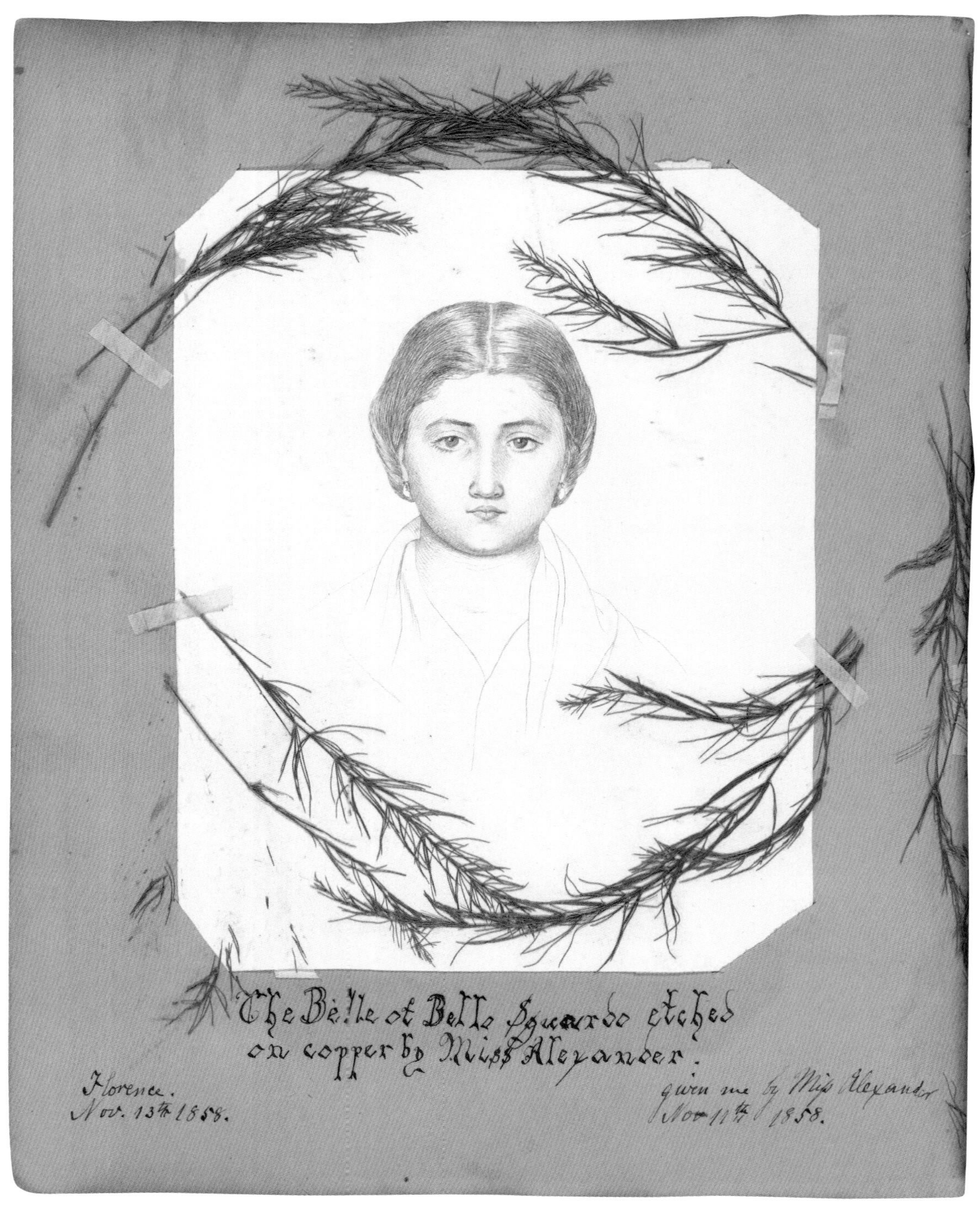

46 Francesca Alexander, *The Belle of Bello Sguardo (Carolina Nardi)*, 1858, etching with dried flowers in Lilly Cleveland's scrapbook, folio 26.5 × 21 cm (10 ⅜ × 8 in), New York Public Library, NY

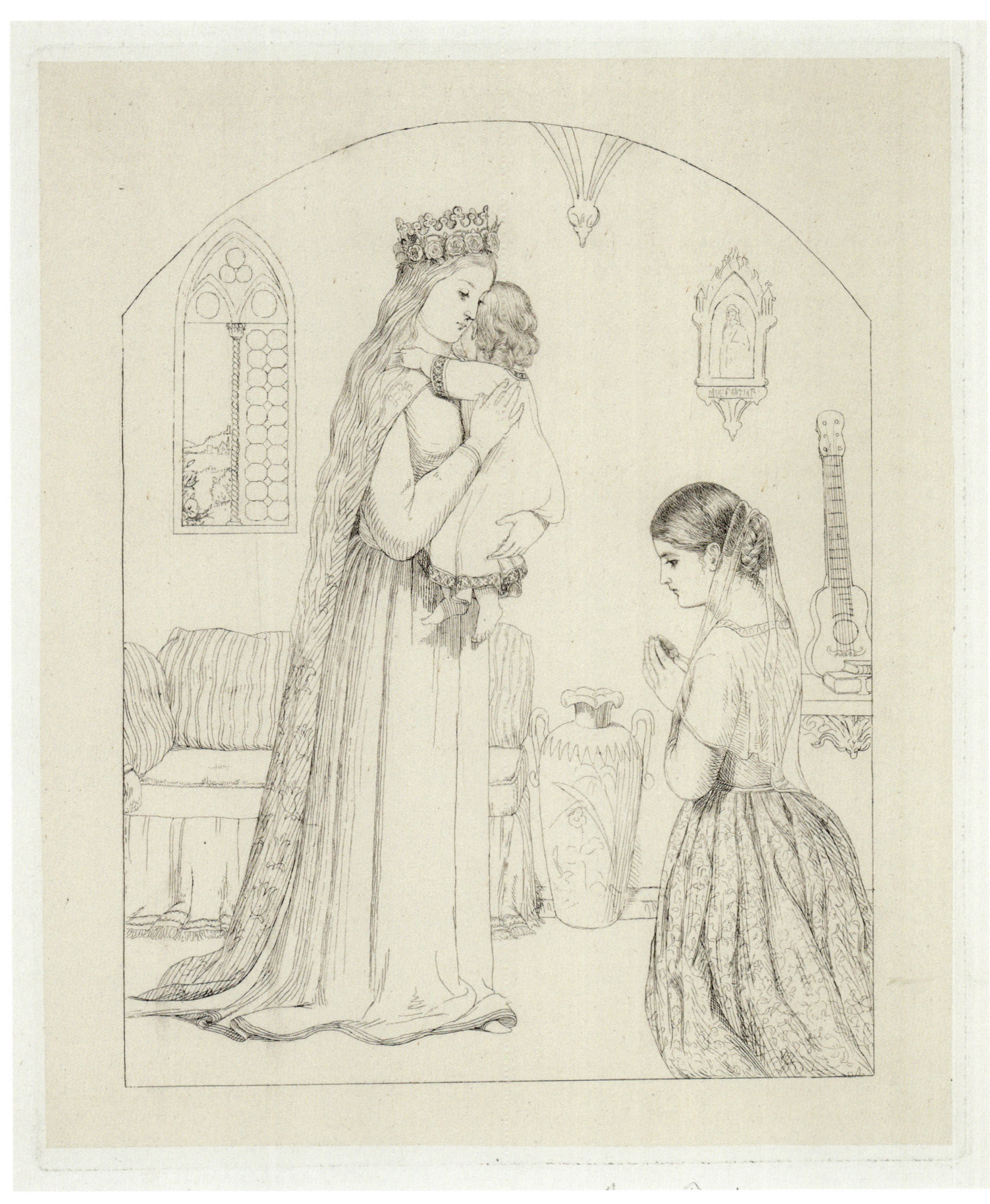

47 Francesca Alexander, *Vision of the Madonna and Child*, late 1850s, etching on chine, platemark 22.5 × 18.1 cm (8 ⅞ × 7 ⅛ in); sheet: 34.6 × 25.1 cm (13 ⅝ × 9 ⅞ in), Museum of Fine Arts Boston, Boston, MA

distant hills on one side and octagonal muntins on the other, and the chamber is furnished with a devotional painting, a cushioned bench, a large vase and a guitar, all elements that appear in her drawings from this period.[119] Although there is little evidence for Fanny's printmaking, the medium was especially suited to her precise linear style and these examples indicate that she was thinking about ways to circulate her work from an early date.

In addition to meeting the Alexanders, the Cleveland visit is notable because they intimately experienced the turmoil of the Risorgimento. They wintered in Rome and on their way back to Florence stopped in Perugia on 14 June 1859, the same day the city expelled its papal representative and declared allegiance to Vittorio Emanuele II. The Clevelands continued their visit undeterred; Perugia was a favorite destination for many travelers, with its ancient past, historic walls and gates, and proximity to Lake Trasimeno. But the papacy, keen to regain hold of the strategically located city, sent in troops on 20 June and Lilly and her family found themselves in the midst of a battle. The troops stormed their hotel, stole their belongings, and killed the owner and a servant; a papal soldier named Conrad Wellauer defied orders and protected the family until they escaped to Florence two days later, where the Alexanders provided clothing and assistance.[120] Lilly described the ordeal in her diary and commemorated it in her scrapbook with Wellauer's *carte-de-visite* and other ephemera.

This incident, which risked damaging relations between the United States and Italy, attracted attention in both countries and generated newspaper accounts and a flurry of correspondence between United States Secretary of State Lewis Cass, Minister to the Papal States John P. Stockton and Cardinal Secretary of State Giacomo Antonelli. The Clevelands claimed a loss of $2425 worth of belongings and were quickly awarded that plus incidental costs but minus the value of the few recovered items.[121] Italy's

Anglo-American population, who had not been involved in Risorgimento battles in this way before, were horrified. Elizabeth Barrett Browning, wanting to offer the Clevelands 'stockings & petticoats & a sympathizing word or two', expressed her concern for them, for the Perugians, and the for Risorgimento cause.[122] Theodosia Garrow wrote an article about the Clevelands' experience, detailing how the hotel owner was stripped and dismembered, other men were thrown from the roof to their death, and the Clevelands were 'barely able to escape with life, amid insults and spectacles of horror'.[123]

Lilly's grandmother never recovered from the traumatic experience, forcing the Clevelands to remain in Florence to care for her. She died that November and was buried alongside so many other Anglo-Americans in the so-called English Cemetery, founded by the Swiss Evangelical Reformed Church in 1827 in what is now the Piazzale Donatello. But this extended visit formed a strong bond between Lilly and Fanny that lasted the rest of their lives. Indeed, it is through Fanny's letters to Lilly, which Lilly carefully kept, as well as Lilly's diaries and scrapbooks, that we know so much about Fanny's art and charity, as well as the minutia of her daily life. For example, Lilly described a visit to Fanny's room in the Villa Brichieri in 1860:

My days there are so unlike other things . . . I got to Fanny's a little before two. Fanny has a passion for taking me into her room, + keeping me all to herself, so in we went, leaving Mrs. A. sewing in the parlour. I was put into an arm chair before the . . . fire. In a minute comes a knock at the door, + Mr Alexander's kind face peeps through, + his tall long person follows with a glass of deliciously sweet wine for me, + Fanny flies off to get a plate of particularly nice cake. Then we are left to ourselves. Fanny's room is quite as original as herself. Long, narrow, high, with one window to look out of, which you must mount a step to reach, + then you have the Val d'Arno, + the distant mountains, now snow white stretched out before you. The furniture of the room is very nice, + such as belongs to any one's room, only the table has a tumbler of oil paint brushes + various artistic implements, + the book case contains rather different books from the general run of young ladies book cases. There in lovely company are the Bible, Dante, Stories of the Padre Santi, 'il Direttore delle Religiose' by Monsignor Francesco di Salis', printed in 1652, + various other volumes of the same order, while one or two curious pictures hang on the wall. First we read Dante together, then I read some of Mrs Browning's poetry to her, then dinner, + after dinner a little general talking, + then Fanny carried me back to her room, where we looked over illustrated French papers, + about 7 the carriage came for me.[124]

Fanny and Lilly also corresponded about the progress of Italian unification and other important events. When the news of Elizabeth Barrett Browning's death on 29 June 1861 reached Lilly, who was then in northern Europe on her way back to the United States, she wrote to ask Fanny about it. Fanny's reply is an indication of the information circulating in Florence at that time, and Fanny's awareness of it:

> I do not suppose I can tell you much more than you have heard already. Her death was quite without warning. She had been in a consumption for a long time and had a very bad cough; but the day before her death she seemed no worse than usual. In the morning, as she was lying in bed with no one in the room but her husband, she had a very violent fit of coughing; he went to her and raised her in his arms and apparently at that very moment she died. He called about for help, not daring to lay her down; the servants came in, but it was too late. That is all I know and I can hardly say that I know that but that is what was told me. Her funeral was very largely attended – both by Italians and foreigners. Among the Italians there was a very great sorrow for her death; she was much loved, I think, by

all, for her own sake as well as for her writings on Italy. Mr Browning left Florence almost immediately, taking his little boy with him. I do not know where they have gone; some say England, others Paris.[125]

On later visits to Florence Lilly must have visited Barrett Browning's grave in the English Cemetery, which was located near her grandmother's plot.

Elizabeth Barrett Browning left a mark on the city long after her death. But Lilly left a mark, too. The Perugia uprising became part of Risorgimento lore, and Lilly's role in it was well known. From then on, Fanny and her Italian friends referred to Lilly as the 'Signorina di Perugia', an affectionate title indicating her ongoing connection to that pivotal event in the popular imagination.

3

Fanny and Her Poor

Although the Alexanders had close friends among the Italian elite, those Fanny referred to as her 'poor' were more important to her. The lush landscape and farms described by Elizabeth Barrett Browning in *Aurora Leigh* emphasized the fact that Bellosguardo, though inhabited by an Anglo-American enclave who lived in considerable comfort, was surrounded by agricultural land. This land was farmed on the *mezzadria* system, where the landowner split the harvest with local *contadini* whom he provided with housing and tools for cultivation. Many of these *contadini* suffered from poverty and needed regular assistance just to survive. Women joined men in the fields or contributed to their households by making the straw hats, baskets and other objects travelers purchased for souvenirs.

Anglo-Americans were intrigued by the lives of these Italians. In 1860 Annie Adams Fields and her husband, the publisher James T. Fields, visited the Alexanders on Bellosguardo and joined them to watch an Italian family press olives to make oil. Fields wrote, 'It was a new glimpse at life as seen from this cottage and though they all seemed happy we turned away more grateful than ever for our blessings'.[1] Although many of these Italians lived in the area around Bellosguardo, Fanny encountered others in the village of Abetone, 50 miles north of Florence in the Apennine mountain range, where the Alexanders summered beginning in 1862.[2] Few Anglo-Americans visited this area until later in the nineteenth century. But Fanny and Francis loved the countryside, and Lucia, who tended to prefer urban destinations where they could socialize with their many friends more easily, at least appreciated its similarities to rural Massachusetts.[3]

The family shared their enthusiasm for Abetone and its inhabitants with others. Writing to Lilly Cleveland, Fanny described it as beautiful, full of people who were 'Kind, honest, gentle and sociable, mostly relatives of each other and all friends, and excessively proud of their mountain country, it is impossible to live among them without growing fond of them'.[4] Florence Freeman and Lizzie Adams dined with the Alexanders soon after this first summer, and Florence wrote to her family:

We had an exceedingly nice dinner, which finished off with some of Mrs A's brandied peaches and cream, and they told us all about their summer at Abbatone, from whence they have just returned. Mr A was very enthusiastic about it, he thought it as beautiful as any place he ever saw. There the country people interested them very much in their rustic simplicity.[5]

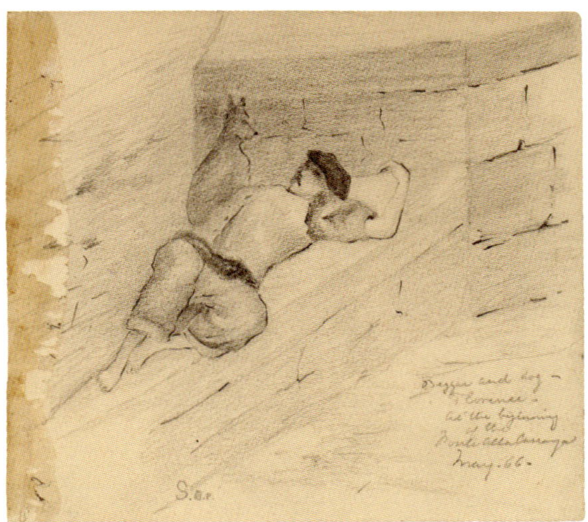

48 Sarah Gooll Putnam, *Beggar and Dog – Florence – at the Beginning of the Ponte alla Carriaja*, May 1866, pencil, approx. 9.5 × 10.5 cm (3 ¾ × 4 ¼ in), Collection of the Massachusetts Historical Society, Boston, MA

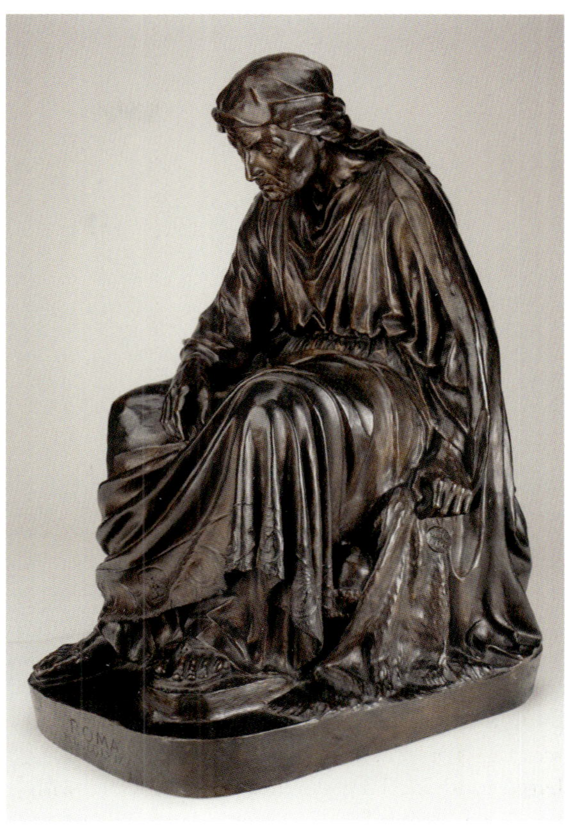

49 Anne Whitney, *Roma*, modeled 1869, cast 1890, bronze, 68.6 × 50.8 × 39.4 cm (27 × 20 × 15 ½ in), Davis Museum, Wellesley College, Wellesley, MA

Such an attitude – on one hand curiosity about lives so different from one's own, and on the other hand a certain distaste for those lives – was common to many Anglo-Americans, who used the presence of so many poor Italians to criticize Italy's lack of a social safety net, though neither the United States nor the United Kingdom were much better.[6] Of course, there were charitable organizations that offered assistance, but they did not have enough resources to care for all.[7] It is therefore no surprise that these Italians appeared in art, as symbols of the troubled country itself. Sarah Gooll Putnam sketched a destitute man she encountered on a Florentine bridge (fig.48), and Anne Whitney modeled a complex allegory of the city of Rome as an elderly beggar woman (fig.49). Novels included them, too. In his *Marble Faun* (1860), Nathaniel Hawthorne rhapsodized that, 'A pre-Raphaelite artist . . . might find an admirable subject in one of these Tuscan girls', the idea being, of course, that they were interesting models for artists but not for any more personal relationship.[8] Perhaps Hawthorne was thinking of Fanny's work with this comment; he and his family knew the Alexanders from their time on Bellosguardo and Lucia once gave their governess Ada Shepard a sprig of jessamine (fig.50).[9] The character of the

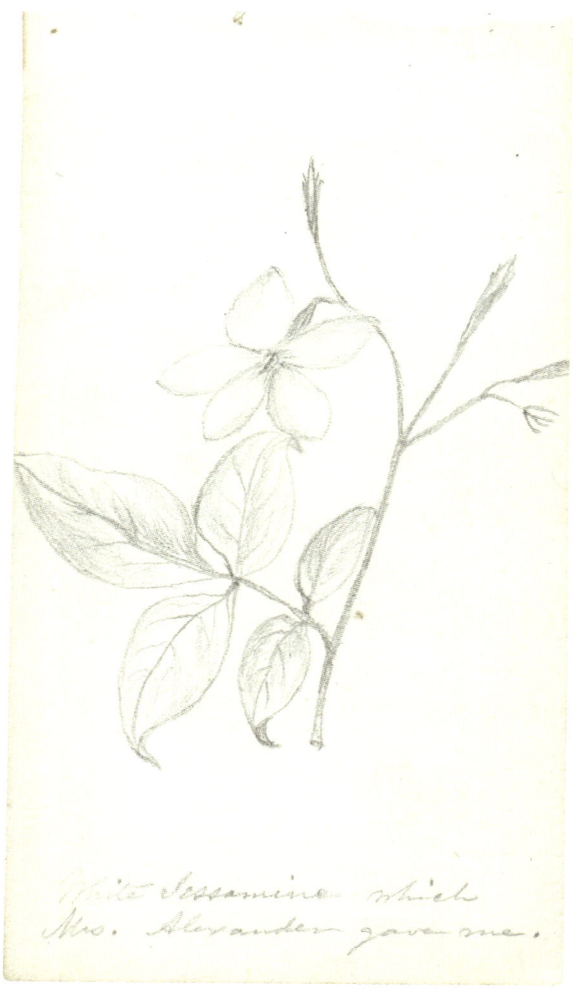

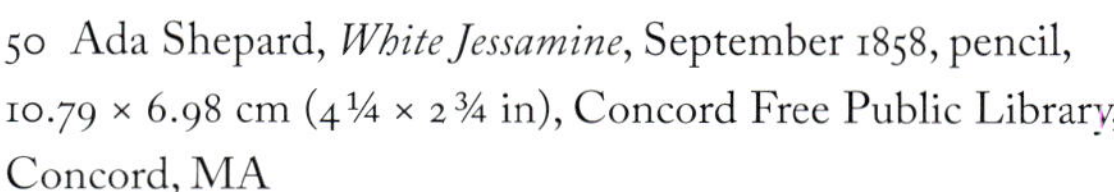

50 Ada Shepard, *White Jessamine*, September 1858, pencil,
10.79 × 6.98 cm (4¼ × 2¾ in), Concord Free Public Library,
Concord, MA

contadina Tessa in George Eliot's *Romola* (1863),
exploited by Romola's corrupt husband Tito and left
to suffer, was another example of the type. Travelers
used both novels, with their extensive descriptions
of Italy past and present, as guidebooks, and they
purchased staged photographs of *contadini* to paste
into their copies to create personalized souvenirs
(fig.51).[10]

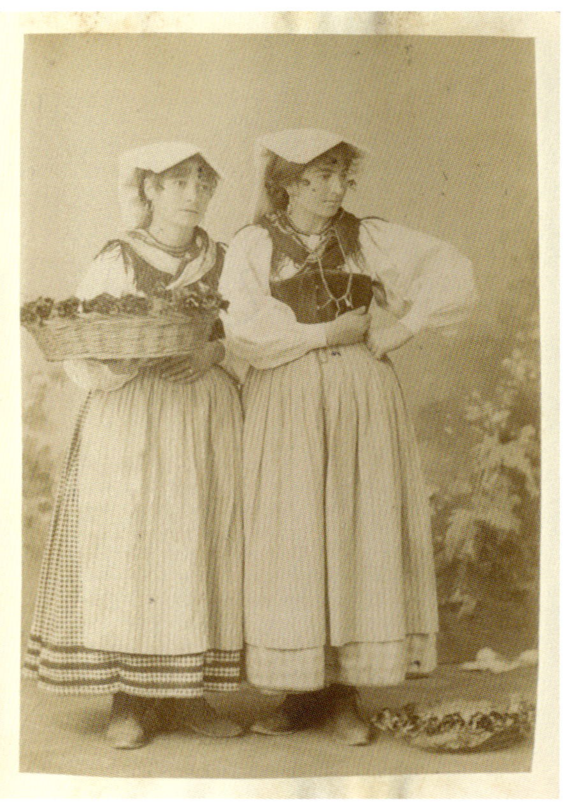

51 Italian, photograph from an extra-illustrated copy of
George Eliot's *Romola* (Leipzig: Tauchnitz, 1863), 8.5 × 12.5
cm (3¼ × 5 in), private collection

But there was a big difference between admiring
a work of literature or art – especially one that made
the reader or viewer feel superior to the subjects – and
engaging in actual relationships with impoverished
Italians. Unlike Putnam and Whitney, Italian artists,
especially those associated with the Macchiaioli
group, ennobled their lives as an opportunity for
social commentary and a statement on honest and
undervalued labor, as Telemaco Signorini did with
his representations of straw workers (fig.52).[11] Fanny
too made these Italians her models; she befriended
and assisted them, and saw them as individuals rather
than symbols, capturing the specific details of their

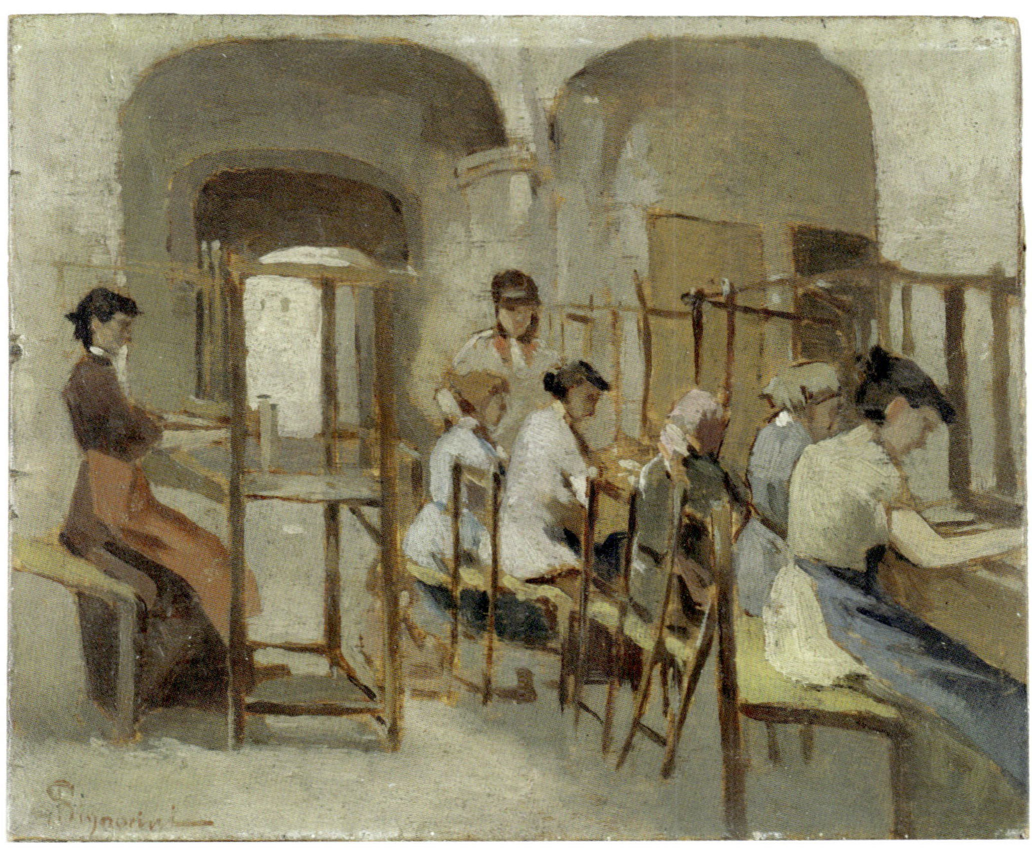

52 Telemaco Signorini, *Straw Weavers*, c.1880, oil on board, 11.5 × 13.5 cm (4½ × 5⅜ in),
Museo del Novecento, Milan

costumes and accessories and focusing on their faces (fig.53). Of course she was not alone in employing Italian models. In Rome, men, women and sometimes children loitered around the Spanish Steps in their traditional costumes to pose for artists in exchange for a few coins a day. But Fanny's relationship with her models was more personal.

Fanny met some of those she helped through her church community. The Alexanders attended Florence's various Protestant churches but beginning in April 1861, Francis and Fanny, if not also Lucia, began to worship at the newly established Evangelical church. Although its leaders included prominent Italians like Count Pietro Guicciardini – who had been persecuted for his beliefs – the space and its furnishings were simple and the congregation was comprised of a significant number of less fortunate Italians. Fanny saw Francesco Madiai on her first visit, and the following year she secured the famous couple's autographs.[12] In 1866 Teodorico Pietrocola-Rossetti, the cousin of English Pre-Raphaelite painter Dante Gabriele Rossetti, became the minister.[13] There were internal conflicts in church leadership over the years, and Guicciardini knew Fanny well enough to

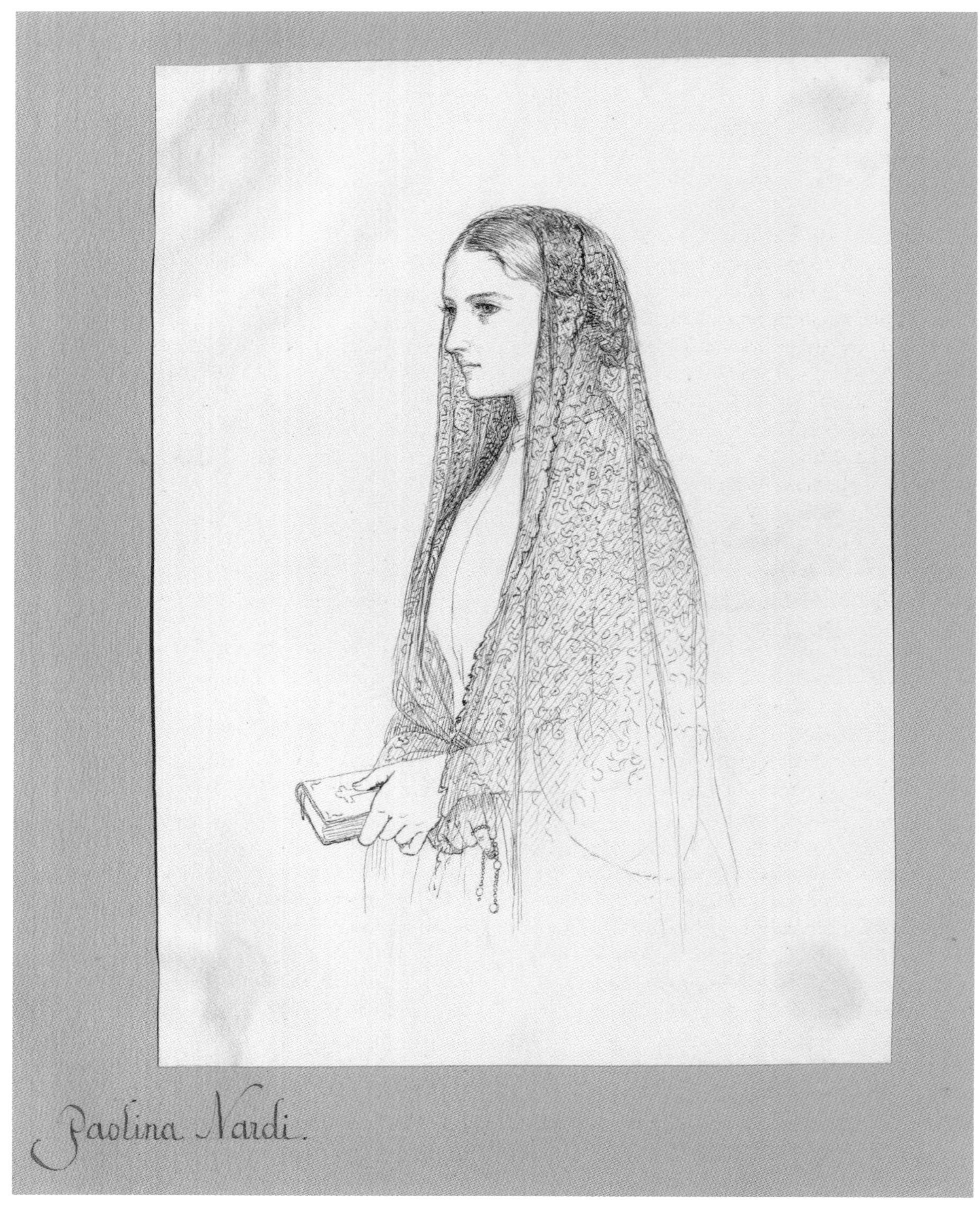

53 Francesca Alexander, *Paolina Nardi*, 1860s, pen and ink, 12 × 17.5 cm (4 ¾ × 6 ⅞ in),
Wellesley College Special Collections, Wellesley, MA

confide in her about this.[14] Despite these conflicts, the institution thrived; in 1879 it acquired part of the former church of Sant'Apollinare near the Bargello, providing a more permanent and centrally located home for the growing community.

Although the Alexanders' Evangelicalism can be difficult to reconcile with their art collection, it is even more difficult to reconcile with Fanny's sympathy for Catholicism, which endeared her to many Italians.[15] She was intrigued by Catholic ceremonies; she walked in sacred processions and attended masses as well as vespers and holy day festivities at the small church of Santi Vito e Modesto – which Fanny referred to as San Vito – a few minutes from her Bellosguardo home, which served the *contadini* population in the area.[16] With its minimal ornament and spartan interior, San Vito echoed the simplicity she recalled from Boston's churches, adding to its appeal. In addition to the art she collected, and the drawings and paintings she made of sacred subjects (fig.54), she owned a Madonna from Germany and a rosary from Rome, which Fanny described as 'the envy of my Catholic friends', both gifts from Lizzie Boott.[17] Fanny also claimed to own fragments of the bones of Saints Clement and Casimir, as well as a lock of Saint Francis's hair and Saint Carlo Borromeo's prayerbook; she planned to leave that book to her friend Domenico Cardinal Agostini, the Patriarch of Venice, for the treasury of San Marco.[18]

Borromeo, perhaps because of his reform efforts and his care for the poor during Milan's 1576 plague outbreak, was a particular favorite of Fanny's. During a visit to Milan in 1882 she received permission from the Archbishop to view his remains and those of fellow saints Ambrose, Gervasius and Protasius, and reported her impressions to Lilly:

> For St Ambrose, I have always had an especial affection and veneration, both as a saint and a poet, and his body, after nearly fifteen centuries, still retains enough the appearance of life to show me how he

must have looked when in the world. A grand looking man, much above the common size, and showing plainly the physical strength which he must have needed for his stormy life of nearly a hundred years. S. Carlo, who has been embalmed, still retains his expression of gentle goodness and charity. The bodies of the two martyrs, who go back to the time of the Emperor Nero, are less well preserved, but it gives one a shiver to see how the bones were broken![19]

Lucia was more skeptical about Catholicism than Fanny; she condemned the behavior of Catholic priests, who overcharged the poor for funerals and took lovers.[20] Mocking Catholic beliefs, she claimed to own

> a little picture of an extremely ugly and sour looking Madonna . . . which is certified to be by St Luke, + also that it shed drops of blood when wounded by a Turkish soldier; it does not retain the slightest scar, which must be also miraculous. I have a saint certified to have frequently spoken, but in these evil days, this picture has maintained a discreet silence.[21]

Despite this sarcasm, Lucia had some sympathy with Fanny's feelings and even gifted her two sacred manuscripts. One was a fifteenth-century illuminated manuscript, which Fanny described as the perfect size 'to use when I go to San Vito. I don't think I ever had a prettier present in my life, or one that was more to my taste.'[22] The second manuscript was Latin and bound in ornate silver, much too fancy for San Vito: 'It is very ancient, and looks like Genovese work, and I never saw any binding half so pretty. I do not mean ever to use it until we have a Te Deum in the Duomo.'[23]

Fanny was aware of the tension her Protestantism created. She witnessed the negative effects some priests had on the lives of her Italian friends, and she disliked their dogmatic sermons; she described these men as *codini*, denoting people with pig tails, a derogatory term for conservative Catholics.[24] The priests at San Vito and a bit further away at Santissimo Crocifisso a Monticelli were particularly problematic. In 1860 Fanny reported that the San Vito priest 'has taken a dislike to us, and scolds when his *contadino*'s children come for me to paint them. He also refuses to confess our servants, and all this without our having given him any cause of offense that I know of.'[25] Things became particularly difficult in 1862, when Fanny repeatedly visited a former servant, who was ill, and read passages from the New Testament to her and her family and friends.[26] Although many of these women were illiterate, Fanny gave those who wanted it a copy of the New Testament in the seventeenth-century Italian translation by Giovanni Diodati. The priests viewed this behavior with suspicion and warned their parishioners not to attend Fanny's gatherings; they confiscated the books and threatened Fanny, but her *contadini* friends vowed to protect her. Lucia wrote a letter – unaddressed, but likely to Florentine officials or the American consul – describing the incident in detail to stress the need to investigate the threat so Fanny could continue her charitable activities safely.[27] Perhaps with this in mind, when Fanny gave a book of psalms to another friend she urged her to show it to her priest to make sure he would approve; the priest confiscated it and sent a note to Fanny telling her he had burnt it.[28] Increased religious freedom later in the century eased this tension, and advertisements in Anglo-American newspapers even suggested that Bibles and other sacred texts were suitable gifts for Italians.[29] But in 1862 Fanny's enthusiastic piety sometimes put herself, and her friends, at risk.

Fanny's close relationships with Italians were unusual. They welcomed her to their weddings – Fanny described in great detail the various events associated with the marriage of her friend Carolina Pistolesi in 1860, including the viewing of her dowry and the ceremony itself – and asked for her help

when their husbands were forced into conscription; they came to revere her as their patron and even named their children after her.[30] Her correspondence includes descriptions of their homes and lives, and details her efforts to support them through their many hardships with money, food, clothing and medicinals.[31] In 1863, she even sent King Vittorio Emanuele II a drawing of a young mother and her child, and a petition describing the difficulties the mother faced following her husband's conscription; although the King did not excuse the man from duty, he did send money and kept Fanny's drawing for himself.[32] Reflecting on this years later, Fanny was surprised by her determination: 'Oh dear, it almost frightens me now, to think of the strange things I did when I was a girl! And now I am so old and sober, I can hardly believe that that enthusiastic young person was myself.'[33]

Fanny's enthusiasm for charity was boundless, and she tried to pre-empt situations like the one facing the young mother by providing those in need with regular assistance. In 1859 she held a festive dinner for 60 *contadini*, decorating her home with flowers and laurel-wreathed engravings of Risorgimento patriots and joining in when her guests sang patriotic songs.[34] Beginning that year, each Christmas she set up a tree with presents to distribute to the needy, and American friends sent funds and gifts to assist.[35] She kept careful records of the toys, clothing and household necessities she purchased and dutifully reported back to her donors; in 1859, she wrote to tell Lilly what she did with each of the toys her friend sent:

> The pretty Noah's ark is to go to the milk boy's little sister, and the doll, who I find can cry, is for that little blackeyed Maria Martelli whom you took a fancy to at our dinner party; she has wanted a doll for a good while; one of the cannon, and I think one of the generals, will be for the little boy over opposite, who has a military taste, and who sings 'Viva la Guerra',

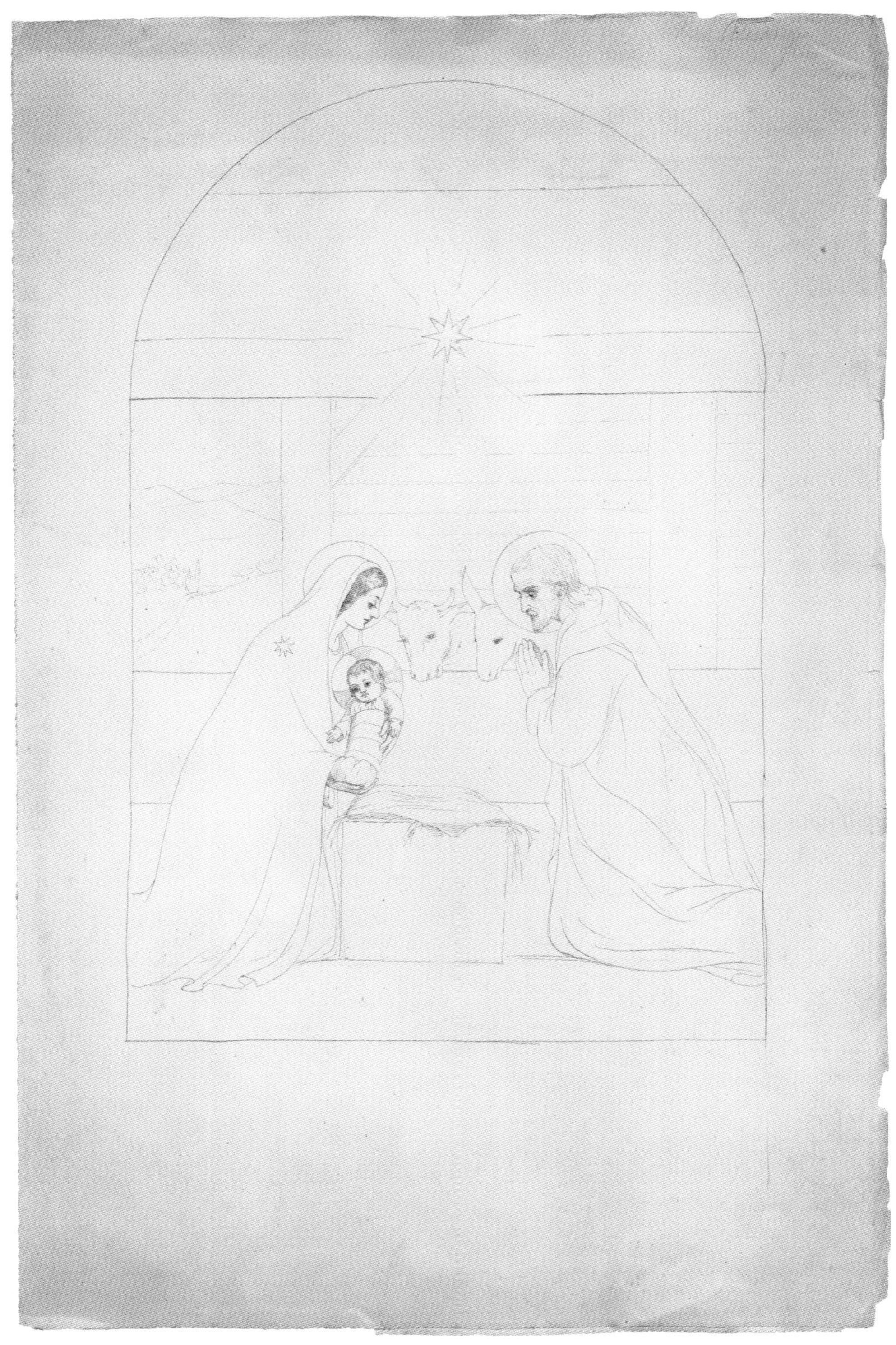

54 Francesca Alexander, *Nativity*, late 185cs, pen and ink, 46 × 30.5 cm (18 ⅛ × 12 in),
Wellesley College Special Collections, Wellesley, MA

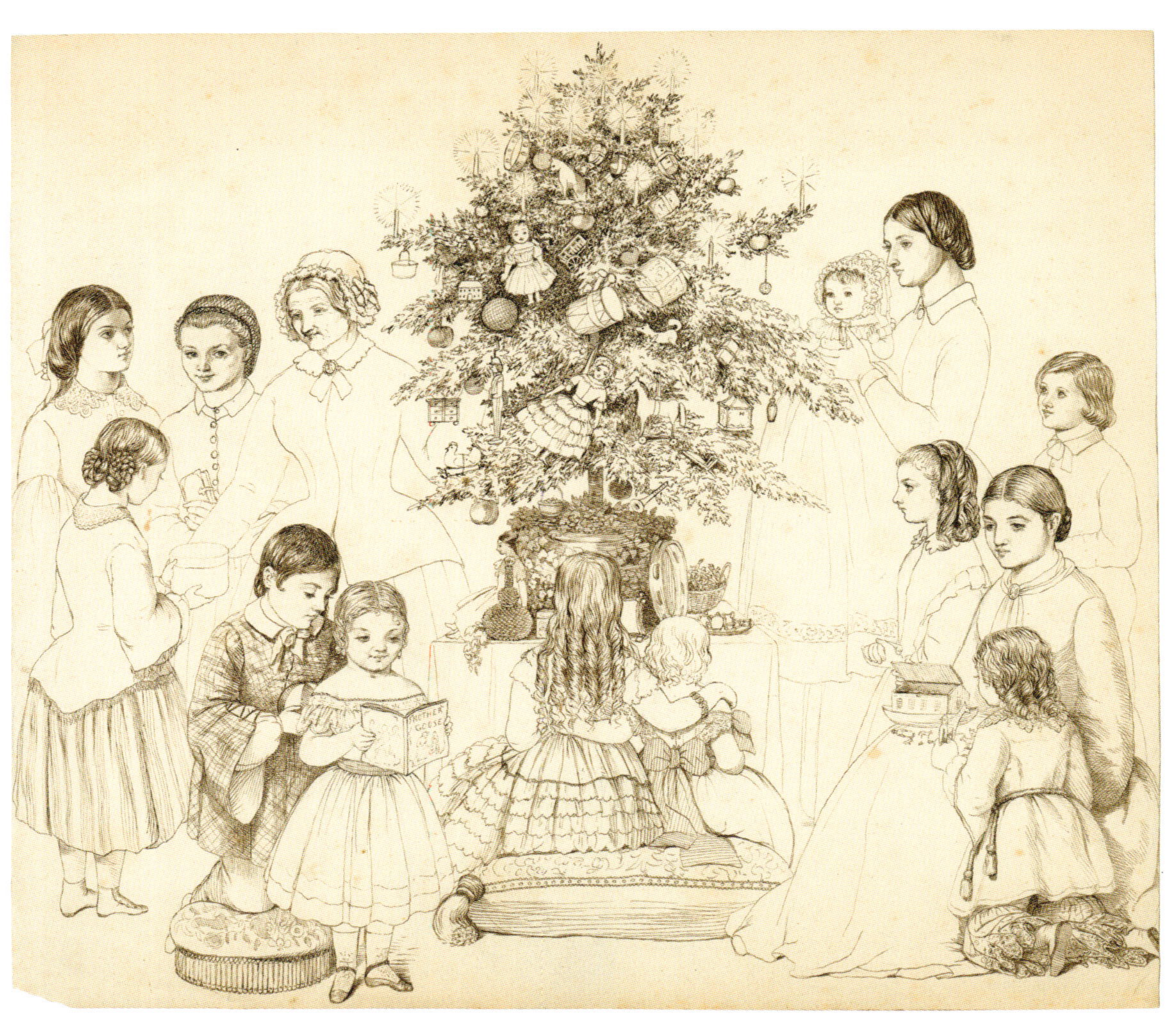

55 Francesca Alexander, *Christmas*, early 1860s, ink on paper, 26 × 30 cm (10 ¼ × 11 ¾ in),
Wellesley College Special Collections, Wellesley, MA

with great spirit. I hope you will not object to giving
the toys to the children yourself, they would think so
much of anything which they received from the hand
of the 'Signorina di Perugia'.[36]

The holiday celebrations were a particularly beloved
ritual for Fanny, one she captured in a drawing of 14
women and children around a candlelit tree, its table
laden with dolls, drums, toy soldiers, a tambourine
and a miniature tea set; the children play with the
tiny animals in a model of Noah's Ark and read from
a book of Mother Goose rhymes (fig.55). Only one
young woman looks out at the viewer, quite possibly
Fanny herself, with dark hair tucked in her customary
net. She holds a small volume with a clasped binding,
suggesting one of her devotional manuscripts. The
older woman standing next to her, a frilly bonnet
on her head, may be Lucia herself, distributing gifts.
Italians in turn regularly filled the Alexander home
with gifts of flowers and foodstuffs, both for special
occasions and for no reason at all, offerings many of
them could ill afford.

Fanny's Italian friends were also eager to be her
models, first for drawings but by the early 1860s
for paintings, too. Although John Lothrop Motley
claimed Fanny was not yet painting in 1855, by 1860
she told Lilly that she was engaged in painting their
contadina friend Paolina in the guise of Sleeping
Beauty and Cinderella.[37] Around this same time,
Fanny reported that a girl came to her door, offered
her flowers and figs, and said, 'If you would like me
in your society, I have three sisters and perhaps we
might do for you to paint. I want to be like the people
you paint.'[38] Following this, Fanny's correspondence
includes references to several paintings with *contadini*
models – she quickly realized she could raise more
funds by making paintings rather than drawings – but
few can be located.

Fanny was never fully confident in her painting
ability. In early 1862 she wrote to Annie Adams
Fields,

I myself am fully occupied in learning to paint, in
which I just begin to see a little improvement; I hope
in the course of a year that I may begin to paint pretty
well. I have a dear little subject now, a pretty little
blackeyed girl of only five years old, whom I am taking
with her dolly in her arms. Of course she cares much
more for the doll's portrait than for her own.[39]

She found it challenging, but a few years later she
confessed to Lizzie Boott that she was willing to
sacrifice her time and effort, and her weak eyesight –
an ongoing concern for the rest of her life – because
'I would rather be a painter than anything else, and I
know there is no other way'.[40]

But Fanny was a bit too modest about her
accomplishments. Her earliest known painting, dated
1861, is already a complex, multi-figured composition,
despite the somewhat awkward perspective and
anatomy that often characterizes her work. In it, a
richly dressed girl – apparently standing in for the
older Fanny – distributes oranges, bread and wine to
four children on a tiled loggia, their simple clothing,
bare feet and earrings identifying them as *contadini* in
need of charity (fig.56). The farm landscape rises up a
hill, past a Madonna and Child sculpture in a flowering
garden to a church with a bell tower at the summit,
standing against the blue sky, a view that likely echoed
what Fanny saw from her Bellosguardo home.

As this painting demonstrates, Fanny took care
to devise her compositions. In 1864, she told Lilly
Cleveland how she planned a now lost painting of
Petrarch's beloved Laura sitting under an apple tree,
using a seamstress friend as her model. To prepare,
she read poetry and looked at other representations of
the same subject around Florence:

You can hardly imagine the amount of pleasure which
one finds in such a work. First, the study of Petrarch
for a day or two to decide on my subject, then, the
composing the picture in my head, which was very
entertaining, though it rather interfered with my

night's sleep. Then the next thing of course was to go
to Santa Maria Novella, down into the green cloister,
with its old frescoes, its green grass, its sunshine and
its perfect quiet, and the square patch of sky always
looking so intensely blue above it; and from thence
into the damp solitary Spanish chapel where I spent a
happy half hour in the tranquil society of Laura herself
[traditionally identified as one of the kneeling figures
in the center foreground of Andrea di Bonaiuto's *Via
Veritatis* fresco], with her fair innocent face looking full
into mine, while I studied the dressing of her golden
hair and the fashion of that green dress embroidered
with violets which Petrarch says he could never see
a bank in spring without thinking of. I chose for my
subject that beautiful scene where Laura sat under an
apple tree, with the blossoms falling all about her.[41]

These paintings attracted notice. In early 1868
the American diplomat and author Bayard Taylor
included Fanny as the only painter, and only woman,
in an article about Florence's artists, alongside the
older and more established male sculptors Thomas
Ball, Pierce Francis Connelly, Joel Tanner Hart,
John Adams Jackson, Larkin Goldsmith Mead
and Hiram Powers:

> I was about to say that we are represented only
> by sculptors in Florence, but must not forget the
> exception made by Miss Alexander, who takes up
> the art which her father seems to have relinquished.
> I had the pleasure of examining a large collection of
> exquisite pen-drawings made by this lady – studies
> from nature, portraits, and illustrative sketches – all
> showing an eye of rarest keenness for seizing form and
> character. The artists who have seen these drawings
> are delighted with them. [English painter William]
> Holman Hunt, especially, was quite unreserved in his
> praise. I have seen but one picture by Miss Alexander
> – a peasant-girl of the Apennines – but it was enough
> to show a genuine feeling for color, in addition to her
> other fine qualities as an artist.[42]

Although that painting cannot be identified, Taylor's
description of Fanny's drawings echoes Motley's
more than a decade earlier and accords well with
her surviving oeuvre. It also testifies to the esteem in
which she was held by her contemporaries.

If Fanny made these early paintings on
commission, the patrons are unknown. Unlike other
Anglo-American artists in Italy, Fanny did not
open a studio for travelers to see her art and make
purchases. She remained outside the art market; while
she accepted commissions and sold what she made,
she also gave it away or used it as part of a more
meaningful exchange. Bostonians were her earliest
patrons, and some paid her more than she requested
with the understanding that the rest would fund her
charity. Lilly Cleveland sometimes sent friends to see
Fanny and purchase her art, and Fanny was grateful
for that; when Lilly's friend Mrs Grinnell visited
Florence and bought a painting, she 'paid me a good
deal more for it than I asked'.[43]

On other occasions, instead of overpaying
for a work of art, these patrons made outright
donations to Fanny's charitable efforts. Fanny was
particularly grateful for these offerings, and in some
instances she thanked the donors with specially
made manuscripts. She had always been interested
in writing. Shortly after arriving in Florence, she
composed a poem about a child named Brondina
who received gifts from fairies at her birth.[44] Around
this same time, she collaborated with her father
on a manuscript entitled 'Hannah Blackstone',
which they dedicated to Lucia. Fanny composed
and transcribed the rhyming text and Francis made
the 90 illustrations in a small notebook they likely
purchased from a Florentine stationer's shop.[45]
It tells the story of virtuous Hannah, who lived
with her in-laws, the Deacon Blackstone and his
wife, while her husband Martin spent several years
prospecting for gold in California. The drawing
of the family group facing the title page might
be a mirror of the Alexanders themselves, the

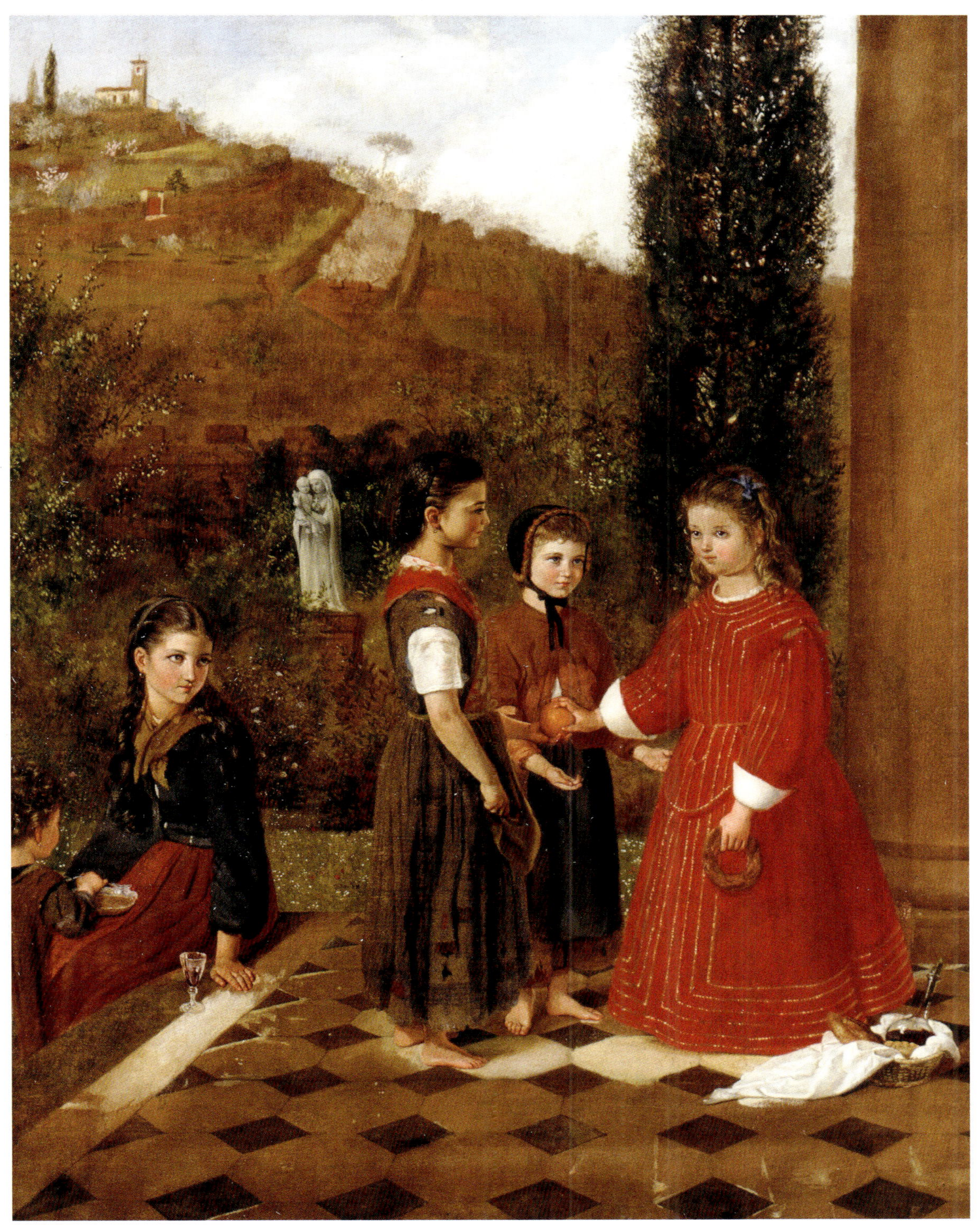

56 Francesca Alexander, *Charity*, 1861, oil on canvas, 72.4 × 57.7 cm (28 ½ × 22 ¾ in), location unknown

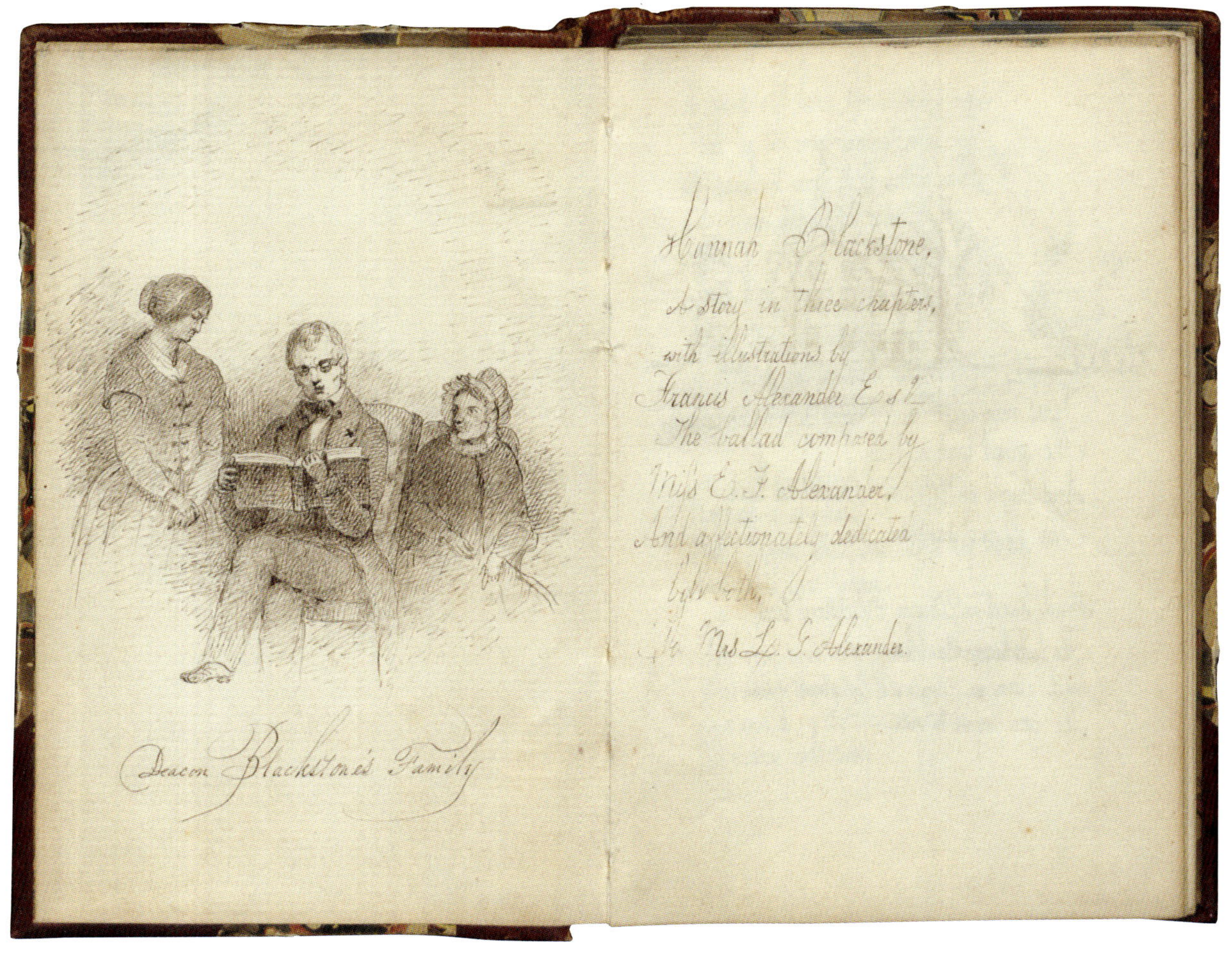

57 Francis and Francesca Alexander, frontispiece and title from 'Hannah Blackstone', *c*.1860, pen and ink, height 17 cm (6 ¾ in), Smith College Special Collections, Northampton, MA

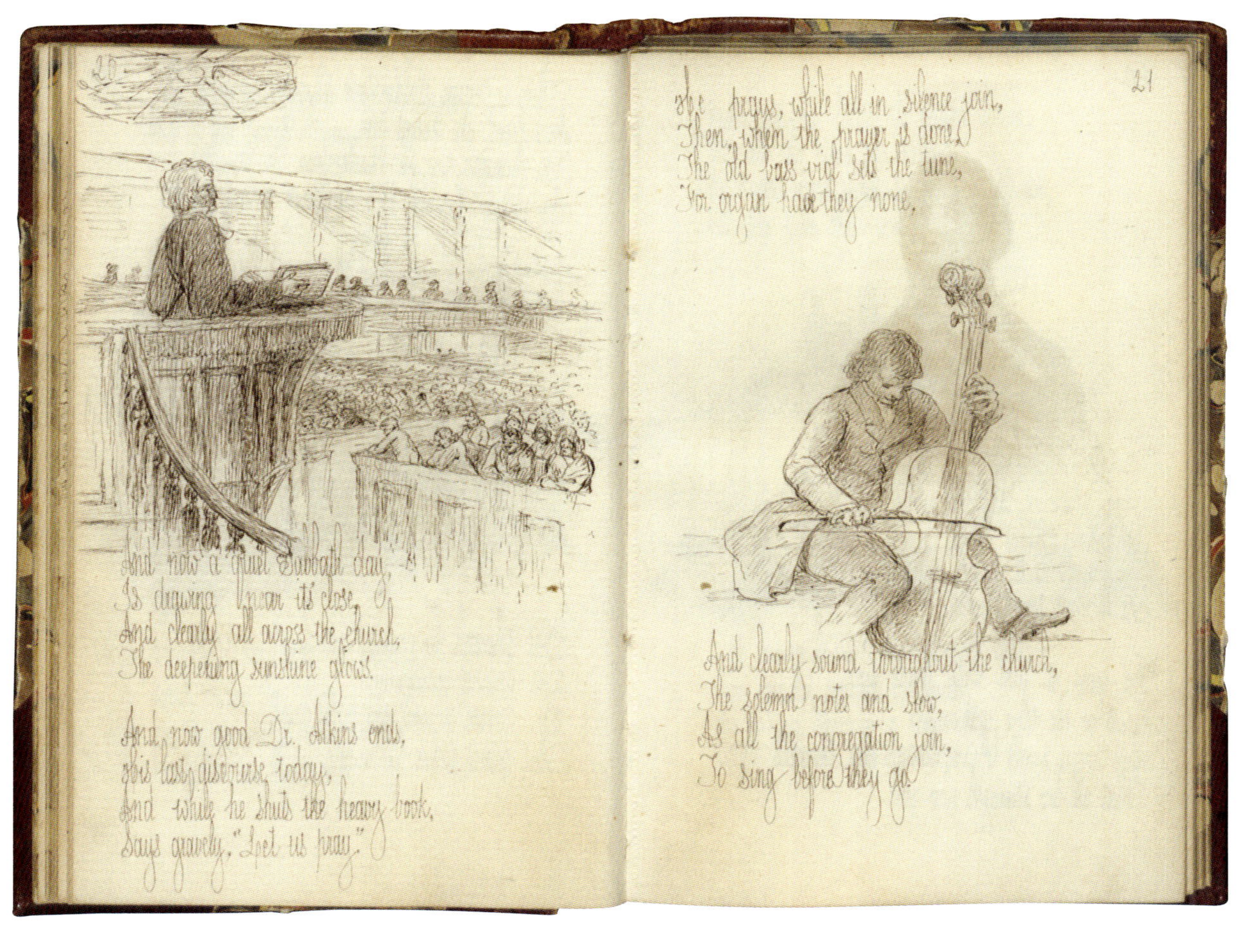

58 Francis and Francesca Alexander, folios 20 and 21 from 'Hannah Blackstone', *c.*1860, pen and ink, 17 cm (6¾ in), Smith College Special Collections, Northampton, MA

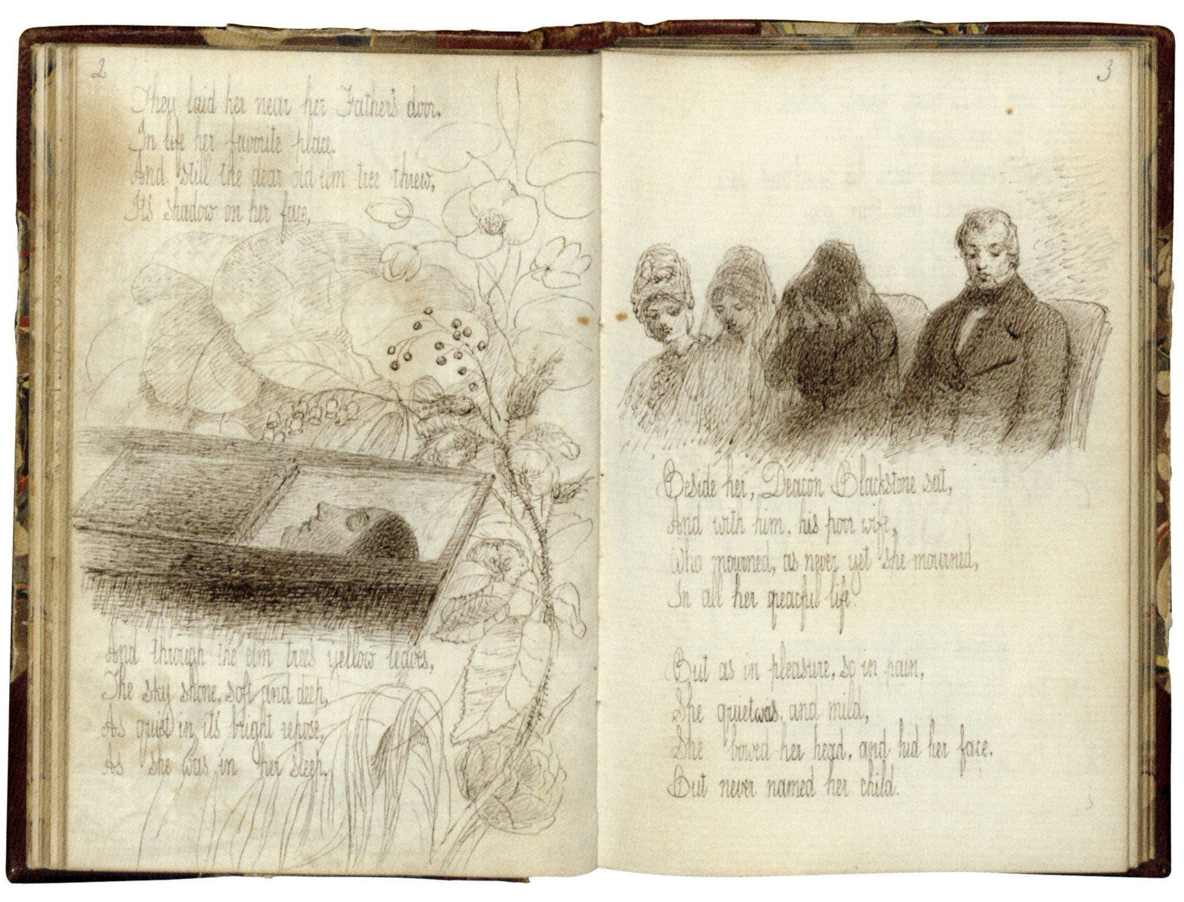

59 Francis and Francesca Alexander, folios 2 and 3 from 'Hannah Blackstone', *c.*1860, pen and ink, 17 cm (6 ¾ in), Smith College Special Collections, Northampton, MA

elders seated and Hannah standing, both women turning to look at the Deacon as he reads to them, presumably from the Bible (fig.57). Hannah was deceived into thinking Martin died in California while fishing on the Sabbath, and she spent the rest of her life atoning for his sins; he returned on the day of her funeral. The subject had nothing to do with Italy or Italian life, but the moralizing tone accorded well with the Alexanders' faith and belief in propriety and charity. On one spread, Francis drew an interior typical of a late eighteenth-century New England meeting house, with the minister in a raised pulpit exhorting his congregation to pray, facing a musician playing the bass viol to accompany the singing congregation, experiences Francis and his family knew from their attendance in New England meeting houses before they moved abroad (fig.58). The floral borders on other folios grow around text and images. In one, sprigs of lily of the valley, a flower Fanny associated with her grandmother's garden in Massachusetts,[46] and rose of Sharon curve around the head of Hannah's coffin on the day of her funeral (fig.59). According to Fanny's verse,

> They laid her near her Father's door,
> In life her favorite place.
> And still the dear old elm tree threw
> It's [*sic*] shadow on her face,
> And through the elm tree's yellow leaves,
> The sky shone, soft and deep,
> As quiet in it's [*sic*] bright repose,
> As she was in her sleep.

The manuscript format must have appealed to Fanny. In 1862 she made her first independent manuscript for Sarah Shaw Russell, a prominent Bostonian well known for her charitable work. Francis had painted portraits of Sarah and her brother Quincy Adams Shaw, and Lilly Cleveland was a friend of Sarah's daughter Emily, so the meeting of the families when the Russells arrived in Florence in fall 1861 is not unexpected. Fanny even drew a portrait of Emily a few months later, focusing on the face but leaving the body in outline in her usual manner (fig.60).[47] That Christmas, Sarah entrusted Fanny with a silk bag filled with 50 silver coins known as *francesconi* to distribute to the poor; a *francescono* was worth a bit more than $1, so this was a significant sum.[48] Dispersing it was a challenge to Fanny, but she was grateful for the opportunity. A few months later she wrote to Lilly:

> [Sarah] has given away a great deal to various poor families since she has been here; but she did not find quite so many poor as she wished to assist – did you ever hear of any one having that difficulty before? – and she gave me a large portion of her charity money to distribute in her place. It was a great pleasure to me, as you can well imagine, going from one poor family to another and leaving them all happy when I came away.[49]

To thank Sarah for her largesse, and to record the distribution of these funds, Fanny created an illustrated manuscript entitled 'History of the Fifty Francesconi Given to the Poor'. The title page, with red initials reminiscent of earlier sacred manuscripts, includes a passage from Matthew 25:40 emphasizing the need to show mercy and charity, a sentiment both Fanny and Sarah took to heart (fig.61). It was bound in parchment with gilt ornament and floral endpapers, with Sarah's initials added to the front cover, likely at Giannini's stationery shop in the Oltrarno, which specialized in similarly bound traveler souvenirs like scrapbooks, photo albums and extra-illustrated novels. Now in prose rather than verse, Fanny's text describes the 17 poor, sick and needy individuals and families whose lives were made better by the donation, with minutely detailed sketches of flowers, people and the Tuscan countryside – farmland, roadside shrines and hilltop

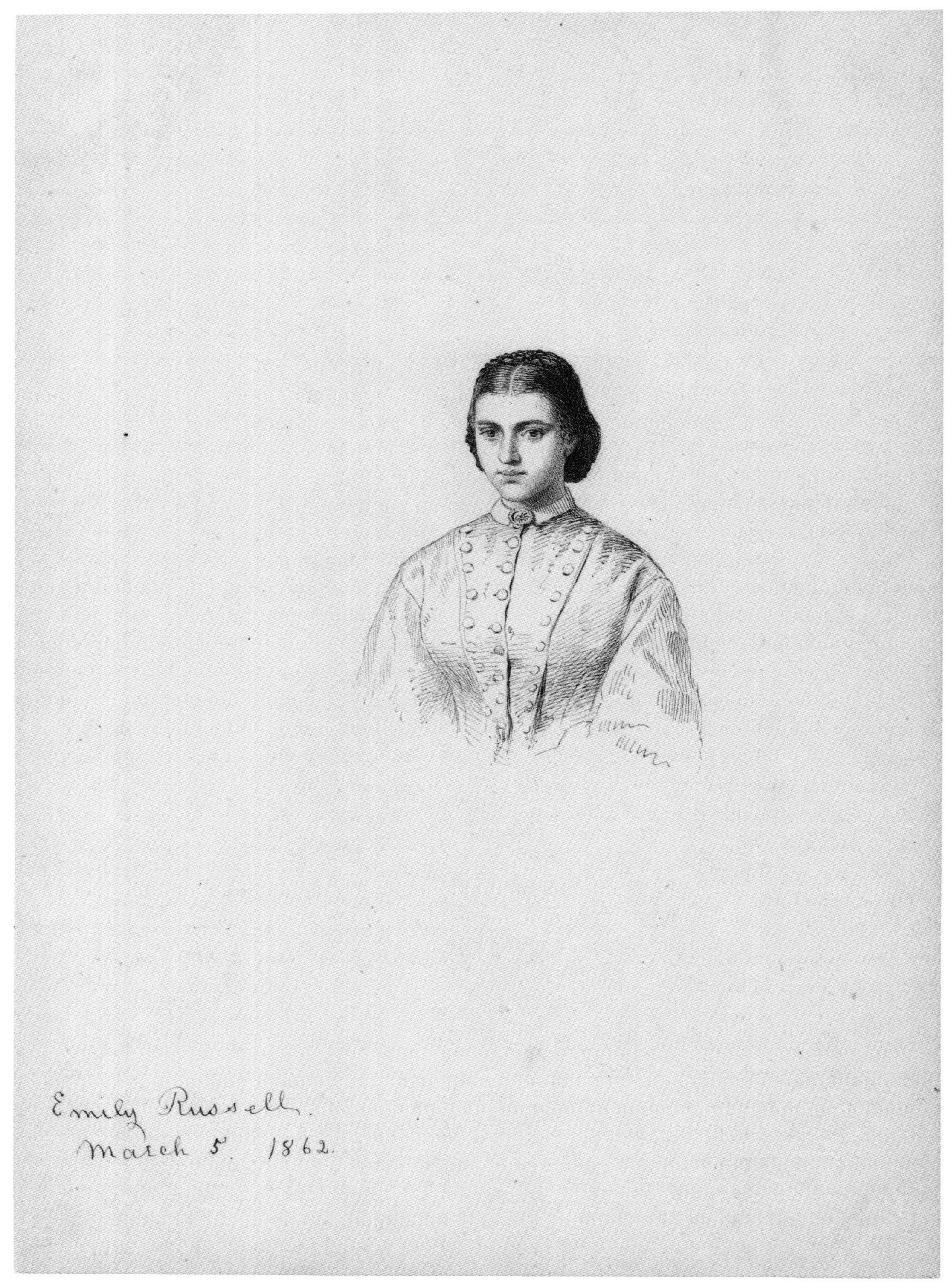

60 Francesca Alexander, *Emily Russell*, 5 March 1862, pen and ink, 28.89 × 20.63 cm (11⅜ × 8⅛ in),
Schlesinger Library on the History of Women in America, Harvard Radcliffe Institute, Cambridge, MA

villages – balancing her calligraphic script, now with the distinctive decorative serifs she would use for the rest of her life (fig.62).

The manuscript opens with a drawing of the silk bag full of *francesconi*, and a description of Angela Manetti, an ailing older *contadina* who 'never asks for anything, not so much . . . from pride as from the fear of giving trouble and from the feeling that she is as well off as she ought to expect, for she is of a very humble and patient disposition' (fig.63).[50] Fanny gave her two of the coins, enabling the grateful woman to buy enough food to improve her health. The manuscript continued, describing the unfortunate Annunziata Brunetti, who married against her family's wishes, with a drawing meant to be the area around her home in Pelago, some 12 miles east of Florence (fig.64). Additional chapters told the story of the sick tailor Pietro Ciari, the widow Angelica Betti, the debt-ridden Assuntina Caretti, the wounded Cesare Pecori, and others, many of whom attended the Evangelical church with the Alexanders. Francis accompanied Fanny as she went from home to home, entering shabby dwellings on dark streets or isolated country lanes, introducing herself to those in need and asking about their circumstances before surprising them by placing a coin or two into their grateful hands. The manuscript ends with a drawing of the empty silk bag, all the coins dispersed (fig.65), and Fanny's reflection on her efforts:

> I have learnt much more than I knew before of the way the poor live; and I have found so much goodness in places where no one would expect it, have met so many good Christians dressed in rags and living in out of the way holes and corners, that I am reminded of the priest in one of my old stories who had some money to distribute to the poor of a certain village and who returned home 'wondering, as he thought of the number of God's hidden servants!'[51]

Fanny later explained the origins of her use of the phrase 'hidden servants', a recurring device in the Bible to describe those God hid away, like David, Elijah and Moses, before they were called to a greater purpose:

> I owe much to a certain old book, which our washerwoman found among the rubbish in her garret, and sold to me for a few soldi, when I was a very young girl indeed. It had seen rough usage, children had scribbled on the pages, it was torn and dirty, and coming out of its yellow parchment binding, and the title page was gone: I should think by the style of printing it was not far from three hundred years old. It contained many curious stories of saints . . . And there was one, too long to tell you now, about one of the holy Fathers of the Desert, who took a journey, in the course of which it was given to him to meet with several very great saints in most unexpected places and conditions; so that, we are told 'he returned home, wondering at the great number of God's hidden servants!' That story took a great hold of my imagination, and I thought, if there were so many hidden servants then, no doubt there must be some now; and it would be a very blessed thing to know them. I began to look for them, and was almost immediately successful, which encouraged me to go on.[52]

This manuscript marked a pivotal moment in Fanny's career as both artist and philanthropist, indeed as a hidden servant herself. Sarah Shaw Russell showed it to her friends, generating additional donations and obligating Fanny to create additional manuscripts, although this is the only one identified today.[53] The Russell and Alexander families remained close, and in 1905 Lucia urged Sarah's daughter Elizabeth Russell Lyman (who also provided funds for Fanny's poor) to publish the manuscript, noting that Sarah's donation resulted in Fanny 'choosing the career which has made her so happy, and such a faithful servant of the Master'.[54]

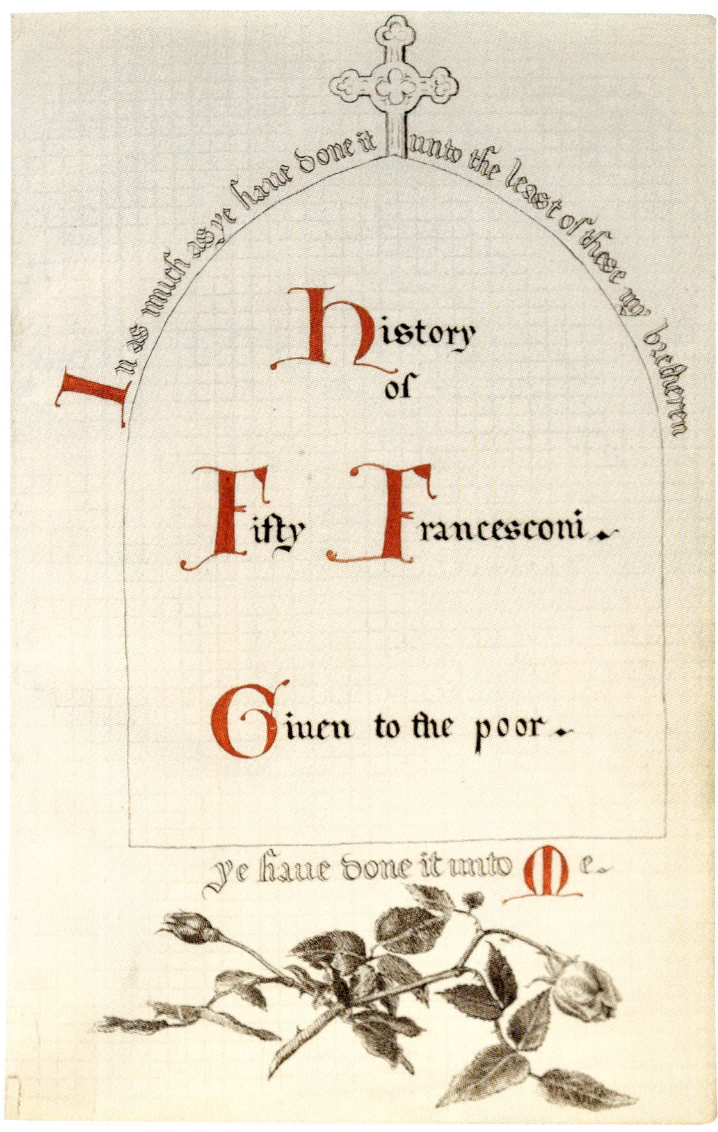

61 Francesca Alexander, title folio from 'History of Fifty Francesconi Given to the Poor', 1861, pen and ink, height 22 cm (8⅝ in), Boston Athenaeum, Boston, MA

62 Francesca Alexander, folio 45 from 'History of Fifty Francesconi Given to the Poor', 1861, pen and ink, height 22 cm (8⅝ in), Boston Athenaeum, Boston, MA

63 Francesca Alexander, folio 1 from 'History of Fifty Francesconi Given to the Poor', 1861, pen and ink, height 22 cm (8⅝ in), Boston Athenaeum, Boston, MA

64 Francesca Alexander, folio 3 from 'History of Fifty Francesconi Given to the Poor', 1861, pen and ink, height 22 cm (8⅝ in), Boston Athenaeum, Boston, MA

65 Francesca Alexander, folio 47 from 'History of Fifty Francesconi Given to the Poor', 1861, pen and ink, height 22 cm (8⅝ in), Boston Athenaeum, Boston, MA

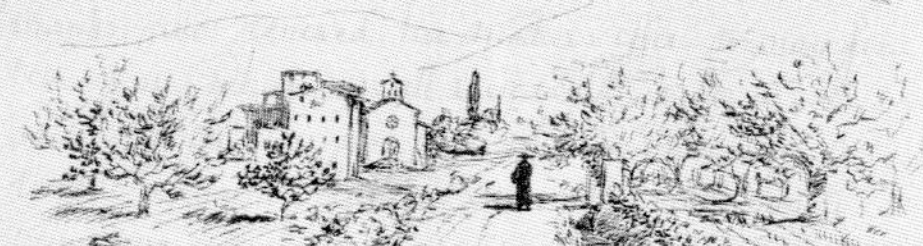

I had now given something to all the poor whom I knew to be in any particular need, and two francesconi still remained. Of these I sent one to Nunziatina Giunti, by one of "i fratelli," who was only too happy to undertake the errand. He brought back word that she was a great deal better, and that he found her sitting up and eating a bowl of soup; indeed I imagine that enough to eat was the principal thing she wanted. She was most thankful for the money. The other francescone I took myself to Angelica Betti. She was not at home; but I saw her daughter, apparently almost as old as the mother, a soft, helpless sort of woman, still somewhat lame from the rheumatism. She was probably rather more energetic than she looked, for she told me she had found a little sewing to do, and had by no means given up finding materials for their usual work. At any rate, she said, she could do any sort of sewing if she could only find it to do. I told her my friend had sent her another

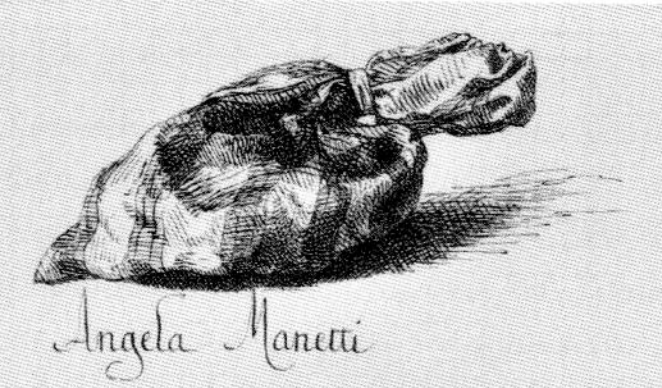

Angela Manetti

The first poor person whom I was able to help was Angela Manetti, a poor old contadina of San Francesco. She is a good old lady, well spoken of by all, living a peaceable hardworking life on the farm where her husband was born. She has been for many years subject to an incurable and very painful complaint, which has been much worse lately, and the coarse food which she is obliged to live on always hurts her. Still she never asks for anything; not so much, I think, from pride, as from the fear of giving trouble, and from the feeling that she is as well off as she ought to expect; for she is of a very humble and patient disposition, and it was only from her daughter Teresina that I heard of her need. When she admitted me this morning, and had shown me the hens, and the dog, and led me into the little garden, I began to make some inquiries. "How are you Angela? Any better yet?" "O! not bad today. Yesterday I was in such pain, but it has gone off with the

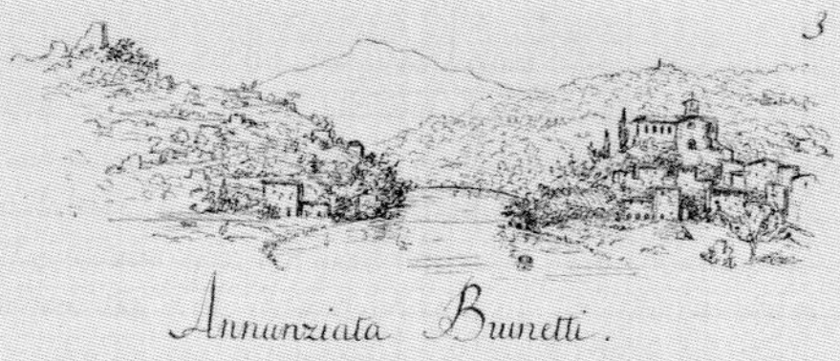

Annunziata Brunetti.

This poor woman is perhaps the most unfortunate of all whom I shall have to help; her whole life has been a series of troubles. She belonged to a respectable contadina family, living near Pelago, about twelve miles from Florence; who supported themselves by raising sheep and goats. When she was only eighteen years old she married, against the wishes of all her family. The man whom she selected was a pigionale, which is a degree lower than a contadino: he had no property and supported himself by working on the roads; but he bore a good character, he was fond of Annunzia, and she was fond of him. It was in vain that her family told her of the hard life she would have before her, and promised to find a much better match for her if she would have patience, and wait. She was satisfied, and she married her pigionale. When he had regular work he was able to support her, but often there was no work to be had, and then they were in great need. As for her rela

money, and was a great deal better in consequence, but she thought it doubtful if he would be able to work well as a mason without hurting himself, and she was trying to find something else for him to do. And now at last, my work about this money, the pleasantest work that I ever had to do is over. I have been able to help seventeen families, for most of whom I had enough to supply all their immediate necessities. Their thanks I have already written down; but I cannot end this account without adding my own for what has been so great a pleasure, and I think also somewhat of a profit to me. I have learnt much more than I knew before of the way the poor live; and I have found so much goodness in places where no one would expect it, have met so many good christians dressed in rags and living in out of the way holes and corners, that I am reminded of the priest in one of my old stories who had some money to distribute to the poor of a certain village, and who returned home," wondering as he thought of the number of God's hidden servants!"

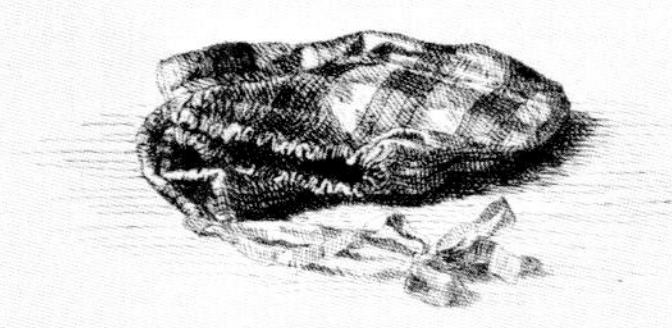

This was certainly not the only time Lucia promoted her daughter's work. In May 1863, she described the Russell manuscript to John Lowell Gardner and his wife Catherine Endicott Peabody, and expressed the hope that they would see it.[55] Both the Gardner and Peabody families, like Lucia, were connected to Salem's maritime trade, and Lucia's letters to them are full of gossip about Bostonians passing through Florence. In that same letter, Lucia described Fanny's many activities: 'Between the poor who are in want, and the rich who are invalids, with her painting and her singing, she is one of the most laborious of the working classes.'[56]

The Gardners were duly impressed. When they visited Florence, they commissioned Fanny for what would become her largest and most complex painting, a group of three *contadine* leaving flowers at a roadside shrine with a view from the hills around Florence in the background (fig.66). Fanny was particularly pleased by what this commission would do for her poor. On 1 November 1864 she told Lilly Cleveland:

> [Mrs Gardner] has given me an order for a large picture, larger than I ever painted yet. It is to represent two contadine arranging some flowers before a Madonna. I have found a lovely model for the eldest girl, only she is in delicate health, and is every now and then confined to the house, so I lose more time than I could wish. But I console myself with the thought that so much beauty is worth waiting for. The price which I am to receive for this picture will be enough to last all the poor people for a great while.[57]

Indeed, the Gardners paid Fanny generously before she finished the painting – Fanny described the amount as 'Mr Gardner's very acceptable present to the poor, for such I must consider all that he has given me beyond the original price of the picture' – and she distributed the funds to her needy friends, many of whom were suffering from the recent flooding of the Arno river.[58] But the painting took more time than Fanny initially anticipated, not only due to her model's health but also, as Fanny wrote to Mrs Gardner, because the young woman '(who knows her own value and torments me accordingly) has had her house overflowed, which she appears to think a sufficient reason for staying in it'.[59]

In January 1865, Lucia sent Mrs Gardner an update, revealing that 'Fanny is at this moment painting a mass of lauristinus [*sic*] – which I believe is a favorite flower of yours – in your picture'.[60] Those flowers appear at top center, growing over the wall alongside the shrine, the branches and flowers forming a natural halo around the standing *contadina*. At this point Fanny was almost done; a month later, Lucia wrote to say the painting was 'finished like a miniature'.[61] In another letter that April, Lucia expressed her condolences on the death of the Gardner grandson (the only child of Jack and Isabella Stewart Gardner) and announced that the painting was finished and on its way to Boston. Lucia described the background as

> a literal copy of the view which you will remember, and there are flowers enough to suit you. On the horizon not far from the tabernacle is a mountain covered with snow shaped like a pyramid, this is 'Le Tre Potenze' because it was formerly the place where the boundary lines met of the three duchies of Toscana, Modena, and Lucca. The first mountain on the right hand from the gap where there is no snow, is 'Il Libro aperto', so called because its two summits resemble an open book, and the next mountain on the right of this is 'Monte Cimone' the highest of the northern Apennines. At the base of the hills, below Le Tre Potenze, is Pistoja, faint in the distance, and above the woods of the Cascine, which you will recognize, of course, is the city of Prato.[62]

If this tabernacle was on one of the roads around Bellosguardo, as Lucia implied – and the settings for Fanny's drawings and paintings were always quite

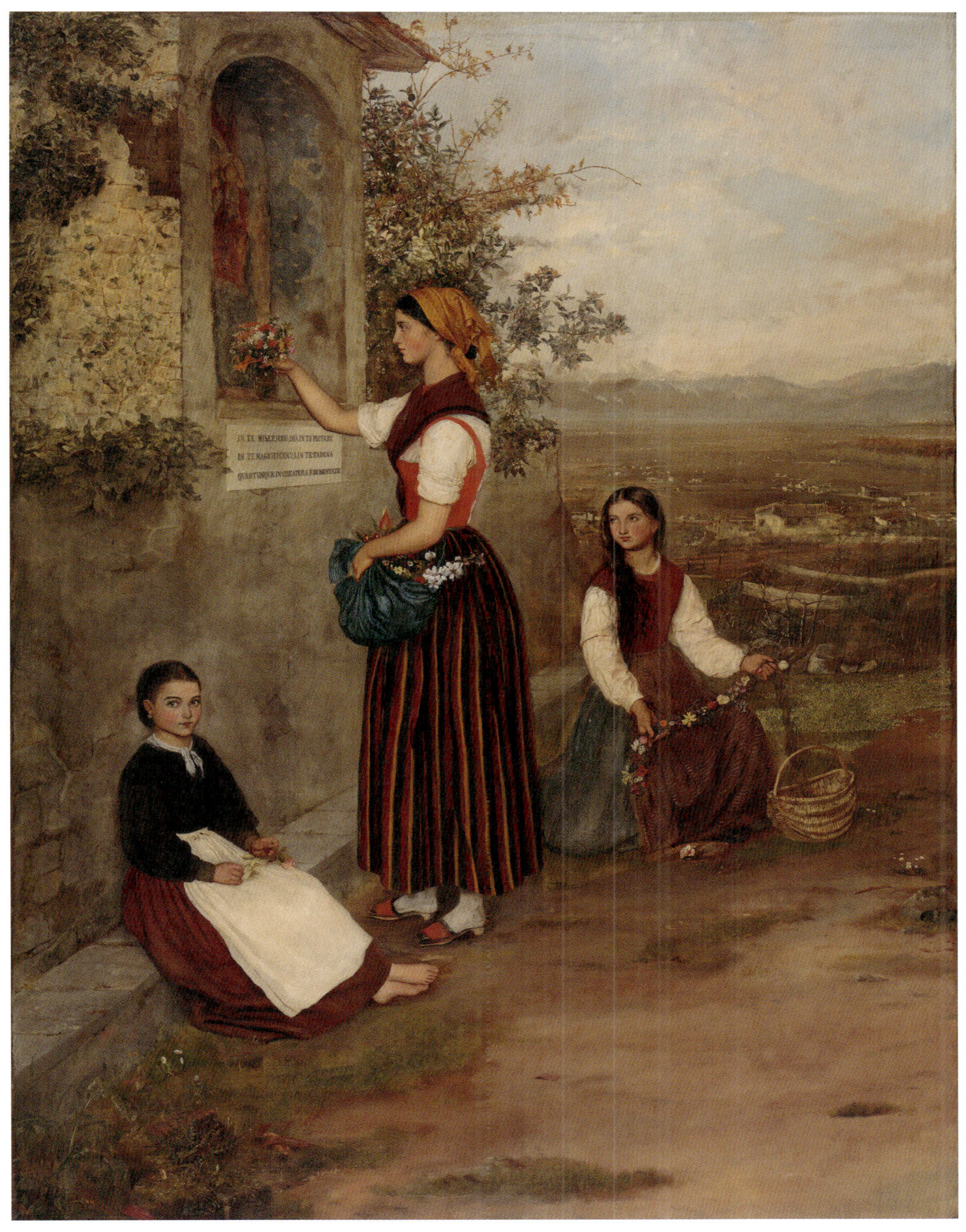

66 Francesca Alexander, *Decorating a Shrine*, 1855, oil on canvas, 125.2 × 93 cm (49 ¼ × 36 ⅝ in),
Isabella Stewart Gardner Museum, Boston, MA

literal, making this likely – it no longer survives. It enclosed a painting of the enthroned Madonna and Child against a starry blue ground, above a plaque quoting Saint Bernard of Clairvaux's prayer to the Virgin Mary from Dante's *Paradiso* (33:19–21). The overt Catholic iconography was somewhat mitigated by the Dante reference, one that sophisticated Bostonians like the Gardners – and their Dantophile daughter-in-law Isabella Stewart Gardner, who inherited the painting – could appreciate.[63]

Lucia continued corresponding with the Gardners, boasting of Fanny's success. In January 1866, she sent another gossipy letter with the news that a number of other Bostonians had acquired Fanny's paintings.[64] Two of these, purchased by Susan Hammond Timmins Perkins and Mr (Gardner?) Brewer, cannot be identified, but two others can. Both represent Fanny's *contadina* friend Clorinda Amadei, who lived near Abetone and taught Fanny popular songs and stories.[65] The first, *Italian Mother* (fig.67), was purchased by Martha Wharton Dow and her husband George Washington Wales and later exhibited in the Boston Athenaeum in 1869 with a lost painting entitled *Italian Peasants*. The second – identified by a verso inscription – was purchased by a Henry Whitney (fig.68). In both Clorinda wears a traditional costume of skirt, white shirt and laced bodice, and even the same flowered scarf. In the Wales painting she sits on a bench in a portico, holding a swaddled child, with a distant view to a villa on a hilltop, while in the Whitney painting she stands at an open door with a glimpse of hills and a potted plant behind her. In 1863, Fanny sold another painting of Clorinda to the Clevelands; in this one, Clorinda stands in a simple church interior, wearing a similar costume but with a veil on her head and a rosary and a devotional book in her hands (fig.69).[66] A related but lost painting represented Clorinda in the same costume reclining in a flowering field, illustrating a popular song.[67] And surely there were more paintings from this period, of Clorinda and

others. But Fanny's inclination to sell or give her art as part of a more personal exchange associated with her charitable efforts, lacking documentation beyond references in correspondence, makes them difficult to locate today.

Lucia's letters to the Gardners betrayed her longing for the United States. And the persecution of Fanny by local priests must have left the Alexanders wondering if they should remain at Bellosguardo, or even in Italy. These feelings surely intensified in 1866, when Lucia's father Samuel Swett died. She and her siblings divided a considerable estate; Lucia's inheritance included portraits of her parents by Gilbert Stuart and other paintings by John Smibert and John Singleton Copley.[68] The combination of these factors, as well as Lucia's health, which suffered from the Villa Brichieri's dampness, prompted the Alexanders to return to the United States in 1868, after almost 15 years abroad.[69] They journeyed north through Paris to London, where they visited Sir John Soane's Museum – its eclectic collection must have appealed to their taste – and sailed from Liverpool to Boston in June.[70] Transportation had improved somewhat since their earlier journey, but a transatlantic crossing still meant up to two weeks at sea.

They remained in the United States for just over a year, much of that time at Winthrop House, a popular hotel on the edge of the Boston Common. They also visited Newport and Swampscott, where they socialized with the family of James Freeman Clarke and Fanny painted a portrait of his teenage niece Elizabeth Huidekoper.[71] They traveled to upstate New York and encountered members of the Tuscarora nation, from whom they acquired various objects made for trade, among them 'Indian babies and moccasins'.[72] Fanny drew a Tuscarora mother and child in a pose reminiscent of Renaissance Madonna and Child paintings and her *Italian Mother* (fig.67), perhaps an indication that she equated them (fig.70). But she also may have been prompted by Lucia's claim of both

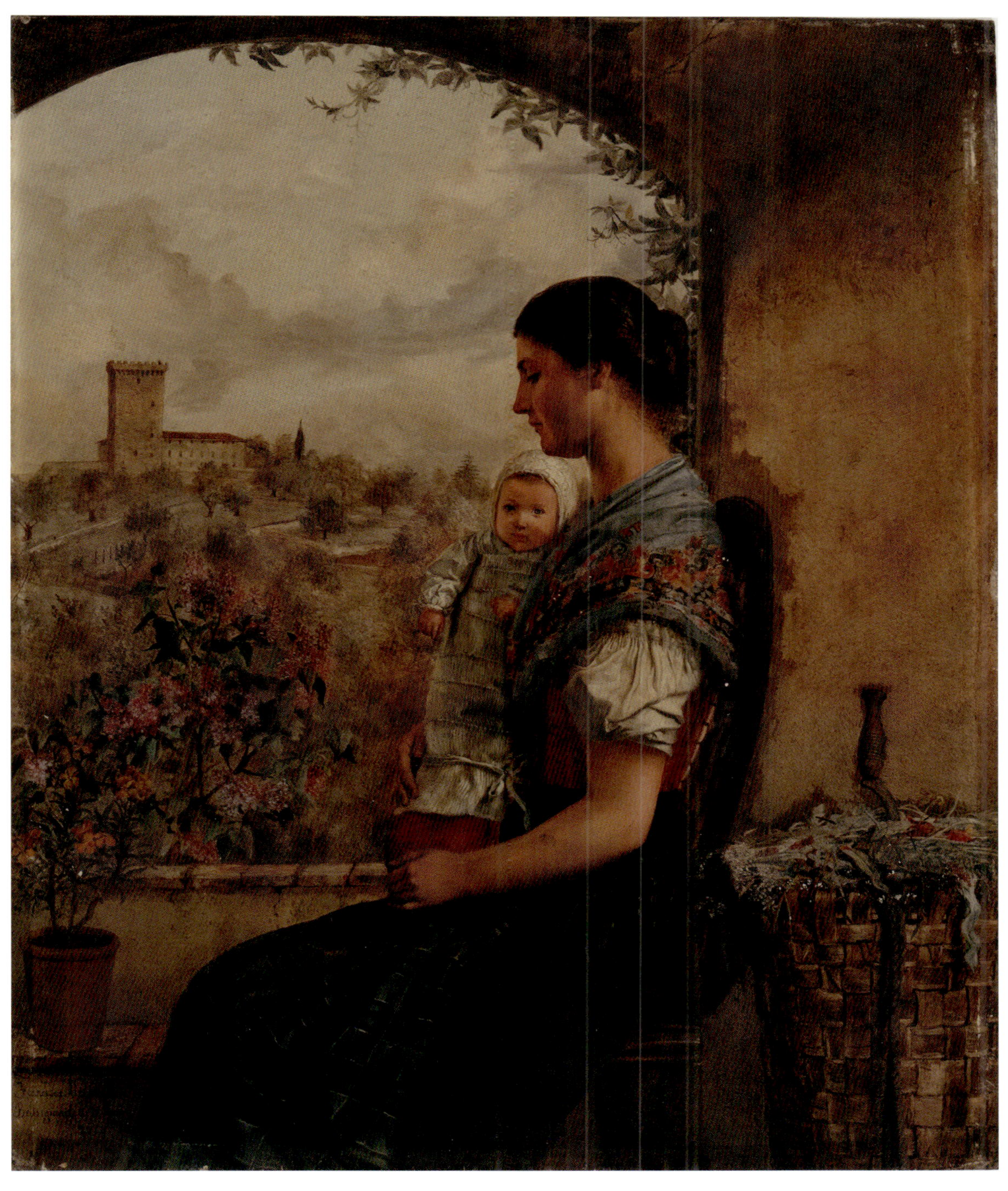

67 Francesca Alexander, *Italian Mother*, 12 May, 1866, oil on canvas, 45.09 × 37.47 cm (17 ¾ × 14 ¾ in),
Addison Gallery of American Art, Andover, MA

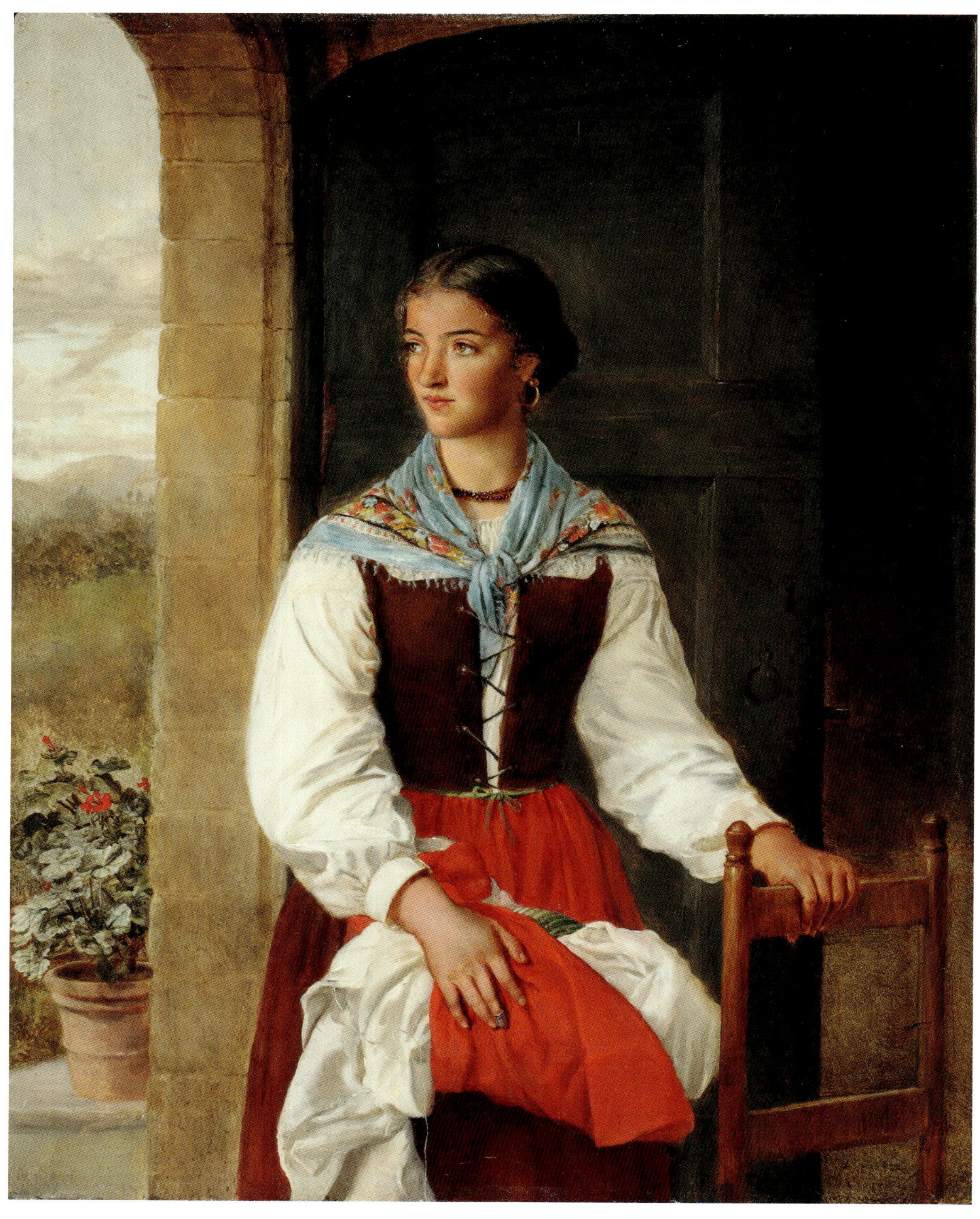

68 Francesca Alexander, *Clorinda Amadei*, August 1865, oil on board, 38.73 × 30.48 cm (15 ¼ × 12 in),
McGuigan Collection, Harpswell, ME

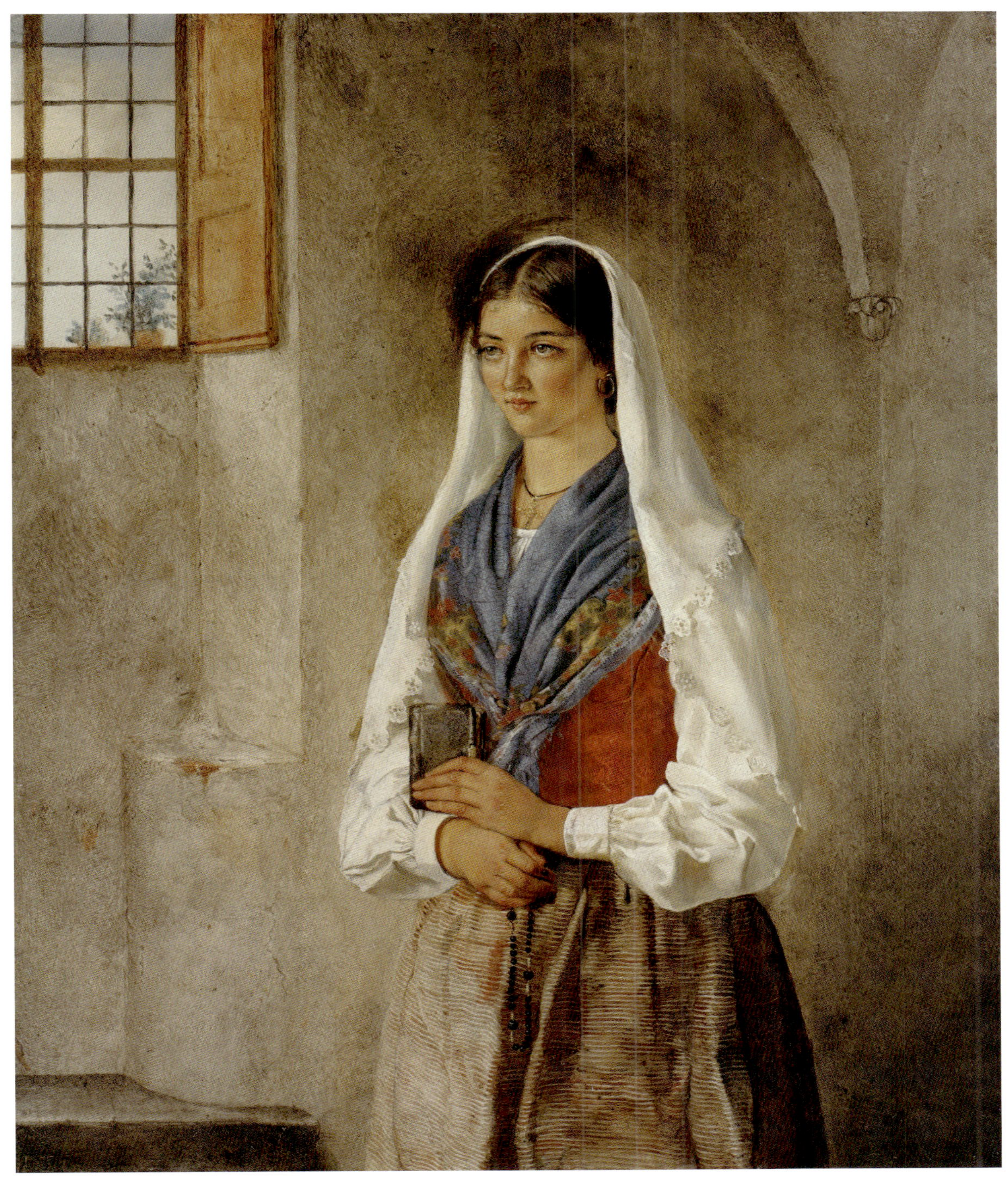

69 Francesca Alexander, *Clorinda Amadei*, 1863, oil on board, 46.7 × 38.6 cm (18⅜ × 15¼ in),
Munson Williams Proctor Arts Institute, Utica, NY

distant Native American ancestry and descent from the seventeenth-century missionary Reverend Richard Bourne, who converted Mashpee Wampanoags to Christianity but also supported their rights to land holdings on Cape Cod.[73]

It is no coincidence that 1869 was the only year Fanny was represented in the Boston Athenaeum's annual exhibition, with five paintings of Italian subjects on display. After her earlier rejection from the Esposizione Nazionale Italiana, even the modest Fanny must have been proud to have her paintings installed there. No doubt she had a slight advantage, since George Washington Wales and Lilly Cleveland's uncle and fellow Perugia evacuee Edward N. Perkins were on the exhibition committee. Wales sent his two paintings by Fanny, W.R. Robeson sent two more entitled *La Fontana* and *Peasant Girl*, and Margaret Grant Chadwick Tucker, an amateur artist whose painting of lilies is in one of Lucia's scrapbooks, sent a fifth, entitled *Saint Zita*.[74] Of these, only Wales's *Italian Mother* can be identified (fig.67).

Despite this success, Fanny missed Italy and her Italian friends, and they missed her. Fanny told Lilly Cleveland that Marianna Capponi Farinola's heart was broken by her absence.[75] In a letter to Diamante Tommaseo she confessed that even her mother's happiness, and time spent with American friends, 'cannot alter my heart from those I have left behind, who are always in my heart'.[76] She worried about those who needed her charity, and she tried to do what she could for them even from a distance. She was particularly concerned for a poor sculptor with a Florence studio named Severino Castorani, who later married her friend Gigina Milli. She urged Caroline Marsh and a Boston friend, a Mrs Ripka, to tell their friends about him.[77] Knowing that the Longfellow family were in Florence during her absence, Fanny also wrote to the poet to ask him to sit for Castorani, though there is no evidence he ever did.[78]

Although the Alexanders originally planned to return to Italy that fall, they decided instead to search for a permanent home in the Boston area.[79] But the search proved daunting, and after more than a year they left to wrap up their affairs in Florence while family members continued to look on their behalf. Always an obedient daughter – though now more than 30 years old – Fanny resigned herself to the idea of living in the United States; in a letter to Niccolò Tommaseo she confessed,

I, for my part, have promised, both to [my mother] and father, to be ready to leave again for America next spring. And I am certain that, after having refreshed my eyes and heart with the sight of the homeland of my affection, and of my loved ones, I will then be able, with God's help, to live contentedly at a distance, because I see that America is too necessary for father and mother.[80]

Believing they would only be in Italy for a short time, the Alexanders left some of their belongings in Boston. But they brought other items back with them, including the Native American objects as well as algae, tree bark and a collection of wood samples supplied by the piano manufacturer George H. Chickering, the brother-in-law of Thomas Ball, to donate to the botanist Filippo Parlatore for the collections of Florence's museum of natural history.[81] They also brought gifts for friends, like beef and celery extract and pineapples for Italian Senator Gaetano de Castillia.[82] Lucia consulted the Boston oculist Henry Willard Williams – whose artist sisters, known as the Misses Williams, lived in Italy for many years and must have known the Alexanders – for a cure for Sigismondo Castromediano's eye ailment.[83] Castromediano was grateful for this kindness, and later mentioned both Lucia and Fanny in his memoirs, claiming that they were known for 'their great heart and beneficence; they love Italy so much!'[84]

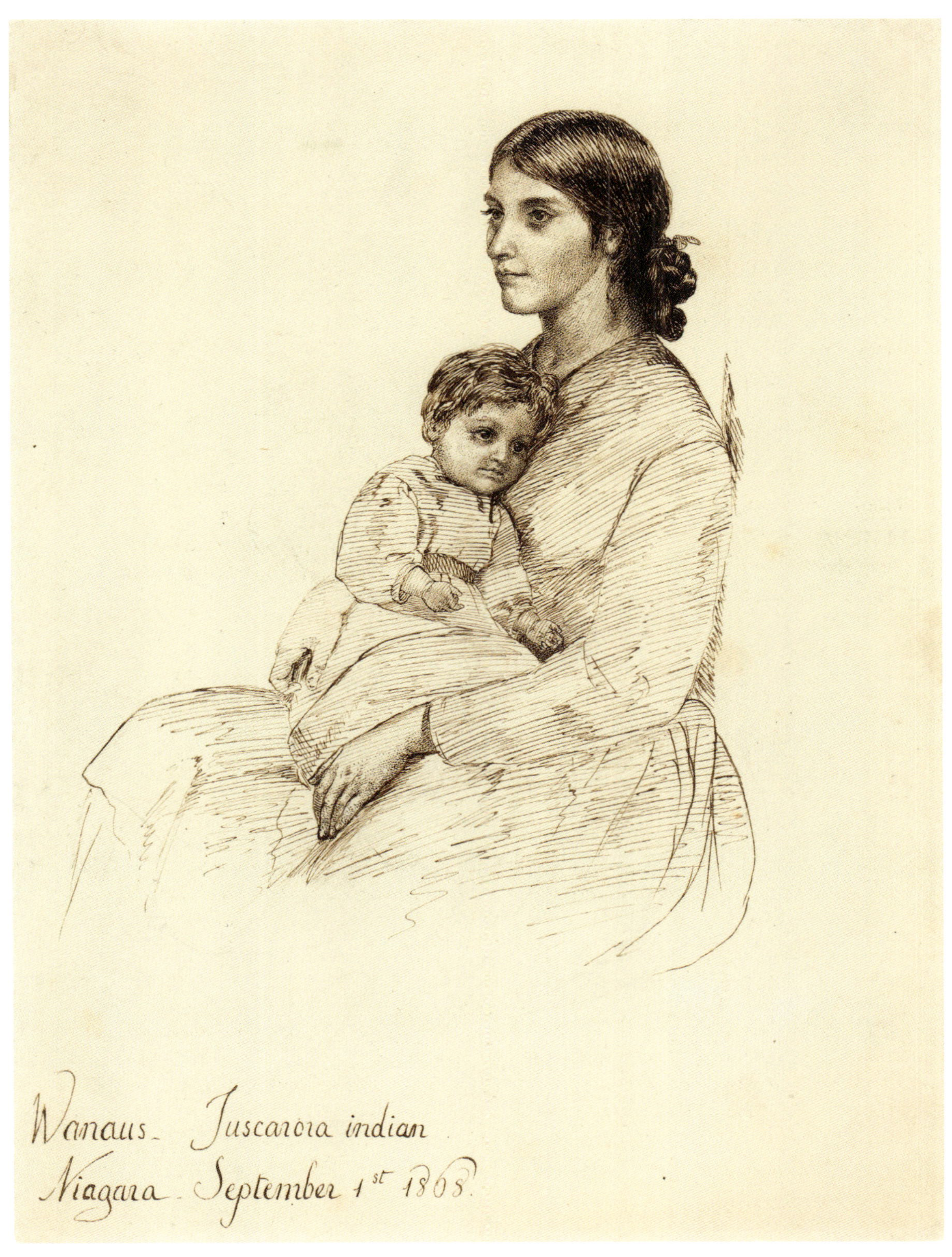

70 Francesca Alexander, *Wanaus, Tuscarora Indian*, 1 September, 1868, pen and brown ink on heavy ivory card stock, 22.5 × 16.6 cm (8 ⅞ × 6 ½ in), National Gallery of Art, Washington, DC

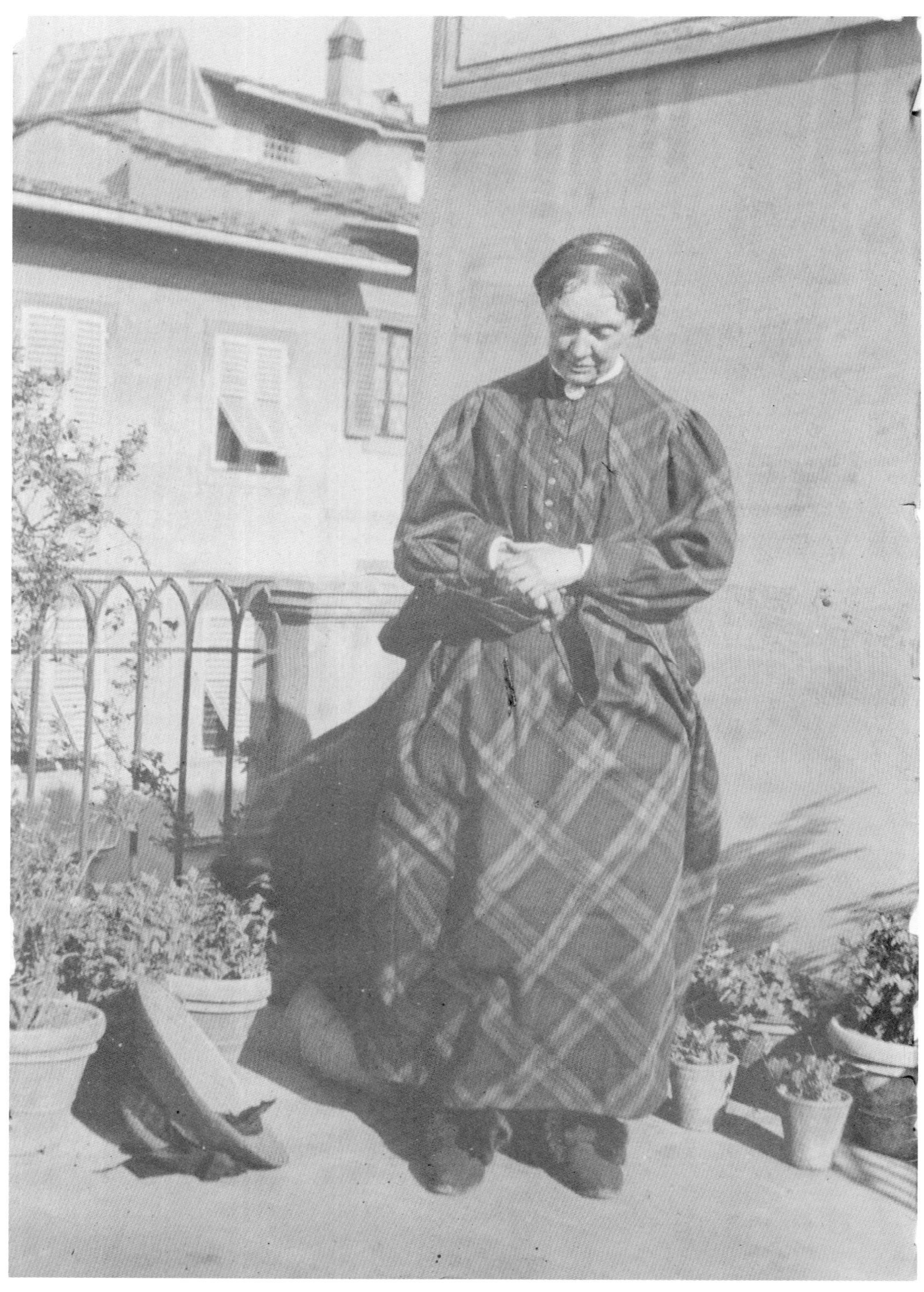

71 *Francesca Alexander in her Sky Parlor*, late nineteenth century, photograph, approx. 12 × 9 cm. (4¾ × 3⅜ in), New York Public Library, NY

On 12 August 1869, Francis applied for a passport on behalf of himself and Lucia, but Fanny applied for her own. It described her as 5 feet 6 ½ inches tall, with a high forehead, light hazel eyes and dark brown hair, a straight nose, large mouth, round chin, oval face and light complexion.[85] Although it is tempting to think that Fanny secured her own document because she wanted the option to remain in Italy longer than her parents, there is no indication that she ever considered this. Despite her love of Italy, if forced to make the choice she would have joined her parents in the United States; the Alexanders were too deeply interconnected to do otherwise. They sailed soon after and, following a short stay in Paris, arrived in Florence on 29 September, where many of their friends waited at the train station to welcome them back.[86]

Remembering the dampness that sickened Lucia at the Villa Brichieri, they took an apartment on the upper floor of the Hotel Bonciani, overlooking Piazza Santa Maria Novella in the heart of the city.[87] According to contemporary guidebooks, the Bonciani was a second-class hotel composed of several interconnected palaces once associated with the Pitti and other prominent Florentine families.[88] The Alexanders' apartment had its own entrance, giving them some privacy from the hotel's more itinerant guests, as well as two bedrooms, a dining room, a drawing room and two additional chambers, with a rooftop garden and studios for both Francis and Fanny.[89] Fanny called that rooftop her sky parlor, perhaps knowing that her former Bellosguardo neighbor Nathaniel Hawthorne used the same term for the tower he built on his home in Concord, Massachusetts, a few years earlier. A photograph of Fanny, taken by a friend or admirer years later, when personal cameras were more widely available, shows her in the sky parlor (fig.71). She wears a dark plaid dress, her head modestly lowered and her hair pulled back in a headband similar to the one worn in the likely self-portrait in the Christmas drawing (fig.55). Fanny stands against what must be the wall of her

studio, alongside an iron railing that kept the many potted plants and sundial at her feet from falling to the piazza below.

This is one of the only known photographs of Fanny, though she apparently did have more formal ones taken. In 1860 she confessed to Lilly Cleveland that a recent photograph came out so badly that she was

obliged to have it destroyed. I hope it was not like me. I don't set up for looks, as you know, but I should be sorry to think I was so very forbidding and disagreeable looking as the picture. At any rate if I ever find myself becoming vain, I mean to go and have a photograph taken, and I'm sure it will be an effectual cure. Papa says he means to try again, and if it is any way tolerable (which I don't think it will be) you shall have one.[90]

More than 30 years later, she told another friend that 'I take very badly in photograph'.[91] This, in addition to her disinclination to self-promotion, may be why she did not have photographic *cartes de visite* made to offer her visitors, as artists like Hiram Powers and Harriet Hosmer did.

Italian friends hoped the Alexanders would change their minds and remain in Italy. Marina Sprea Baroni Semitecolo even offered them a wing of her Villa Rezzonico in Bassano as a permanent residence.[92] But the search for a Boston home continued. In 1870 Lucia wrote to John Greenleaf Whittier about an offer they made on a house but she admitted that if it was not accepted, 'we shall most likely not cross the water again. Fan is happier here, Mr A's heart almost fails him, I have gone through the agony of leaving every thing I love in one country + dread going through the same experience a second time.'[93] Although this offer was indeed declined, the following summer she wrote again to say that they were now negotiating to purchase a house near the Clevelands in the Jamaica

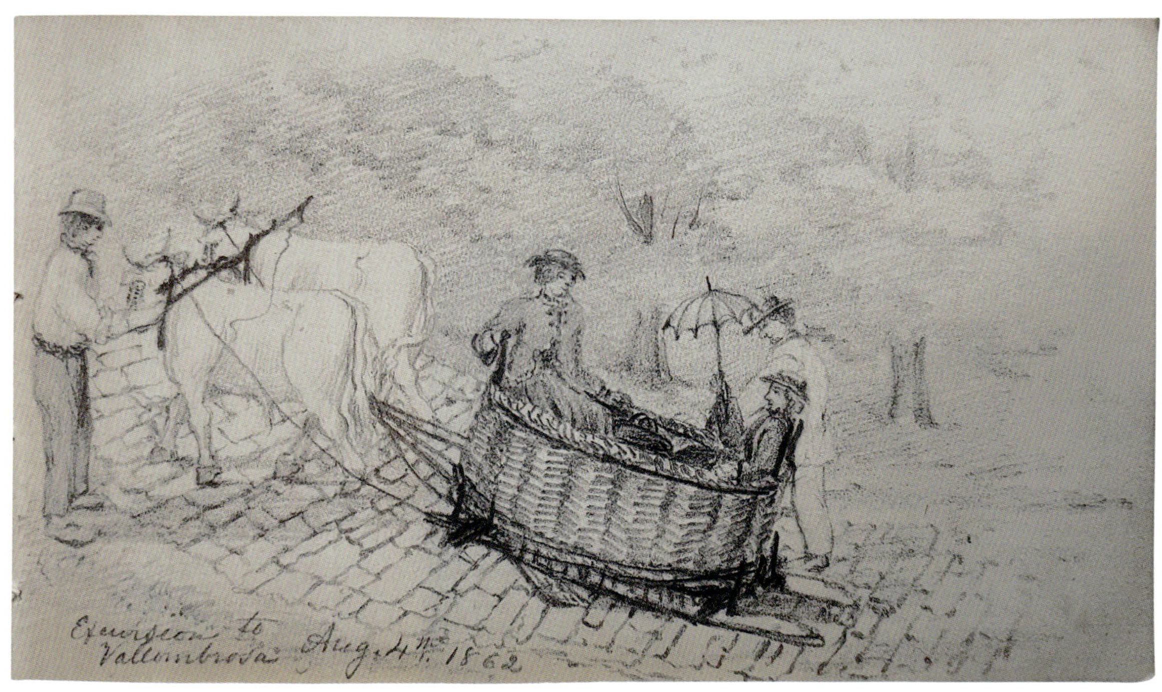

72 Mary Elizabeth or Abigail Osgood Williams, *Excursion to Vallombrosa*, 4 August 1862, pencil,
15.24 × 9.52 cm (6 × 3¾ in), Cucurullo collection

Plain neighborhood of Boston; when this too fell through Lucia finally resigned herself to remaining in Florence, though she referred to it as 'this life of exile'.[94] But the family quickly re-established their familiar routines. They enjoyed Florence during the spring, fall and winter, and traveled during the summer to escape the heat. In addition to Abetone and Bassano, they began to spend more time in Venice, where Marina's gondolier rowed them around the canals and Lucia described the basilica of San Marco as 'very near heaven'.[95]

Francis and Fanny were comfortable wherever they went, but Lucia was somewhat less adaptable. After several weeks near the Benedictine abbey of Vallombrosa during the summer of 1871, she was relieved to leave the hilltop: 'we came down in a picturesque procession composed of white oxen and a military escort and I have no wish ever to see the place again.'[96] This procession was one undertaken by many Anglo-Americans – the military escort was protection against bandits in the remote locale – and it was captured in a drawing by one of the Misses Williams, representing two women (presumably the sisters, or a sister and a traveling companion) seated in a large basket on runners, protected by a parasol, as a pair of white oxen pull them up the path (fig.72). Lucia found such conveyances less than ideal, and the mountaintop isolating.

The Hotel Bonciani became home, and photographs of their salon give a sense of how they lived in it. This was a crowded space, with paintings hung salon-style on the walls alongside *ferri* in the shape of winged dragons holding aloft porcelain vases (fig.73). These *ferri* were either modern copies or Renaissance

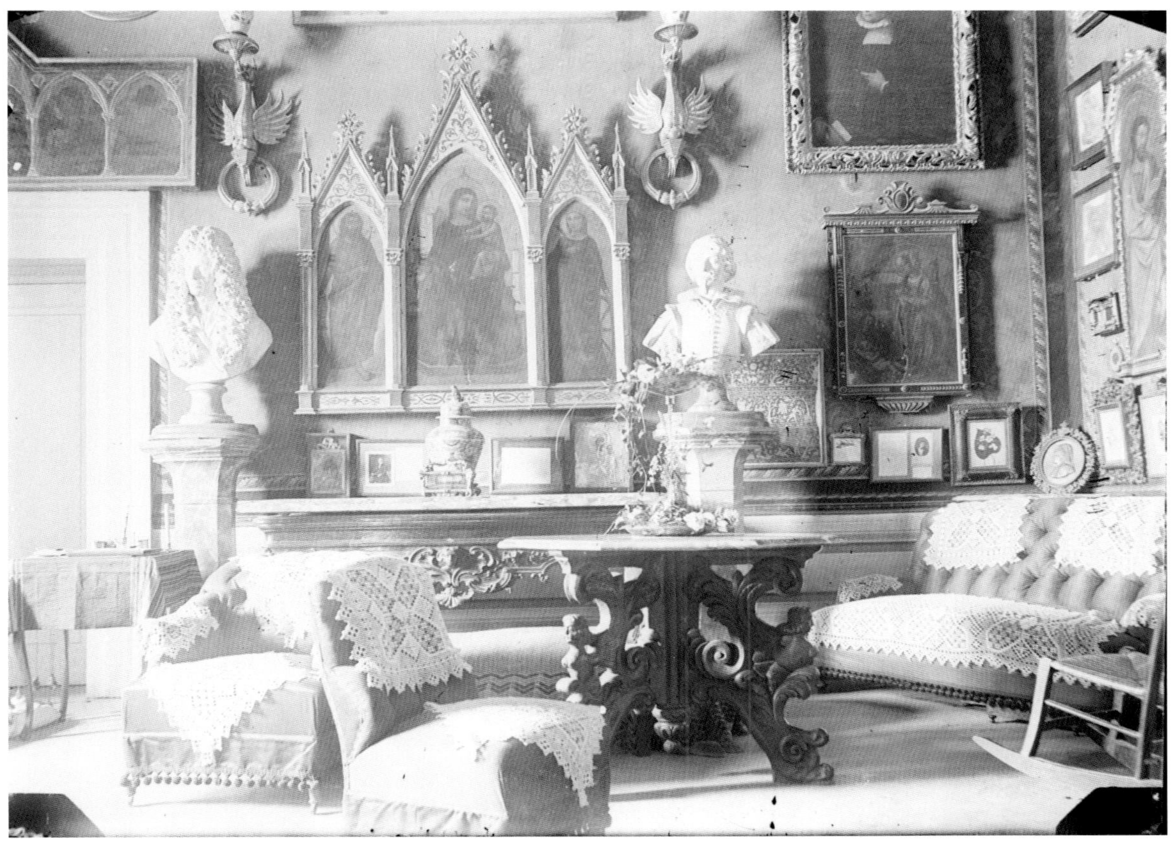

73 Harriet Georgina Ellis Caetani, *The Alexanders' Drawing Room at the Hotel Bonciani, Florence*, between 1869–84, photograph from a glass negative, New York University Acton Photograph Archive, Villa La Pietra, Florence

examples removed from palaces demolished during the urban renewal undertaken when Florence was capital of Italy. Taking advantage of the high ceiling, the Alexanders placed Cole's *Tornado in the Wilderness* over a portal; framed photographs and documents were scattered about, carved antique furniture mixed with contemporary upholstered chairs covered in lace antimacassars, and marble busts, assorted decorative objects and floral bouquets rested on tabletops, mantles and even the floor (fig.74). Other rooms in the apartment would have been similarly furnished; one held a group of ancient vases Sigismondo Castromediano gifted to Lucia (fig.75).[97]

Fanny readily adapted to this new residence and appreciated the space it provided for her friends to gather. In early 1870 she wrote to tell Lilly Cleveland,

We could hardly be more pleasantly situated from our windows we can see across the piazza and the buildings beyond to Bellosguardo where we used to live, and see our old house, and most of the other houses about it which are associated with my old happy life, which all seems very natural and home like. The church [Santa Maria Novella] is a never failing comfort, almost a second home, for I can go and sit there at any time when I am tired or have a wish to

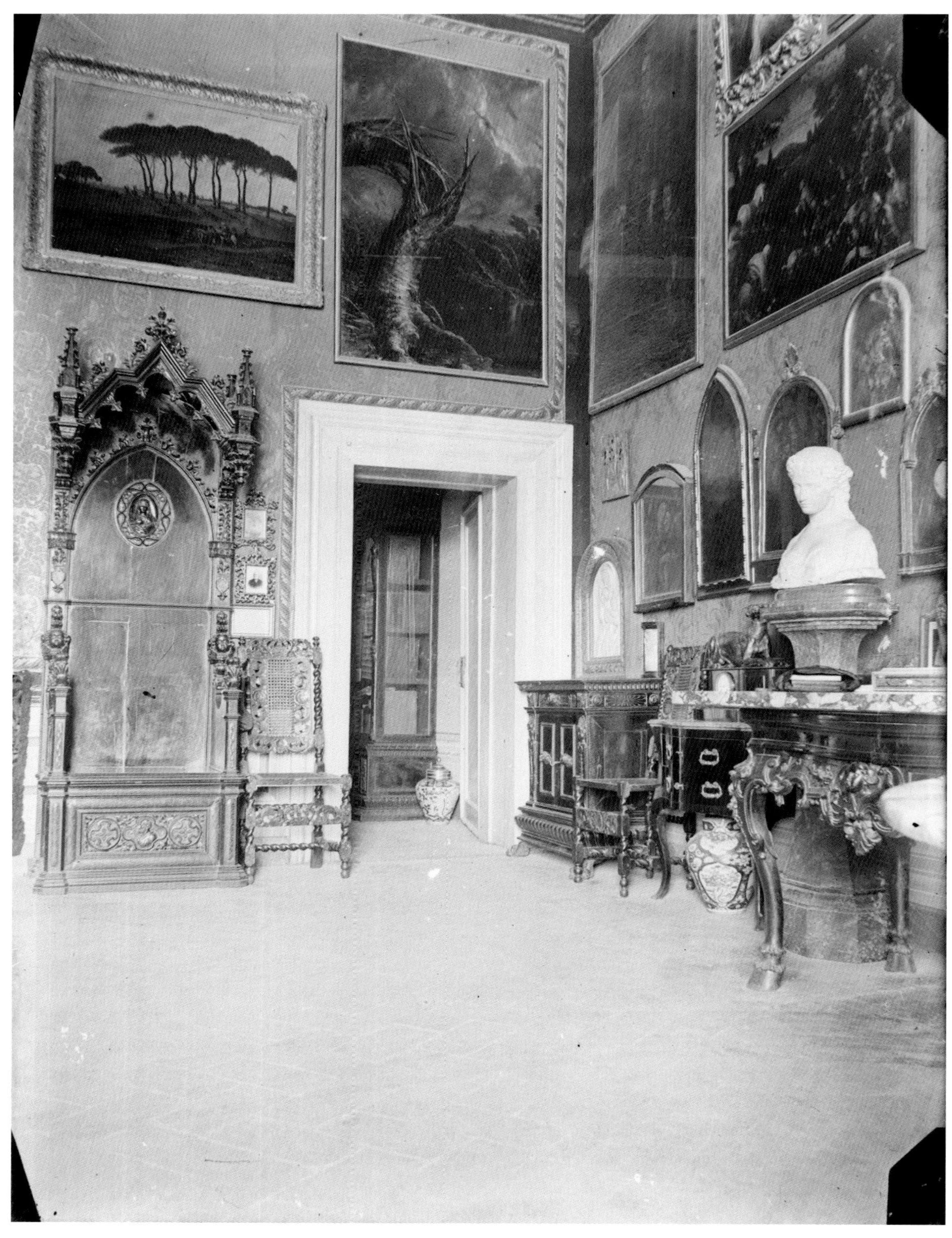

74 Harriet Georgina Ellis Caetani, *The Alexanders' Drawing Room at the Hotel Bonciani, Florence*, between 1869–84, photograph from a glass negative, New York University, Acton Photograph Archive, Villa La Pietra, Florence

be quiet. When I was in America I used to miss these churches always open. Then I have a painting room, where I pass my working hours, and that is a constant place of resort for all my friends, who bring all their friends, and as they entertain each other, and never expect me to make company of them, they do not disturb my work, and the time passes quite gaily.[98]

One of these friends was a young seamstress named Ida. Like many of the Italians Fanny knew, Ida worked hard for minimal wages and needed Fanny's charity. Tragically, Ida fell in love with a philandering soldier who deceived her, and she died in 1872 of a respiratory ailment, seemingly brought on by the many hardships she endured. Her death weighed heavily on Fanny, who continued to take care of Ida's family for many years.[99] In 1875 Fanny composed a manuscript describing her friend's life and death, and their friendship, and made a number of now lost portraits of her, too.[100]

As her relationship with Ida suggests, Fanny recommended her charitable work following her return to Florence, providing whatever she could to those in need. The seemingly miraculous – but really only commonsense – cures she suggested for the sick made the grateful recipients view her as a veritable saint.[101] She funded some of her efforts by gathering small tokens like wood carvings and mosaics and shipping them to her Boston friends, who sent back more money than they were worth, knowing she would use it for charity.[102]

Political events continued to cause turmoil, and the Alexanders again assembled medical supplies for the Italian troops marching on Rome during the climactic battles of 1871. Their donation was timely; only a few days later Fanny wrote,

as I sat at my work in my little painting room, I heard some one calling in the street 'The Italians are in Rome!' and then one after another, the bells of the various churches began to ring and as I went to the

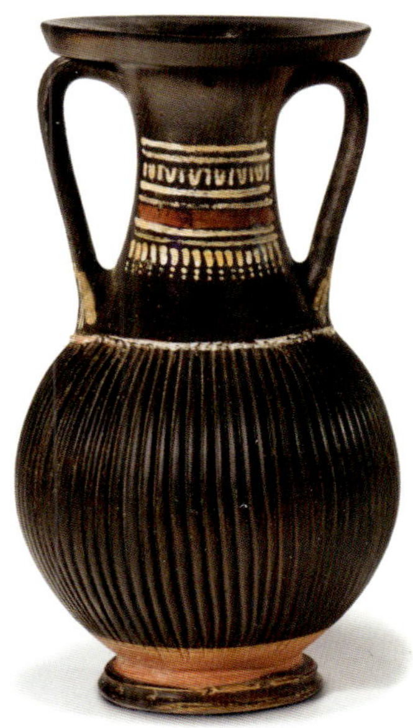

75 Follower of the Louvre Bottle Painter (attrib.), Pelike, late fourth–early third century BCE, terracotta, height 22.2 cm (8¾ in), location unknown

window I saw a number of men and boys, like a swarm of black flies, covering the top of Giotto's campanile, where they were raising the Italian flag. And I knew that Italy was all one at last![103]

Knowing they had played some small part in these events must have been gratifying.

Fanny's art and charity were intertwined in the minds of many. Lydia Maria Child commented on this in a letter to Francis in 1877: 'I have been glad to hear how much comfort you had in your excellent and gifted daughter, and how much comfort she had in the love of her parents, the cultivation of her artistic taste, and her assiduous ministry to the welfare of others.'[104] A few years earlier, James Russell

Lowell, a childhood friend and neighbor of Lucia, visited Florence and witnessed Fanny's efforts, and her singing, first-hand. While there he composed a sonnet praising her character, her art and her care for the needy:

> Unconscious as the sunshine, simply sweet
> And generous as that, thou dost not close
> Thyself in art, as life were but a rose
> To rumple bee-like with luxurious feet;
> Thy higher mind therein finds sure retreat,
> But not from care of common hopes and woes;
> Thee the dark chamber, thee the unfriended, knows,
> Although no gaping crowds thy praise repeat:
> Consummate artist, who life's landscape bleak
> Hast brimmed with sun to many a clouded eye,
> Touched to a brighter hue the beggar's cheek,
> Hung over orphaned lives a gracious sky,
> And traced for eyes, that else would vainly seek,
> Fair pictures of an angel drawing nigh![105]

The subsequent publication of this poem in *The Atlantic Monthly* kept Fanny in the public eye, as did her art. This was a particularly productive period for her. In 1871, she sent a painting called *The Father's Dinner* to Childs and Jenks Gallery in Boston – a gallery that handled several women artists – to sell; the model for this lost painting was a young girl near Abetone, who posed with a basket of food as if waiting for her father to come home from working in the fields.[106] In 1876, the Centennial Exhibition in Philadelphia displayed three of her drawings, owned by the Waleses, Caroline Brewer and Reverend Arthur Lawrence, and one painting, a copy of a Renaissance Madonna in a Gothic frame owned by James Davis.[107]

In 1878, Fanny described working on 'several small pictures'.[108] One, identified with an inscription as a representation of 16-year-old Paolina Pistolesi – the sister of Emilia, the Madonnina – shows the *contadina* in profile against a glowing yellow ground (fig.76). She stands within a narrow arch, like a saint in a side panel of a Renaissance polyptych but with the sickle and sheaves of wheat associated with the Old Testament heroine Ruth. Fanny had earlier experimented with this iconography and was attempting a series of illustrations of the Book of Ruth, too, though she feared that she did not know enough to represent biblical stories.[109] This painting, with the focus on Paolina over her attributes and no attempt at a narrative, may have seemed like an easier option. Given Ruth's reputed charity and her position as a woman in a foreign land, her appeal to Fanny is not surprising.[110] But Ruth was also popular among American male sculptors, who had succumbed to what one reviewer described as 'Ruth fever'; Randolph Rogers, for example, created more than 30 copies of his marble Ruth.[111] Fanny seems to have been responding to this interest.

A second painting from this period represents Paolina sewing, seated in the corner of a room with heavy wooden furniture, a well-stocked bookcase and two paintings on the wall (fig.77). Years earlier, Fanny had drawn Paolina's seamstress mother Carolina in a similar pose, with the familiar Bellosguardo view through the window (fig.78). The painting, however, must have been set in Fanny's sky parlor at the Bonciani, where Paolina would have been one of the many friends who gathered to work on domestic tasks like sewing. Both drawing and painting include the tools necessary for the piecework so many *contadine* took on to earn money. In Paolina's case, the table holds a pin cushion, scissors, thimble and thread, as well as a straw basket containing a lace-edged handkerchief, a length of green ribbon, a photograph and a small bound volume, perhaps one of the sacred texts Lucia gave Fanny years earlier, used here as a prop to affirm Paolina's piety.

Fanny also continued to accumulate the stories and songs of her *contadini* friends, now with the goal of a publication. Niccolò Tommaseo may have encouraged her to do this, as a way to update his own publications and bring them to a broader audience, or she may have been inspired by the bilingual edition of Armenian songs her friend Ghevont Alishan published decades earlier.[112] Fanny learned them from publications by Tommaseo and others, as well as directly from her *contadini* friends and from the broadsides she purchased from booksellers and street vendors.[113] In a letter to her friend Sally Hayward in 1871, Fanny confessed that she was busy 'writing down a curious collection of legends and poetry, which I learnt long ago at Abetone, and which it seems a pity should be forgotten. I think that I shall have it printed some time, but how or where, I have not the least idea.'[114] She confirmed this the following year, in a letter to Lilly Cleveland:

> For about a year I have been engaged, during all my spare time, in writing down and arranging all the curious old legends and poetry which I have collected during many years of familiar intercourse with the mountain people. They seemed too valuable to be lost, and I mean in the course of the present year to have them printed or, at least, to offer them to a printer. Only think of your Fanny coming out literary! But I had a particular reason for wanting to have them published just now: I will tell you all about it when I see you.[115]

Presumably that reason had to do with her charitable efforts; publishing it for sale would generate more funds for her poor. But the project moved slowly. Three years later, Lilly shared a letter Fanny wrote about Abetone's annual outdoor *giostra*, or play, with James Russell Lowell. Lowell was entranced by Fanny's vivid description of the event, a dramatization in verse and music of the French Revolution. The letter described the plot, as well as the local men and boys who acted in it, and the enthusiastic audience who sobbed out loud during the final scene of the king's beheading.[116] Lowell urged Lilly to send the description to *The Nation* for publication: 'Having done this + got [Fanny's] forgiveness (you may make

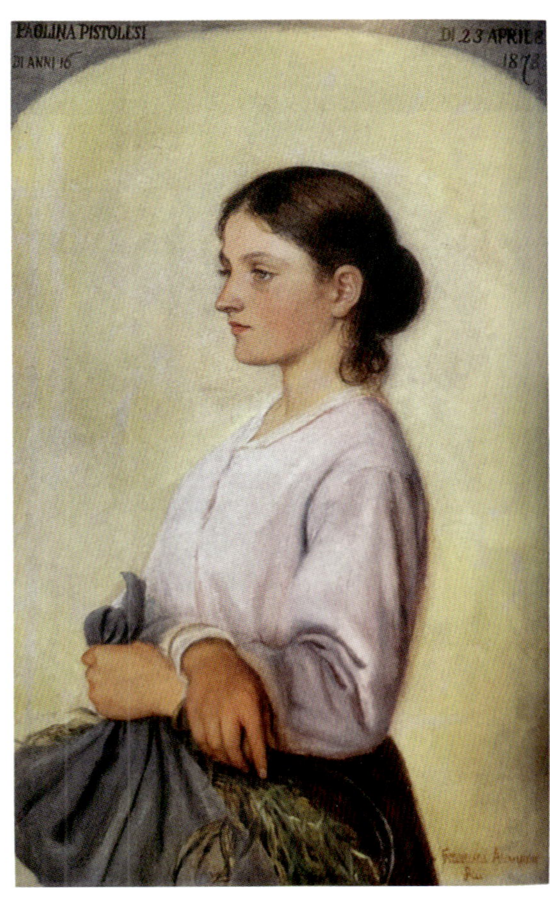

76 Francesca Alexander, *Paolina Pistolesi as Ruth*, 23 April 1878, oil on canvas mounted on masonite, 45.1 × 26.7 cm (17 ¾ × 10 ½ in), location unknown

me the scape goat if you like) ask her for more.'[117] But Lilly knew Fanny better than Lowell did, and she asked for permission first, which both Lucia and Fanny denied. Lucia admitted she was assembling this kind of material herself, because 'Fanny has certainly seen many out of the way things, + people, + places, that should not be forgotten or unrecorded, and I trust they will not remain so much longer'.[118] In fact, from their time on Bellosguardo, the two women had transcribed a wide assortment of anecdotes like

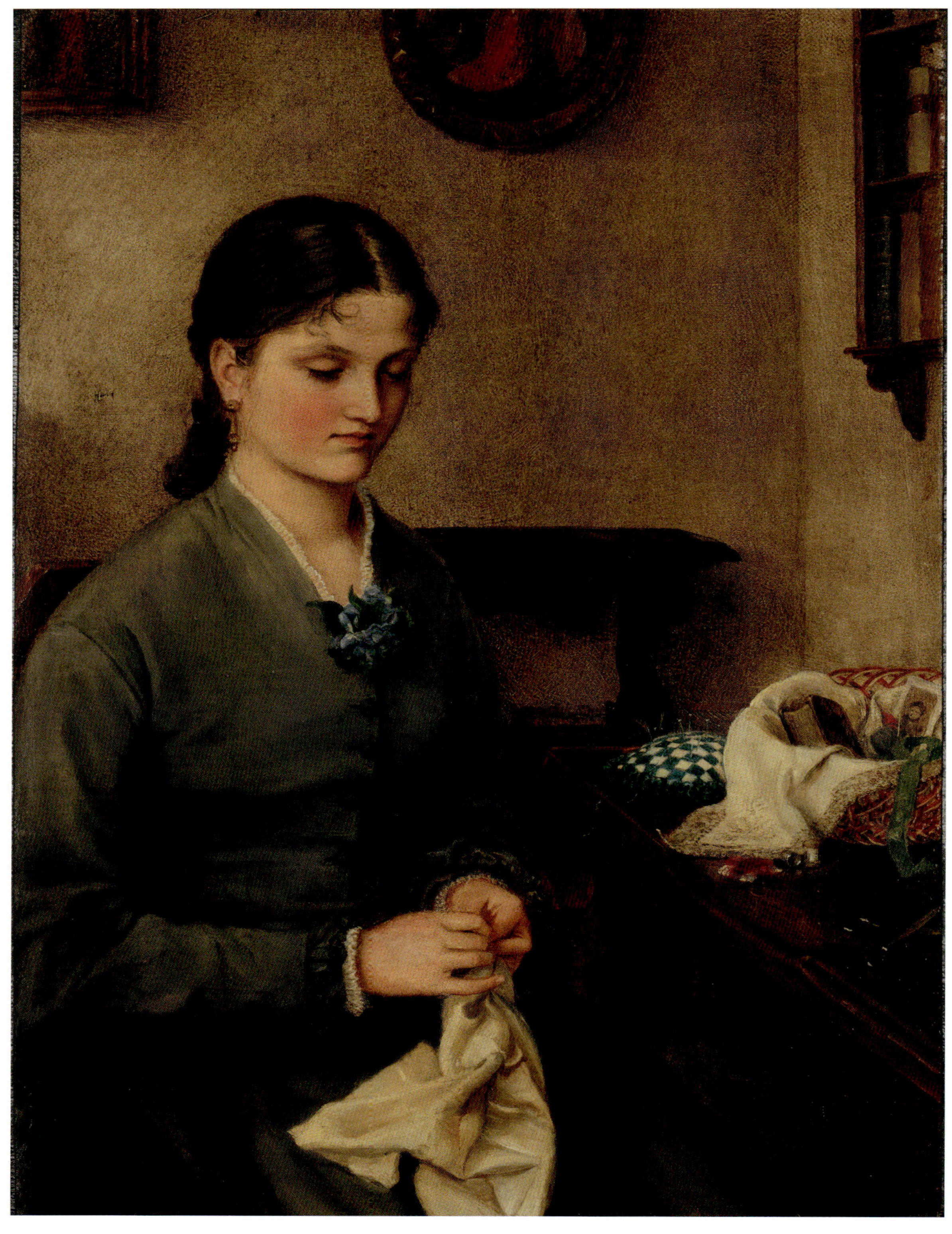

77 Francesca Alexander, *Paolina Pistolesi*, c.1878, oil on canvas, 32 × 23.7 cm (12 ⅝ × 9 ⅜ in), Brooklyn Museum, New York, NY

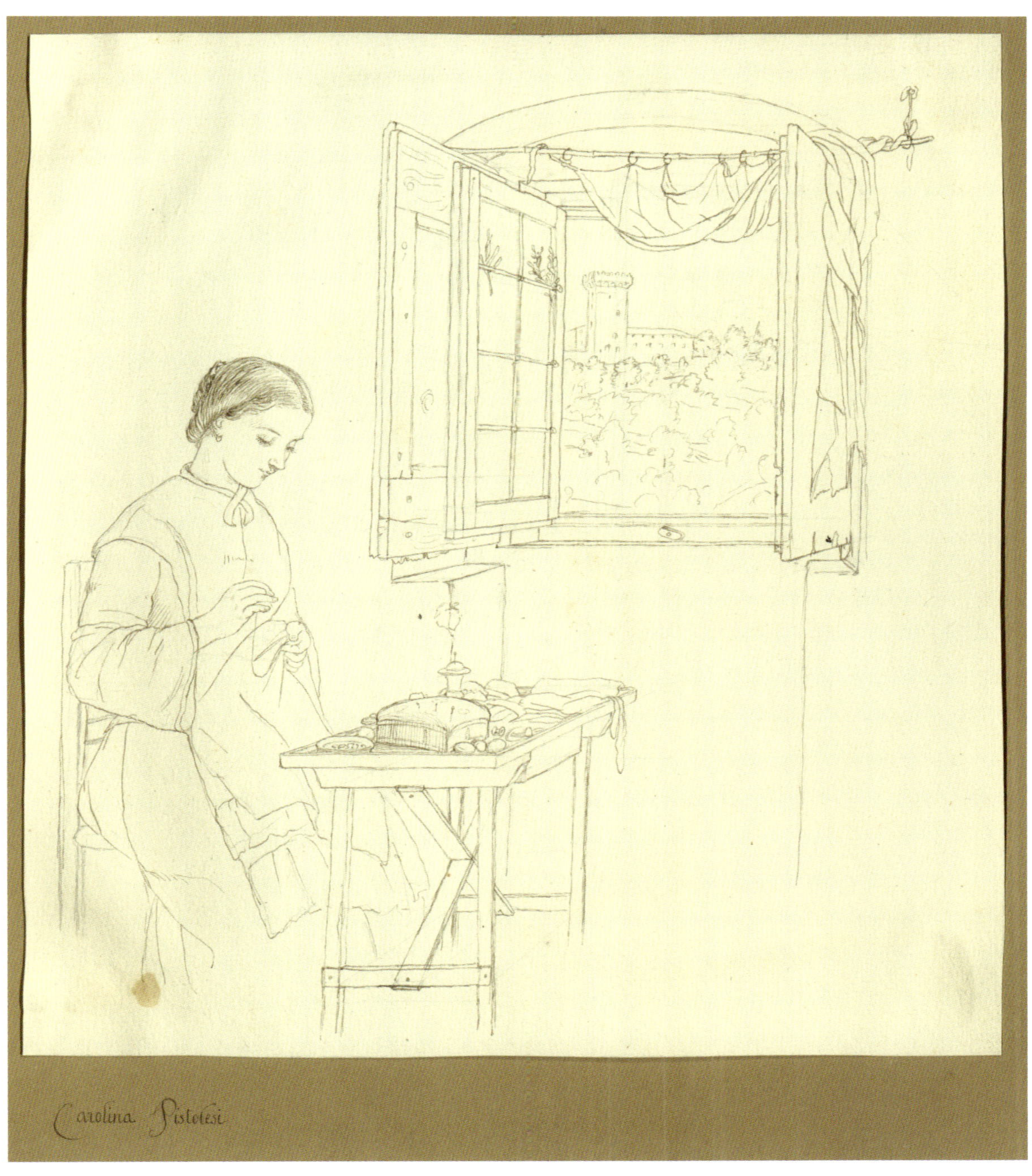

78 Francesca Alexander, *Carolina Pistolesi*, *c.*1860, pen and ink, 19 × 20.5 cm (7 ½ × 8 ⅛ in),
Wellesley College Special Collections, Wellesley, MA

this in a notebook, on topics as diverse as the behavior of Catholic priests, the activities and superstitions of their Italian friends and neighbors, and the cannonballs found on the banks of the Arno river, apparently with the thought of a future publication of stories and songs.[119]

This evolved into two separate manuscripts, one a single story and the other a collection of songs, both with a combination of bilingual text and illustrations and both larger and more complex than the earlier volume for Sarah Shaw Russell. The first to be completed, entitled 'La Sorellaccia', is a moralizing tale like the earlier story of Hannah Blackstone but now set in Italy; Fanny learned it from *contadini* in the village of Boscolungo, near Abetone. The story was apparently well known in certain circles; the English author and Florence resident Lucy Barnes Baxter, who published under the name Leader Scott, included an abridged version in her book *A Nook in the Apennines* (1879).[120] Fanny's 63-folio manuscript includes a frontispiece with a view of the mountains blocked by a lace-edged cloth displaying the title, suspended between two rough wooden poles wound with flowers and vines (fig.79). The base of one pole is surrounded by sacred items, including books, a rosary and a crucifix, while the other has household implements, among them a distaff, knitting supplies and kindling, hinting at the central conflict of the story. It described the life of a widowed mother of ten young children, worn down by her many domestic obligations, whose friar brother reprimanded her as a *sorellaccia*, or bad sister, for neglecting her religious duties in comparison to their nun sister, who devoted herself entirely to God. The brother offered to watch the children so the *sorellaccia* could attend church, but in her absence he was quickly overwhelmed by the many tasks she bore without complaint. When she returned to relieve him, he announced that she was more virtuous than either he or their sister: 'You need not go to church any more! If you can keep your patience with these children, you will go to heaven before I shall!' But he was

nevertheless astonished when Saint Peter welcomed the *sorellaccia* to heaven even more enthusiastically than he welcomed her nun sister, and Peter had to remind him of the many hardships she endured.[121]

This was a challenging project. In a letter to Caterina Tommaseo in September 1875, when the Alexanders were in the Apennines, Fanny wrote,

> I'm working so hard, making drawings for a book, and these drawings must be finished before leaving, and time is very limited. I will then be so pleased to show you my drawings, when I see you in Florence, which I think you will like, which are based on a legend that I wanted to learn from a girl in the village here … Among other things, I had to draw many of these very delicate flowers of the town, to make the border on the pages.[122]

The borders are a much more elaborate version of those her father included on some of the folios of the Blackstone manuscript. On one, delicate stalks of lily of the valley grow between the bilingual text blocks (fig.80).[123] Some folios begin with large letters looming somewhat incongruously in tiny, framed landscapes, while others integrate the letters into floral arrangements or vignettes, like the letter A placed near a bird's nest tucked under rafters, with five chicks clamoring for food like the *sorellaccia*'s children (fig.81). Many folios have figural scenes, and 12 of these are full-page illustrations; in one the friar, unable to control his nieces and nephews, sits helplessly as his sister returns to release him from household duties after her day at church (fig.82).

Fanny wrote to Caterina again in October, explaining that she was still 'very busy making the drawings for that book which, it seems to me, you have seen begun, and which is still missing a last bit, although it has been sold for more than six months'.[124] The buyer was Pauline Agassiz Shaw, and her early purchase apparently enabled Fanny to use at least some of the five Shaw children as models for the *sorellaccia*'s children.[125] Fanny claimed this 'very happy occupation'

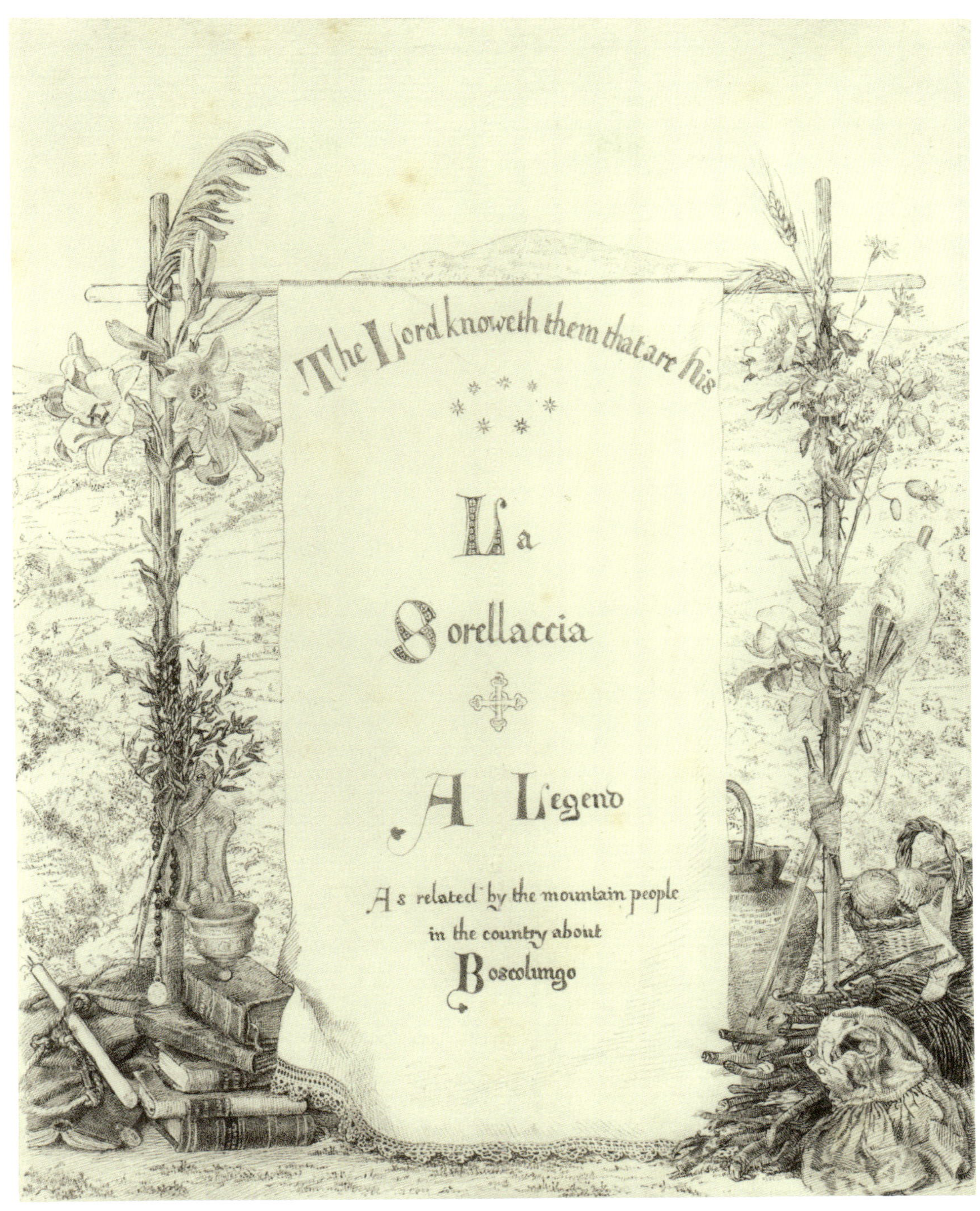

79　Francesca Alexander, title folio from 'La Sorellaccia', 1877, photogravure, 40 × 46 cm (15 ¾ × 18 ⅛ in), Wellesley College Special Collections, Wellesley, MA

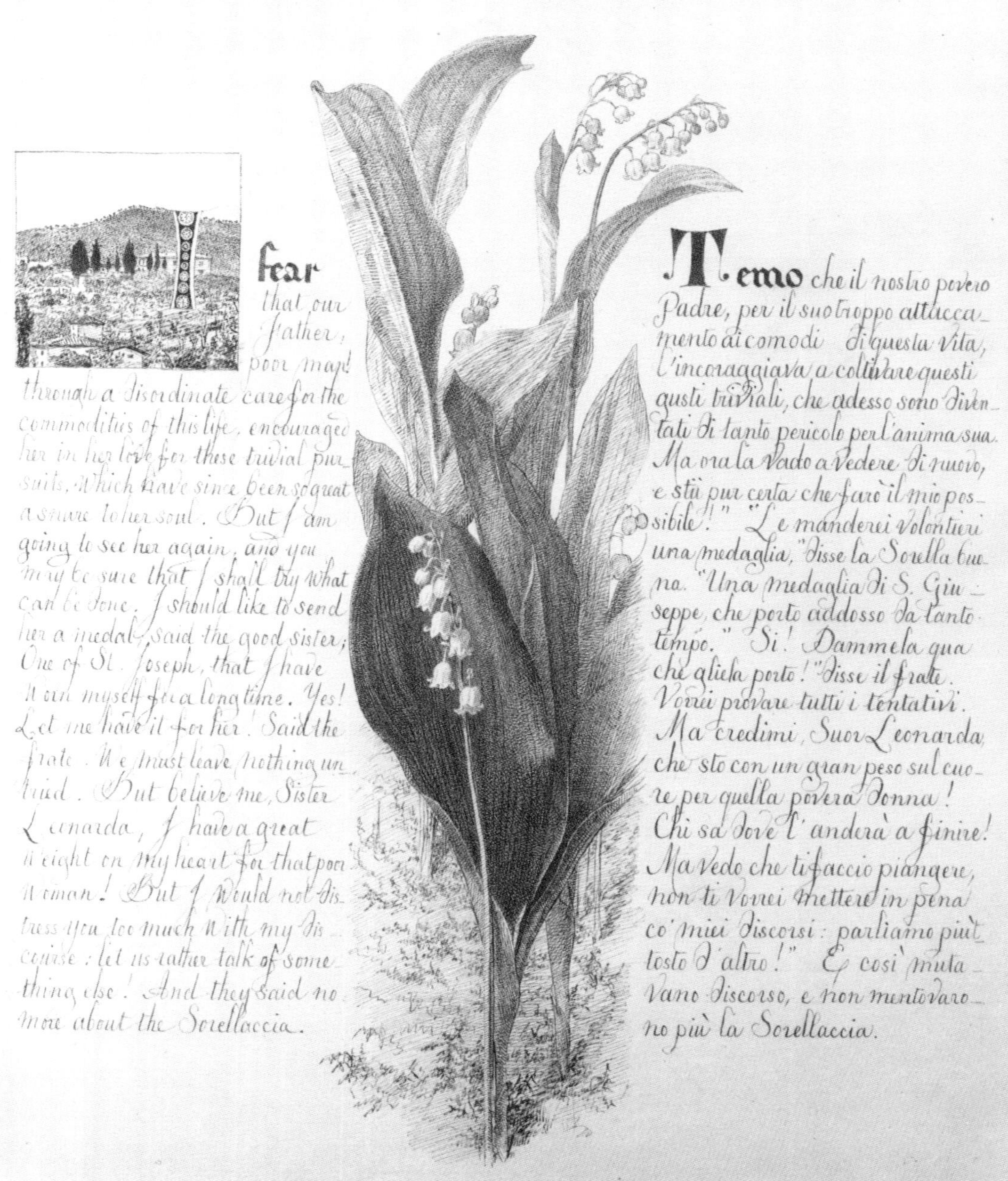

80 Francesca Alexander, folio 33 from 'La Sorellaccia', 1877, photogravure, 40 × 46 cm (15 ¾ × 18 ⅛ in), Wellesley College Special Collections, Wellesley, MA

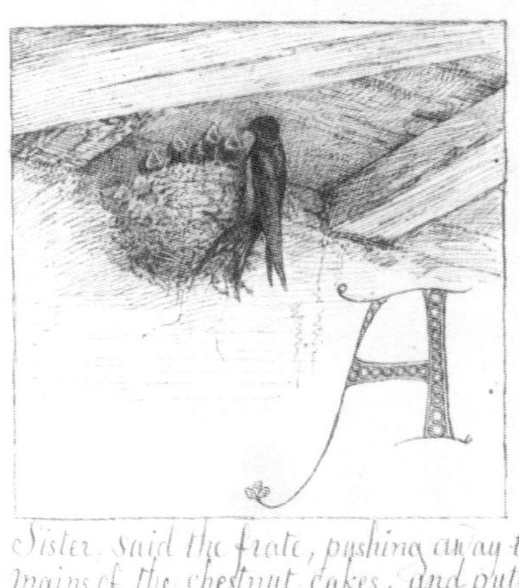

81 Francesca Alexander, folio 21 from 'La Sorellaccia', 1877, photogravure, 40 × 46 cm (15 ¾ × 18 ⅛ in),
Wellesley College Special Collections, Wellesley, MA

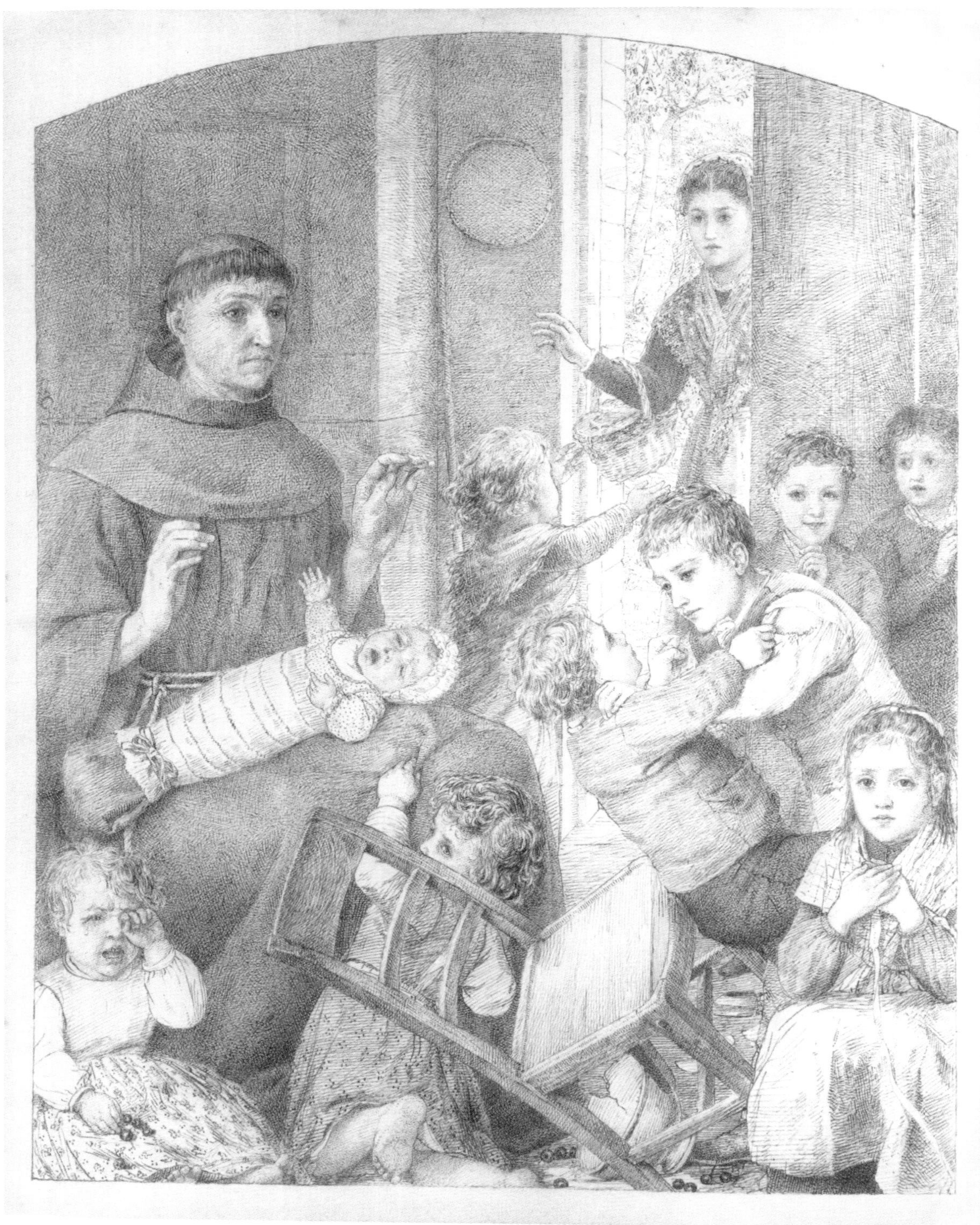

82 Francesca Alexander, unpaginated folio from 'La Sorellaccia', 1877, photogravure, 40 × 46 cm (15 ¾ × 18 ⅛ in), Wellesley College Special Collections, Wellesley, MA

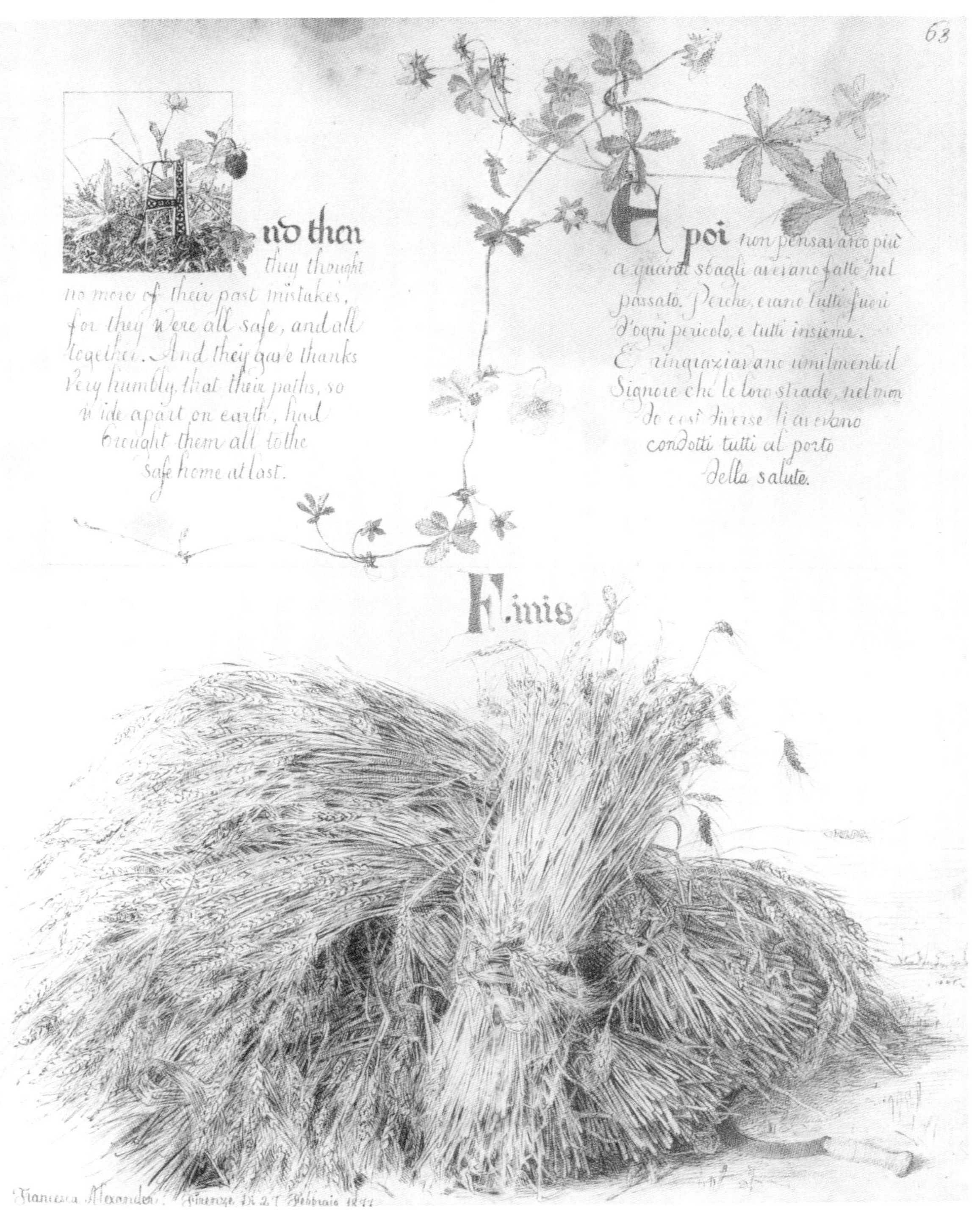

83 Francesca Alexander, folio 63 from 'La Sorellaccia', 1877, photogravure, 40 × 46 cm (15 ¾ × 18 ⅛ in),
Wellesley College Special Collections, Wellesley, MA

took a year and a half to complete.[126] She signed with her Italianized name Francesca and the date 27 February 1877 on the last folio, below sheaves of wheat, the sickle used for harvesting half in shadow (fig.83).

Pauline, the daughter of Harvard scientist Louis Agassiz and his first wife Cecile Braun, was the wife of copper-mining investor Quincy Adams Shaw Sr. She surely knew the manuscript Fanny made years earlier for her sister-in-law, Sarah Shaw Russell. Like Fanny, Pauline was deeply engaged in charitable work, in her case focused on immigrants and education in Boston. The women met in Florence by January 1866, when Fanny wrote to Lilly, 'I have seen Mrs. Shaw, who brought me fifty francs from you. She and her daughter gave me 200 francs for the poor, which I imagine I owe to you also who have no doubt spoken a kind word for me. We have made great friends and talk about you all the time.'[127]

'La Sorellaccia' arrived in the United States by June 1877, and Pauline wrote an enthusiastic note of thanks to Fanny, apologizing that it took her five days to do so but she had 'been so busy looking at it + reading it + showing it to other people . . . It is so beautiful and grows more so each time I look at it.'[128] The manuscript created much excitement in Boston, and Lucia's scrapbooks include letters from friends praising it, further evidence of the close connections the Alexanders maintained in the United States and of course the great appeal of Fanny's art. Some, like the Clevelands and Margaret Grant Chadwick Tucker, already owned work by Fanny, but others wrote too, including author Thomas Gold Appleton (Henry Wadsworth Longfellow's brother-in-law), Katherine Sergeant Cram (wife of lawyer Henry Augustus Cram), and Marianne Wells Healey (sister of reformer Caroline Healey Dall).[129] When the scientist and later politician Theodore Lyman, husband of Sarah Shaw Russell's daughter Elizabeth, wrote to thank Fanny for sending him a box of medicinal extracts in 1878 – most likely from the Santa Maria Novella pharmacy, around the corner from the Hotel Bonciani – he added, 'I have enjoyed examining your wonderful book of the story of the two sisters – it is quite your masterpiece – though to me your portrait of Cora is much more valuable.'[130] Lyman's daughter Cora was born in Florence in 1862, but she died in Boston in 1869, so this lost portrait must have been made either in Florence or during the Alexanders' Boston visit.

In 1895 Pauline was in Florence with her stepmother Elizabeth Cary Agassiz, the cousin of the Alexanders' old friend Charles Callahan Perkins. Elizabeth, who had been one of the founders and the first president of Harvard Annex – which became Radcliffe College – enjoyed spending time with Lucia, whom she described as 'a bright old lady'.[131] The Boston visitors joined in the Alexanders' charitable work and together they arranged an Easter dinner for 70 needy children. Elizabeth described the dinner:

> Each [child] had three presents apiece and an orange – and then there was a surprise which Pauline had prepared, a plant in flower for each child. That carried the day – nothing they had received seemed to give them the pleasure that these growing plants did – so they went off, a floral procession, each child bearing his or her pot all in bloom. Indeed I hardly know how they managed to bear away their treasures. They had full hands + full hearts, I think. The rounds of applause were loud and long.[132]

Even if the flowering plants were Pauline's idea, this was a feature in which Fanny would have delighted, and indeed some of those plants must have come from her rooftop garden.

The 'Sorellaccia' manuscript solidified this bond between the families, and it achieved lasting fame. Pauline loaned it for an exhibition at Boston's Museum of Fine Arts in 1883 and donated a photogravure copy to the Boston Public Library in 1902.[133] According to Lucia, who hoped it would one day be published, the Shaws had 13 photogravure copies made by 1899; in addition to the copy given to the library, one went to each Shaw child and others to the Alexanders and the city of Florence.[134] The Shaw children made a bequest to Boston's Museum of Fine Arts in 1917 that included a group of Jean François Millet paintings and Donatello's marble *Madonna of the Clouds*. However, while the Shaw collection is usually associated with Quincy Adams Shaw Sr, Pauline was the buyer of Fanny's manuscript; it did not form part of that bequest and it cannot be traced.

'La Sorellaccia' was Fanny's first concerted effort to capture one of the stories circulating among Italy's *contadini*. But, as she told Sally Hayward and Lilly Cleveland, she initially planned to assemble a combination of stories and songs. Perhaps she changed her plan to focus solely on this story at Pauline Agassiz Shaw's request. Whatever the reason, it did not deter her from returning to songs for her next project. Her persistence is really no surprise. She had always enjoyed singing, and she was drawn to Italian songs about love, loss and patriotism from her earliest years abroad.[135] When Louise Winsor Brooks was in Florence in 1854 – soon after the Alexanders arrived in the city – she described several visits with the family, including an evening when Fanny sang: 'Her voice is very powerful + with cultivation + modulation will prove something extraordinary. She is a very singular girl, quite simple and childlike.'[136] This was, presumably, an Italian song; John Lothrop Motley reported that she was already translating both *rispetti* (songs in eight iambic lines) and *stornelli* (songs in three verses) in 1855.[137] One of her early Florentine drawings, of a young woman on her deathbed, clutching a cross and surrounded by loved ones, is pasted into a scrapbook above two songs of longing and regret, with a translation on the facing folio (fig.84). Those songs appeared, with variations, in Giuseppe Tigri's *Canti popolari toscani* (1856), a rich source for the songs sung by Italy's *contadini* as they went about their work and play, and one was included in Isa Blagden's novel *The Cost of a Secret* (1863),

indicating that they were known in both Italian and Anglo-American circles.[138]

Other women in the Anglo-American community were interested in songs, too. Elizabeth Barrett Browning referenced the patriotic 'O bella libertà' in her poem *Casa Guidi Windows* (1851), while Elizabeth Kinney incorporated lines from other songs in her poems 'To the Boy Who Goes Daily by My Windows Singing' and 'To an Italian Beggar Boy' (1854), and Theodosia Garrow Trollope planned but never published an illustrated translation of several songs under the title *Canzoni popolari toscani*.[139] Janet Ross, who oversaw a working farm during her years in Florence and listened as her employees sang, published some of these songs and performed them for guests at her receptions.[140]

In fact, many Anglo-Americans enjoyed performances by Italians, especially by the women who composed and sang extemporaneous songs of their own devising, who were known as *improvisatrici*.[141] The eponymous *improvisatrici* heroines in Germaine de Staël's novel *Corinne, ou l'Italia* (1807) and Elizabeth Barrett Browning's *Aurora Leigh* (1856), and the songs and singers in *A Village Commune* (1881), a popular novel by English author and Florence resident Maria Louise Ramé, who wrote under the pen name Ouida, stimulated additional interest. Although Fanny would have read at least some of these texts, she would have been less interested in fictive heroines and more interested in actual singers, like Maria Beatrice Bugelli Bernardi, better known as Beatrice di Pian degli Ontani, and Giannina Milli.[142] Both of these celebrated *improvisatrici* became her friends, and she learned many songs from them directly.

The Alexanders met Beatrice in 1862, during their first summer in Abetone. She was a *contadina* who spent her life working in the fields and taking care of her eight children; Beatrice only discovered her gift for improvisation as an adult and though it brought her fame she earned little money for her efforts.

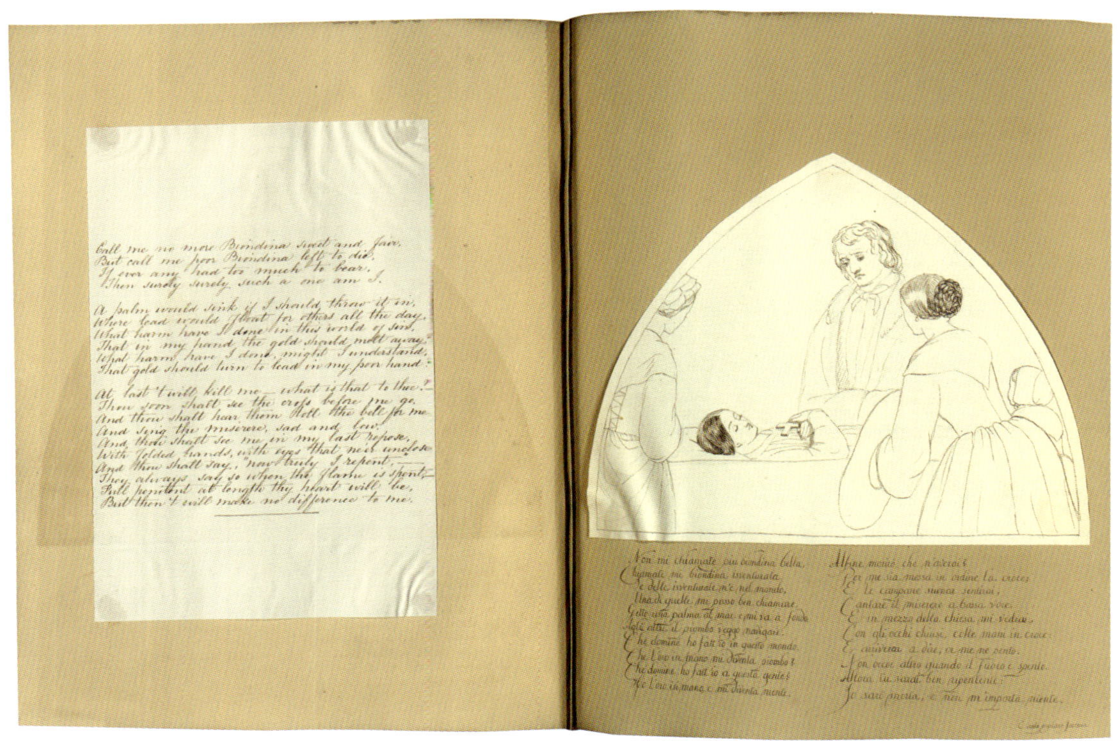

84 Francesca Alexander, transcription and translation of songs with a deathbed scene, *c.*1860, pen and ink, 24 × 30 cm (9 ½ × 11 ¾ in), Wellesley College Special Collections, Wellesley, MA

Fanny described her excitement about this encounter in letters to Lilly Cleveland – how the Alexanders walked miles over mountainous terrain to reach Beatrice's farmhouse and found her raking a hay field – and how she sang a plaintive farewell to them when they returned to Florence at the end of the summer:

> we walked part way home with her and took leave of her at last in a wild pasture on the side of a mountain. Papa said, 'Beatrice, you must sing us one ottava to take leave of us'. It seemed to me quite solemn: the solitary place, the grand mountain ridges about us, the clear evening sky, all in a glow overhead, and the perfect stillness all around; as Beatrice, after bidding us stand so that she could see us all at once (she was a little notional about the positions of her auditors) stood quite still with her eyes on the ground for a moment, and then, with that peculiar lighting up of the face which always came with her ottave, sang such a beautiful addio! She made it up as she went along, of course, but it was so full of feeling, and so simply and naturally expressed, that I cannot tell you the effect it had on all of us. Then, after many tears and good wishes, she left us, wiping her eyes as she walked quickly up the steep narrow path, and in a few minutes was out of sight.[143]

The women grew close, and each summer Beatrice posed for Fanny and taught her new songs. Then, in 1864, Fanny met Giannina Milli through their mutual friend Marina Sprea Baroni Semitecolo.[144] Giannina's life was very different from Beatrice's; she was from the city of Teramo and had a musical education. Her intellect and talent put her in contact with prominent Risorgimento patriots and intellectuals, and she later held positions in Italy's educational system. But Fanny described Giannina's life as exhausting:

> She travels from city to city, giving what she calls her 'academie'. She can only improvise by throwing herself into what she calls a 'deliro', in which she becomes unconscious of everything about her, and she described

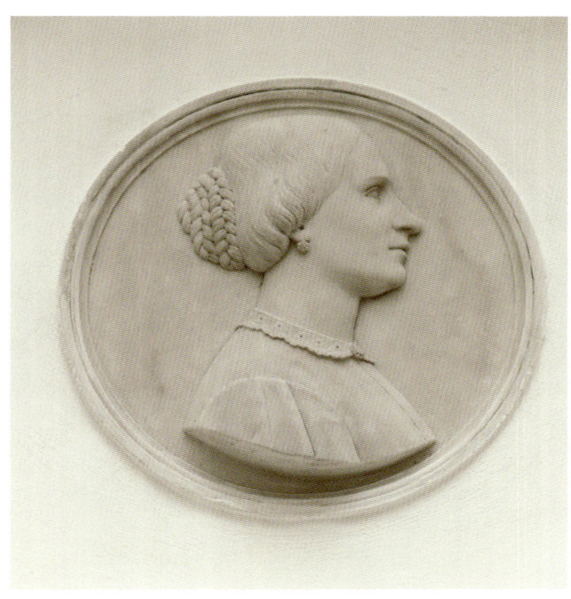

85 Severino Castorani, *Giannina Milli*, c.1863, marble, dimensions unknown, Biblioteca Delfico, Teramo

> the effort as painful in the extreme. I thought it seemed a comfort to her to talk over her troubles and to find people who would sympathise with her. One trouble she did not think to tell us, but [Marina] did. Her eight brothers and sisters all think they have a right to live on Giannina's talent, and she also supports her old parents: ten people to be provided for by one unlucky girl![145]

Giannina lived for some time in Florence, as did her younger sister Luigina, known as Gigina. It was Giannina who found the Alexanders their apartment at the Hotel Bonciani when they returned from the United States. At some point Gigina's husband, the sculptor Severino Castorani, gave Fanny one of the two marble portraits he carved of Giannina (fig.85).

It must have been with much excitement that Fanny orchestrated a meeting between Giannina and Beatrice in Abetone on 9 August 1867. She later described how the two women embraced and sang songs to each other with great emotion.[146] The Alexanders commemorated the event in a document, headed (in Italian) 'In memory of this delicious day' and signed by all present – the Alexanders, the two women and several Italian friends – though Beatrice did so only with a cross because she was illiterate.[147]

It is therefore no surprise that Fanny created a song manuscript. In its original 122 folios, this manuscript, which Fanny titled 'Tuscan Songs', was much grander in scope than 'La Sorellaccia', but she composed it with some of the same features. Figure and landscape scenes, and musical notation arranged by Fanny's friend Sestilia Poggiali, take up all or part of the folios. Bilingual text blocks are set as if on placards hovering in space, with flowers, vines and grasses growing around, behind or in front of them. The order of the flowers was carefully planned; Fanny used knowledge gained from years of gardening to draw native Tuscan plants on each folio in order of their bloom, from winter-blooming snowdrops in the first folios to fringed gentians in the last.[148]

Each folio is unique. For example, on the folio with the song 'Per la Natività di Nostro Signore' ('For the Birth of Our Lord') – first published, as a note at the foot explains, in a volume of sacred music by Matteo Coferati in 1675 – Fanny drew four crocuses growing through dense vegetation, one leaning over to obscure the edge of a placard, below the music and between the text (fig.86). As always, Fanny's Italian friends served as models; she referred to them as the 'originals' of the saints and commoners they represented.[149] Paolina Pistolesi modeled for several folios, including one where she stands at a window, gazing at a tall blooming lily – a more extravagant bloom than in Fanny's earlier drawing (fig.2) – illustrating one of the two songs included on placards below, with three sprigs of wild pinks between them (fig.87).[150] The setting seems to be the room represented in the painting of Paolina sewing (fig.77),

with the same straw basket set on the same table with curved legs. While some of these figural folios have landscape backgrounds, others focus on landscape for its own sake, with no connection to the song, as in the folio with a fragment of a patriotic tune about replacing the Austrian flag with that of Italy, a version of which Fanny heard *contadini* singing in the fields in 1859 and shared with Lilly Cleveland (fig.88).[151] This minutely rendered view of rolling hills, with a few farm buildings and plowed furrows, includes a woman carrying a large sheaf of wheat on her head as she walks down a tree-lined path, presumably singing the song.

According to Lucia, Fanny spent 20 years collecting these songs (although, if Motley was correct, she spent even longer), and another four creating the manuscript, at the cost of about $500 annually for supplies and models.[152] Always the proud mother, Lucia claimed that the academic painter Nicolò Barabino, who designed the mosaics over the three portals of Florence cathedral, believed this manuscript was better than anything he had ever made.[153] Barabino's knowledge of the manuscript and his relationship with the Alexanders further indicates the family's connections to the Italian community in the city and the recognition of Fanny's talent.[154]

The great reception 'La Sorellaccia' received must have prompted the Alexanders to consider publishing this manuscript to reach a wider audience. They discussed the possibilities with the English painter Frederic Leighton, perhaps when they were all in Abetone in 1879.[155] On his return to England, Leighton brought one of Fanny's drawings to Thomas Way, a London lithographer who later worked with James Abbott McNeill Whistler, to attempt a reproduction. But the ink she used, and probably her very fine lines, apparently resulted in a poor print.[156] Lilly Cleveland also tried to assist; her mother Sarah wrote to a friend:

if only Fanny was not the most impractical of humans something could be done to bring them out a treasure

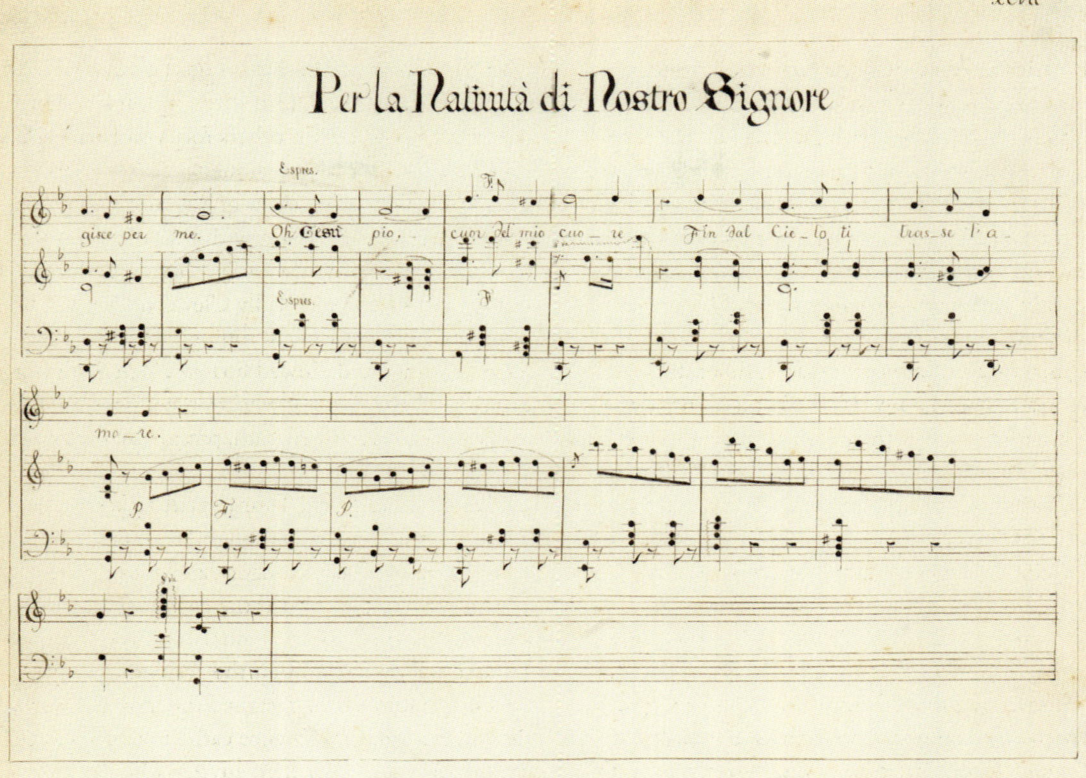

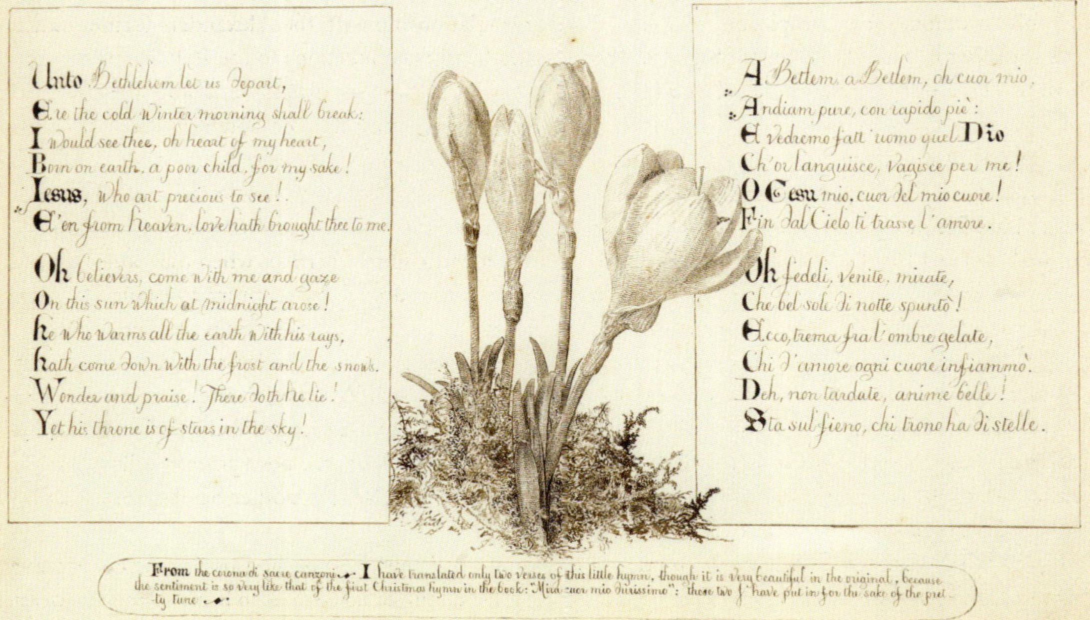

86 Francesca Alexander, 'Per la Natività di Nostro Signore', folio from 'Tuscan Songs', before 1883, pen and ink,
38.4 × 27.8 cm (15⅛ × 11 in), Brooklyn Museum, New York, NY

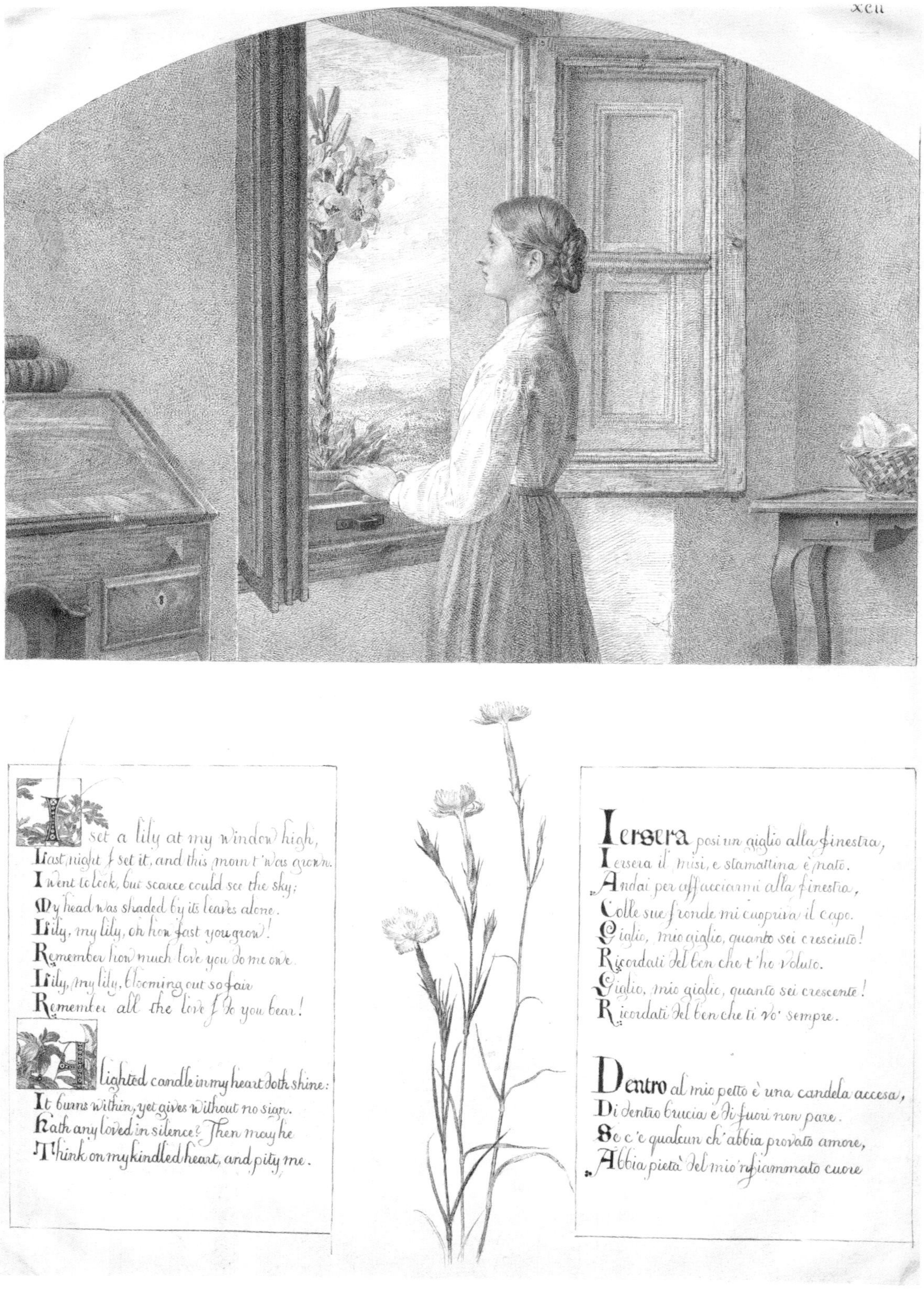

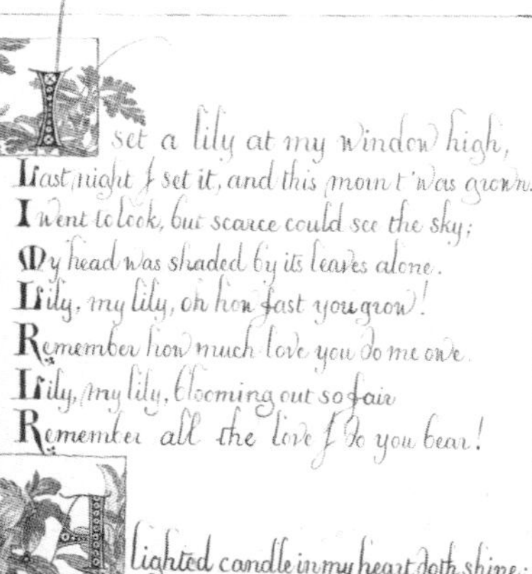
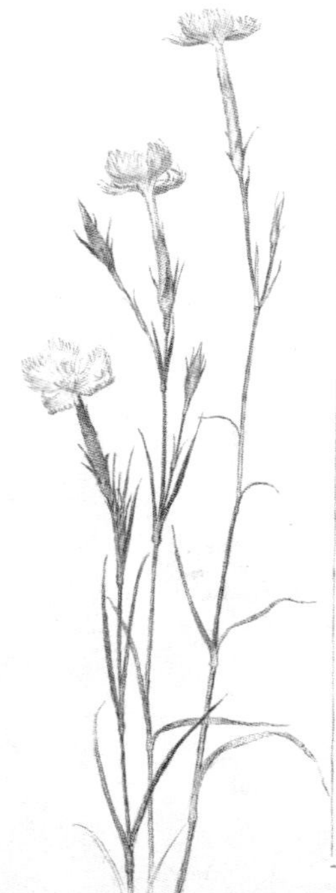

87 Francesca Alexander, 'Iersera posi un giglio alla finestra', folio from 'Tuscan Songs', before 1883, pen and ink, 38 × 27.5 cm (15 × 10 ⅞ in), Wellesley College Special Collections, Wellesley, MA

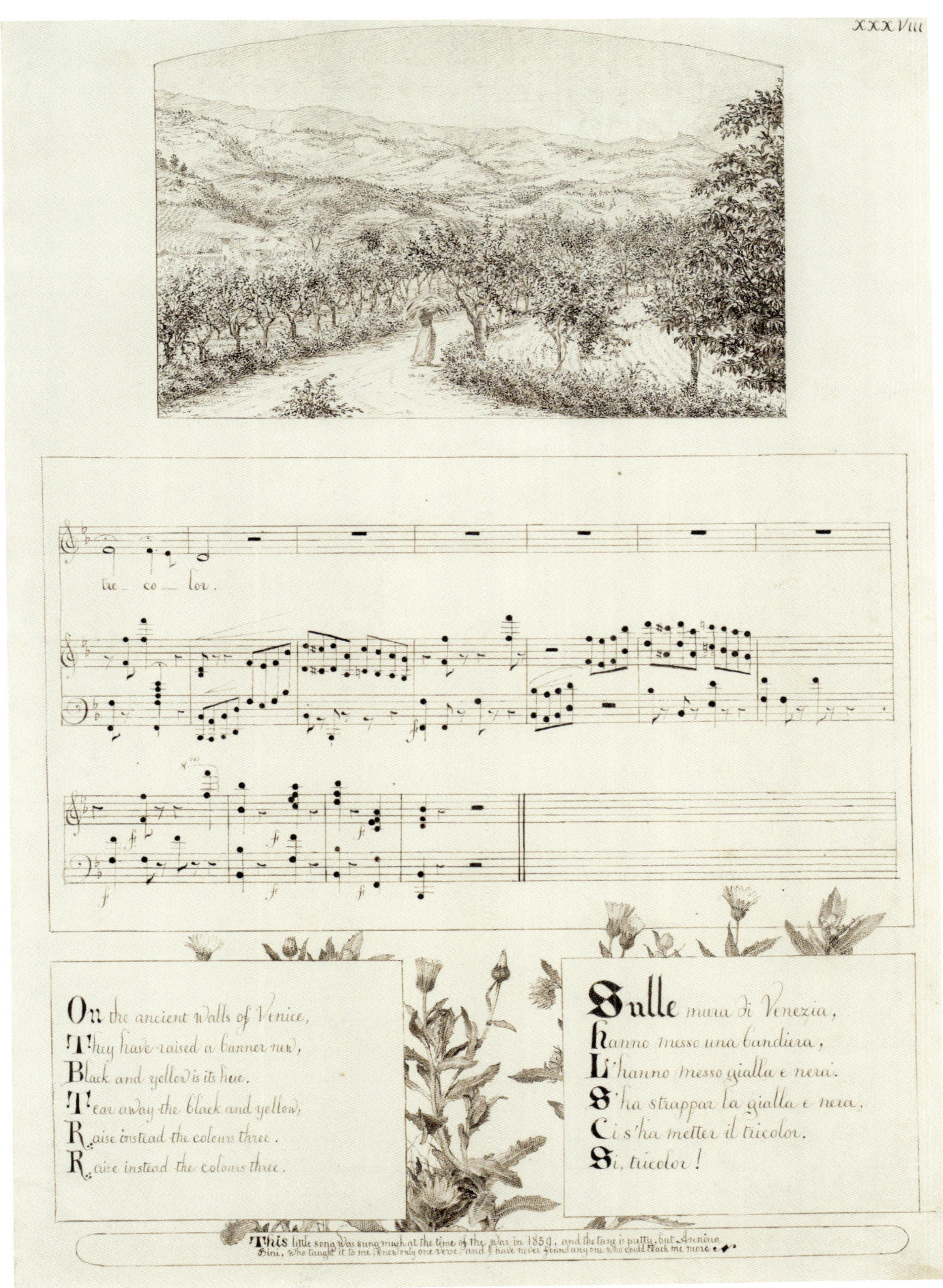

88 Francesca Alexander, 'Sulle mura di Venezia', folio from 'Tuscan Songs', before 1883, pen and ink, 38.6 × 27.3 cm (15 ¼ × 10 ¾ in), Harvard Art Museums/Fogg Art Museum, Cambridge, MA

for all time + all the world. She will sell them for publication for a sum + Lilly is going to try + see what can be done – Lilly has thoughts of heliotyping the drawings + that could be done by [Boston publisher James R.] Osgood – Any how what can be done must. The illustrations are fully equal to the Sorellaccia + so various + fascinating that each seems more perfect and beautiful than the last.[157]

In light of the great effort Fanny put into the manuscript, Francis set the price at £600 before she even finished it.[158] But then tragedy struck. Francis had long suffered from various ailments, but his health declined significantly in 1879 and he died on 27 March 1880. A few months later Fanny wrote to Lilly, using black-bordered mourning stationery, and described his illness, death and burial, emphasizing the solace of their religion and the assistance they received from friends. The English Cemetery where Lilly's grandmother was buried (as well as Fanny's cousin Walter Eldredge Alexander) stopped receiving burials in 1877, so Francis was interred at the Cimitero Evangelico agli Allori, a mile outside Florence's Porta Romana. Fanny wrote,

> There we went and there he was laid by the side of his old friend and minister Mr. [Cesare] Magrini, who died a few weeks before him. Mr. Rossetti, who is our minister at present, prayed, and made a short discourse on the words 'Whether living or dying, we are the Lords'. Another brother of the church prayed also, a few passages of the bible were read, and then we all sang a hymn. It was one of the loveliest spring days that ever I felt, with a clear soft sky, and the fruit trees all in blossom on the hills around us: and through all the praying and the singing we heard the sound of the Easter bells in Florence, recalling to us our Lord's victory over the grave. We all remained there while the grave was filled up, and the earth piled in a mound above it, and then Angelina Puccio and I arranged the flowers on and about it, and we all came away. I think

that no one who was present at that funeral service will ever forget it.[159]

Francis's grave was marked by a marble cross with trilobed terminals, the Christian symbols alpha, omega and Chi Rho, and an inscription in recessed lead:

> In
> memory of
> Francis Alexander
> of Killingly Connecticut USA
> died March 27th a.d. 1880
> aged 80 years
> his dying words were
> I put all my trust in the Lord

The loss of husband and father – so soon after Magrini's death, the leader of Florence's Evangelical community – was devastating to the Alexander women. But they found solace in their religion and in Fanny's song manuscript. Writing to Sarah Cleveland a few months later, Lucia called it 'the principal interest that remains to us, when that is finished I hope we shall be able to decide something for the future'.[160] Lucia, at least, seemed to be contemplating moving back to Boston, and a reunion with family and friends, as a way to manage their grief.

4

Francesca

'Tuscan Songs' continued to occupy Fanny in the immediate years after Francis's death. Then, in October 1882, the Alexander women had a pivotal meeting with the English aesthete John Ruskin on what became his final visit to Florence. After Ruskin departed, he and the Alexanders maintained a regular correspondence encompassing advice on Fanny's art and eventually her books, as well as news about family and friends, gardening, health and other matters. This continued until 1889, when illness made it impossible for him to write, though the Alexanders continued writing to him and exchanging letters with his family and friends.

At the time of this first meeting, Ruskin was 63 years old and suffering from intermittent bouts of mental illness. He had already authored several influential studies of Italy and Italian art that were read on both sides of the Atlantic – including an eager circle of admirers in the Alexanders' native Boston – and many artists followed his precepts regarding truth to nature. There is no indication that Fanny read Ruskin's books prior to their meeting, and she never engaged with the theoretical underpinnings of contemporary art movements. But perhaps this lack of awareness was one of the things that attracted Ruskin, since her art effortlessly reflected many of his ideals.

When Ruskin arrived in Florence with his friend and future biographer, the painter William G. Collingwood, they were welcomed by Henry Roderick Newman, who had long been inclined to Ruskinian thought. Newman must have met the Alexanders when he moved to Florence in 1870 and moved into the Hotel Bonciani.[1] He also knew Fanny's song manuscript; according to Fanny, he 'had been in love with my book for a good while'.[2] Thinking both would interest Ruskin, he arranged a meeting on 8 October, which Collingwood later described as 'the great event' of Ruskin's journey.[3] Certainly Lucia, in her role of proud mother, would have shown Ruskin as much of Fanny's work as possible; she even shared James Russell Lowell's sonnet with him.[4] The next day, Ruskin wrote to Lucia to confess his delight in Fanny's work:

> I've taken a new pen – it is all I can! – I wish I could learn an entirely new writing from some pretty hem of an angel's robe – to tell you with what happy and reverent admiration I saw your daughter's drawings yesterday; reverent not only of a quite heavenly gift of genius in a kind I had never before seen, but also of the entirely sweet and loving spirit which animated and sanctified the work, and the serenity which it expressed in the purest faiths and best purposes of life (fig.89).[5]

was, Ruskin was particularly appreciative of Fanny's use of her *contadini* friends as models to express these ideas. He believed this set her work apart:

> Miss Alexander represents everything as it would have happened in Tuscany to Tuscan peasants, while our English Pre-Raphaelites never had the boldness to conceive Christ or His mother as they would have looked, with English faces, camping on Hampstead Heath, or confused among a crowd in the Strand: and therefore, never brought the vision of them close home to the living English heart.[8]

For Ruskin, as for Fanny, the employment of models whose own lives echoed those of the 'originals' they were meant to represent was vital.

Fanny's art and writing also accorded well with Ruskin's publications from this period, which focused on what his early biographers referred to as studies of peasant life.[9] These included sections of his *Fors Clavigera* (1871–84) and *Bibliotheca Pastorum* (1876–88), both meant to educate the minds and morals of Britain's laboring classes, as well as his editorial work on Julia Firth's translation of Swiss author Jeremias Gotthelf's story of the farmer Ulric (1886) and what became three volumes by Fanny. In fact, Ruskin believed Firth's Protestant subjects and Fanny's Catholic subjects were complementary, demonstrating the connections between the two faiths.

Like many of Ruskin's activities, his purchase of 'Tuscan Songs', and its price, was reported in the press. Anglo-American newspapers in Europe were the first to circulate this information, likely because their correspondents knew the parties involved. In March 1883, an article in *The Roman News* commented on Ruskin's 'many years prejudice against women in general, and American men or women in particular' but affirmed that prejudice was overcome thanks to his acquaintance with Newman and Fanny; it claimed the song manuscript would 'carry her name down to a distant posterity'.[10] A few months later, a briefer note

89 Letter from John Ruskin to Lucia Alexander, 9 October 1882, pen and ink, 17.78 × 11.43 cm (7 × 4½ in), Wellesley College Special Collections, Wellesley, MA

Unsurprisingly, given this enthusiasm, Ruskin decided to purchase the manuscript for his St George's Museum in Sheffield, founded the previous decade to promote art for the benefit of local laborers.[6] As he explained to Lucia, 'one of my chief objects in obtaining the book will be the conveying to the mind of our English peasantry (not to say princes) some sympathetic conception of the reality of the sweet soul of Catholic Italy'.[7] Patronizing as this

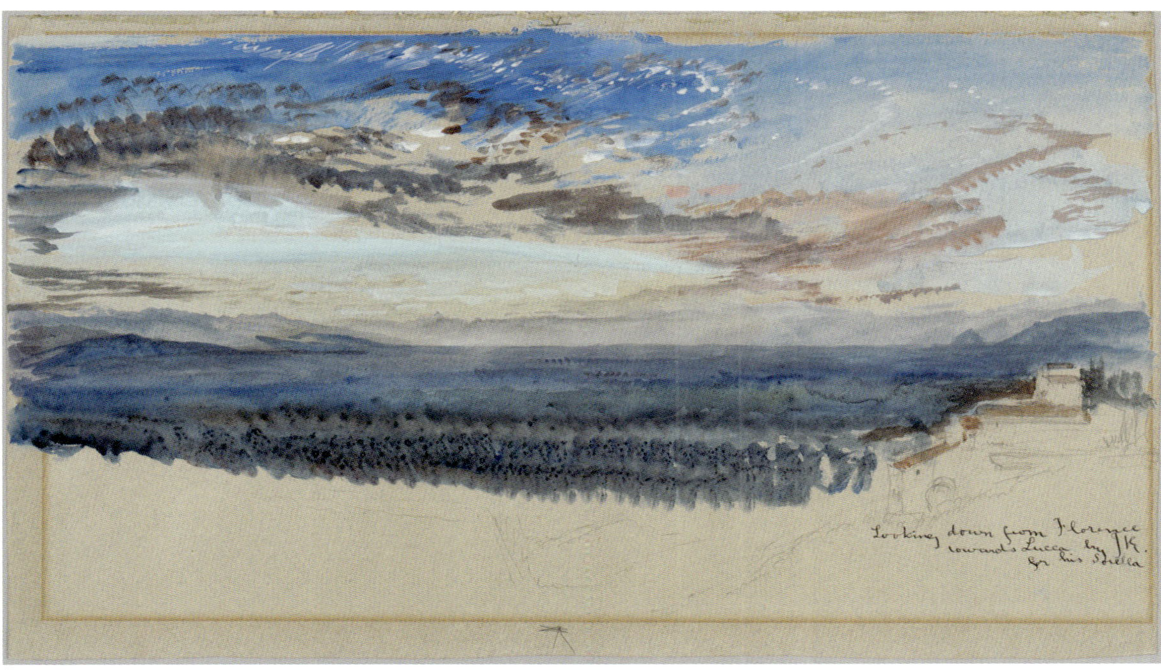

90 John Ruskin, *Looking Down from Florence Towards Lucca*, 1882, watercolor and gouache over graphite on blue wove paper, 28.7 × 49.4 cm (11¼ × 19½ in), Harvard Art Museums/Fogg Art Museum, Cambridge, MA

in *American Register* claimed the manuscript 'contains the folk lore of the Tuscan contadini. The text, music, and pictures are done by Miss Alexander in pen and ink. The verses are framed or separated by exquisite drawings of the beautiful mountain plants indigenous to the region.'[11] As these quotes indicate, the reports could be hyperbolic, but Ruskin may have encouraged some of that himself. He often referred to Fanny as a 'girl', implying her youth made her achievements all the more remarkable, when in reality she was 45 when they met.[12]

Ruskin was also drawn to the Alexander women. He told his cousin Joan Severn they were 'such kind people – gave me Ices, and American Raspberries – and Aleatico – besides the tea'.[13] The raspberries were likely grown from seeds in Fanny's garden, and the sweet red wine known as Aleatico was from the Tuscan town of Montepulciano, so these were particular treats for the visiting Englishman. He met with the Alexanders several times during his Florence stay, and was so taken with the women that he confessed to his friend, Harvard professor Charles Eliot Norton, 'I've been actually obliged to run away from Florence lest I should be converted into an American-citizen. There are two such precious American women there, M^rs & Miss Alexander, besides Newman, who is a great sweet – and doing lovely things.'[14] The Alexanders were equally enamored and gave Ruskin a marble pelican, which he placed in the dining room of Brantwood, his home in England's Lake District.[15] Ruskin was delighted with the gift, and described it using the infantilizing language he employed in his correspondence with Joan and, later, in his letters to Fanny:

> the kind peepies gave me . . . the marble pelican that used to be over the altar at Orvieto – its a little pelly-welly about a foot high – and little under in the wings – and three little-little-little pelly wellies being fed, oo know – di ma – and there's the ruffled place in the plumes, – and its all so booty – Giovanni Pisanos I suppose – anyhow a master's work.[16]

They quickly adopted terms of endearment: Fanny became *sorella* (sister) to Ruskin, and he even inscribed an unfinished watercolor of the countryside around Florence made during this visit, 'for his Sorella' (fig.90). He was *fratello* (brother) to her and *figlio* (son) to Lucia (though Lucia was only five years his senior); Lucia was *Mammina* (little mother) to both of them and Joan was *cugina* (cousin). These names, and the baby talk, reflect Ruskin's often problematic relationships with women. His correspondence with Fanny, Lucia and Joan (and several other women) often devolved into a petulant dialogue that perpetuated his fantasy of their relationships, or perhaps helped him keep them at a distance, apart from any potentially sexual feelings.[17] The annulment of his marriage to Effie Gray in 1854 and his obsession with Rose La Touche, almost 30 years his junior, whose death in 1875 contributed to his mental decline, were the basis for much gossip in Britain. But it is unlikely that the Alexanders followed this gossip, relying instead on his version of events and always doing their best to comfort him. His letters were at times confessional and strikingly intimate, particularly regarding his sorrow over Rose, his interest in young girls, and his mental state. He occasionally included cryptic statements, as he did

in one letter to Fanny in 1888: 'the fact of me that neither of you know is so different from what you believe, that after knowing me a little better I'm afraid you'll think I had better have stayed away'.[18]

Ruskin championed several women artists besides Fanny, including the illustrator Kate Greenaway, often for reasons other than their innate talent.[19] Anna Lloyd, one of the first five women to enroll at Cambridge's Girton College, was an amateur artist who occasionally studied with Ruskin. She claimed he believed 'it is the simple duty of every woman who has a gift for drawing to learn the elements thoroughly, and then be ready and earnest to teach others, more especially the children of the well-to-do lower classes'.[20] His belief in a woman's duty to better the general public, while still maintaining traditional roles, was certainly one reason for his fascination with Fanny. But her devotion to her charitable work, and its intimate connection to her art, was just as important.

Ruskin was so enthralled by 'Tuscan Songs' that Edwige Gualtieri gave him the name 'Signore del Libro' ('Gentleman of the Book').[21] He had to leave the manuscript in Florence for Fanny to complete when he traveled back to England later that fall. But he carried home her shorter manuscript about her *contadina* friend Ida and immediately began to prepare it for publication. For Ruskin, Ida – and by extension Fanny – represented ideal feminine virtue, and her unselfish actions fit well with contemporary notions of innocence and self-sacrifice. But he also recognized the commercial potential of Ida's story – indeed, of all of Fanny's work – and the almost predatory enthusiasm he expressed for it seemed to sustain him in these last years of his life.

Fanny was immune to much of this, however. In a letter to Lilly describing her first meeting with Ruskin, Fanny revealed,

> He said a good deal about my little story of Ida, which he had just read, and quite took my breath away by

proposing to take it away and have it printed. He said it would be a very useful religious book (which you may believe I was glad to hear), especially from the absence of all sectarian feeling in it; and he seemed much pleased at the strong friendship and religious sympathy between Ida and myself, belonging as we did to two different and usually opposing churches.[22]

This sacred aspect was emphasized by the sole illustration in the manuscript, representing Ida on her deathbed (fig.91). The light from a window shines on the young woman, propped against pillows with hair falling over her shoulders, flowers and rosary beads twining around her bed-frame and a copy of the New Testament in her lap, which Fanny read to comfort her friend and which, she implies in the text, ultimately provided the young woman with salvation. Ruskin must have recognized the uncanny similarities between this portrait and his own drawing of Rose La Touche on her deathbed, which may be why he worried it might 'trespass on her peace' to include it in the book.[23] But, ultimately, he decided to use it as the frontispiece. He added his own preface, stressing the truth of the story as well as the union of Catholic and Protestant that Fanny described to Lilly. He also claimed he did nothing to the text beyond adding 'a naughty note or two'.[24] There are occasional footnotes, signed with his initials, but correspondence between Ruskin and Fanny suggests he did much more; he asked for clarification and information on details to add to the text, a task he described as both a pleasure and a duty.[25]

While working on this manuscript, Ruskin resumed his position as Oxford's Slade Professor, a prestigious post that required him to deliver six lectures in 1883. These lectures, which were printed and widely circulated, were ostensibly about contemporary English art, but he referred to Fanny in two of them. He did not name her in the first, on 9 March, which otherwise focused on Dante Gabriele Rossetti and William Holman Hunt as representatives of the 'Realistic Schools of Painting'.[26] Ruskin shared the Ida frontispiece with the audience, promising they could soon read the book, and enthusiastically described Fanny and her relationship with Italy's *contadini*:

> They come to her as their loving guide, and friend, and sister in all their work, and pleasure, and – suffering. I lean on the last word. For those of you who have entered into the heart of modern Italy know that there is probably no more oppressed, no more afflicted order of gracious and blessed creatures – God's own poor, who have not yet received their consolation, than the mountain peasantry of Tuscany and Romagna . . . Among them, as I have told you, this American girl has lived – from her youth up, with her (now widowed) mother, who is as eagerly, and which is the chief matter, as sympathizingly benevolent as herself. The peculiar art gift of the younger lady is rooted in this sympathy, the gift of truest expression of feelings serene in their rightness; and a love of beauty – divided almost between the peasants and the flowers that live round Santa Maria del Fiore . . . She has thus drawn, in faithfullest portraiture of these peasant Florentines, the loveliness of the young and the majesty of the aged: she has listened to their legends, written down their sacred songs; and illustrated, with the sanctities of mortal life, their traditions of immortality.[27]

This lavish praise was meant to excite his audience, as well as those who later read the published lecture, for the forthcoming publications, though many of them must have found it odd that he included an American 'girl' in his lecture on English art. Ruskin shared more information about Fanny in his third lecture, on Frederic Leighton, Lawrence Alma-Tadema and the 'Classic Schools of Painting', delivered twice on 19 and 23 May. Now he teased his audience with drawings from 'Tuscan Songs', which he had only received a few days earlier, including several of Saint Christopher, claiming they were 'the

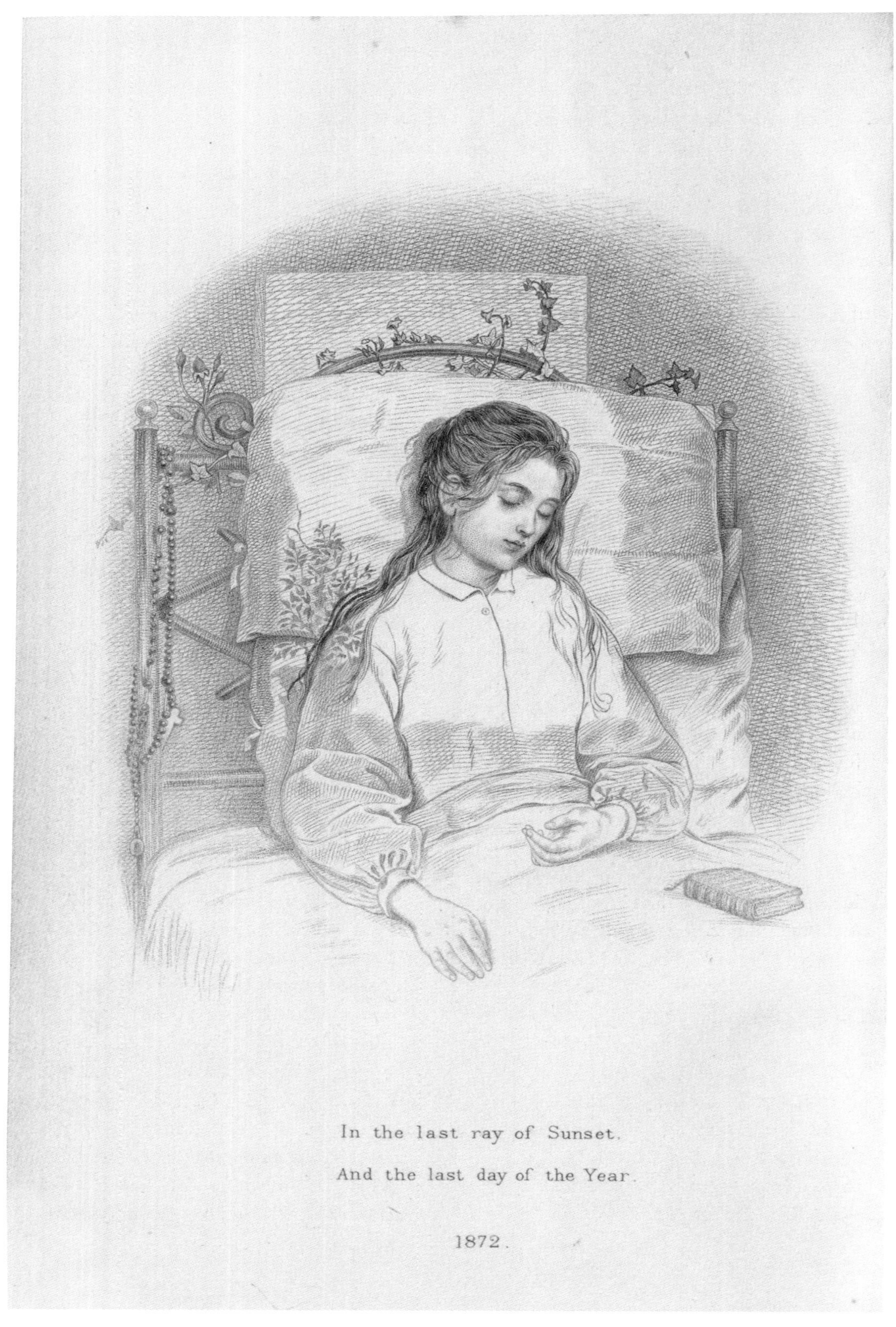

91 Francesca Alexander, frontispiece from *The Story of Ida*, ed. John Ruskin (Sunnyside, Kent: George Allen, 1883), photogravure, 18.5 × 12 cm (7 ¼ × 4 ¾ in)

most beautiful renderings of the legend hitherto attained by religious imagination'.[28] He now referred to the artist as both 'Miss Alexander' and 'Francesca'. Italian friends (and occasionally Americans like John Greenleaf Whittier) had called her by the Italian Francesca for many years; in 1866 she signed a letter to Lilly as Francesca 'in Italian through force of habit', and she signed 'La Sorellaccia' as Francesca, too.[29] But once Ruskin used this name, everyone else followed; she will be referred to as Francesca for the rest of this book, too.

Ruskin was a savvy promoter. Within days of this lecture, *The Story of Ida* was published, the title page identifying 'Francesca' – no last name – as author and him as editor. It was immediately acclaimed and reprinted in multiple editions over several decades in both Britain and the United States, and within a year it was translated into Italian.[30] Ruskin did not purchase this manuscript from Francesca; instead, he apparently brought it out with his usual publisher, George Allen, as both a labor of love and a way to interest readers in the forthcoming song manuscript. He instructed Allen to send the profits to Francesca, a further indication that it remained her property.[31]

On 1 June, Ruskin wrote to tell Francesca that he had already received 'the loveliest letters about Ida' and promised to send them to her, confirming his belief that the book would find wide appeal.[32] For Protestant readers, Francesca's admittedly mild criticism of the priests who allowed Ida to suffer justified their suspicions of Catholicism, and ministers like Samuel Edward Herrick of Boston's Congregational Mount Vernon church recommended it to their congregations.[33] Emily Dickinson, whose writing expressed some sympathy with Catholicism, referred to it as an 'etherial [sic] volume'.[34] Yet Catholics found much to admire in Ida's biography, too; Cardinal Henry Edward Manning, the leader of the Catholic Church in England and a friend of Ruskin, praised it extravagantly and compared it to the writings of Saint Francis of Assisi.[35]

The Alexanders gave signed copies of *Ida* to friends in Florence. Additional copies were mailed to others in the United States with the help of the publisher and Charles P. Bowditch, the Boston lawyer who, with his brother Alfred, served as the Alexanders' legal representatives and financial managers. Lucia's scrapbook includes letters from many of the recipients, including Americans Thomas Gold Appleton, George Chickering, Frances Boott Greenough, Oliver Wendell Holmes, Elizabeth Russell Lyman, Ellen and Ida Mason and George Washington Wales; Britons Frederic Leighton, Anna Lloyd and Georgina Forbes; and Italians Luisa Rasponi Murat and Sigismondo Castromediano.[36] Ghevont Alishan was so moved by Ida's story, in part because she reminded him of a beloved deceased niece, that he began sending small gifts to Ida's niece, or 'Ida seconda'.[37] Other letters came from complete strangers, among them the sister-in-charge at Cottage Hospital in Cushendall, Ireland, who shared the book with her indigent patients, and the vicar Hardwicke Drummond Rawnsley, who sent along a poem, too.[38] The book was cited in a variety of publications, including a review in the form of a mock dialogue – where Francesca was likened to Hilda in Hawthorne's *Marble Faun* – in a monthly newspaper for members of the Anglican Church.[39] And it was read aloud to factory girls and women in Boston's Resolve Club in efforts to improve their lives.[40]

Bostonians were especially thrilled by the achievement of their friend in Florence. In July, John Greenleaf Whittier wrote to Annie Adams Fields, 'We have been reading with interest & sympathy Francesca's beautiful and touching story, under the pines near the lake, with the plaintive song of the wood-dove as accompaniment.'[41] A month later, he wrote directly to Francesca, claiming the book would 'do more good, than all the volumes of theological controversy and speculation which have appeared for half a century. Every body is reading it, and it will be reaching and melting human hearts long after the writer shall have joined her beloved young friend.'[42] Whittier enclosed his poem, 'The Story of Ida', which he published later that year, with his letter:

Weary of jangling noises never stilled,
The skeptic's sneer, the bigot's hate, the din
Of clashing texts, the webs of creed men spin
Round simple truth, the children grown who build
With gilded cards their new Jerusalem,
Busy, with sacerdotal tailorings
And tinsel gauds, bedizening holy things,
I turn, with glad and grateful heart, from them
To the sweet story of the Florentine
Immortal in her blameless maidenhood,
Beautiful as God's angels and as good;
Feeling that life, even now, may be divine
With love no wrong can ever change to hate,
No sin make less than all-compassionate![43]

These accolades overwhelmed the modest Francesca, who was still mourning the death of her father. She wrote to Lilly,

in the midst of my sad thoughts I have a great comfort; [Ida's] story is doing good, a great deal more than I ever hoped or imagined. In America they have two ten-cent editions now, besides the more expensive one, and I have heard things about it that make me feel as if I never ought to stop giving thanks . . . To think of my poor Ida, who thought her life had been of no use, coming to this![44]

In June 1883 Ruskin delivered a lecture described as 'Fairyland and art, and their effect upon child-life' to a large audience of friends and admirers, including Leighton and Edward Burne-Jones, at the London home of Mrs W.H. Bishop. While the first half of the lecture examined the stated topic, the second half discussed Francesca's song manuscript at length. He cited Cardinal Manning's praise and enthusiastically shared 20 of the folios with his audience. Ruskin commended her drawings of nature, but apparently he could not resist some criticism of her rendering of anatomy, which one of the newspaper reports of his lecture echoed: 'Since Leonardo da Vinci's flower studies, we can recall no drawings of the "herb of the field" equal to "Francesca's" for strength and delicacy, for truth and the reverence that comes of truth; though she has perhaps somewhat to learn in expressing human form.'[45]

The Alexanders and Ruskin exchanged dozens of letters that summer, with his forwarded to the women in Abetone and Venice. They were joined at Abetone by Eunice Whitney Farley, wife of Cornelius Felton (the son of Harvard president C. Conway Felton), who likely met them through her Agassiz relatives. Eunice later reminisced about her time with vivacious Lucia and plain Francesca, echoing so many others when she observed that they 'seemed like people who had remained in some peaceful dream, while the rest of the world hurried on, but thankful for an occasional glimpse of this Arcadian innocence'.[46]

Other Americans in Florence were very aware of Ruskin's interest in Francesca. Joseph Pennell, who was eager to get Ruskin's approval, lamented that the man never responded to his etchings, because 'he was then too much interested in Miss Alexander, and her stories and drawings of Florence, to bother about me'.[47] American journalist, artist and diplomat William James Stillman and the bibliophile Willard Fiske were more generous in their assessments. In an article about their visit to Abetone that summer, Stillman reflected on the close relationships Francesca had with the residents, and the care she gave to the sick and needy among them. As Francesca herself had noted years earlier, Stillman claimed the Italians saw her 'as a miracle-worker, and the effect of her prescriptions as due to a divine grace'.[48] While there, he and Fiske enjoyed what the latter described as an 'American lunch (oysters, salmon, corn etc.)', during which Lucia and Francesca waited on them 'as if they were two contadine'.[49] Acknowledging Francesca's

sudden acclaim, Fiske identified her as 'just now
Ruskin's pet craze', who had been 'Ruskined into
fame'.[50] They spent some time discussing the plans for
the song manuscript. Fiske wrote, 'Ruskin is seeing
[Francesca's] book of Rispetti (lovers' songs), with
the illustrating heliotyped, through the press. Mrs.
A. read us those letters from R. received the previous
day, and showed us proofs of the illustrating.'[51] Fiske
seemed as charmed by the Alexanders as others were.
When he called on them again that fall in Florence,
they served him catawba grapes, an American variety
grown near the city, and introduced him to Princess
Luisa Rasponi Murat's daughter, Countess Letizia
Rasponi Murat, who promised to show him her
family heirlooms.[52] Knowing Fiske was assembling
a library, Lucia later gifted him a rare and valuable
Petrarch volume he had been seeking.[53] This may have
been a book the Alexanders acquired years earlier,
when old volumes could be purchased for very little
money, or perhaps it was gifted to them, as was the
case with a sixteenth-century culinary manuscript
they received from a woman in Bassano.[54]

Despite the omission of Francesca's surname
on *Ida*'s title page, she was quickly identified as
the author. She never listed her studio address in
the English-language newspapers or guidebooks,
a common practice for artists who hoped to lure
potential clients, because she never needed, or even
wanted, to promote herself. And although her studio
was in her home, that address appeared only rarely
in resident lists published by those same sources,
and not until 1894.[55] Of course, as hotel residents,
the Alexanders did not fit easily into the established
categories; when they did appear in the newspaper
lists, it was as visitors, alongside a changing cast of
other Bonciani guests.

But travelers easily found her, as they always had,
whether by word of mouth or perhaps the circulation
of her calling cards (fig.92). Both Francesca and her
studio became sites to be seen like the city's churches,
palaces and works of art, and the hospitable women

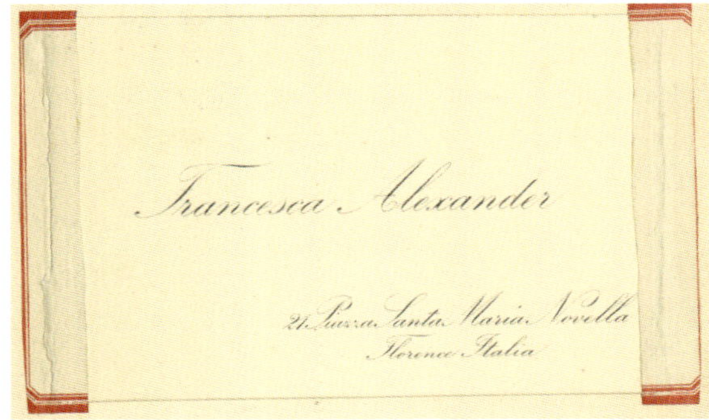

92 Francesca Alexander's calling card, in Constance
Grosvenor Alexander's copy of *The Hidden Servants and
Other Very Old Stories* (Boston, MA: Little, Brown & Co.,
1900), 6.5 × 10 cm (2 ½ × 4 in), Wellesley College Special
Collections, Wellesley, MA

accommodated these travelers with a regular open
house. Francesca's studio was particularly evocative,
with its assortment of tapestries, paintings and gifts
from her Italian friends. Francesca described it to
a friend as 'a pretty little room, and always full of
flowers, so that it looks like a garden . . . I have a few
little presents there, almost all from poor people;
those which I receive from the rich are disposed of
in the room down stairs, but my little painting room
is the poor people's room especially.'[56] According to
one American couple, the room, which was filled
with Italian women sewing, was 'very small, decorated
with all manner of things + many flowers. On one
wall I counted more than 75 objects hanging –
paintings, cabinets, photographs, brackets, etc.'[57] The
Englishwoman Matilda Lucas, who with her sister
Anne visited 'the authoress of *Ida*', described it as:

in great confusion, full of flowers, shells, books, a
crucifix & old pictures, while behind the door hung
a large bundle of 'Comforting assurances' like railway
texts [presumably sacred broadsides] – On the floor

was a charming portrait of Ida in a red dress & white
chemisette, painted in a very subdued key. The face is
far prettier than the book portrait in which the hair
is drawn off the forehead. Here it falls a little in the
way you often see in Italy, much more becoming to the
Italian face.[58]

That portrait, now lost, was part of a shrine Francesca
set up to honor her dead friend, accompanied by
a framed lock of Ida's hair, her favorite lilies and a
rosary.[59]

Travelers gathered to watch Francesca draw, and
if they were fortunate they left with a work of art or
flowers from her garden.[60] Ruskin, eager to publish
the song manuscript, worried about these distractions,
and tried to exert control over Francesca's art. He
insisted that she not publish 'La Sorellaccia', which
the Alexander women or perhaps the Shaws were
considering, because 'it would come blundering out as
an American speculation – spoiling and caricaturing
all my work on [the song manuscript] – and giving
me no end of irritation + trouble'.[61] He cautioned that
Francesca was 'frittering herself away . . . and being
made a prey and savoury morsel and marrow-bone of
by the worldly multitude'.[62] That multitude apparently
wanted copies of the *Ida* frontispiece, among other
things, and Francesca worked hard to oblige.[63] Ruskin
urged her to avoid making drawings for magazines
– *The Century* had requested a contribution – and to
send her drawings first to him so he could critique,
price, sell and occasionally exhibit them.[64] His long-
standing desire to teach drawing, whether formally or
informally, found a target in Francesca.[65]

Despite this, Ruskin made no impact on
Francesca's art. Her style was fully formed before she
met him, and it remained unchanged throughout her
life. But his role in the promotion of her work was
immediately acknowledged, and people assumed her
prices rose accordingly. In July 1883, John Milton Hay
wrote to fellow American diplomat William Dean
Howells to ask for Francesca's address: 'I would like to
write to her and ask her for a drawing. Do you think
she would do one for me for 500 francs? or has the
rapturous screaming of Ruskin put her out of reach?'[66]

For her part, Francesca was bewildered by this
rapturous screaming. She was still the same woman
she always was – she changed very little throughout
her long life – but Ruskin amplified her, bringing
notice of her art and life to his large audience. She
described this attention, and her reaction to it, in a
letter to Lilly:

After the good fortune which had befallen me became
known, my work and myself became objects of general
curiosity, and my peaceable little room was filled, from
one week's end to another, with the strangest variety
of people that you can imagine of every possible
nationality. At first they used to try to obtain an
introduction; afterwards they laid aside all ceremony,
and simply walked in: often there would be as many
as four languages talked at once; and one gentleman,
who came with a party of Russians, spoke nothing
that any one could understand excepting a little rather
peculiar French, and as this was soon exhausted, he
responded to everything with a low and solemn bow.
After people heard that Mr Ruskin had looked over
me while I worked, everybody else wanted to look over
me, and it never made the smallest difference what
I was doing. I remember one day a party of english
people came to look at me while I was copying out a
list of names for my index, and they said it was most
wonderful! The only wonderful thing about it was that
I could do it without making a mistake, when those
people were looking at me all the time and talking to
me. And there were so many near sighted people, that
would put their heads between me and the paper that
I was working upon, and then expect me to go on just
the same; and other people would carry off two or three
of my pens to try . . . I was always finding myself short
of pens, in consequence! But such a strange variety of
people as I have seen! There were Mr. Ruskin's adorers,
who would ask where he stood when he came to my

room, and then, with much solemn emotion, would go and stand in the same spot. And then there were his enemies, some of whom regarded me with positive malignity, made up faces at my work, and accused me of not doing it as I said I did; while others looked upon me as an innocent victim, and warned me sadly of the ill-treatment that I must shortly expect to receive. Then there were the professional sightseers, who looked on Edwige and myself exactly as they would have looked on any kind of curious wild beasts, and appeared to be taking notes of our habits. I remember one old lady, who, after reading some of the little songs, asked who translated them; and on hearing that I had done so, remarked to the people near her: 'Oh! Then she is a poetess; I never saw one before, and I have always wanted to; I must have a look and see what she's like!' And, arranging her spectacles, she turned, and took a long comfortable stare at me. But she made no further remark, and, I fear, was not pleased, and did not think I looked poetical. Some people seemed mortally afraid of me (only think of me an object of terror!) and kept at a distance, and talked in whispers, and changed colour painfully if I spoke to them. Others paid me extravagant, and not always intelligible compliments. I have been much puzzled to know what one gentleman meant, who, after remaining silent until near the end of his visit, began to say in an impressive manner: 'If Fra Bartolomeo could come out of his grave' . . . and then did not finish the sentence. He repeated the same words again however after a short interval, and yet again several times, until I asked him what there was that made him think of Fra Bartolomeo, and he then said, 'If Fra Bartolomeo could come out of his grave, I think he would want to take drawing lessons!' Dear Lilly, I am sure you must think that I am exaggerating, but I assure you that it is not so, and that all which I tell you really happened, just as I tell it! So I feel now as if I had been, temporarily, on the list of distinguished people![67]

Bolstered by the success of *Ida*, and a timely inheritance of $25,000 from two of Lucia's relatives,

the Alexander women decided to remain in Florence, by that time their home for three decades.[68] This decision was not without some regret on the part of Lucia, who had maintained her account with Boston grocer S.S. Pierce, perhaps as a way to promise herself an eventual return.[69] They were certainly not the only female Anglo-American household in Italy. During their years abroad, in Florence, in addition to Isa Blagden and her friends on Bellosguardo, others included the American Jane M. Healey Jackson, widow of the sculptor John Adams Jackson, who lived with her daughter Margaret, and the Scottish sisters and authors Susan and Joanna Horner. In Rome, the actress Charlotte Cushman shared her home with a changing cast of friends and lovers she called 'jolly bachelors', among them sculptors Harriet Hosmer and Emma Stebbins. The number of these households only continued to grow as travel became easier.

The decision to remain in Florence made the Alexanders reassess their belongings. Francesca wrote to Anna Lloyd, 'we have taken our rooms by the year, and are having them repaired and newly painted, and we are going to move in all our things that have been packed so long . . . when we are once settled I hope we shall have a home for life. So many many years we have been without one.'[70] Matilda Lucas confirmed that the Alexanders were starting a new phase that fall: 'They were just settling their things in for tho' they have lived there many years they are only just putting in their old furniture.'[71] Some items came to them from the United States, where they had been in storage for many years, including the portrait of Lucia's mother by Gilbert Stuart, which went into Francesca's bedroom, and an assortment of animal horns as well as weapons from a Pacific island, the last likely acquired years earlier by Lucia's seafaring relatives and subsequently gifted to Ruskin.[72] But other items had been lost in Boston's devastating 1872 fire.[73] They also unburdened themselves of some of their possessions. Lucia donated two eighteenth-century samplers stitched by relatives of

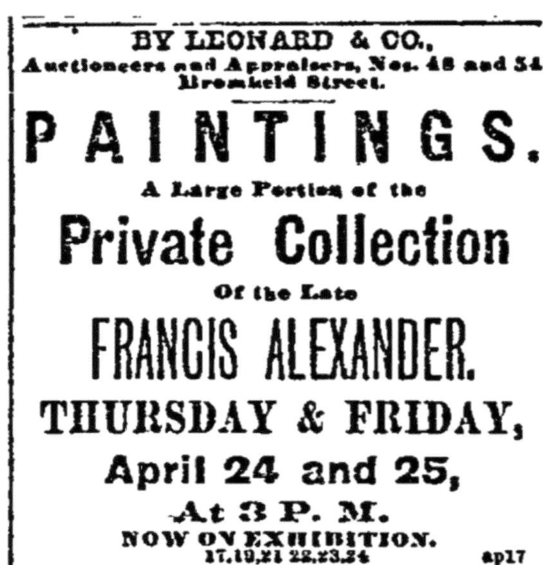

93 Advertisement for the auction of Francis Alexander's painting collection in *Boston Daily Journal*, 23 April 1884

Massachusetts governor Thomas Hutchinson to the Massachusetts Historical Society.[74] She sent a box made from the wood of the USS *Constitution*, and a medieval medical manuscript, to Oliver Wendell Holmes.[75] And Francesca donated a plaster hand by Italian sculptor Luigi Pampaloni, probably something Francis acquired on his first trip, before Pampaloni's 1847 death, to the city of Florence.[76]

The women had paintings to dispose of, both the remains of Francis's collection that had been left in storage and others in Florence they no longer wanted. They arranged for an auction of 93 paintings in Boston – encompassing portraits, still lifes, landscapes, genre scenes and sacred subjects – in April 1884 (fig.93).[77] None were by Francis, perhaps because the women could not bear to give up his paintings, and most were unattributed. Lucia

identified the artists of 11: two by Thomas Cole (including his *Tornado in the Wilderness*), three by John Singleton Copley, and one each by Émile François Dessain, Jean-Baptiste Greuze, Camille Roqueplan, and the more ambiguously designated 'Leslie', 'René' and 'Zucchero'. Inscriptions identified five more as the work of Agnolo Bronzino, George P.A. Healey, Onorio Marinari, Joos de Momper and Luis de Morales.[78] The income from this sale must have further secured the Alexanders' future in Florence. But comments by later visitors indicate that they still had an enormous quantity of paintings in their home; in 1894, they even had another Copley in storage at the Bonciani.[79] An article from 1889 described their crowded rooms, but Lucia worried that it gave the wrong impression; she insisted that their home, excepting Francesca's studio, was decorated sparingly, with only one object per tabletop, though photographs belie that claim.[80] Indeed, Lucia seemed to share the collecting impulse that motivated Francis to fill their homes with so many things from the time they arrived in Florence. She even decorated the rooms they rented during the summer months, one year buying Japanese plates, lacquerware, ostrich eggs and peacock feathers to display around their Venetian rental.[81]

As Francesca dealt with her new fame and the logistics of the decision to remain in Florence, she was also finishing 'Tuscan Songs' and working with Ruskin to bring it to publication. This was a complex project for both of them. Ruskin's queries and requests for additional information formed a large part of their correspondence for almost three years. At Christmas 1882, Francesca wrote her preface, which consisted of a biography of Beatrice di Pian degli Ontani and an explanation of her process and premise:

These songs and hymns of the poor people have been collected, little by little, in the course of a great many years which I have passed in constant intercourse with

the Tuscan contadini. They are but the siftings, so to
say, of hundreds and hundreds which I have heard and
learnt, mostly from old people: many of them have
never, so far as I know, been written down before, and
others it would be impossible now to find . . . there are
others who will collect and preserve the thoughts of
the rich and great; but I have wished to make my book
all of poor people's poetry, and who knows but it may
contain a word of help or consolation for some poor
soul yet? However that may be, I have done my best to
save a little of what is passing away.[82]

She illustrated the preface with drawings of the
two sites where she worked on the manuscript: the
mountains around Abetone (fig.94) and the Hotel
Bonciani, represented by a view from her sky parlor
of the Piazza Santa Maria Novella (fig.95).[83] The
placement of these drawings at the start served as
acknowledgment of Francesca's debt to her Italian
friends, and Italy itself. Ruskin, who was so charmed
by the arches to the left of the church facade that
he had Henry Roderick Newman paint them years
earlier, declared the second drawing 'the only bit of
interesting Italian building' in the entire manuscript.[84]

Francesca continued to work on the manuscript
until mid-April. Then, at Ruskin's request, she
composed biographies of her models. She readily
admitted that this request puzzled her:

I had not the least idea whether he wanted them
written in a book that he could lend to those who
saw the large book, or only to read himself and tell
the stories to people, and I did not know at all how
I ought to write them. So I ended by writing a series
of contadino biographies, in the style of the letters
which I write you, and I should not imagine he could
find them very interesting, but I hope they are what he
wants. It took me a good fortnight to write all these
out in a plain clear hand in a little blank book, and
writing is much harder work for me than drawing.[85]

She purchased this parchment-bound and
ornamented blank book from Giannini's shop; the
word 'NOTES' on the spine is an indication that
Giannini produced these books with English-
speaking clientele in mind (fig.96). Francesca filled
193 pages in her precise handwriting, with anecdotes
about the lives of 27 of her models and their
relationships with her; the first, appropriately, was
about Beatrice di Pian degli Ontani (fig.97). On the
final page she wrote, in her modest manner,

And so now I have finished all the stories of these hard
and obscure lives, which most people care so little to
hear about . . . I wish that I could think they might
induce any one who may happen to see them to feel
kindly towards my poor friends, and others who are
like them; and that is the most that I desire for them.[86]

Ruskin did not trust the manuscripts to the mail,
so he arranged for Anna Lloyd, who was in Florence
visiting the artist Alicia Hewitt Townsend Morgan
(a sister of a Girton classmate), to retrieve them and
transport them to England.[87] Anna was enchanted
by Francesca, whom she described as 'a tall lady with
beautiful brown eyes, a pleasant smile, dressed very
simply in rather an old violet silk dress, her hair drawn
back plainly into a net', and by the song manuscript
itself.[88] She departed Florence on 30 April 1883, and
Ruskin had the manuscripts in his possession by 13
May. He promptly wrote to Francesca:

I have no words to tell you how precious it is to me:
but if I am spared in strength to complete my work in
Oxford this spring, you will soon know how precious it
is to become to uncountable multitudes. The songs will
not be forgotten nor will these Italians pass away. They
will not all be taken to Heaven, yet – their song shall
still be heard in the springtime of their native land
. . . I am for the present too much bewildered by the
beauty of it all to write more than that.[89]

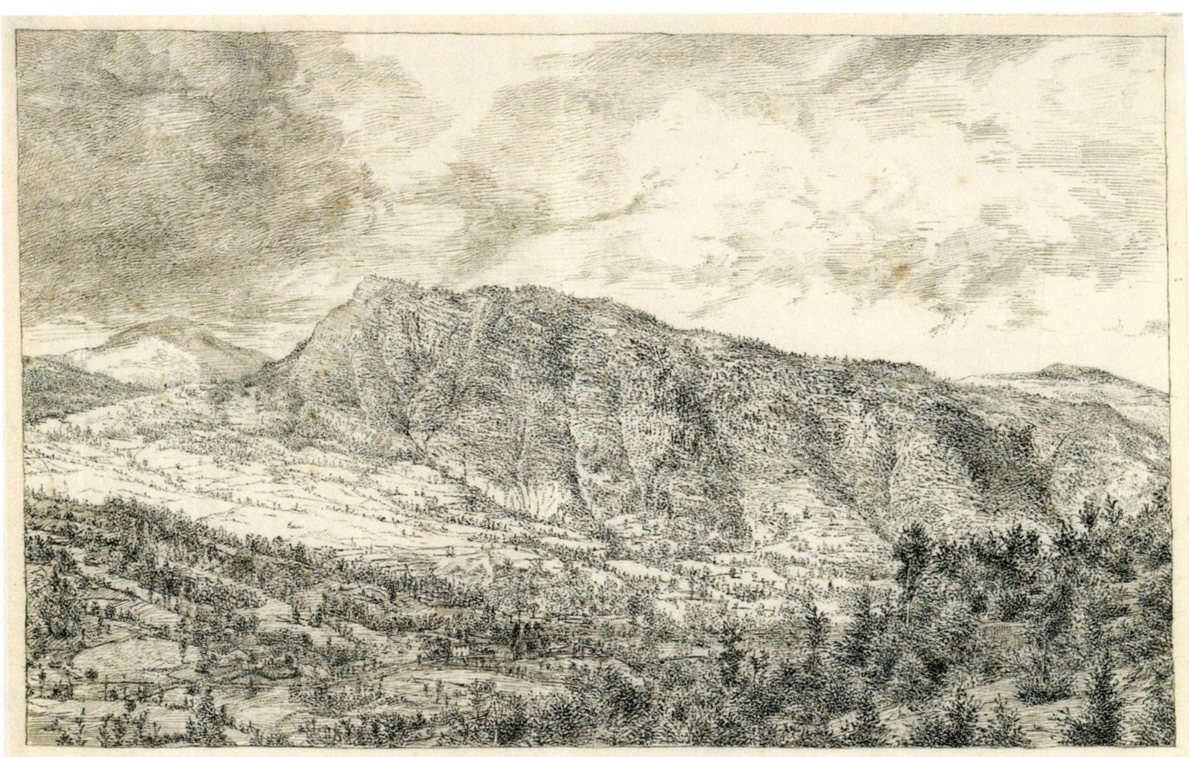

PREFACE

These songs and hymns of the poor people have been collected little by little, in the course of a great many years which I have passed in constant intercourse with the tuscan contadini. They are but the siftings, so to say, of hundreds and hundreds which I have heard and learnt, mostly from old people; many of them have never, so far as I know, been written down before, and others it would be impossible now to find. A great many were taught me by the celebrated improvisatrice, Beatrice Bernardi of Pian degli Ontani, whose portrait I have placed in the beginning of the book.... One of the most wonderful women whom I ever knew!. This Beatrice was the daughter of a stone mason at Melo, a little village of not very easy access on the mountain side above Cutigliano; and her Mother having died in Beatrice's infancy, she became, from early childhood, the companion and assistant of her Father, accompanying him to his winter labours in the Maremma, and, as she grew larger, helping him at his work by bringing him stones for the walls and bridges which he built.... Carrying them balanced on her head. She had no education, in the common sense of the word, never learning even the alphabet, but she had a wonderful memory, and could sing or recite long pieces of poetry. As a girl, she used in summer to follow the sheep, with her distaff at her waist; and would fill up her hours of solitude by singing such ballads as "The War of St. Michael and the dragon," the creation of the world and the fall of man" or, The history of San Pelegrino, son of Romano King of Scotland": and now, in her old age, she knows nearly all the new testament history; and much of the old, in a poetical form. She was very beautiful then, they say, with curling black hair and wonderful inspired looking eyes, and there must always have been a great charm in her voice and smile; so it is no great wonder that Matteo Bernardi, much older than herself, and owner of a fine farm at Pian degli Ontani, and of many cattle, chose rather to marry the shepherd girl who could sing so sweetly, than another woman whom his family liked better, and who might perhaps have brought him more increase of worldly prosperity. On Beatrice's wedding day, according to the old custom of the country, one or two poets improvised verses suitable to the occasion, and as she listened to them, suddenly she felt in herself a new power, and began to sing the poetry which was then born in her mind and having once begun, found it impossible to stop, and kept on singing a great while; so that all were astonished, and her uncle, who was present, said; "Beatrice, you have deceived me! if I had known what you were I would have put you in a convent. From that time forth she was the great poetess of all that part of the country, and was sent for to sing and recite at weddings and other festivals for many miles around; and perhaps she might have been happy; but her husband's sister, Barbara, who lived in

94 Francesca Alexander, preface with view of Abetone, folio from 'Tuscan Songs', 1882, ink on paper, 37.9 × 27.9 cm (14 ⅞ × 11 in), Collection of Deborah and Joseph Goldyne

Preface

the house, and who had not approved of the marriage, tried very wickedly to set her brother against his wife, and to some extent succeeded. He tried to stop her singing, which seemed to him a sort of madness, and at times he treated her with great unkindness; but sing she must and sing she did, for it was what the Lord made her for; and she lived down all their dislike: her husband loved her in his old age; and Barbara, whom she nursed with motherly kindness through a long and most distressing illness, was her friend before she died. Beatrice is still living at a great age now, but still retaining much of her old beauty and brilliancy, and is waited on and cared for with much affection by a pretty grand daughter bearing the same name as herself. As for the other songs, I have explained in the notes which I have written under them all the little that I know about them. The tunes, with the exception of those which I found printed in the Corona di Sacre Canzoni, I learned from the poor people themselves, and wrote down as well as I could: most of them, (though they sound very sweet to me, bringing back the very feeling of the air in the fir woods, or on the farms, where I have been used to hear them) are nothing more than plaintive monotonous little chants; but a few of the airs are very pretty; the accompaniments have been nearly all composed by Sig.ra Sestilia Poggiali. And the pictures sufficiently explain themselves; they are likenesses, nearly all, of the country people in their every day clothes and with their every day surroundings; while as to the ornamenting of the pages, it seemed natural that road-side songs should have borders of road-side flowers. Of the four long ballads, the Madonna and the Gypsy, St. Christopher, St. Zita, and the Samaritan, I have put in only one (the Samaritan) at full length, and of St. Christopher I have left out all the last half, which describes his preaching and his martyrdom, both because it was so very long, and because the details were so painful. Already the old songs are fast being forgotten; many of them it would be impossible now to find, and others are sung only by a few aged people who will soon be gone, or in some remote corners of the mountains; and in a few years they will probably be heard no more. They have served their time, and many people laugh at them now, and some have told me that I should have done better to spend my time and work on something more valuable: but in their day they have been a comfort to many. Labouring people have sung them at their work, and have felt their burdens lightened; they have brightened the long winter evenings of the poor women in lonely houses high among the mountains, when they have been sitting over their fires of fir branches, with their children about them, shut in by the snow outside, and with their men all away in the Maremma; and I have known those who have been helped to bear sickness and trouble, and even to meet death itself with more courage, by verses of the simple old hymns. I have heard Beate Leonardo's hymn to the cross sung in chorus by a party of pilgrims, men and women together, going to the mountain of San Pellegrino on a still moonlight night in August, when it has sounded to me as sweet as anything that ever I heard. It seems to me that there are others who will collect and preserve the thoughts of the rich and great; and I have wished to make my book all of poor people's poetry, and who knows but it may contain a word of help or consolation for some poor soul yet: however that may be, I have done my best to save a little of what is passing away.

Florence, Piazza Santa Maria Novella

December 25th 1882

Francesca Alexander

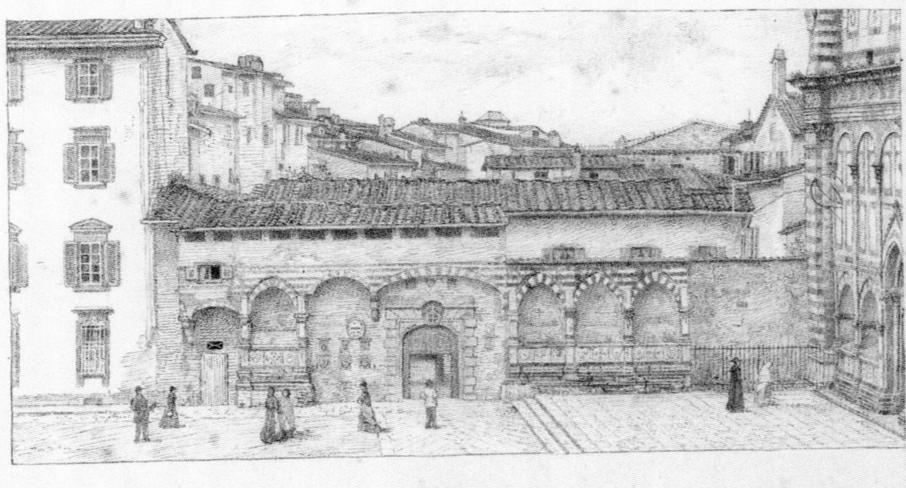

95 Francesca Alexander, preface with view of Piazza Santa Maria Novella, folio from 'Tuscan Songs', 1882, ink on paper, 37.8 × 27.6 cm (14 ⅞ × 10 ⅞ in), Collection of Deborah and Joseph Goldyne

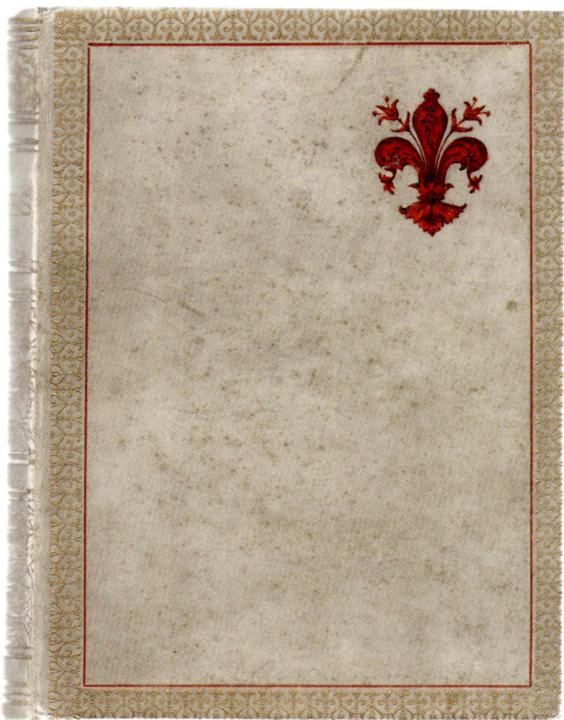

96 Francesca Alexander, 'Some Account of the People Whose Portraits are Given in the Roadside Songs', manuscript bound in parchment at Giannino Giannini's stationery shop in Florence, 1883, 10.5 × 16 cm (4 ½ × 6 ¼ in), private collection

Despite Ruskin's enthusiasm, it took him months to prepare the manuscript for publication and, as Francesca implied in her letter to Lilly, she was not always fully aware of his efforts. That October, she wrote to Anna Lloyd: 'Some portion of the "Roadside Songs" are going to be printed, with pictures reproduced in photograph; I do not know how much, or what ones; but I took the impression, from what Mr. Ruskin said in a few words that he wrote about it, that it was to be printed in separate numbers.'[90] This was not a complaint; Ruskin purchased the

manuscript so she believed all decisions were his.[91] As he worked, Ruskin took apart and dispersed the folios, despite his initial plan to donate the entire manuscript to his St George's Museum. Some folios are indeed there, but others went to Oxford and Cambridge colleges and he kept, gifted and sold the rest.[92] The dispersal happened quickly; by late 1884, a friend of Lilly Cleveland reported seeing four drawings in Ruskin's bedroom, and 35 more around Oxford University.[93]

Beginning in April 1884, Ruskin published what he now called *Roadside Songs of Tuscany* in ten installments, followed by a complete volume in September 1885. He reordered some of Francesca's folios and removed others entirely, integrated her additional biographies and some excerpts from her letters, and inserted his own preface and explanatory essays. He also limited the illustrations to two per installment. The cost of platinum photography reproductions – deemed the best option at that time – played a part in his decision, as it would have been too costly to reproduce all of Francesca's original 122 folios.[94] Without their accompanying illustrations, Ruskin decided many of the songs were also unnecessary.[95] This fundamentally changed the manuscript; it shifted the focus to text, much of it written or at least edited by Ruskin, rather than Francesca's drawings and the bilingual song verses and music. Ruskin deliberately created a very different volume, one for which he became co-author.[96]

However, Ruskin did retain Francesca's focus on Beatrice, with her portrait as the frontispiece to the first installment (fig.98). Seated diagonally to the picture plane, her sleeves pushed up to expose her strong arms and her hands together in her lap, Beatrice wears the traditional clothing of a *contadina*, but one dressed for a special occasion, with a fringed plaid scarf over her shoulders and tucked into her skirt and a multi-strand garnet necklace at her throat. She resembles a description Francesca wrote about their first meeting in 1862:

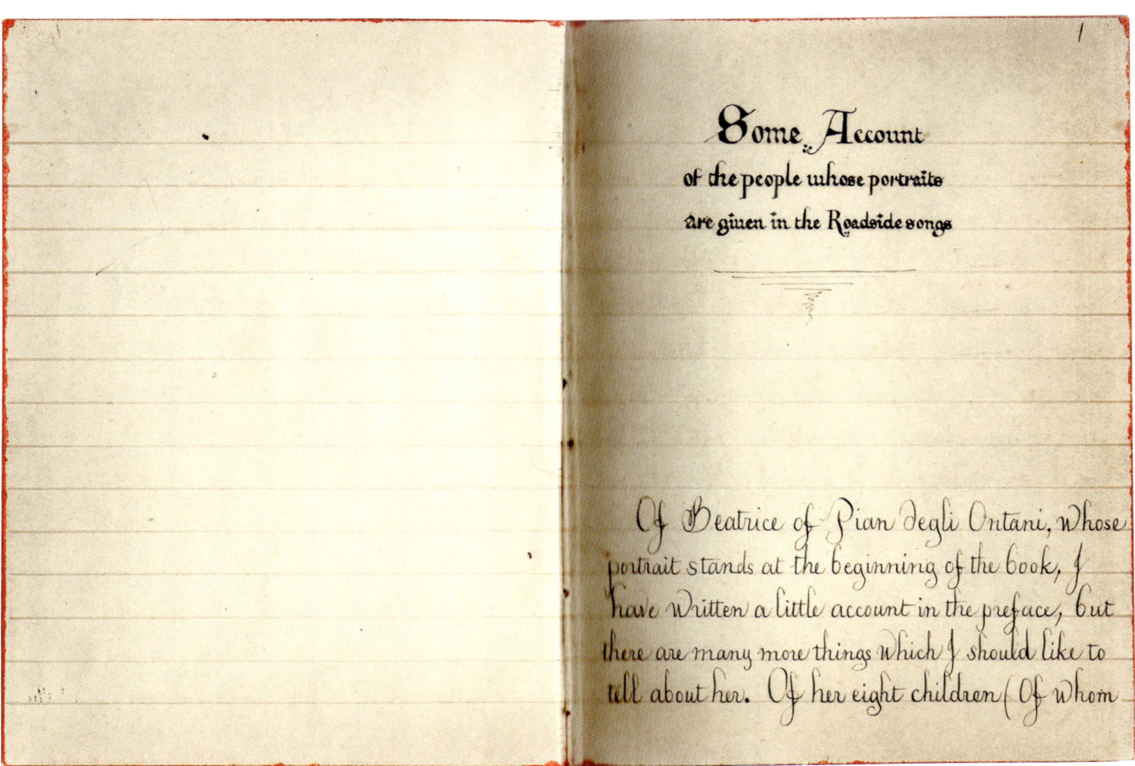

97 Francesca Alexander, folio 1 from 'Some Account of the People Whose Portraits are Given in the Roadside Songs', manuscript bound in parchment at Giannino Giannini's stationery shop in Florence, 1883, 10.5 × 16 cm (4 ½ × 6 ¼ in), private collection

She says that she is sixty, but she looks at least ten years younger; her eyes are her great beauty, large, dark and brilliant, full of fire; I did not wonder that Tomaseo called them inspired. For the rest of her face, she has a pretty little straight nose, rather strongly marked eyebrows, and a mouth so sweet in expression that I really cannot say whether it is pretty or not, one never notices the shape of it. She is very brown, that I cannot deny, and her skin has become polished through long exposure to the weather, but she has plenty of color in her cheeks . . . Her head is always covered with a handkerchief, from under which her beautiful gray hair falls in natural curls about her face.[97]

The text for this installment began, as Francesca's original manuscript did, with her author's preface, but it continued with Ruskin's editor's preface, in which he detailed his acquisition of the manuscript and introduced it to the reader. He then inserted material related to the Lucchese Saint Zita – the subject of the Tucker painting exhibited at the Athenaeum in 1869, who figured later in Francesca's original manuscript – for the remainder of this installment and the entirety of the second, too. Ruskin used Francesca's biography of her model for the saint, her friend Lucia Santi, a hard-working young woman who lived at Abetone, and added his own commentary on Lucia's life. This was followed by the saint's biography – with information

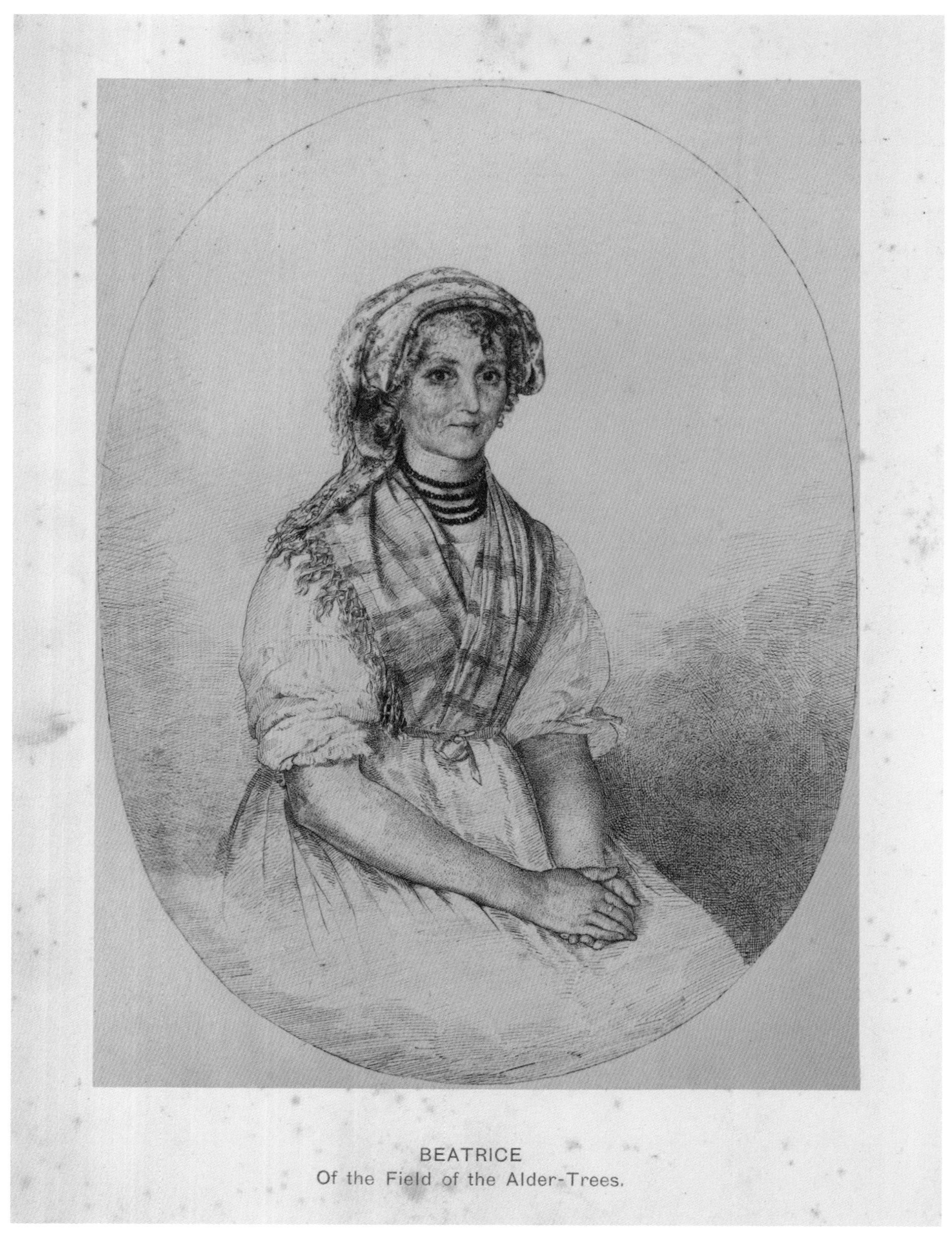

98 Francesca Alexander, 'Beatrice of the Field of the Alder-Trees', from *Roadside Songs of Tuscany* (Sunnyside, Kent: George Allen, 1885), photogravure by Frederick Hollyer, 22.5 × 16.5 cm (8 ⅞ × 6 ½ in), Rijksmuseum, Amsterdam

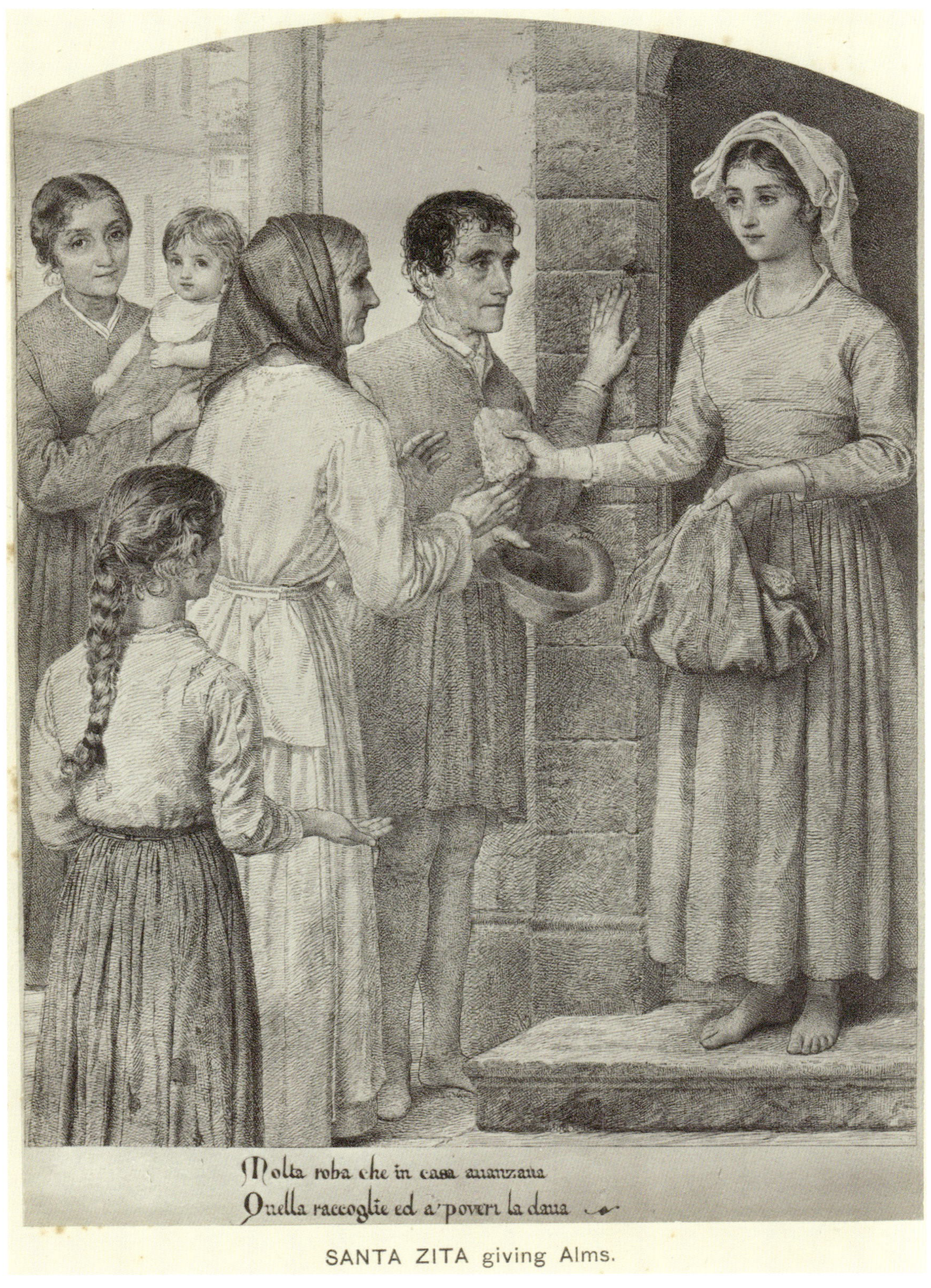

SANTA ZITA giving Alms.

99 Francesca Alexander, 'Santa Zita Giving Alms', from *Roadside Songs of Tuscany* (Sunnyside, Kent: George Allen, 1885), photogravure by Frederick Hollyer, 24.2 × 17.5 cm (9 ½ × 6 ⅞ in), Rijksmuseum, Amsterdam

from Francesca and other sources as well as his own writings and experience in Lucca, a seventeenth-century song about Zita by Guaspari di Bartolomeo Casentini in both Italian – from a cheaply printed version published by Francesco Bertini in Lucca – in 1820 – and Francesco's English translation, and his postscript glossing the translation and quoting further information from Francesca. Ruskin ended by drawing parallels between Zita and the Italian servants of his friends Rawdon Brown and Henry Roderick Newman, as well as Francesca's companion Edwige; his interest in these Italian servants may well be why he moved Zita's material to the first two installments. He also included three illustrations, one of which represents the saint distributing bread to the needy on her doorstep (fig.99). Following Francesca's biographical manuscript, Ruskin identifies the woman at far left as Edwige, with one of her five children in her arms, though he placed Edwige's biography in edited form in his sixth installment.[98] A similar assortment of texts, songs and illustrations, rearranged and at times overwhelming Francesca's original work, continued through the remaining installments.

Roadside Songs found a ready audience and, following the success of *Ida*, further secured Francesca's fame. It was advertised widely – always under Ruskin's name – and articles in newspapers and magazines shared information about Francesca with curious readers. Of course, that information was not always correct; Francesca described one of these articles as 'all a romance, from beginning to end, and of the most poetical description'.[99] But the praise continued, too, from Francesca's friends as well as strangers. Lilly Cleveland's uncle, Monsignor George Hobart Doane, a prominent Catholic official, read parts of it to his congregation in Newark, New Jersey.[100] One woman in England, worn down by family duties, claimed to be brought back to health after reading it, stating, 'It's like being on an Alpine pasture again!'[101] Constance Fenimore Woolson's sister described the thrill of living at the Villa Brichieri, with its associations with

Elizabeth Barrett Browning, Henry James and 'Miss Alexander whom Ruskin has written so much about. We have her desk to write upon . . . Do you wonder that my excited, trembling fingers can hardly hold a pen or write a word in such surroundings?'[102] Queen Victoria even knew about Francesca: probably at Ruskin's urging, and with the assistance of her friend Lady Margaret Crawford, Francesca sent a signed copy of *Roadside Songs*, specially bound at Giannini's shop in parchment with gold-stamped ornament and a painted Saint Edward's crown on the front and a fleur-de-lis on the back, to the sovereign during her 1888 visit to Florence. Lucia pasted the note of thanks from the Queen's private secretary Sir Henry Ponsonby into one of her scrapbooks.[103] The English artist George Frederic Watts allegedly told Ruskin that 'I would rather have drawn the face of the Madonna in the design of the Madonna and the Rich Man [fig.100] than all the things I have done, put together.'[104]

The model for that Madonna, the same Emilia who posed for the *Madonnina* (fig.1), like many of the Italians who posed for Francesca, became a minor celebrity. Ruskin's philanthropist friend Fanny Talbot, who later made the first donation of property to Britain's National Trust, was so charmed by the stories of Francesca's 'poor friends' that she regularly sent funds to assist them, and purchased clothing they made. Writing to thank Talbot, Francesca confessed, 'It is the first time in my life that I ever was helped in this way by one whom I had never seen.'[105] But other donations soon followed, including £1.50 from a Scottish gentleman and his young daughter 'for the poor of Tuscany'.[106]

Ruskin and the Alexanders continued to exchange letters filled with news and gossip, as well as gifts like a Hebrew scroll, jewelry from an archeological dig in Cyprus, and flowers and seeds to plant in each other's garden.[107] They exchanged art, too. In 1885, Ruskin sent Francesca a group of studies he described as 'a little lot of leaf sketches'.[108] He often gave Francesca advice about her art, noting that her landscapes were

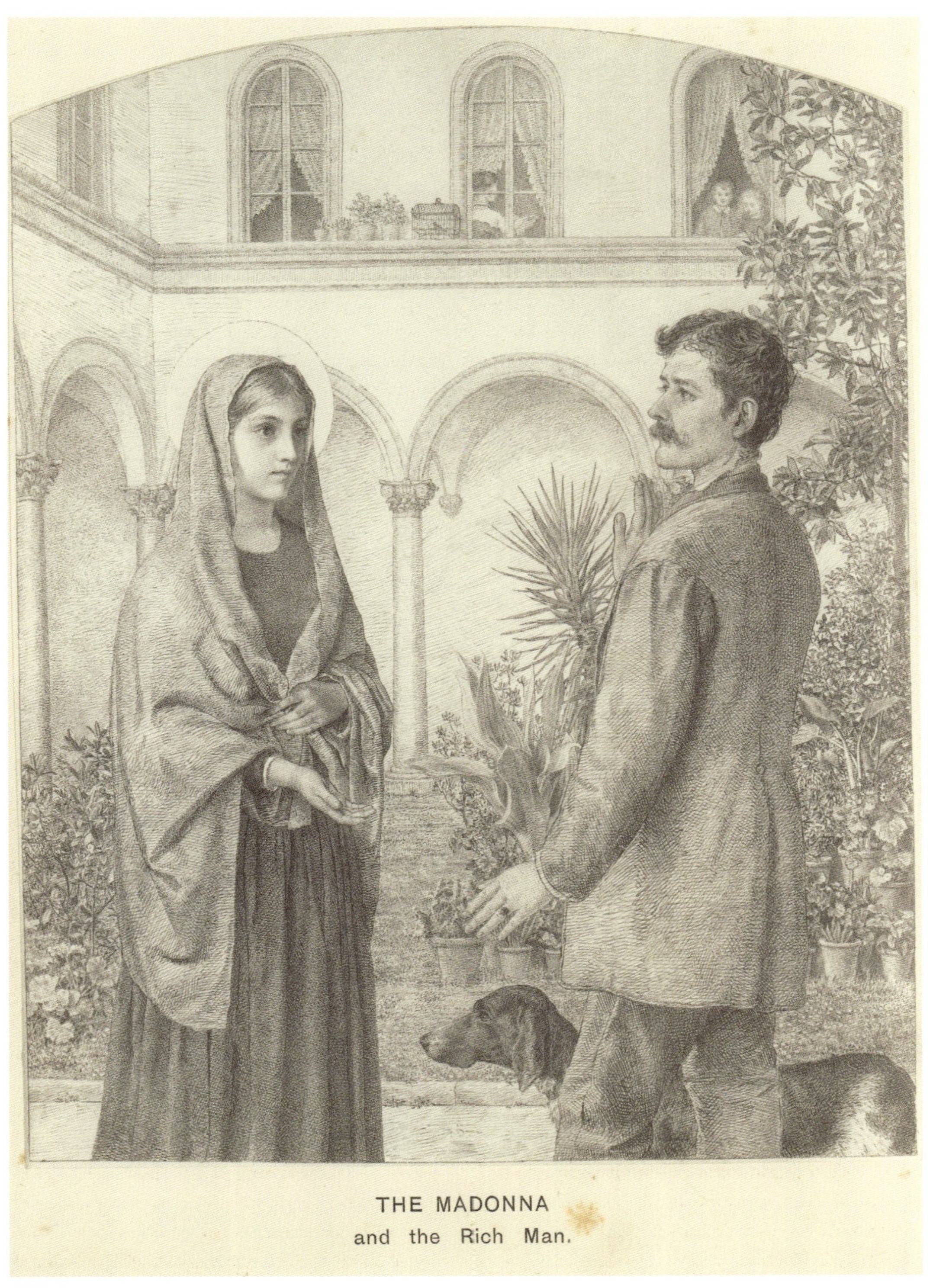

100 Francesca Alexander, 'The Madonna and the Rich Man', from *Roadside Songs of Tuscany* (Sunnyside, Kent: George Allen, 1885), photogravure by Frederick Hollyer, 22.5 × 17.6 cm (8 ⅞ × 6 ⅞ in), Rijksmuseum, Amsterdam

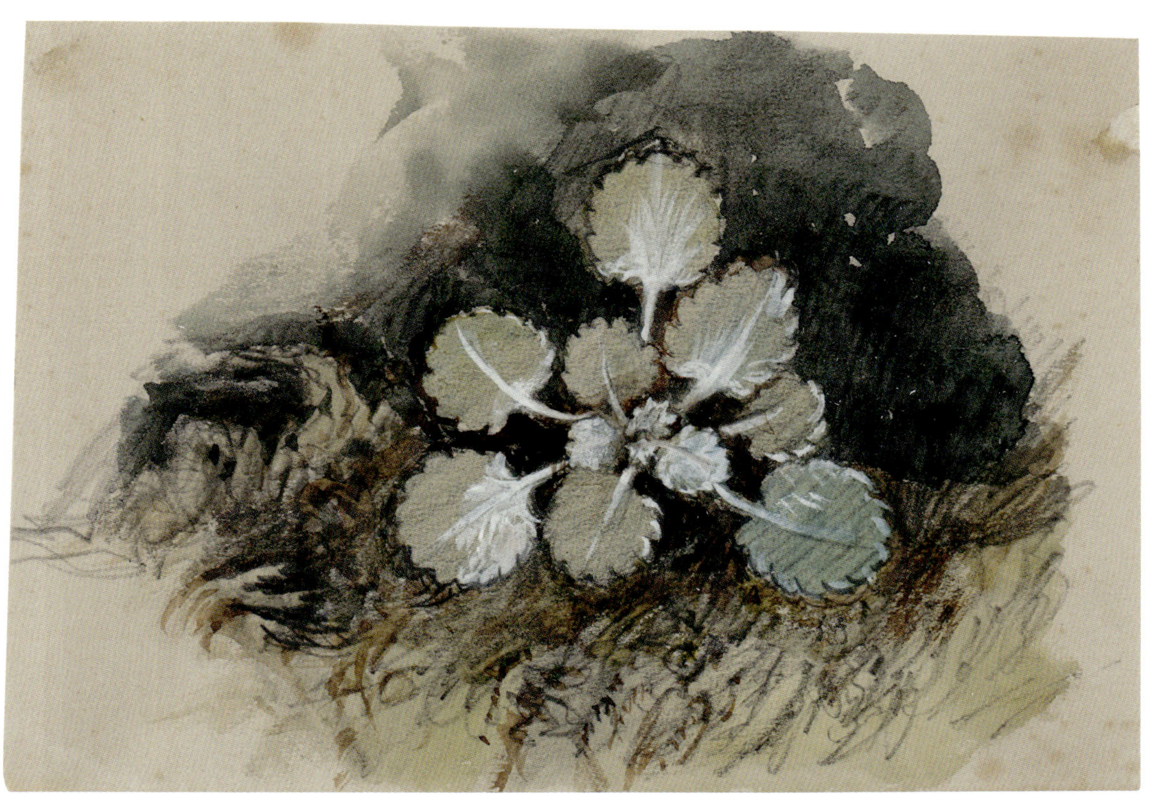

101 John Ruskin, *Leaf Cluster*, *c.*1885, graphite pencil and watercolor on paper, 10 × 14.1 cm (3 ⅞ × 5 ½ in), Museum of Fine Arts Boston, Boston, MA

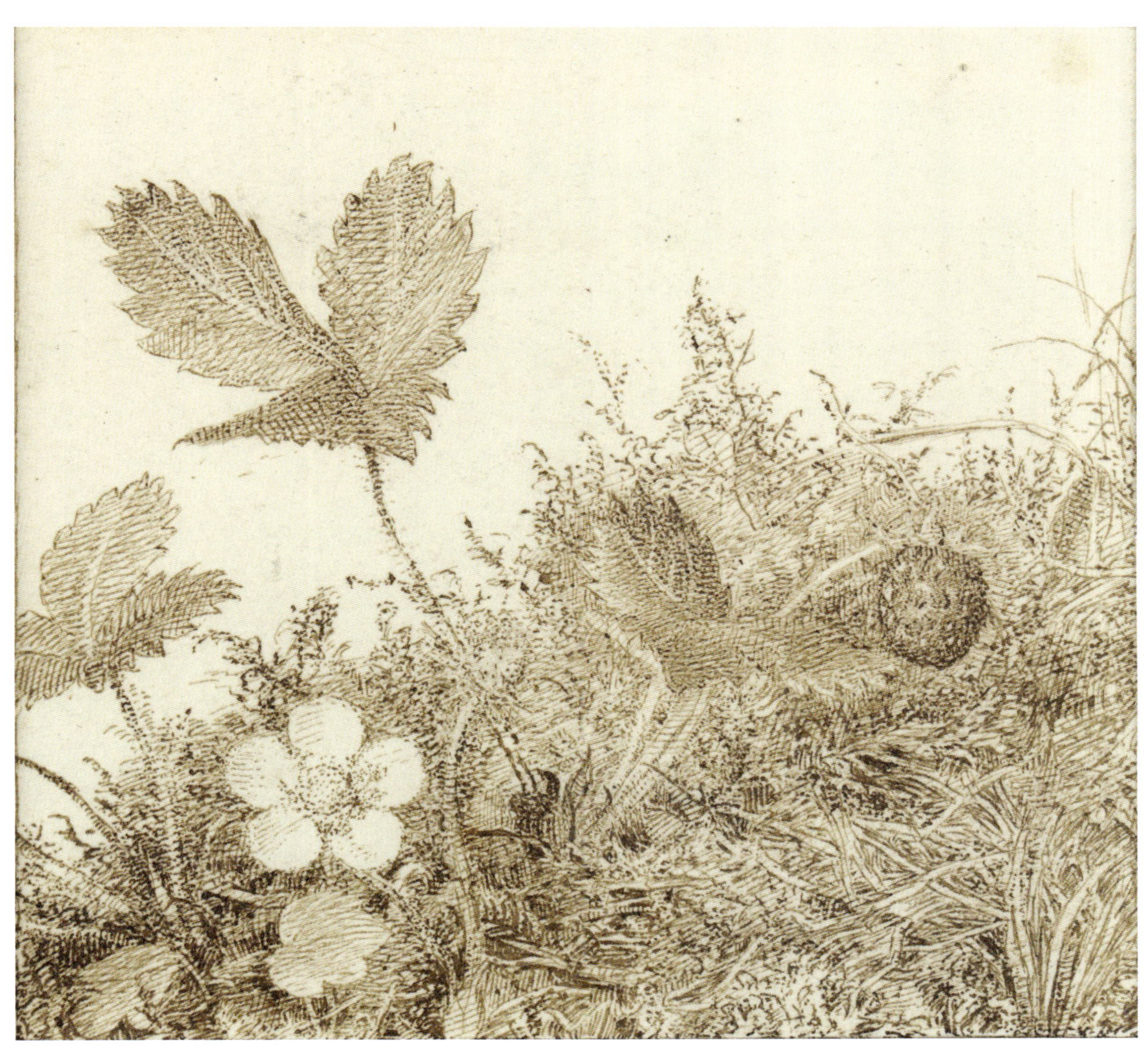

102 Francesca Alexander, *Study of a Wild Strawberry Plant*, c.1870s, pencil and ink, 5.4 × 6.35 cm (2 ⅛ × 2 ½ in),
Victoria and Albert Museum, London

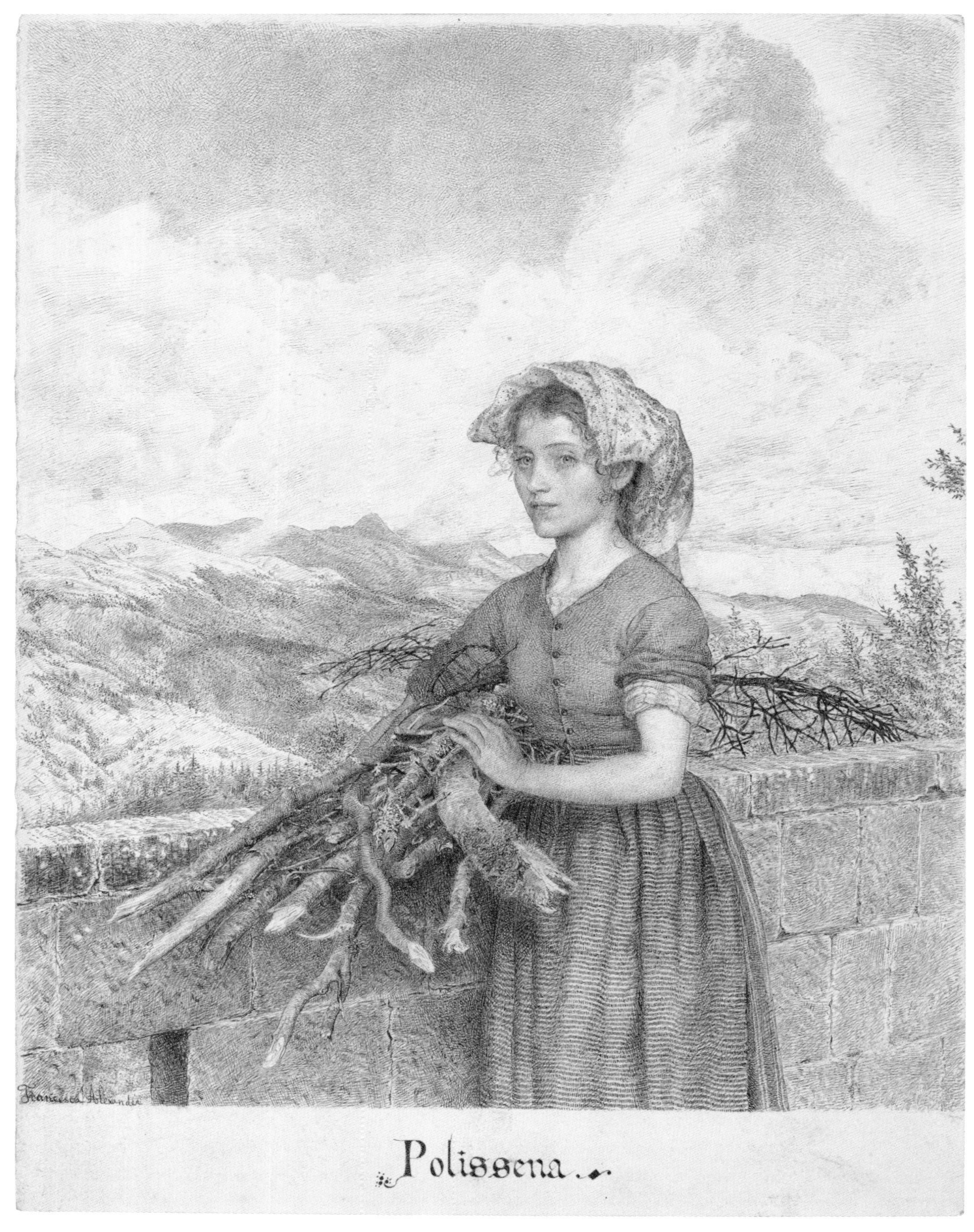

103 Francesca Alexander, *Polissena*, *c.*1884, pen and ink, approx. 30 × 23 cm (11 ¾ × 9 in),
Wellesley College Special Collections, Wellesley, MA

weak, instructing her to practice more, or to copy flowers from paintings by Renaissance artists like Sandro Botticelli and Fra Filippo Lippi.[109] But these sketches, including one of saxifrage with its distinctive serrated edges (fig.101), are in varying stages of finish and could not be intended as models for her work. Instead, it seems he simply gathered up these sheets, which seem to be related to the drawings and outlines of plants he included in his *Proserpina* (1875–86), and put them in an envelope with one of his letters.[110] Francesca reciprocated, at one point sending a tiny pen and ink of a strawberry plant, a densely rendered representation of nature taken from a low vantage point as if to give an insect's view, with two of the plant's stalks looming up at left (fig.102). That close attention to natural detail had long been Ruskin's taste, and it is rendered here in her precise style, with forms delineated by outline, cross-hatching and stippling to create a variety of shades, from very dark in the areas of the densest cross-hatching where the plants are near the ground or shadowed, to very light where the strawberry petals and some of the stalks and grasses are formed by reserved paper.

Francesca also continued to send Ruskin stories about the lives of her Italian friends. There were so many that he decided to assemble what he called her 'word-portraits, finished as tenderly as her drawings, and of even higher value in their accuracy of penetration', into a third publication entitled *Christ's Folk in the Apennine* (1887).[111] Francesca explained Ruskin's process, and her removal from it, to Lilly: 'Mr Ruskin selects out of my letters to him any scraps that take his fancy; and often I can't imagine what he selects them for; but I suppose he knows best, and I never make any suggestions.'[112] Although Ruskin added occasional commentary and notes, his claim that he changed none of her writing is probably true because his health was again failing.[113] This may also be why the arrangement is so haphazard, with stories about many of Francesca's friends – including Maria Zanchetta, who ran an orphanage for girls in Bassano,

Giannina Milli, several of Edwige's family members, and others from Florence and elsewhere – and a number of popular songs, gathered together without a consistent organizing principle.

Christ's Folk was also a serial publication, released in six installments from March 1887 to November 1887 and then assembled as a volume that year; although he planned to continue the installments to assemble a second volume, only one more appeared in 1889. Neither the installments nor the first volume was illustrated, but a combined edition, which came out in 1901 after Ruskin's death, had one illustration, Francesca's portrait of her friend Polissena, a *contadina* from the Abetone region with a difficult life whom Francesca nevertheless described as the happiest person she knew (fig.103). Ruskin had requested this drawing of Polissena in a landscape when he was thinking of publishing the young woman's story separately, as a companion to *The Story of Ida*, in 1884.[114] In 1892, William G. Collingwood, who hoped Francesca might continue the installments herself, told Lucia that Ruskin had copied out many of Francesca's letters, 'but it wants editing. I don't understand enough about Italy + the Italians. If somebody doesn't do something, all Mr. Ruskin's trouble will be lost.'[115] But Francesca would have had little interest in doing this, and the preparatory work Collingwood described has not been traced.

Ida, *Roadside Songs* and *Christ's Folk* required a great deal of collaboration, sometimes resulting in multiple letters and page proofs crossing land and water each week. It was fortunate that Ruskin and Francesca were so dedicated to their correspondence because they only saw each other once more, in September 1888, when Ruskin met the Alexanders at the home of Marina Sprea Baroni Semitecolo in Bassano. He was feted by the Alexanders and their Italian friends, whom he described as 'among the kindest people in the world'.[116] Yet he was deeply unhappy, and he departed unexpectedly to make his way back to England. Of course, after meeting in person only four times almost six years earlier, this gathering must have felt somewhat awkward. Surely his illness was evident, but Francesca later described it in positive terms:

> He seemed not so strong as I could have wished, (though mentally quite well,) but he liked the place, and the people; and he gained all their hearts, with his kind ways . . . It was a week never to be forgotten, and which I can hardly hope will ever be renewed, and he did not think Italy suited him, and therefore will probably not return to it.[117]

Indeed, following this journey Ruskin never fully recovered, and he died in January 1900.

5

'A Medieaval Saint'

John Ruskin must have earned significant profits from his work on *Roadside Songs* and *Christ's Folk*, and though both he and the publisher wrote to tell Francesca of the strong sales, there is no indication that she shared in those profits beyond an occasional gift from Ruskin.[1] In fact, Ruskin told Francesca that he was keeping the profits from *Roadside Songs*, 'till you can be quite sure I'm paid scot and lot for every jot of trouble I had with it'.[2] But the Alexanders were financially secure; they had income from their savings and investments, as well as Francesca's earnings from *The Story of Ida* and the art purchased by the many travelers who came to their door. They could afford their modest lifestyle as well as Francesca's charitable work.

As they aged, however, they faced several health problems. Francesca's vision was increasingly poor, exacerbated by both her drawing method and what was described as an accident with a stove in Bassano.[3] In 1890, after months of debilitating pain, Lucia had a large benign tumor removed in a risky operation in their home; the surgeon cautioned that there was a 75 per cent chance Lucia would not survive, but that she would surely die within months without intervention.[4] During her long recovery, she required constant care from Francesca, Edwige and others. At the same time, the Alexanders were grieving the loss of many of their friends; by 1888, Beatrice di Pian degli Ontani, Marianna Capponi Farinola, Caterina Percoto, Gigina Milli Castorani and Giannina Milli, among others, were dead. Francesca tried to console herself with the knowledge that 'it is very pleasant to have so many friends in heaven, and to think that, if ever it pleases the Lord to take me there, I shall not be a stranger'.[5] But this must have been an incredibly challenging period.

Perhaps prompted by these medical emergencies and losses, the Alexander women endeavored to put their estate in order. Some of their efforts were small; in 1896, Lucia sent a Hayward engagement ring she had inherited back to that family.[6] But other efforts were more involved; in 1891 Francesca wrote out their wills and had them witnessed by consular officials.[7] Despite their long residence in Italy, they described themselves as Bostonians in these wills. Many Florentines thought of them in this way, too; when Mrs Felton visited them in 1903, a grocer directing her to their home described them as *forestieri*, or foreigners.[8] The women left everything to each other, and, if there was no survivor, to descendants of Lucia's brothers. Curiously, the wills provided no charitable bequests to institutions in Italy or in the United States, despite Francesca's lifelong efforts to help the needy.

But their connection to Italy remained strong. They continued to be part of the congregation at Florence's Evangelical church and were offered a leadership role that would have required them to interact with the city government on behalf of the institution; Francesca demurred, stating that such positions were not for women.[9] She much preferred engaging in charitable work in a less official capacity. In her letters to Ruskin and Constance Oldham, she described the help she gave cholera victims and those suffering from Florence's harsh winters, the funds she provided to Bassano's Cucina Economica to feed the needy, and the money she sent to a sick *contadina* so the girl could make a restorative seaside visit.[10] In 1891, echoing William Stillman's earlier assessment, Thomas Ball wrote that Francesca was still 'devoting her time and talents to charity, principally among the poor contadini, who little less than worship her as a Saint'.[11]

The Alexanders continued to leave Florence during the warmer months. But their Abetone summers came to an end in 1887, when the increasing number of tourists changed the character of the place and a crime wave forced them to hire an escort to get home.[12] They began to spend more time in Venice, where they enjoyed visits with friends and the monks at San Lazzaro.[13] They also traveled to various Alpine towns and to Bassano, where they stayed in their own wing of Marina Sprea Baroni Semitecolo's Villa Rezzonico. Anna Lloyd described a humble meal she shared with them there in 1898:

> It looked lovely to begin with, set out in a cool quiet room with a charmingly decorated ceiling. The table cloth was not white, but a siena red, and there were grapes, and peaches, and vases of flowers, and different coloured plates . . . The pudding [Francesca] had made herself. She took us into her kitchen, where she helps the contadini to prepare the dishes she and her Mother can eat.[14]

Marina's daughter Silvia often joined them during these visits, and it may have been through her that the Alexanders met the Italian poet Giosuè Carducci, who received a Nobel Prize in literature in 1906. A year earlier they sent him a gift of salmon, and he described Francesca in a letter as 'the famous American who speaks and writes Italian so well'.[15]

Francesca's celebrity persisted. In 1890, Horace E. Scudder, editor of *The Atlantic Monthly* and a prominent Boston literary figure, invited her to write a biography of either the Dominican friar Girolamo Savonarola or Saint Francis of Assisi for a series of children's books published by Riverside Library. Francesca certainly was familiar with both men. In Savonarola's case, she knew the recent biography by another Florentine resident, senator and historian Pasquale Villari, and she probably knew Villari and his wife, the Englishwoman and author Linda White, too. But in the case of Saint Francis, she had long felt an affinity with the friar, an affinity Cardinal Manning noted years earlier when commending *The Story of Ida*.[16] Nevertheless, she turned down Scudder's invitation: 'I do not think that I should succeed very well in historical writing; it would be quite new to me, and such faculty as I have is rather for describing people whom I have known, and places which I have seen.'[17] This had been true for her art, too; she always preferred to draw or paint those she knew. Instead, she debated putting together some of the legends associated with Francis from various books she had collected, and from consultation with friends in the Franciscan order, to demonstrate his enduring relevance, but nothing came of this.

For many travelers, the purchase of a work of art was still the best reminder of a meeting with Francesca. She did draw several portraits in the late 1880s, all with minimal settings and her familiar dense cross-hatching and stippling of facial features and costume. One, identified by an inscription as her friend Assuntina from Viterbo, is accompanied by lines from a popular Tuscan song (fig.104).[18]

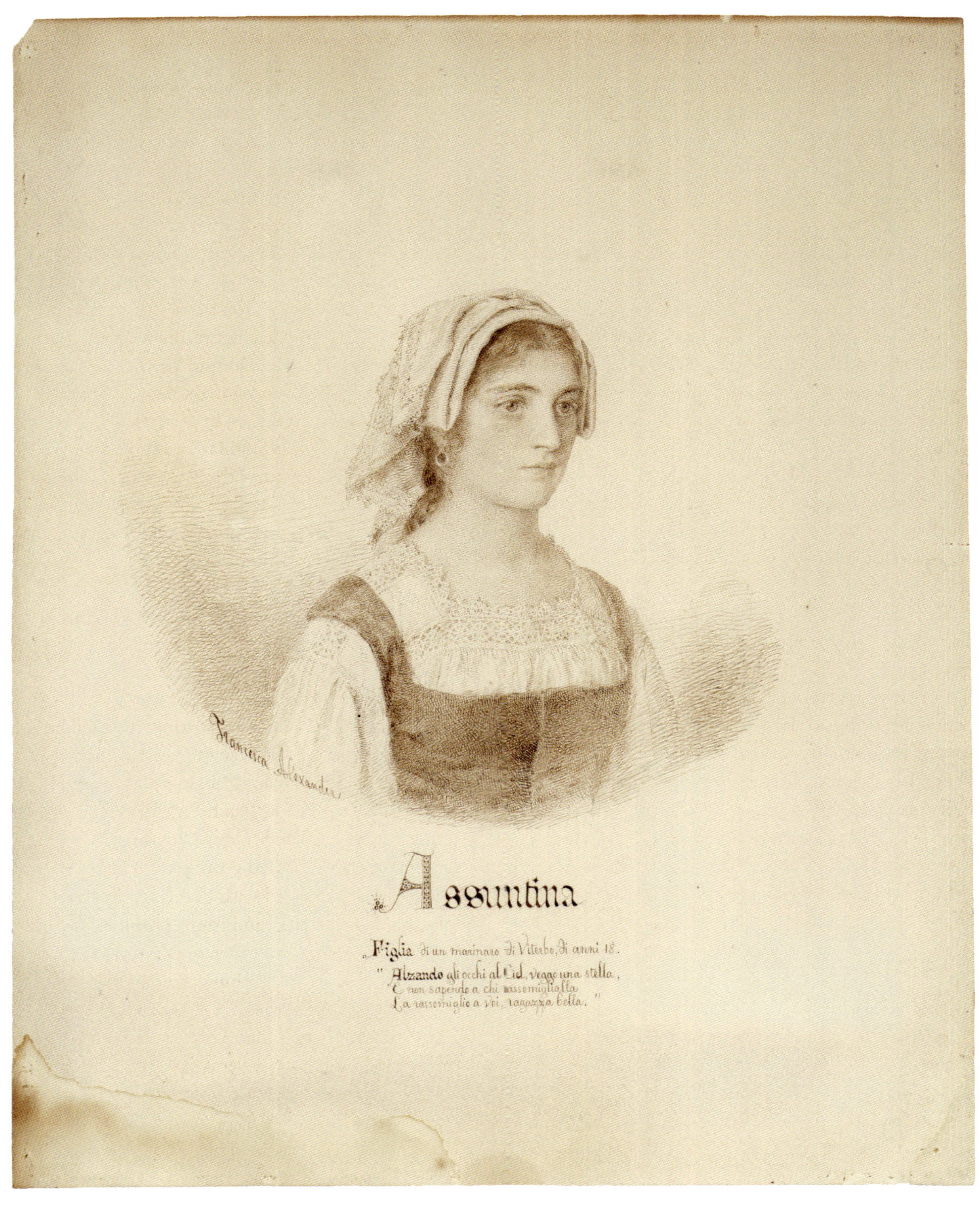

104 Francesca Alexander, *Assuntina*, 1880s, pen and ink on heavy stock paper, 31.5 × 25.1 cm (12 ⅜ × 9 ⅞ in), McGuigan Collection, Harpswell, ME

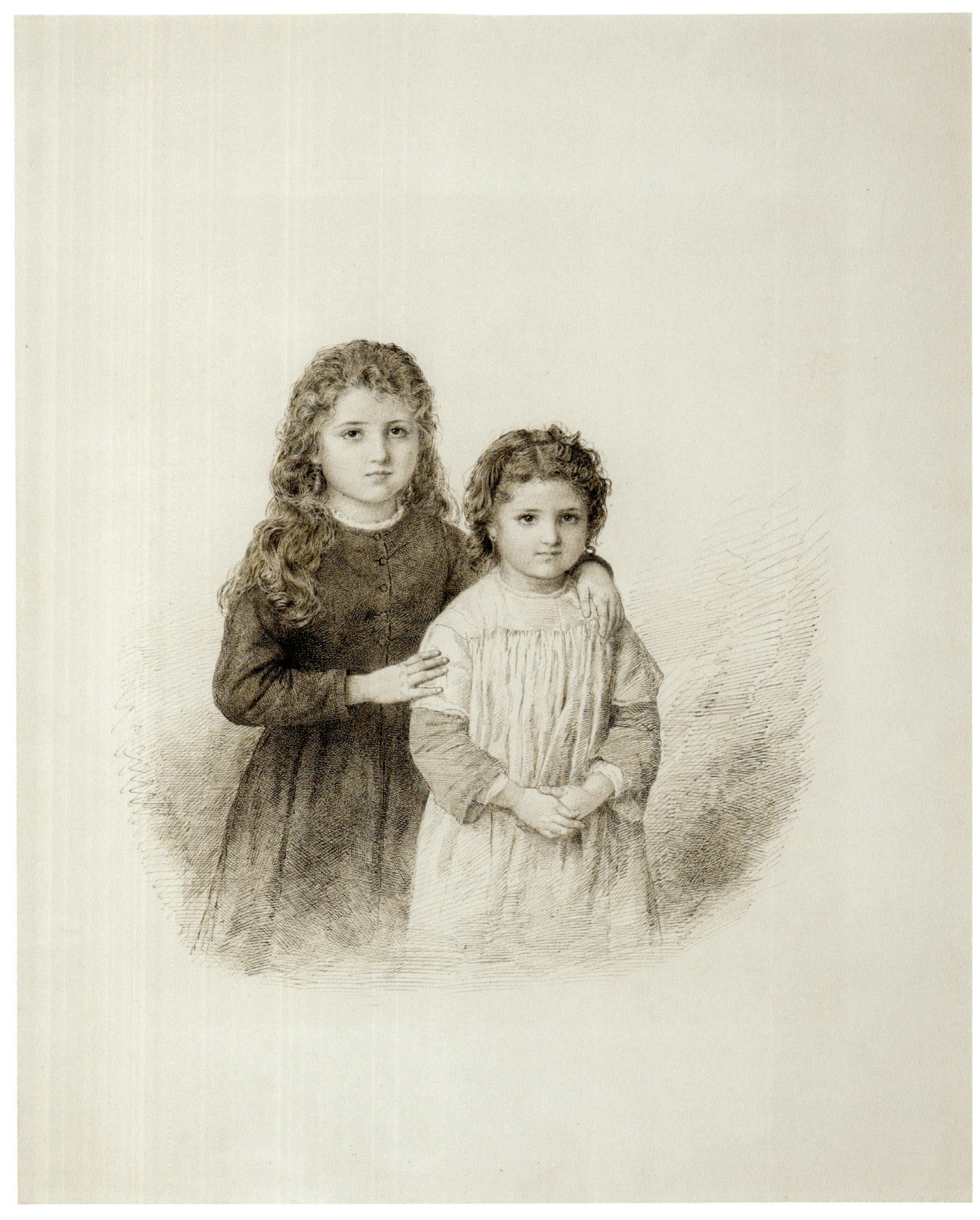

105 Francesca Alexander, *Two Sisters*, 1880s, pen and black ink on paper, 50.7 × 39.4 cm (20 × 15½ in), Museum of Fine Arts Boston, Boston, MA

Another, larger drawing, her most accomplished from this period, represents two young girls, likely sisters, their earrings, simple dress and loose dark hair almost certainly marking them as Italians, perhaps two of Edwige's grandchildren, or children from one of the families Francesca assisted with charity and friendship (fig.105). Although the pose differs, this drawing may be an homage to Washington Allston's painting of two sisters, her father's first major purchase and one Francesca would have remembered from her childhood; Allston painted the women from behind while Francesca drew them from the front, but in both the taller figure has her arms around the shorter to imply a tight bond.

In 1889, Francesca sent a drawing of Edwige's seven-year-old granddaughter Sandrina, wearing earrings and a smocked dress, her long hair over her shoulders, to the author Charles Warren Stoddard (fig.106). He had gifted her a copy of his book, *The Lepers of Molokai* (1885), about the Belgian priest (and now saint) Father Damien, who selflessly ministered to a leper colony in what was then the Kingdom of Hawai'i.[19] Francesca was thrilled by the book – Stoddard included an enthusiastic quote from her in a later edition – and, when Father Damien died shortly after this, she grieved with Stoddard.[20] At this date she was still hopeful her sight would improve; she told Stoddard her drawing was the only finished 'little head' she had left, but she did not want to send an unfinished one, 'as there is just a chance that I may be able, some day, to work again'.[21] Stoddard described the gift to a friend: 'the gentle Francesca of Florence has sent me one of her exquisite pen and ink sketches: you know Ruskin raves over them'.[22]

In 1890, after lamenting the departure or death of sculptors Hiram Powers, Joel Tanner Hart, John Adams Jackson, Edward Thaxter and Launt Thompson, and painters Lizzie Boott, Frank Duveneck and Ross Turner, journalist Theodore Stanton wrote about the American artists still active in Florence, noting that, 'Miss Alexander still works on in her small studio on the top of the hotel where she lives, patiently and nobly as ever, doing good to all men and women, whether or no they be of the household of Faith.'[23] However, as Francesca herself noted, her eyesight had failed. In 1893, her old friend Georgina Forbes wrote that Francesca 'no longer creates saints with her pencil she lives the life of one wh[ich] is better'.[24] The great strain caused by years of creating detailed drawings and fine calligraphy in poorly lit interiors had taken a toll. In the early 1870s she began to write letters in what she called 'blind writing', scrawled without looking to lessen eye strain. When it was particularly bad, her mother or a hired scribe wrote on her behalf.[25] She met with several specialists in Venice and Switzerland, who implied that her vision might improve if she took better care of her overall health.[26] But this never happened, and no art can be dated to the last decades of her life.

Some travelers were persistent in their efforts to secure these few remaining drawings. Chicagoans Frances and John Glessner and their daughter Frances (later Frances Glessner Lee, the founder of the first department of forensic science in the United States and the creator of the *Nutshell Studies of Unexplained Death*) met Francesca in 1890. They had extensive social contacts in the Boston area, and it is likely that one of those friends advised them to visit Francesca during their tour of Italy. They carried with them an address book with recommendations for dressmakers, restaurants and more, including Francesca's name, address and reception hours, noting she was 'The Authoress of the "Roadside songs of Tuscany"' who was 'Always glad to meet Americans'.[27] However, perhaps because they associated her with Ruskin, they confused her nationality (and, unlike many, underestimated her age): 'Found her a substantial English woman about 48 years old, of the artistic coming to pieces appearance, who received us most cordially.'[28]

The Glessners claimed their visit to Francesca's studio, together with a stop in the Bargello and a

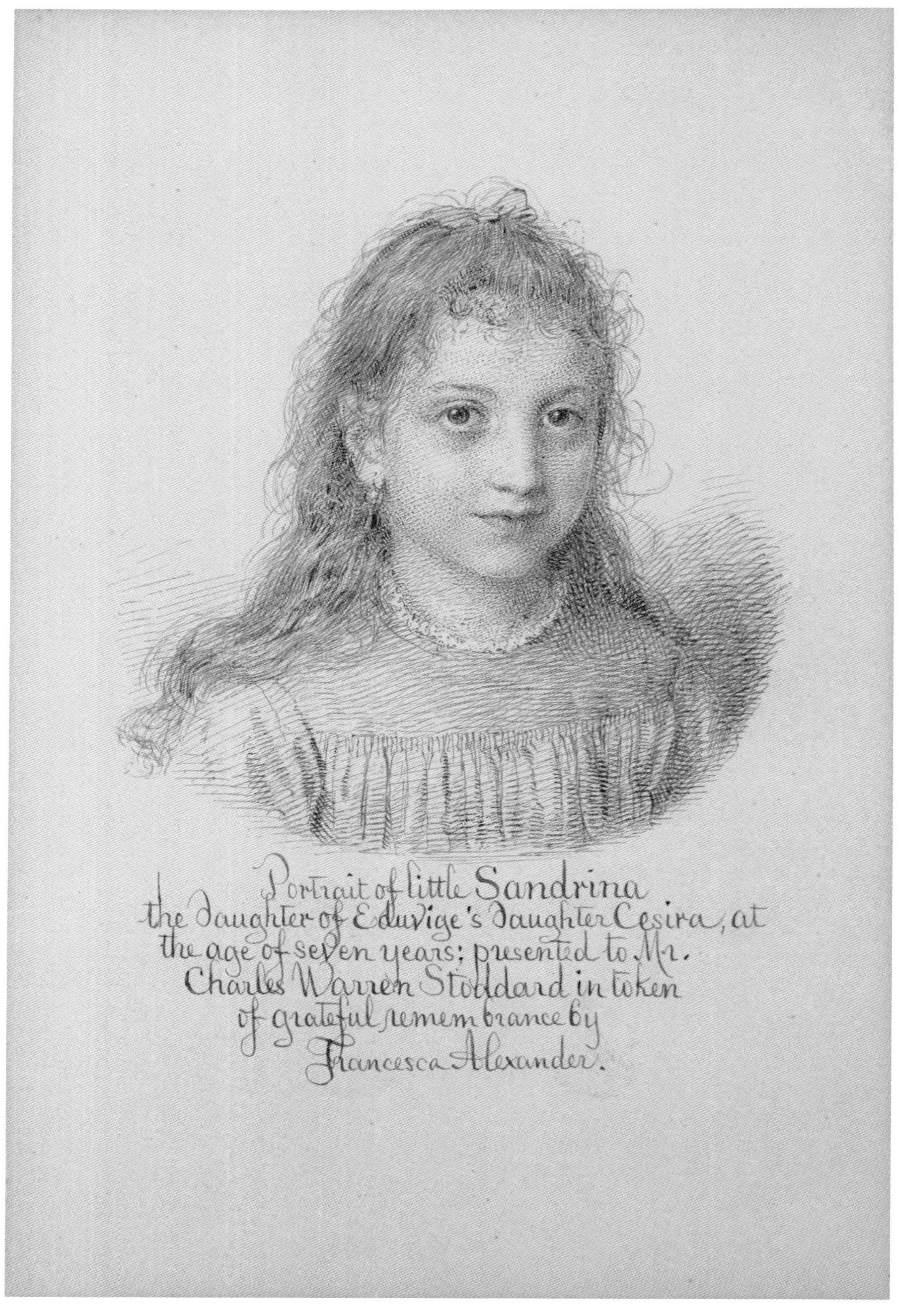

106 Francesca Alexander, *Little Sandrina*, 1880s, pen and ink, 18.73 × 12.7 cm (7⅜ × 5 in),
McMullen Museum of Art, Boston College, Boston, MA

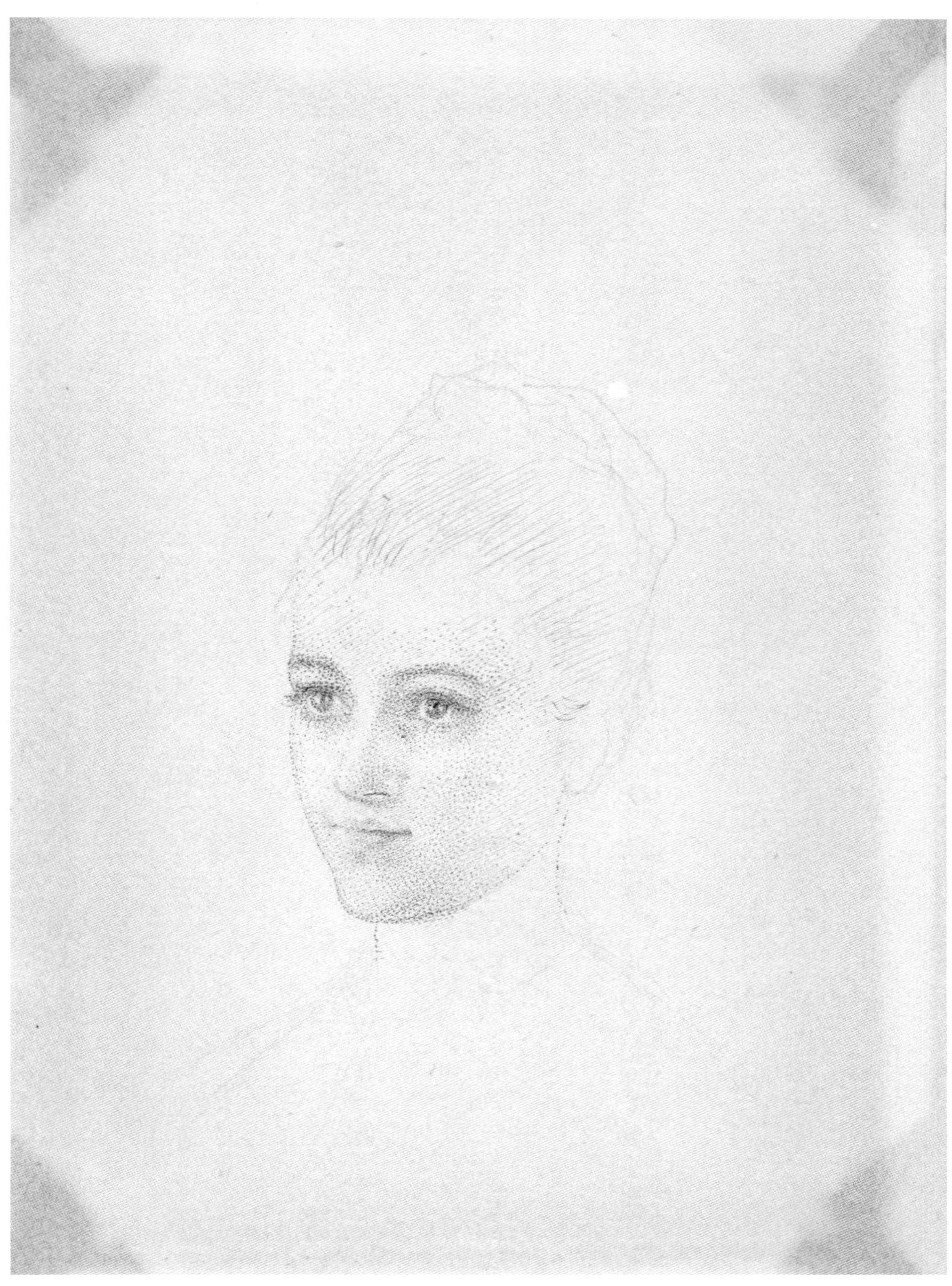

107 Francesca Alexander, *Unidentified Woman*, 1860s?, pen and ink, 13.3 × 9.2 cm. (5 ¼ × 3 ⅝ in), Glessner House, Chicago, IL

carriage ride to Bellosguardo, was 'more to our taste than most of the sightseeing'.[29] But they had trouble obtaining a souvenir of their experience. Francesca said that she had only a few unfinished drawings on hand, which were part of a series – if that were true, nothing ever came of it – and she could not part with them. Unwilling to take no for an answer, the Glessners sent their daughter's companion to the Bonciani with a great bouquet of flowers, and Francesca agreed to sell two drawings. The first, from several decades earlier, represents a young woman with her hair stylishly piled high, presumably a portrait of a friend or patron but left unfinished (fig.107). The second, signed and in the same format as other portraits from the 1880s, depicts an older woman in three-quarter view from the chest up, her eyes lowered, a simple ruff peeking out from the neck and placket of her bodice (fig.108). The Glessners described it as the head of a peasant woman, but it is certainly Edwige, recognizable from *Roadside Songs* (fig.99) and a contemporary photograph.[30] They left a standing order for anything else she might have to sell, and in 1892 Francesca offered them a drawing of Ersilia di Cola from Abetone, 'a little wild mountain girl who used to earn her living . . . by carrying great loads of wood down the steep paths on her shoulders' (fig.109).[31] According to Francesca, Ersilia 'was not beautiful and looked rather thin and feeble', but she priced the drawing at 100 francs because 'I am not likely ever to draw anymore'.[32] The Glessners, who also owned a copy of *The Story of Ida*, were pleased with this drawing, and Lucia placed Mrs Glessner's letter of thanks in one of her scrapbooks.[33]

Most of Francesca's art, however, circulated in the Boston area. Bostonians occasionally saw it on display at the Museum of Fine Arts. Caroline Brewer loaned four of her drawings in 1885; in 1894 Elizabeth Brooks, the wife of architect Edmund March Wheelwright, loaned Francesca's painting of a Madonna and Child – likely the painting formerly in the Davis collection – and Lucia's niece Mary Coolidge Swett sent two paintings by Francesca, and three by Francis, to that year's annual loan exhibition.[34] Articles about her art and life continued to appear in the popular press, echoing the awestruck comments made by many of her visitors.[35] Some of these visitors were other Anglo-American residents of Italy. In 1892, Newport native Olivia Cushing Andersen wrote at length about mother and daughter in her diary:

Miss Alexander is like a little child + has almost angelic simplicity. I can imagine how all her poor people must adore her. Their rooms are filled with all sorts of pictures, books + old curiosities. On the roof Miss A. has a lovely little garden. Mrs A says she has started numberless gardeners in the neighborhood. Every day a number of dinnerless people come + are fed by her + helped in different ways. They both take the greatest interest in art + letters, Miss A writes + has published a good many of her experiences with the poor. She seems almost an ideal person, with such sweetness, one of those who go through the world + see nothing but good in it. When she sees misery, her mother told us, she does not shrink from it but is almost glad as she thinks how much she can relieve it. We happened to mention turquoises + Mrs A. immediately said: 'Francesca, dear, you know that tin box downstairs, go + get it for me + I'll see what I've got in it.' So Francesca got her the box + she found two dear little turquoise bracelets of which she gave one to [Lucia Lice, the muse of Olivia's brother-in-law, the artist Hendrik Christian Andersen] + one to me, + then a dozen + ½ silver buttons to [Lucia] + a little silver nécessaire to me. Hers seems a life worth living . . . Miss A. seems utterly to ignore her goodness, to take for granted that anyone w[ou]ld do the same.[36]

Other travelers were enchanted by similar gifts, like the strings of coral, card case, purse and brooch, and flowers from the sky parlor, given to Anna Lloyd's niece and her friend, or the bookmark Francesca painted with Renaissance ornament and an

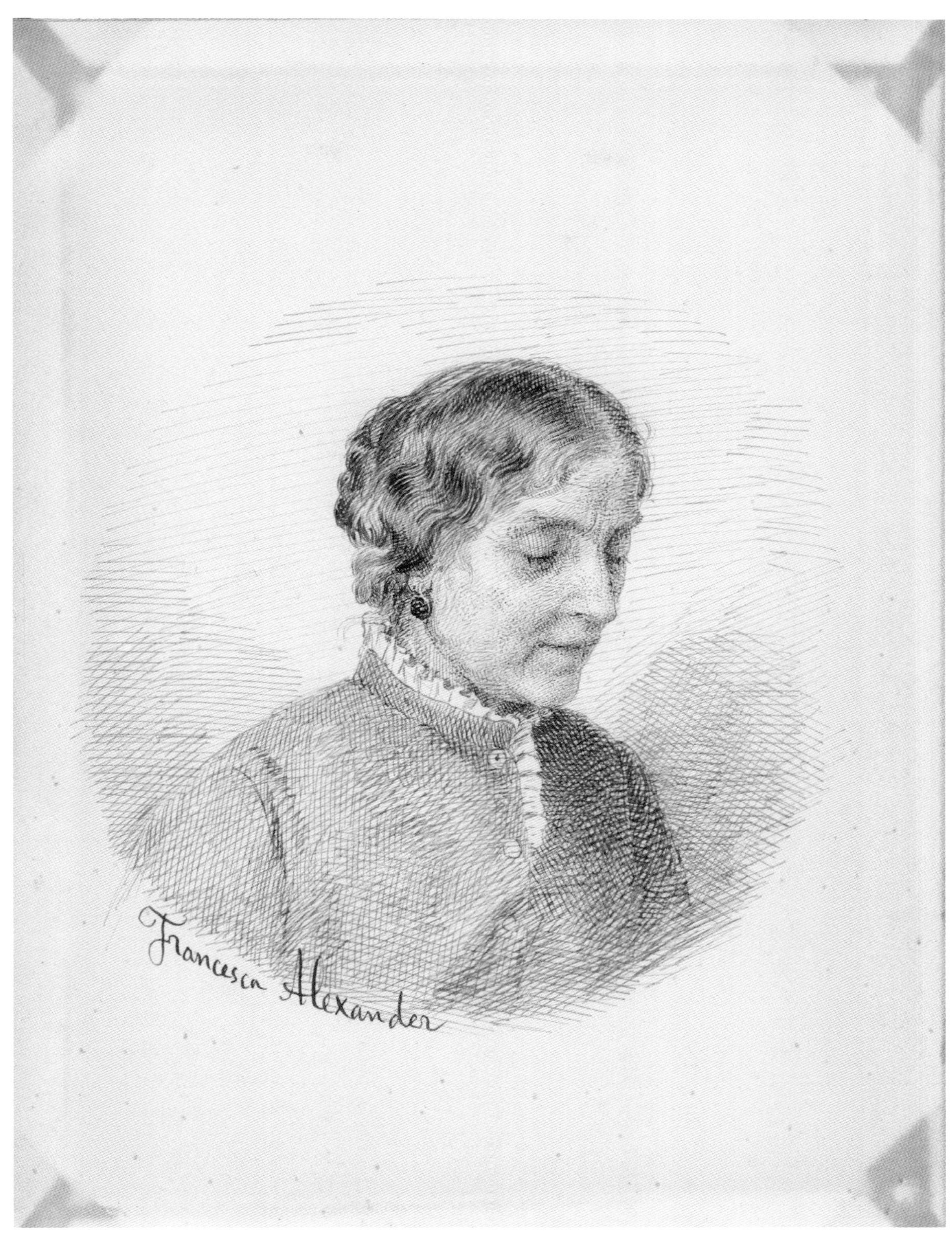

108 Francesca Alexander, *Edwige Gualtieri*, 1880s, pen and ink, 19.37 × 13.9 cm (7⅝ × 5½ in), Glessner House, Chicago, IL

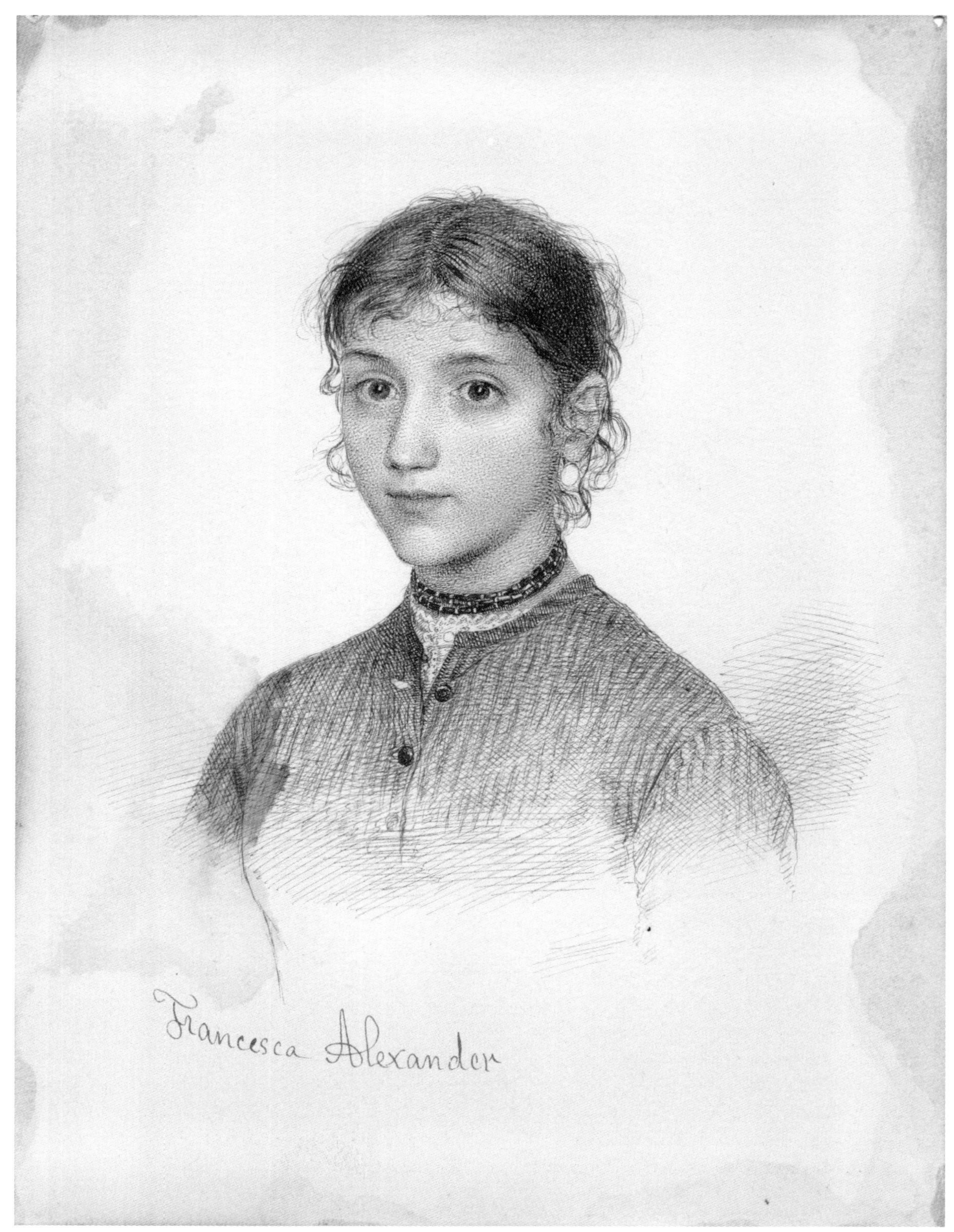

109 Francesca Alexander, *Ersilia di Cola*, 1880s, pen and ink, 20.6 × 15.6 cm (8 ⅛ × 6 ⅛ in), Glessner House, Chicago, IL

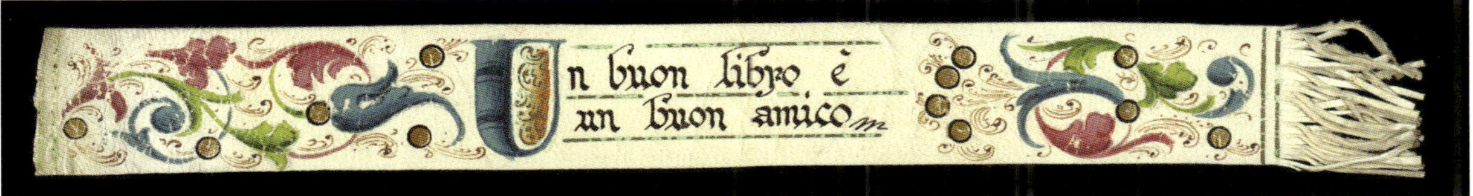

110 Francesca Alexander, hand-painted bookmark, in Constance Grosvenor Alexander's copy of *The Hidden Servants and Other Very Old Stories* (Boston, MA: Little, Brown & Co., 1900), leather, 21.5 × 2.5 cm (8 ½ × 1 in), Wellesley College Special Collections, Wellesley, MA

inscription for her cousin Constance Grosvenor Alexander (fig.110).[37] On other occasions, the women sent their servants to the train station with baskets of food for departing friends.[38]

The American author Lilian Whiting was introduced to the Alexanders through their mutual friend, the Florence-born singer Isabel MacDougall, whose father, Reverend John Richardson MacDougall, was associated with the Scottish Presbyterian Church there. Whiting was struck by Francesca's appearance and character:

> In her absolute simplicity of dress, with hair black as a raven's wing, and arranged after the Madonna fashion, she seemed to have just stepped from the walls of Santa Maria Novella, or some other *chiesa*, where saints most do congregate in pictorial evidence … She was reticent, yet cordial, and at times very fluent in conversation. She was the friend of the poorer people, who adored her … that particular order of the universe which we know as the great world made no impression at all upon her; she would have treated the poorest peasant with the utmost courtesy; she could not have done more for one of the Strozzi princesses. She lived in a world where conventional distinctions had little recognition.[39]

This impression of a sanctified aura was emphasized by Lucia's niece and namesake Lucia Gray Swett, who later wrote Francesca's biography.

She visited mother and daughter in Italy and mined that experience as the basis for several poems in her collection *Sisters of Reparatrice* (1902), including one, simply entitled 'To Francesca', about her cousin:

> Peace and joy, beloved Francesca,
> Ev'ry mercy crown this day.
> Thy own heart reflect the sunshine
> Shed about thee on thy way.
> And as thou art nobly using
> Those great gifts bestowed on thee,
> Gladdening this world of sorrow,
> Heaven grows more fair to see.
> For the angels paint in glory
> Pictures, that the saints above
> May know all thy deeds of kindness
> And thy patient works of love.[40]

Francesca's visitors continued to treat her as one of Florence's attractions; they were happy to be in her saintly presence. Around 1890, Eugenia Brooks Frothingham described her as 'indeed a saint, as good a one as Saint Francis, if not so great'.[41] In 1892, the Alexanders spent time with Bostonian Margaret Cabot and her family in Venice, where Francesca brought them to San Lazzaro and Ghevont Alishan gave them a tour of the complex and its gardens. Margaret was as entranced by Francesca as she was by the monastery:

Miss Alexander is just like a Medieaval saint, a fitting
guide to such a place. Coming home slowly in the
twilight Miss A. sang hymns to us with a sweet strange
voice. She did'nt [*sic*] sing them to us, she sang them
to Spirits in Heaven, leaning forward + holding her
hands up with a rapt expression in her eyes. After
singing 'Lead Kindly Light' she said, 'that's a good one
for me, I have so many waiting for me up there'.[42]

Margaret and her family were so fond of their friends
that when they parted she wrote that they 'were torn
asunder from the Alexanders with grief'.[43]

The American painter Joseph Lindon Smith and
his brother also enjoyed the Alexanders' company.
The men arrived in Florence in 1889 with a letter of
introduction, perhaps from John Greenleaf Whittier,
a cousin of their mother, Emma Greenleaf Smith.
Smith found Francesca's art 'commonplace', but he
was charmed by her nonetheless: 'She is very queer
looking and has funny strange ways. I should have
said she was in a dream or trance – she had such
a very "far away" look in her eyes and though she
made a few leading questions and remarks, I did
most of the talking.'[44] The Alexanders and the Smith
brothers were in Venice that summer, all residing at
the Palazzo Dario, across the Grand Canal from San
Marco in the Dorsoduro area. Ruskin admired and
painted the palace and its polychrome ornament,
which was owned at different times by his friends
Rawdon Brown and Fanny Talbot, so it is not
surprising that the Smiths and the Alexanders all
chose to stay there (fig.111). In a letter to his parents
from Venice, Joseph described Lucia as:

a funny little old lady . . . She is rather short and has
brownish hair in wave-like forms on her forehead and
falling down on either side, partly hiding her ears. She
wears what looks exactly like a tidy from the arm of
an armchair. She talks a good deal and very rapidly
and had a good deal to say to me. I found her very
interesting indeed and as bright as a dollar.

He continued with another description of Francesca,
who 'sat with her back to the light, making a stocking.
She is very picturesque though not good looking
and wears her hair in a net which is real, one of
the invisible kind. I should rather like to paint her
portrait though it would be difficult for me to tell
you why.'[45] Though he apparently never painted
that portrait, the families grew close; the Smith
brothers showed the Alexanders their sketches
and the Alexanders sent them a bottle of tamarind
syrup, which was used as both a summer drink and a
laxative.[46]

Smith returned to Florence in 1894 and reported
to his mother, who had apparently visited the
Alexanders the year before:

I sat again in the old fashioned seeming dining room
and Francesca had bought strawberries specially for
the feast and they heaped two platefuls for me, and
how good they were! I had all sorts of Boston news to
tell Mrs Alexander – I thought items up beforehand
and she was as deeply interested as ever – and when
she had pumped me dry began herself and talked as
she is able to until Francesca took me up upon the
roof to her beloved garden – and we sat in her quaint
little studio room and she told me a charming peasants
ghost story. How out of this century she is – I couldn't
help feeling it as I sat there in her room filled as it
is with old pictures and remembrances of friends of
hers long since dead – and sitting in front of me the
interesting preRaphael like woman telling this strange
tale – in a voice so full of quaint mannerisms and
charm . . . I wish I could come to Florence sometime
and meet no one except the Alexanders.[47]

Smith repeated some of these impressions in
his diary, echoing Margaret Cabot by referring to
Francesca as medieval.[48] In fact, this was a common
sentiment among so many who encountered
the Alexanders. Charles Peirson, the husband of
Francesca's old friend Emily Russell, accompanied his

wife on a visit to the Alexanders in 1898 and described
both mother and daughter as medieval in his diary.[49]
Francesca's cousin Constance Grosvenor Alexander
later described her similarly as a 'Mediaevalist, with
the naïve outlook of a cloistered nun or a child-saint
of centuries ago'.[50]

Medieval here, of course, referred to that same
interest in *bric-à-brac*, in collecting objects from
what today would be described as the medieval and
Renaissance periods, objects that reminded viewers
of the romanticized European past. In the United
Kingdom this was closely tied to Victorian taste, to
Ruskin, William Morris and the Pre-Raphaelites,
and its popularity was readily replicated in the United
States. Francesca's appearance, her behavior and her
art all made that connection for her contemporaries;
she was medieval in the best sense of that term.

The Alexanders' lawyer Charles P. Bowditch and his
family were also frequent visitors during this period.
In 1898 the families socialized in Florence, Venice and
Lugano.[51] His daughter Cora described a May trip to
Florence, the first time she met the Alexanders:

> At last we have seen the long heard of 'Francesca' + her
> mother – The former welcomed us and we had a most
> attractive dinner – very filling – strawberries + whip
> cream! Mrs A. did not appear until afterwards – Miss
> A. most unique – hair in a net + sloping shoulders +
> low collar to the dress – most pleasant! Talkative – Mrs
> A. very bright + interested in everything – Showed us
> their pictures which were charming – They seem to
> love everything they have about them.[52]

A few days later, the families met again in Venice,
where they visited San Lazzaro and Ghevont Alishan
showed them the gardens, printing press, library
and even the herd of Swiss cows.[53] Cora sketched
Alishan and Lucia, the thin monk with his long
beard holding the hand of stout Lucia (fig.112), and
Francesca, in a modest view from behind, her blouse
cinched into the waist of her long skirt and her hair
tucked away in a net (fig.113). Later that summer, the

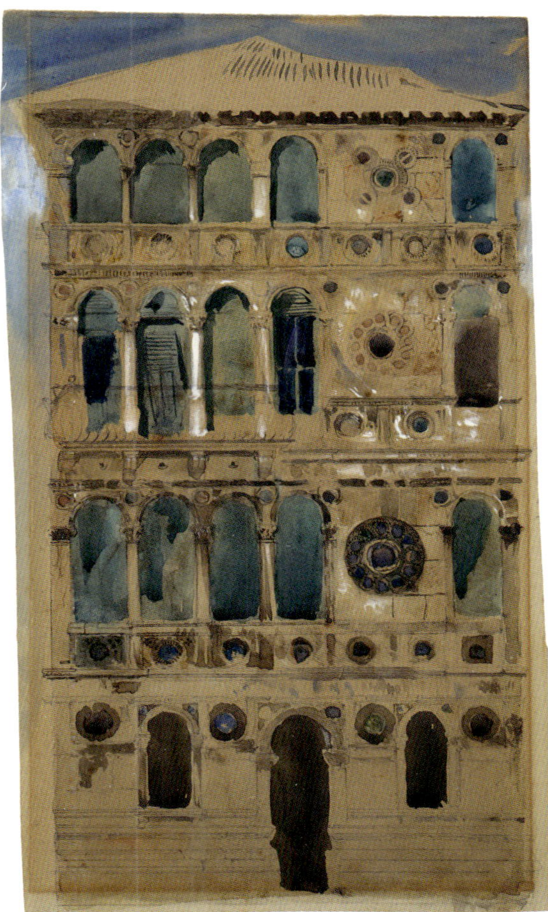

111 John Ruskin, *Palazzo Dario*, Venice, n.d., pencil, ink,
watercolor and bodycolor, 23.5 × 13.4 cm (9 ¼ × 5 ¼ in),
Lancaster University, Lancaster

families met again in Lugano, where they found the
Alexanders,

> ensconced in three small dark rooms on the front of
> the Hotel Washington, with a nice balcony + charming
> view. The rooms were rather desolate + we were rec[d] in
> Mrs. A. bed room after passing through Francesca's but
> as they told us we were the first people who had called
> on them, perhaps they need no better accommodation.
> They seemed well happy + were glad to see us + called
> on us the next day after dinner.[54]

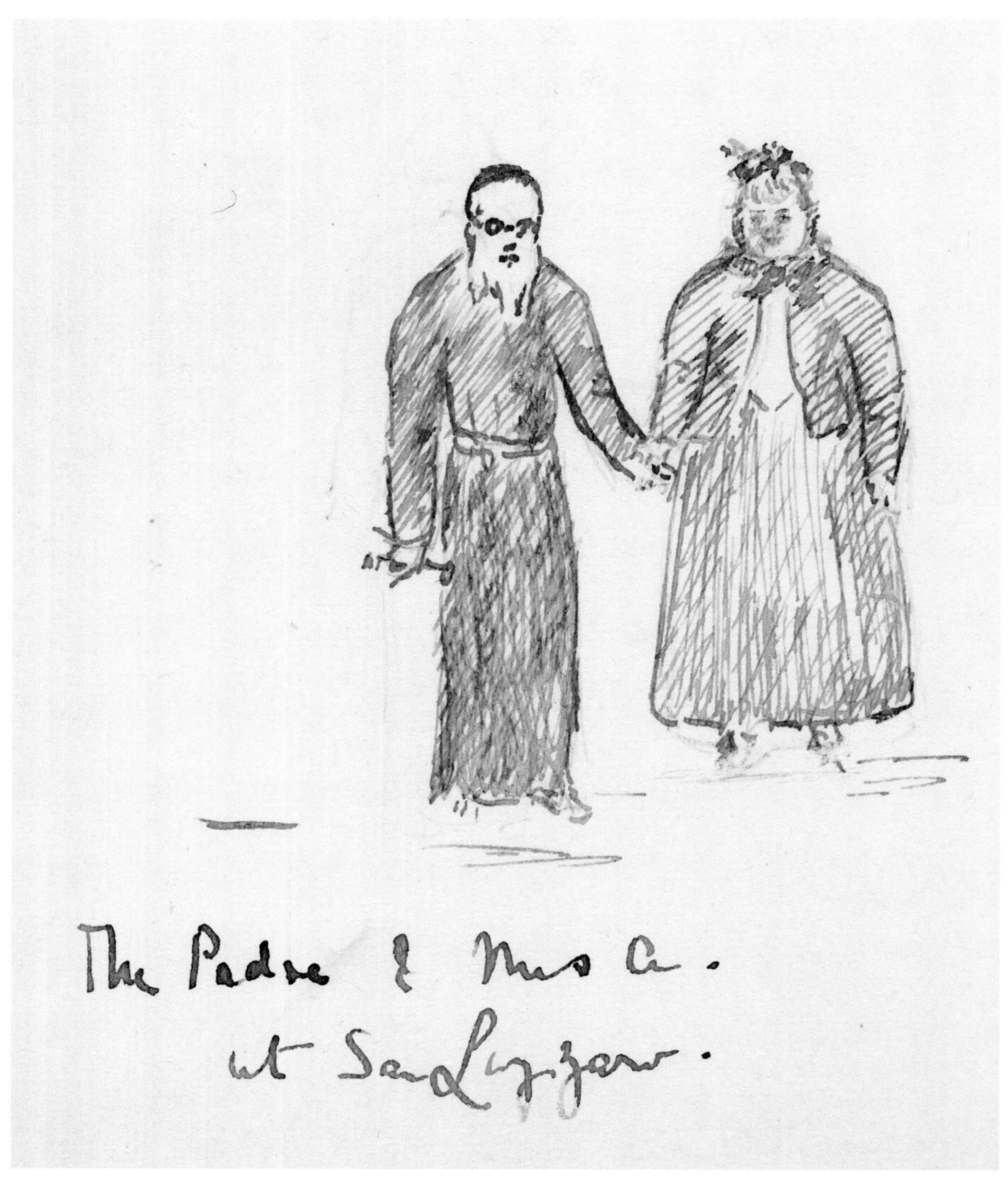

112 Cora Bowditch, *Lucia Alexander and Ghevont Alishan at San Lazzaro*, 22 June 1898, pen and ink in a travel diary, folio approx. 20 × 16 cm (7 ⅞ × 6 ¼ in), Massachusetts Historical Society, Boston, MA

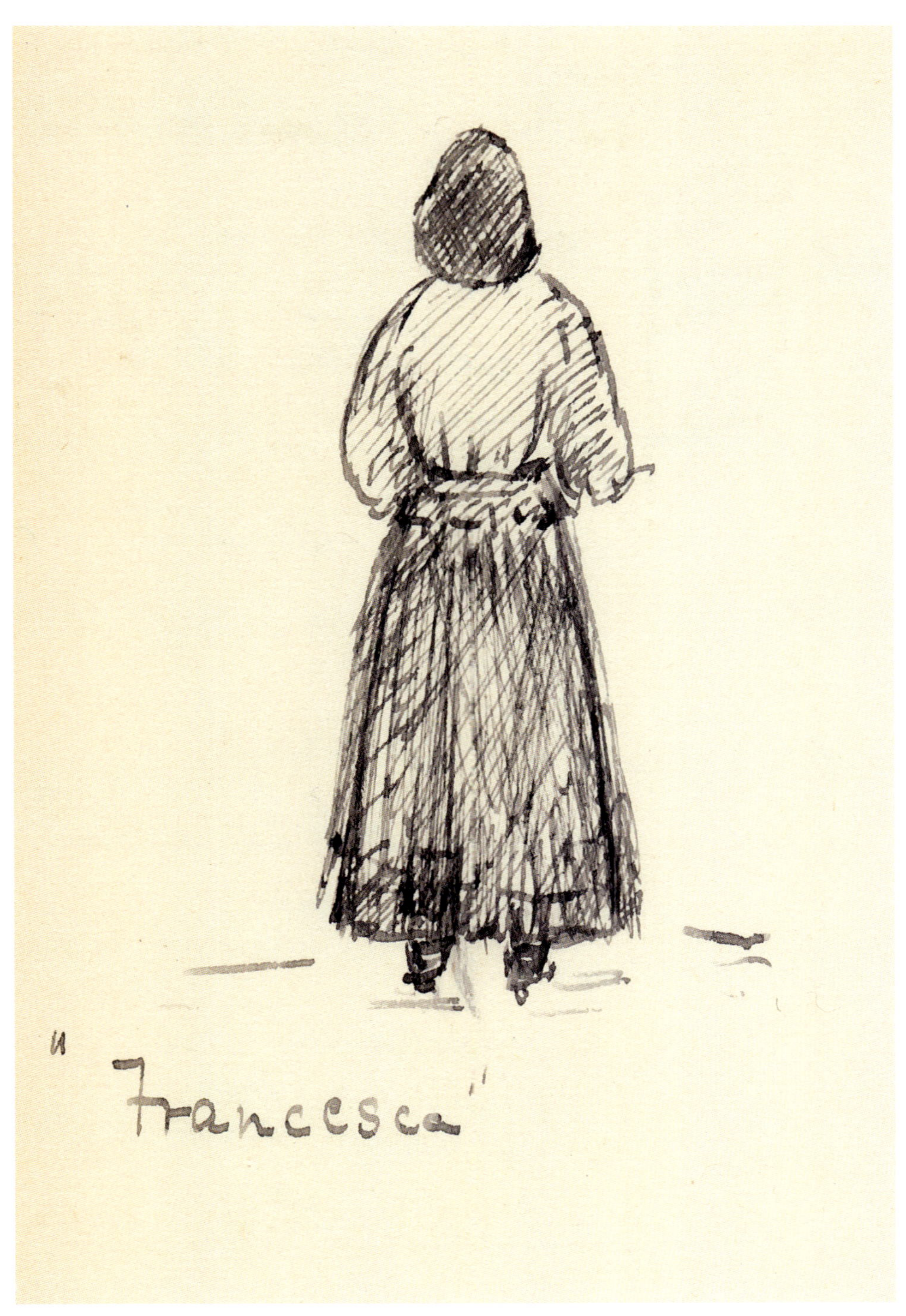

113 Cora Bowditch, *Francesca*, 24 June 1898, pen and ink in a travel diary,
folio approx. 20 × 16 cm (7⅞ × 6¼ in), Massachusetts Historical Society, Boston, MA

Clearly the Alexanders, who gifted Cora and her sister with old coins and fans painted with Venetian scenery, captivated the Bowditch family, just as they captivated so many others.[55]

Francesca's vision continued to deteriorate during this period, but she was unconcerned. Repeating a saying she learned from Edwige, she later noted, 'when the Lord took from me one faculty He gave me another; which is in no way impossible. And I think of the beautiful Italian proverb: "When God shuts a door He opens a window."'[56] Her window, in this case, was her prodigious memory. She used that memory to take on small projects, like translating several poems by her friend Vittoria Aganoor.[57] But she also began to compose verses in her mind, writing them down whenever she was able. In this way she became an *improvisatrice*, like her friends Beatrice and Giannina, both now deceased.[58] She had, of course, shown a talent for poetry as early as her work on the Hannah Blackstone manuscript. But now it was her only creative outlet.

This led to her fifth and final book, a versification of 12 Italian folk tales titled *The Hidden Servants and Other Very Old Stories* (1900). Ruskin's health was too poor to assist, so the Alexander women had another friend, a Mr Samuel in London, guide them through the publication process.[59] The title of this volume – and its first chapter – came from Francesca's earlier manuscript for Sarah Shaw Russell, which ended with her comment on the importance of God's hidden servants, a conceit she brought up in the last installment of *Roadside Songs*, too. Now, she used it as the theme for a collection of stories of a diverse group of those servants – hermits, beggars, orphans, farm laborers, widows, nuns, saints and others – told in lively rhyming verses. In her preface she referred to herself as 'the old story-teller', and defined her increasingly limited world from the Hotel Bonciani sky parlor:

> In my upper chamber here,
> Still I wait from year to year;

> Wondering when the time will come
> That the Lord will call me home.
> All the rest have been removed,
> Those I worked for, those I loved;
> And, at times, there seems to be
> Little use on earth for me.

She continued with a description of her beloved view – this, at least, she still could see – and the ways in which Florence had changed since her arrival in 1853, though she had not:

> From my window I look down
> On the busy, bustling town.
> But beyond its noise and jar
> I can see the hills afar;
> And above it, the blue sky,
> And the white clouds sailing by;
> And the sunbeams, as they shine
> On a world that is not mine.
> Here I wait, while life shall last,
> An old relic of the past,
> Feeling strange, and far away
> From the people of to-day

Yet despite this, she admitted that her life 'still has pleasures of its own', among them the many children who come up the stairs, wanting to hear her stories, which in turn prompted her to write this book.[60]

Francesca had known these stories for years, either through the antique books she collected or through her Italian friends. For example, she learned about Suora Marianna, who dozed off cooking broth over a fire for a sick woman and woke to a vision of the Christ Child tending the pot for her, from an old woman in the village of San Marcello in the Apennines. In fact, she had mentioned Marianna in a letter in 1871; at that time she was making a drawing of the story to send to Child's Gallery in Boston to sell.[61] She eventually sold it in Italy, not in Boston, but she made another version in 1883 and it is probably

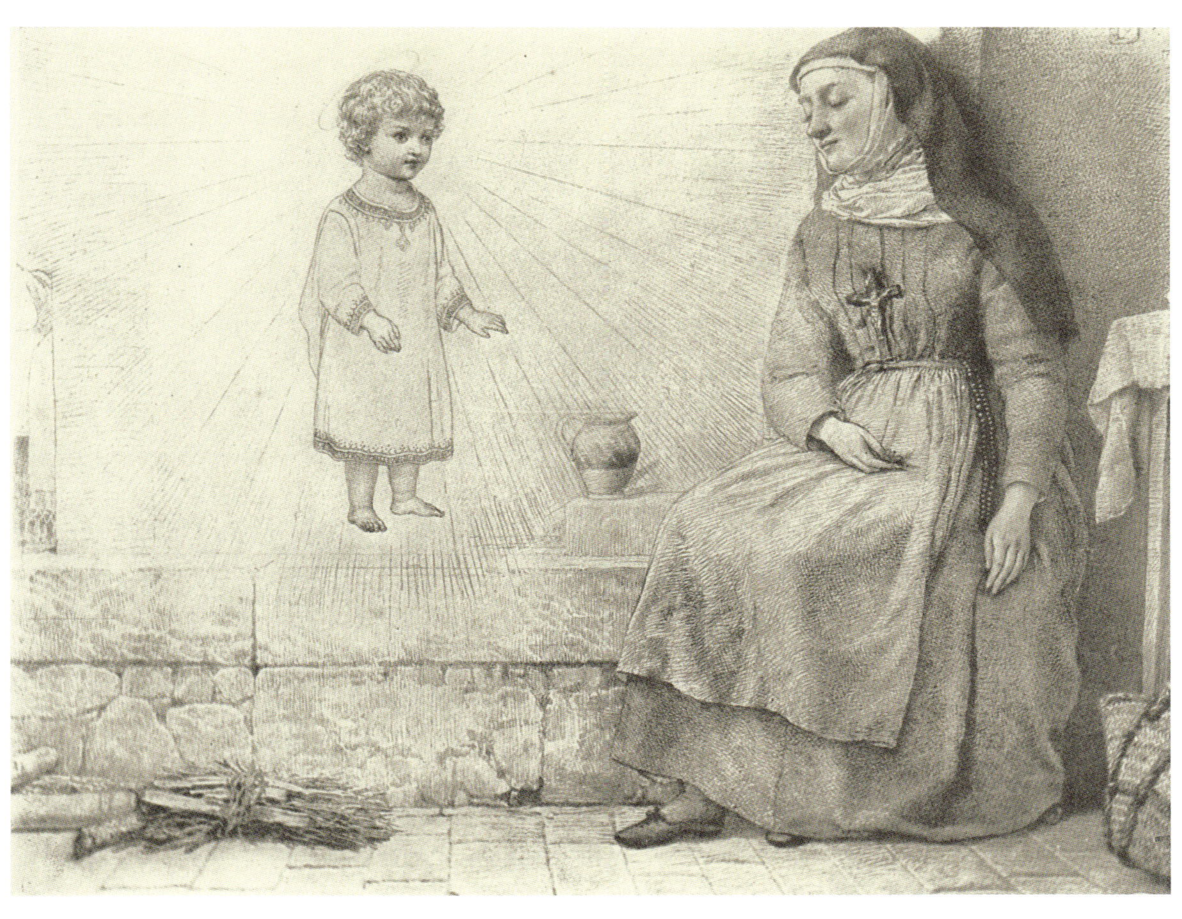

114 Francesca Alexander, frontispiece from *The Hidden Servants and Other Very Old Stories* (Boston, MA: Little, Brown & Co., 1900), photogravure, 19 × 13 cm (7½ × 5⅛ in)

this one that became the book's frontispiece and only illustration.[62] It represents the exhausted Marianna, in her habit with a crucifix on her chest and a rosary at her waist, kindling and a willow basket full of supplies on the floor, dozing at the hearth while the Christ Child hovers over her (fig.114).

The book was lauded in the popular press, particularly for its religious sentiment.[63] Lucia claimed that they received so many letters about it, running the gamut from positive to heretical, that she was 'half tempted to immortalise them in an article for some magazine'.[64] Perhaps remembering the Italian translation of *Ida*, in 1906 the women asked the publisher for permission to publish an Italian translation, which was granted.[65] Between 1908 and 1910, 10 of the 12 chapters appeared as individual, cheaply printed booklets, most translated into Italian by Francesca's friend, Professor Pasquale Lefons. This took no effort on her part, and it is unlikely that she earned much, if anything, from these booklets, but together with the earlier translation of *Ida* they gave her an Italian audience.

While Francesca was working on *Hidden Servants*, Lucia was bolstering her daughter's fame in another way. In 1889, Ruskin, though in a severely compromised mental state, began to make plans to publish the verses he had removed from *Roadside Songs*, and although Lucia offered to send whatever information he needed, nothing came of it.[66] Lucia never said anything to Ruskin, but she had been dissatisfied with his editorial interventions on the song manuscript; she regretted that the manuscript had been disassembled and was distressed that Francesca earned virtually nothing from the popular publication.[67] In 1890, Lucia shared her regret, and her plan to remedy it, with Joan Severn:

> I wish I had known sooner, and then the scattering and loss – for the present certainly, and perhaps forever – of the work of F[rancesca]'s life, and most of its best years, might have been so easily prevented. If

ever it shall be possible the work of mine shall be its reproduction and consequently preservation entire. I shall spare no pains and no money. I deeply grieve and blame myself every day, and I only hope by working and spending to remedy the effects of what I see now to be my criminal carelessness – if the time ever does come I know you will help me. It is the last plan and hope of my life.[68]

Joan proved to be an ally, and arranged photography of many of the folios still in the United Kingdom.[69] Lucia lobbied William G. Collingwood to help her find the remainder and to advise her on publishing the manuscript in Francesca's original format.[70] By 1892, those friends had located 108 of the 122 original folios; Collingwood believed another nine were untraceable, but he continued looking for the remaining five, assuring Lucia that at least their dispersal '[spread] Miss Alexander's reputation, and [gave] far more pleasure to more people than if they were all in a cupboard at [Ruskin's home]'.[71] As a last effort, late that year he placed a series of notices in *The Academy*, *The Athenaeum*, *The Daily Graphic*, *The Times* and *The Magazine of Art* – whose editor was Francesca's admirer Marion H. Spielmann – on the premise that their readers, engaged as they were in the arts and literature, were most likely to help.[72] And indeed in December 1894 another notice in *The Magazine of Art* announced that four more folios had been found, and urged the owner of the last one to come forward.[73]

Collingwood estimated it would cost $2500 to bring this slightly curtailed version of Francesca's original manuscript to press.[74] Although the technical process had improved since the publication of *Roadside Songs*, it was still a costly venture; if Francesca's earlier books had not been so successful it is doubtful any press would have taken the chance. However, in October 1896, with the assistance of Charles Callahan Perkins, Lucia signed a contract with the Boston publisher Houghton Mifflin & Co.;

she supplied photographs of the folios and the press covered the cost of making photogravures from them, as well as the printing, binding and advertising.[75] It appeared as *Tuscan Songs* – Francesca's original title – with 108 folios, largely in her original order with a few new songs but none of Ruskin's material.[76]

Recognizing the appeal of a volume with this new, fully illustrated format, the publisher advertised it widely and even produced a limited edition of 50 signed copies, with gilt fleur-de-lis on cream vellum binding and protective tissue between each page. It was printed in time for the Christmas season, and advertisements quoted from the many reviews that celebrated its charm and beauty (fig.115). Even the occasional critical review, noting the awkwardness of Francesca's figures or the errors of her 'Pre-Raphaelism', found much to commend in the volume overall.[77] The limited edition was especially sought after; Francesca's patron George Washington Wales included his copy in a bequest to the Museum of Fine Arts in Boston.[78] Lucia's efforts to publish Francesca's original manuscript – with the assistance of friends and strangers in three countries – further indicate her pride in her daughter's accomplishments.

But by this time life was difficult for the Alexander women. Their beloved Edwige, a celebrity herself due to her inclusion in Francesca's books, fell ill with a heart problem in Lugano in 1897. She died in 1899, after 40 years with the Alexanders; her daughter and granddaughter continued working for the family in her place but this was a hard loss.[79] Francesca had described Edwige as 'First servant, then friend, finally she has become to me like a relation; yet never ceasing to be servant through it all . . . humble, gentle and retiring, as on the first day when she came to us.'[80] This tragedy was followed the next year by Ruskin's death on 20 January 1900, the 27th anniversary of Ida's death, making it doubly painful for Francesca. She sent a garland of olive branches she cut from a tree in her sky parlor to be placed on his grave.[81] He had been in poor health for some

HOUGHTON, MIFFLIN & COMPANY

Invite attention to a work of very remarkable character, one of the finest of the Holiday Books of the season

Tuscan Songs

Collected, translated and illustrated by

FRANCESCA ALEXANDER

A large quarto volume with 108 Photogravure Etchings, exquisitely reproducing Miss Alexander's designs. Price $25.00 *net.*

The EDITION DE LUXE of this work is a sumptuous volume, brought out with the utmost care to produce a perfect result of bookmaking art. The designs are printed on Japanese paper, artist's proofs, and the work has Miss Alexander's autograph. It is bound in vellum, artistically stamped in gold, and is a gift fit for a king. Price, $100.00, *net.*

From the New York Tribune

This collection of folk-songs from the roadsides and fields of Tuscany is one of the most enchanting ever made. . . . Her peasants are true peasants of Tuscany, and added to the careful portraiture is that naive charm which lies in all really sympathetic studies of the Italian rustic. The effect of the pictures and the text is enhanced by the lovely floral decorations flung gracefully on every page. Altogether the study of these songs is rendered more and more delightful by the editor's artistic accompaniment. The songs themselves belong among the tenderest and most exquisite flowers of artless poetry. . . . The magic of beauty is over them all. It may be added that this beauty has received sympathetic handling in the present volume. It is superbly made.—*New York Tribune.*

From the Nation.

In reproducing Miss Alexander's designs in their original size, the publishers have made a noteworthy contribution to the small number of American specimens of first-rate book-making, and what is more, they have perpetuated a unique and in some respects precious work.

Unique it surely is, for a Mediæval missal, with its illuminated text and music and pictures of sacred scenes, does not more faithfully represent the spirit of worship in a bygone age than do these songs and pictures and exquisite flowers represent the spirit of the lowly in modern Tuscany. . . . The whole is like a veritable piece of Tuscan life, perennially enchanting to any one who has known it, and delightful to every one sensitive to beauty.

Sold by Booksellers. Sent, postpaid, by

HOUGHTON, MIFFLIN & CO., Boston

115 Advertisement for *Tuscan Songs* in *The New York Times. Saturday Review of Books and Art*, 18 December 1897

time, making collaboration and even correspondence impossible, but the Alexander women were kept apprised of his condition.

Following Ruskin's death, Joan Severn and Charles Eliot Norton, as his executors, grew concerned about some of his letters to the Alexanders, and their potential harm to his reputation, perhaps thinking of the sort of scandal Henry James described in his thinly veiled story about the fate of Percy Bysshe Shelley's letters in *The Aspern Papers* (1888). Severn and Norton asked the Alexanders to relinquish their letters, but Francesca refused and promised to safeguard them instead: 'They are among the most precious things that I possess; but I think I would rather see them all in the fire, than in the hands of a stranger.'[82] Clearly Ruskin felt the same; though some letters have been lost, hundreds between him and the Alexanders survive. In 1905 she also refused to send any of the two dozen or so Ruskin drawings and watercolors she owned to England; these were too precious to relinquish, too.[83]

The Alexanders may have wanted to keep these objects in part because their world was growing narrower. Summer travel may have ended in 1908, when Francesca had a bad fall that left her disabled and incapable of negotiating the many steps from their apartment to the street without assistance.[84] But even before this she often stayed in the apartment for long stretches of time, taking advantage of her rooftop when she wanted air.[85] She continued to exchange flowers, seeds and bulbs from her garden with friends, including the chrysanthemums, columbines and bulbs of what she identified as *Gesneria odorata* sent to Lady Walburga Paget, the German wife of the former British Ambassador to Florence who lived near Francesca's former home on Bellosguardo.[86] She was particularly pleased with the oil she made from balsam apple (*Momordica balsamina*), grown from seeds a friend acquired from an Indian woman – more likely Romani – in 1904. Francesca harvested the fruit and steeped it in oil for a year to create a salve for cuts and skin diseases, which she then offered to her friends.[87] But her mobility continued to deteriorate; by 1913, servants had to pull her in a chair through her cluttered, flower-filled home.[88]

Despite these ailments, Lucia stressed Francesca's positive outlook in 1911: 'for a long time Francesca seemed between life and death, but now she looks and seems more like her old self. She is crippled and half blind, but she is the happiest of happy, and contrives

to do a wonderful amount of work for others, and you may see another book by her before very long.'[89] This last comment is especially tantalizing. In Bassano in 1902, Francesca began writing a biography of her old friend Marina Sprea Baroni Semitecolo, and Lucia described how 'Late at night when all in the house are asleep, [Marina and Francesca] walk up and down the immense dimly lighted hall and she tells Francesca all her memories, which she writes down the next day, to be worked up into a book hereafter, and this uses up all her disposable eyesight'.[90] If Francesca completed this biography, or another volume like *Hidden Servants*, using her exceptional memory to retain the verses she composed until she could commit them to paper, there is no trace.

In fact, the only new book published in this period was by Lucia. In 1892 she sought out Collingwood's advice about an appropriate venue for an article she wrote on the soup kitchen at Bassano – she pasted two meal tickets from the organization in one of her scrapbooks – but nothing ever came of it.[91] For many years, however, she had been translating sacred stories, and finally published them as *Il Libro d'Oro* (1905). This almost 500-page volume contains 125 stories about those destined for heaven, from the well-known like the three Magi to a variety of more anonymous monks, friars and others, compiled from four seventeenth- and eighteenth-century Italian volumes of saints' lives in the Alexanders' library. It received considerable notice on publication, with several reviewers identifying the author as Francesca's mother, an indication of her enduring marketability.[92]

Francesca also had an enduring influence. The Scottish editor and stained-glass designer Grace Warrack published her own translations of Italian songs in 1914 and 1925, incorporating Francesca's work as well as that of several Italian authors. The women had known each other since at least 1890, when Warrack wrote a poem about Francesca.[93] Warrack praised her in both books and named her as one of

the first book's dedicatees; she included a photograph
of Edwige in the first book, and a reproduction
of Francesca's drawing of Polissena in the second.
Warrack visited the Abetone area to meet Francesca's
friends and noted that the women and men
introduced themselves by the names of the characters
they modeled for in *Roadside Songs*.[94]

The Alexanders continued to welcome visitors
to the Bonciani. On the occasion of the feast day of
Saint Lucy in 1906, Lucia reported on the gifts she
received, many of them from *contadini* who had little
to spare: 'I had 20 letters, 10 telegrams or picture cards
of various dimensions – 12 bouquets which comprised
many orchids, and splendid rare flowers – 4 plants
rather inconveniently large, and nine presents, ranging
from a superb and very large bed quilt, a beautiful
imitation of old lace, all made by hand, to six eggs and
a ball of butter.'[95]

Other visitors were Bostonians who knew them,
or knew of them. Although their dear friend Henry
Wadsworth Longfellow had died in 1882, Lucia and
Francesca happily received his relatives for many
years. When one of his nephews visited in 1893, they
enjoyed 'quite a festa', and his daughters Edith and
Alice dined with them in 1899; a few months later,
they met up with Alice again in Venice, where they all
dined with Fannie Coddington Browning, the widow
of Elizabeth Barrett and Robert Browning's son
Pen.[96] Alice returned in 1913, this time with her niece
Erica Thorp (the daughter of Alice's sister Anne),
who wrote to her family,

> we called on a lovely old Mrs. Alexander who is 99
> and just as clear headed and alert, running her house,
> making jokes and awake to everything. She is perfectly
> remarkable! Mamma probably knows of her . . . Her
> daughter Miss Francesca, who has written sonnets and
> drawn lovely things and is half-blind and stricken with
> rheumatism has one of the loveliest characters I ever
> hope to see.[97]

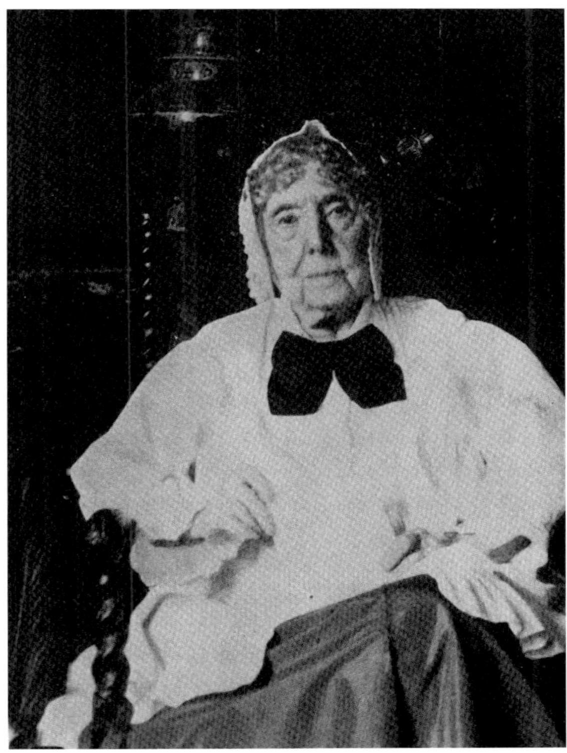

116 *Lucia at Age 100*, 1914, from Constance Grosvenor
Alexander, *Francesca Alexander. A 'Hidden Servant'*
(Cambridge, MA: Harvard University Press, 1927)

The following week, Alice described a second
visit in more critical terms, hinting at the reduced
circumstances the Alexanders lived in at this point:

> I sent by [Erica] a Thanksgiving cake + some flowers
> to the Alexanders. Even I have succeeded in mounting
> the stairs, but nearly froze in Francesca's room. Wasn't
> it dreary + disorderly + dark, + such a frowzy bed – but
> Francesca bright as a little bird, though very emaciated.
> Mrs. A. lively as ever . . . She is 100 in April – I
> thought it was 90.[98]

Indeed, Lucia's 100th birthday was marked by celebrations and reported in newspapers.[99] In a photograph from that occasion, Lucia is ensconced in a carved wooden chair in front of some of their porcelain collection, dressed in a loose-fitting white garment with a dark bow at her neck and a scarf – that armchair tidy Joseph Lindon Smith mentioned – over her curls (fig.116).

The Alexanders continued their charitable efforts as long as they were able. By this time, Francesca's interest in the disadvantaged and downtrodden was widely known. In 1897 Sydney Cockerell, Ruskin's friend and later director of the Fitzwilliam Museum, sent her a copy of William Morris's *Dream of John Bell* (1888), a novel about a revolt of fourteenth-century English peasants; in thanking him she noted that she was a pacifist, like Saint Francis, 'but still I find so much in that book that I think we can all be the better for laying to heart!'[100] She was certainly thinking of the similarly dire conditions under which many of her *contadini* friends lived as she read it. In 1905, after an earthquake in Calabria, she sent an appeal to the *Boston Evening Transcript*, describing the devastation and asking for funds to help residents of the small town of Piscopio.[101] A week later the Bowditch brothers, who served as her intermediaries in the United States, reported that $373 had been contributed by individuals, among them Francesca's friends and patrons in the Appleton, Coolidge, Eliot, Lee and Wheelwright families.[102]

Francesca and Lucia also helped those closer to home. During their summers in Bassano, Lucia marked their friend Marina's name saint day by arranging a lottery to distribute gifts to the local *contadini*.[103] Anxious that a servant in the Hotel Bonciani planned to send his infant daughter to a wet nurse in the countryside – because, he claimed, his wife was a Swiss Evangelical and therefore not allowed to nurse – Lucia purchased a goat and the infant was instead raised on goat milk at home.[104] Appreciative of the efforts of the Italians who served

them so long and faithfully, Lucia arranged to provide some with money and even houses.[105] In 1911, she wrote to a friend in Boston, stressing the sacrifice they made for their philanthropy by quoting the long-dead Ida: 'You cannot imagine how much I envy you living among your own people, but as Ida said, "God knows what He does" and [Francesca's] place here would not be easily filled.'[106] Indeed, Francesca continued her charity work until the end of her life; an article published in 1916 described her, blind and wheelchair-bound, sitting next to a basket of money she distributed to the needy.[107]

Although the world around the Alexanders had changed, they had not, and they knew it. In 1906, Lucia acknowledged this in a letter to Charles Bowditch's wife Cornelia Rockwell, writing, 'Francesca says we have outlived our world, and belong to another century.'[108] Others in the Anglo-American community agreed with this assessment. The Florence-born British aesthete Harold Acton, who was only a child when the women were alive, must have been repeating local gossip when he later claimed that the Alexanders refused to ride in a car or take advantage of inventions like electricity.[109] As the years passed, and the Anglo-American residents of Florence the Alexanders knew best moved away or died, few still knew who they were, and they even stopped registering with the American consulate.[110] In 1913, a relative of Anna Lloyd claimed Francesca 'feels the last of her race'.[111] Lilly Cleveland's death the following year, Francesca's friend and correspondent for more than half a century, must have been another difficult blow.[112]

Around this time, Alfred Bowditch reached out to a colleague to find a Florentine lawyer to assist with the inevitable tasks he and his brother would face when the Alexanders died. International cooperation of this sort was still unusual, and there was a clear distrust of Italians, reflected in his colleague's reply: 'It seems rather odd to apply the word "Florentine" to a lawyer – it seems to fit better, perhaps, with art objects, but I sincerely hope it will not turn out that the lawyer whose name I get you will be artful.'[113] Nevertheless, the colleague suggested F.G. Coselschi – perhaps a relative of Eugenio Coselschi, a lawyer and later member of Benito Mussolini's government – and Bowditch probably met Coselschi when he traveled to Florence that spring.

Bowditch was wise to make this arrangement. By early 1916, the Alexanders' few remaining friends in the city asked the United States consul, Frederick T.F. Dumont, to intervene in their situation. Dumont began his post in 1914 so it is no surprise that he did not know the women well. He later claimed with no basis that they 'were believers in Spiritualism and mediums', probably because such beliefs had been popular in the Anglo-American community decades earlier. But he also, more accurately, stated that they had lived in Florence for so long that they were 'Italian in sympathy and feeling'. Dumont believed that their limited mobility and the perception of their wealth put them at the mercy of 'A certain set of young Italians, not particularly reputable', led by a Neapolitan lawyer named Lefons – the brother of Francesca's translator Pasquale Lefons – who took control of their lives and limited their contact with more honest friends: 'the whole thing became almost a public scandal in that no one seemed able to interfere'.[114]

Of course, Dumont was protecting his office and himself, explaining the circumstances to deflect future criticism if the situation escalated. As much out of prejudice against Italians as out of concern for the Alexanders and their heirs, Dumont pointed out that their situation was not unique: 'Florence has several elderly American women in similar situations whose cases may from time to time come before the Department.'[115] These women, both American and British, who made Florence their home – the type immortalized by E.M. Forster's Misses Alans in his *Room with a View* (1908) – were increasingly dependent on consular officials, but there was little these officials could do.

On 19 May 1916, at the extraordinary age of 102, Lucia died of an intestinal obstruction.[116] An Irish friend in Florence, Mrs Knox Johnson (Mary Elizabeth Constance Burtchaell), wrote to friends and relations on Francesca's behalf to report that Lucia died peacefully: 'Her breathing just went fainter and fainter till it stopped . . . she was so breathless, Francesca would not let her repeat the prayer they always said together, but said it for her, and then Mrs. Alexander murmured "I am content, and very thankful for all" and afterwards spoke no more.'[117] Lucia was buried at the Cimitero Evangelico agli Allori, alongside Francis, two days later. The service was presided over by Gaspare Pult, an elder at Florence's Evangelical church, together with Presbyterian minister J.M. Blake and Scottish physician Dr Alexander R. Coldstream (one of the surgeons who treated Lucia's tumor years earlier); an obituary written by Pult appeared in the church's newspaper *Il Cristiano*, emphasizing Lucia's unstinting faith.[118] Other notices, published in newspapers in the United States and the United Kingdom, improbably claimed that Lucia left behind an estate valued as high as $85,000,000.[119]

These exaggerated reports certainly contributed to the tragic situation described by Dumont. He and Coselschi were concerned that Francesca – essentially naive, blind and immobile – would allow Lefons, 'Miss Alexander's best friend and attorney in all negotiations', to take control of the estate, or might even give it to him. They insisted that it first pass through the executors, which triggered a complete inventory and appraisal. Coselschi, assisted by the consulate, began the process in Florence, keeping a watchful eye on Lefons and the servants to make sure items did not disappear, while Bowditch assessed their holdings in the United States.[120]

Virtually nothing is known of Francesca following Lucia's death. A photograph taken from around this time shows her seated in her salon, in front of a carved wooden cupboard on which rests a framed bas

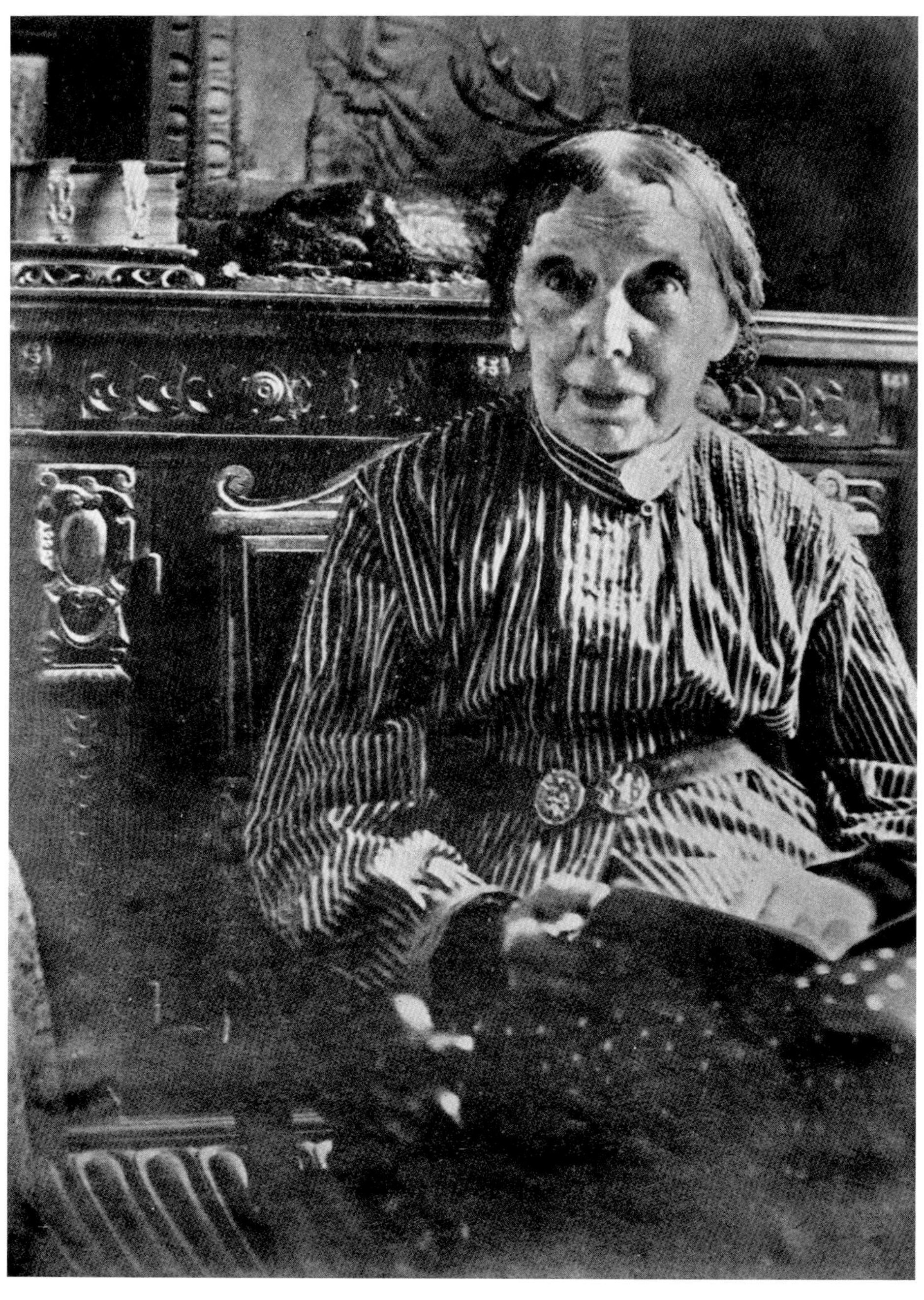

117 *Francesca at Age 79*, 1916, from Constance Grosvenor Alexander, *Francesca Alexander. A 'Hidden Servant'* (Cambridge, MA: Harvard University Press, 1927)

relief of the Madonna and Child (visible in fig.20), perhaps their alleged Donatello, looking frail and holding a book or manuscript in her lap, though she could no longer read (fig.117). Francesca had admitted to Constance Oldham that 'there are only two of us, and we never part, even for one day'.[121] So it is not surprising that she outlived her mother by only eight months, succumbing to bronchial pneumonia at age 79 on 20 January 1917. According to Mrs Johnson, again writing to friends, she too died peacefully, 'her last words being "Pray, Pray"'.[122] The next day a notice appeared in the Florentine newspaper *La Nazione*, inviting friends to attend services at her home and then at the Cimitero Evangelico agli Allori on 23 January; a second notice, this time in English, was printed in the 23 January edition with the same information.[123] Coselschi made the arrangements for her burial, which was officiated on that snowy day by J.M. Blake, and an unnamed mourner read James Russell Lowell's poem at the graveside; the family requested services conducted by the Scottish Presbyterian Church, indicating that at least one relative was with Francesca at the end of her life.[124]

But her death went largely unremarked. If those in Florence's Anglo-American community did not hear of it from friends and did not read *La Nazione* (and few did, since it was an Italian paper), they did not learn of it until after her burial, from a brief notice in *The Florence Herald and Italian Herald* on 27 January, where she was described as 'the last survivor of a group of "intellectuals" who from the days of Robert Browning and Ruskin onwards, had made Florence a sort of Mecca of artistic & literary culture'.[125] A second, more extensive and effusive, obituary appeared in the same paper a week later, identifying her as 'one of the ideal characters of the past century, which were in the world but not of it'; the anonymous author quoted Lowell's poem and emphasized Francesca's role as one of God's hidden servants.[126]

Friends in Boston were alerted via an even briefer notice in *The Boston Journal*.[127] An obituary in the *New York Sun* claimed, 'her salon at Florence was a place of assembly for prominent literary men and women and the Italian nobility', but it confused her publications with Lucia's.[128] It was the height of World War I, and newspapers like *The Times* of London, which would have surely marked her passing, were instead reporting war dead and military movements. An anonymous letter printed in the *Manchester Guardian*, apparently written by a friend in Florence who attended the services, lamented that no notice was made of her death.[129]

The estate inventory begun after Lucia's death was not completed until after Francesca's. On 27 February, the appraisers filed their report, stating that the estate was worth $194,537.97 with an additional $6500 in Boston real estate. Much of this was in stocks and bonds – they were heavily invested in railroads and utilities – but the appraisers also included $25 from the copyright of *Tuscan Songs* and $200 for a silver coffee pot and negatives, presumably of the photographs made for that publication. But they provided no further information on the contents of their home, only noting 'Personal effects, furniture, painting, &c at Florence, Italy, not yet in possession of executors, of uncertain value', which Dumont claimed an antiquities expert estimated was worth at least $15,000 if sold in Florence and up to $40,000 if sold in the United States. Clearly the estate value was far less than the millions some of Lucia's obituaries claimed, but also far more than Dumont implied in his statements, where he described the women as living 'in a style which might have been that of a very poor Italian laboring family'.[130]

The estate was difficult to settle. Not only did the women die within eight months of each other, but they did so in Italy, and war made travel and communication between the United States and Italy especially challenging. In 1918 Alfred Bowditch died, leaving his brother Charles to sort through the inventories, appraisals, sales and distributions. The final settlement did not happen until 1920, by which

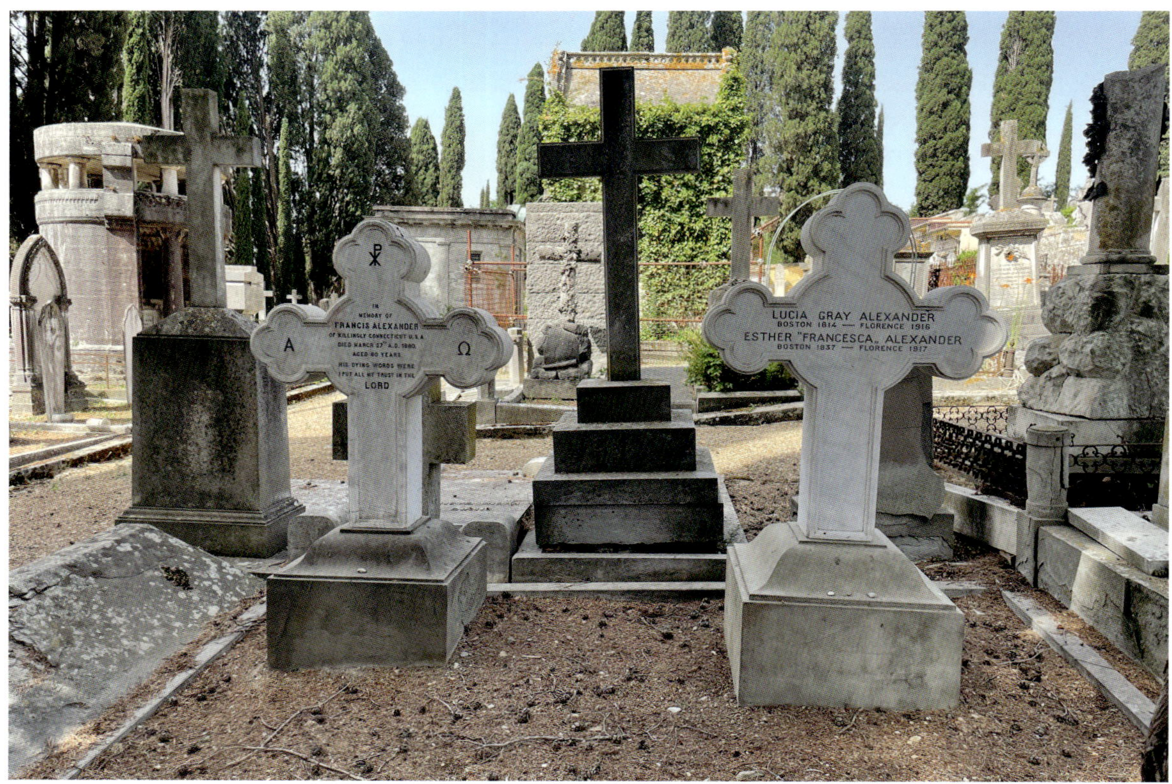

118 Gravesite of the Alexander family, Cimitero Evangelico agli Allori, Florence

point the estate was worth $287,541.63; certain stocks and bonds had increased in value, and 60 cases filled with their property in Florence were shipped to the United States, appraised and sold or distributed among their heirs, including collections of laces (estimated at $3194), books ($1305) and the ambiguous 'personal effects, furniture, etc' ($49,091.92).[131] The lace was appraised by Samuel B. Dean, the books by Charles E. Goodspeed, the china and glass by Leonard & Co. (the same auction house that sold Francis's collection in 1884), and the paintings by Robert C. and Nathaniel M. Vose. The heirs – Charlotte W. Hallowell, Barnard French, Mary Coolidge Swett, Lucia Gray Swett, William L. Swett and Samuel Swett – each received money, stocks, bonds and personal effects.[132] Consular reports for other American deaths in Florence do include more detailed inventories. When Gertrude F. Stark died in October 1915 at age 54, the consul turned over the estate to the local bankers; this may be why Stark's estate inventory – which included everything from three porcelain buttons (1 *lira*) to a ring with two diamonds (2250 *lire*) to trunks of clothing and other objects, among them dresses, corsets, books, a feather boa, seven pieces of maiolica and a plaster cast (valued together at $50) – is in the consular report, while the Alexanders' inventory, undertaken between officials in Boston and Florence, is not.[133]

Although some of their art collection was sent to
the United States in those 60 cases and distributed
to their six heirs – for example, Mary Coolidge
Swett inherited several of the ancient vases[134] – a
significant part of it remained in Florence. At least
some of those objects were purchased by Harold
Acton's parents, the English collector and dealer
Arthur Acton and American heiress Hortense
Mitchell, who had lived with their sons at the Villa
La Pietra since 1903. Both Arthur and Hortense
were interested in Renaissance art and they must
have visited the Alexanders at the Hotel Bonciani.[135]
But what they bought from the Alexanders, beyond
the paintings cited earlier in this book, and when
they bought it, is uncertain. The Villa La Pietra
and its contents were bequeathed to New York
University at Harold Acton's death in 1994, and
many Alexander paintings are still there today.
Francesca, under the influence of Lefons or others,
may have sold objects to the Actons or others
following Lucia's death, although legally she was
not allowed to disperse anything until the inventory
was completed.[136] Or, after Francesca died, the estate
executors may have determined that selling some
of the objects in Florence would be easier than
bringing them back to the United States.[137] Further
information about the scope of the Alexander
collection may be found when the Acton archives
are reopened for research in the future. [138]

Inseparable in life, the three Alexanders were
also inseparable in death, buried alongside each
other with two identical markers in the Cimitero
Evangelico agli Allori, Francis under one and Lucia
and Francesca under another (fig.118). There they
are surrounded by many of their Italian friends,
and many of the other Anglo-Americans who
made Florence their home. Their relatives could
have chosen to bring their bodies back to Boston
for burial; the official paperwork filed by the
American consulate when citizens died in Italy
noted that bodies might be disinterred after a year

for repatriation with the payment of a fee. But those
same relatives must have known how fitting a resting
place this was, especially for Francesca, given the
importance of Florence, and Italy, to her art and life.

Epilogue

Francesca Alexander lived in Florence for almost 64 years, from 1853 to 1917, a time of momentous changes not only in Italy but also in her native United States. She was certainly well informed of these changes, primary among them the American Civil War and Italy's fraught progress toward unification and independence, but she was most interested in the effects these and other changes had on her Italian friends. For example, she worried about the Civil War largely because it meant fewer Americans could travel to Italy, reducing the money straw-weaving *contadine* could earn and sending them further into poverty, and she feared the drawn-out conflicts of the Risorgimento and its resulting conscription took men away from their needy families.[1] Francesca was always concerned for those around her, and she put so much effort into her art not to promote her own fame but instead to enable her charitable endeavors and share Italian songs and stories with the wider world. Her friendship with John Ruskin, his enthusiasm for her work, and her resulting celebrity allowed her to do this in ways she would never have dreamed of prior to their meeting. These activities made her seem like a saint, whether modern or medieval, and this further set her apart from her contemporaries.

Francesca's saintliness was especially obvious by the late nineteenth century, when Florence was home to a number of women who were notable for their independence and the ways in which they overcame societal strictures. They represented the type of 'new women' popularized in books by authors like Henry James and paintings by artists like John Singer Sargent, both of whom had close ties to the city of Florence.[2] It is perhaps telling that there is no character like Francesca in James's novels, and no painting of her by Sargent, though the two men must have known or at least known of her during their many years in Florence. She was simply not the type of woman that interested them; she was no Daisy Miller or Vernon Lee. Francesca had been shaped by very different circumstances. At mid-century, when she first arrived in Florence, many of the Anglo-American women there engaged in charity, or devoted themselves to raising a family while their artist husbands were busy in their studios, or viewed their experience as a sort of finishing school before they went back to their home countries to marry. By the late nineteenth century, however, Italy was an especially hospitable place for a new generation of Anglo-American women, where they could be both intellectually stimulated and socially audacious. And though these women – whether fictional or real – achieved considerable acclaim themselves, none achieved the celebrity Francesca did at the pinnacle of her fame.

A number of these women knew Francesca, and they reacted to her in various ways. German-born Helen Zimmern translated Friedrich Nietzsche into English and edited *The Florence Gazette*, among her many accomplishments. In 1890, she penned a long, flattering article about Francesca, 'the simple story of a saintly American's life', repeating many of the familiar tropes and concluding that, by this date, 'Miss Alexander knows instinctively that she is out of harmony with the times, though the outside world little touches her and her tranquil secluded life'.[3] Helen understood, and appreciated, Francesca's by then outmoded life, even if it was so different from her own.

Others were not so complimentary. In 1894, Radcliffe-educated American art historian Mary Costelloe and her then lover and later husband, the connoisseur Bernard Berenson, came to the Alexander home to see a painting allegedly by the sixteenth-century artist Lorenzo Lotto, probably because Berenson was in the midst of researching his book on Lotto. But the painting did not meet their approval; Mary called it 'a XIV century daub!' (strangely, since Francesca surely knew the difference between fourteenth- and sixteenth-century paintings) and made no comment on the women themselves.[4] Nor were they impressed by Francesca's art. In 1903 they visited George B. Dorr in Boston, presumably a relative of Sarah Hayward Dorr, who spent time with the Alexanders in 1859; the Dorrs apparently acquired one of Francesca's drawings, because, according to Mary, Dorr 'showed us one of those awful drawings by Miss Fanny Alexander, Ruskin's pet. [Bernard] said right out that he loathed it.'[5] Mary clearly had no interest in Francesca and her world.

In yet another instance, American author Mabel Dodge Luhan must have met the Alexanders when she lived at the Villa Curonia near Arcetri in the hills south of Florence from 1905 to 1912. A vast gulf separated Francesca and Mabel in behavior and outlook. But Mabel, who welcomed the artist and poet Mina Loy and the author Gertrude Stein to her villa, found Francesca intriguing. In 1925 she published an essay entitled 'The Story of Francesca'.[6] Although the broad outlines can be recognized as Francesca's biography, most of the details are fiction. The Alexanders become the Endicotts, from Salem, and Francis a ship captain lost at sea; the widow and her daughter moved to Florence's Piazza Santo Spirito, and a few years later, after 19-year-old Francesca's drawings were displayed in the Uffizi, an Italian count introduced them to Ruskin. This almost certainly is not Mabel misremembering; instead, she is dissembling to create a better story. Sadly, by this date, other than Francesca's two cousins, who were about to publish their own biographies, there were few people alive who would notice the errors.[7]

So it is no surprise that Francesca all but disappeared in the years since her death. Part of this is due to her habit of selling or gifting her drawings and paintings to friends and acquaintances. Some of these have by now made their way through donations and sometimes purchases to public institutions, but many more must still be in private hands. Other contemporary women artists, those who participated in the art market with varying degrees of success – including her painter friend Lizzie Boott and the sculptor Harriet Hosmer – are certainly better known today. But Francesca's disappearance is also related to her own self-effacing habits. She included details of her life in her books, but her real subjects were her Italian friends, not herself. And although she shared much information in her correspondence, only a small, edited, portion has been published.

Francesca Alexander was so different from those around her, so enigmatic, that neither her contemporaries nor later authors knew how to explain her. Some marveled at her other-worldliness, as Helen Zimmern did. Others dismissed her as an amateur, a mere pet of Ruskin, as Mary Berenson did. Still others romanticized her biography, ignoring facts for an interesting narrative, as Mabel Dodge Luhan

and, to a certain extent, her own cousins did. Yet
Francesca was far more complicated. Very few Anglo-
Americans took part in Italian life as enthusiastically
and sympathetically, or for as long a period of time.
She engaged with an international community of
artists, politicians and intellectuals, and she was
determined to use her talents to provide friendship
and charity to Italy's neediest, while sharing their
stories with a wide audience who would have had no
knowledge of them otherwise. She may have outlived
her world, but she worked her entire life to make it a
better place.

Notes

All archival references have been abbreviated in the notes; for the full details, see Archival Source Abbreviations.

PROLOGUE

1   M.H. Spielmann, 'Francesca Alexander, and "The Roadside Songs of Tuscany"', *Magazine of Art* 18 (June 1895): p.299.

2   E.M. Forster, *A Room with a View* (London: Edward Arnold, 1908), p.76.

3   E[dwin].B[ale]., '"Madonina" by "Francesca" Alexander', *The Magazine of Art* 12 (September 1889): p.392. The single 'n' in Madonina seems to have been an error on the part of the journal, so I have opted to use the correct spelling, Madonnina.

4   FASA, fols 22–3.

5   Francesca Alexander to William Dean Howells, 15 December 1883, HFP; on Mildred, see Polly H. Howells, 'Mildred Howells as the Father's Daughter: Living Within His Lines', *Harvard Library Bulletin* 5, no.1 (Spring 1994): pp 9–28.

6   Willard Fiske to Charles [Warner?], 8 September 1883, DWFP.

7   Constance Grosvenor Alexander's *Hidden Servant*, typographical work of Bruce Rogers, DTPP.

8   Francesca Alexander to Joan Severn, 23 July [1906?], CLFAJS.

I FROM BOSTON TO FLORENCE

1   Catherine W. Pierce, 'Francis Alexander', *Old-Time New England* 44, no.2 (October–December 1953): pp 29–46, and 'Further Notes on Francis Alexander', *Old-Time New England* 56, no.2 (October–December 1965): pp 35–44; and, for an allegedly autobiographical account of his early career, William Dunlap, *A History of the Rise and Progress of the Arts of Design in the United States* (New York: George P. Scott and Co., 1834), vol.2, pp 426–33.

2   20 September 1825, JSCDLB.

3   Megan Marshall, *The Peabody Sisters* (Boston, MA: Houghton Mifflin, 2006), p.169; and Scrapbook no.2, PAF; for a later memory of their friendship, see Lydia Maria Child to Francis Alexander, 1 July 1877, ALC.

4   *A Catalogue of the First Exhibition of Paintings in the Athenaeum Gallery* (Boston, MA: William W. Clapp, 1927).

5   21 March 1829, WFM; and 'The Editor's Table', *The American Monthly Magazine* 2, no.5 (August 1830): p.364; this poem was pasted into Scrapbook no.2, PAF.

6   Theodore E. Stebbins Jr and Melissa Renn, *American Paintings at Harvard* (Cambridge, MA: Harvard Art Museum, 2008), vol.1, pp 44–5.

7   Dunlap, vol.2, pp 432–3; and Francis Alexander, 15 October 1831, USPA.

8   *Letters of Horatio Greenough American Sculptor,*

ed. Nathalia Wright (Madison, WI: University of Wisconsin Press, 1972), p.110; Henry T. Tuckerman, *A Memorial of Horatio Greenough* (New York: G.P. Putnam & Co., 1853), p.21; and Richard P. Wunder, *Hiram Powers. A Life* (Newark, DE: University of Delaware Press, 1991), vol.1, p.95.

9   Tim Barringer, 'Thomas Cole's Atlantic Crossings', in Elizabeth Mankin Kornhauser and Tim Barringer, *Thomas Cole's Journey. Atlantic Crossings* (New York: Metropolitan Museum of Art, 2018), p.47.

10   Dunlap, vol.2, pp 432–3. Francis exhibited the Magdalene sketch in 1834; see *Catalogue of Paintings at the Artist's Exhibition, in Harding's Gallery, School Street, Boston. May, 1834* (Boston, MA: J.H. Eastburn, 1834), p.4.

11   Amasa Hewins, *Hewins's Journal. A Boston Portrait-Painter Visits Italy*, ed. Francis H. Allen (Boston, MA: The Boston Athenaeum, 1931), pp xiv and 89–98; and *The Letters of Ralph Waldo Emerson*, ed. Ralph L. Rusk (New York: Columbia University Press, 1939), vol.1, p.392.

12   Francis Alexander, 26 August 1833, NYAPCL.

13   'An Hour in a Painter's Study', *American Ladies' Magazine* 7, no.2 (February 1934): p.85; *A Catalogue of the First Exhibition of Paintings in the Athenaeum Gallery* (Boston, MA: William W. Clapp, 1927), nos 46 (by this date the Reni was in the possession of a Dr Harwood) and 127; and Thomas Ball, *My Threescore Years and Ten* (Boston, MA: Roberts Brothers, 1891), pp 70–71.

14   Sarah Freeman Clarke to James Freeman Clarke, March [1834], 'Letters of a Sister', JFCAP.

15   *Catalogue of the Seventh Exhibition of Paintings in the Athenaeum Gallery* (Boston, MA: John H. Eastburn, 1833).

16   Robert F. Perkins Jr and William J. Gavin III, eds, *The Boston Athenaeum. Art Exhibition Index 1827–1874* (Boston, MA: The Library, 1980), pp 9–10.

17   *Catalogue of Paintings at the Artist's Exhibition, in Harding's Gallery, School Street, Boston. May, 1834* (Boston, MA: J.H. Eastburn, 1834).

18   Receipt from Francis Alexander to William Lloyd Garrison, 24 September 1834, ASC.

19   Louis L. Noble, *The Course of Empire, Voyage of Life, and Other Pictures of Thomas Cole* (New York: Cornish, Lamport & Company, 1853), p.185.

20   Theodore E. Stebbins Jr and Melissa Renn, *American Paintings at Harvard* (Cambridge, MA: Harvard Art Museum, 2008), vol.1, pp 45–6.

21   Sylvia E. Crane, *White Silence. Greenough, Powers, and Crawford, American Sculptors in Nineteenth-Century Italy* (Coral Gables, FL: University of Miami Press, 1972), p.186.

22   Francis Alexander to Hiram Powers, 10 October 1838, HPP; and Richard P. Wunder, *Hiram Powers: A Life* (Newark, DE: University of Delaware Press, 1991), vol.1, p.95.

23   Leonard & Co. (Boston, MA), *A Large Portion of the Private Collection of Paintings of the Late Francis Alexander*, 24–5 April 1884.

24   Noble, p.142; see *The Token and Atlantic Souvenir* (Boston, MA: Charles Bowen, 1837), p.65. Alexander put it on exhibition immediately, together with a number of other paintings he owned or painted himself; see *Catalogue of the First Exhibition of Paintings in the American Gallery of Fine Arts. Summer Street. Opened June 17th, 1835* (Boston, MA: W.W. Clapp, 1835).

25   *Exhibition of Pictures, Painted by Washington Allston, at Harding's Gallery, School Street* (Boston, MA: John H. Eastburn, 1839), p.7; and Stebbins and Renn, vol.1, pp 60–61.

26   Francis Alexander to Hiram Powers, 4 February 1839, HPP.

27   Perkins and Gavin, p.177.

28   Christie's (New York), *American Art*, 23 May 2017, lot 6.

29   *A Catalogue of the First Exhibition of Paintings in the Athenaeum Gallery* (Boston, MA: William W. Clapp, 1927), no.114; and James Jackson Jarves, *Italian Sights and Papal Principles Seen Through American Spectacles* (New York: Harper & Brothers, 1856), p.105.

30   *Letters of Horatio Greenough American Sculptor*, ed. Nathalia Wright (Madison, WI: University of Wisconsin Press, 1972), p.303; and Richard H. Saunders, *Horatio Greenough. An American Sculptor's Drawings* (Middlebury, VT: Middlebury College Museum of Art, 1999), pp 92–3.

31   *Letters of Horatio Greenough to his Brother, Henry Greenough*, ed. Frances Boott Greenough (Boston, MA: Ticknor and Company, 1887), p.121.

32   Scrapbook no.2, PAF.

33   Francis Alexander to Hiram Powers, 10 October 1838, HPP.

34   Francis Alexander to Hiram Powers, 4 February 1839, HPP.

35   Deborah Jean Warner, *Alvan Clark & Sons. Artists in Optics* (Washington, DC: Smithsonian Institution Press, 1968), p.113.

36   Leah Lipton, 'The Boston Artists' Association, 1841–1851', *American Art Journal* 15, no.4 (Autumn 1983): pp 45–57.

37   *The Letters of Henry Wadsworth Longfellow*, ed. Andrew Hilen (Cambridge, MA: Harvard University Press, 1966), vol.2, p.385.

38   Francis Alexander to Henry Wadsworth Longfellow, [Summer 1849], LHWL.

39   Scrapbook no.2, PAF; and Francesca Alexander to Henry Wadsworth Longfellow, 12 June [1849] and 7 March 1869, LHWL.

40   Eunice Farley Felton, 'Mrs. Alexander and Her Daughter Francesca', *Cambridge Historical Society Publications XIV. Proceedings for the Year 1919* (Cambridge, MA: The Society, 1926), p.113. Alice owned a copy of Constance Grosvenor Alexander's biography of Francesca.

41   On Dickens in Boston, see Christie's (London), *Fine Printed Books and Manuscripts Including the Works of Charles Dickens*, 1 June 2009, lot 90; and G.W. Putnam in 'Four Months with Charles Dickens', *The Atlantic* 26 (October 1870): pp 476–9.

42   Charles Dickens to Lucia Alexander, 25 February 1842, CDC.

43   Catherine Dickens to Lucia Alexander, 22 August 1870, IMC.

44   See, for example, April Masten, *Art Work. Women Artists and Democracy in Mid-Nineteenth-Century New York* (Philadelphia, PA: University of Pennsylvania Press, 2008).

45   Similar scarves, associated with the Caribbean, appear in nineteenth-century portraits of blacks in both Europe and the United States; see Denise Murrell, *Posing Modernity: The Black Model from Manet and Matisse to Today* (New Haven, CT: Yale University Press, 2018).

46   For this area, see James Oliver and Lois E. Horton, *Black Bostonians* (New York: Holmes & Meier, 1979), pp 1–13; and Adelaide M. Cromwell, 'The Black Presence in the West End of Boston, 1800–1864', in Donald M. Jacobs, ed., *Courage and Conscience. Black and White Abolitionists in Boston* (Bloomington, IN: Indiana University Press, 1993), pp 155–67.

47   For contemporary recipes, see *Mrs. Putnam's Receipt Book* (Boston, MA: Ticknor, Reed, and Fields, 1850), pp 99–100.

2 'TRULY AN ARTIST'S HOME'

1   Francis Alexander to Hiram Powers, 10 October 1838, HPP.

2   Constance Grosvenor Alexander, *Francesca Alexander. A 'Hidden Servant'* (Cambridge, MA: Harvard University Press, 1927), p.56; and Lucia Gray Swett, *John Ruskin's Letters to Francesca and Memoirs of the Alexanders* (Boston, MA: Lothrop, Lee & Shepard Co., 1931), p.219.

3   Francis Alexander, 28 May 1853, USPA.

4   This sketchbook and 35 loose drawings from the Alexanders' first year abroad were on the art market in 1977, but neither it nor many of those drawings can be traced; see *Francesca Alexander* (Boston, MA: Childs Gallery, 1977).

5   *Handbook for Travellers in Northern Italy* (London: John Murray, 1852), p.449.

6   Anne Lohrli, 'The Madiai: A Forgotten Chapter of Church History', *Victorian Studies* 33, no.1 (Autumn 1989): pp 29–50.

7   For example, see Elizabeth Kinney to Sarah Dodge, 15 March and 26 October 1854, ECSP.

8   For the Evangelical church in Florence, see Theodosia Garrow, *Social Aspects of the Italian Revolution* (London: Chapman and Hall, 1861), pp 141–3 and 177–81.

9   Annie Adams Fields to her mother, 24 January 1860, AAFP.

10   Annie Adams Fields to her family, 4 April 1860, AAFP.

11   Francesca Alexander to Lilly Cleveland, 28 July and 11 September 1860, JRC.

12   Scrapbook no.121, FAS ('Dunque, signore, accettera

di buon cuore questo poco che abbiamo potuto fare per quelli che fanno tanto per noi. Dico per noi, perche sono certa che i miei genitori sentono come me che chi fa per l'Italia fa per noi; che questa Italia l'abbiamo sempre sul cuore come se fosse patria nostra: che iddio ci conceda di vederla libera fra poco!'); see also Francesca Alexander to Lilly Cleveland, [July 1866], JRC.

13 Ellen Perkins to Caroline Crane Marsh, [1867], CFP.

14 Swett, 1931, pp 293–301; and Lucia Alexander to John Greenleaf Whittier, 16 March 1870, PWP.

15 D. Medina Lasansky, 'Reshaping Attitudes Towards the Renaissance. The Fight Against "Modern Mania" in Florence at the Turn of the Century', in Yannick Portebois and Nicholas Terpstra, eds, *The Renaissance in the Nineteenth Century* (Toronto: CRRS, 2003), pp 263–98.

16 Francesca Alexander to Sally Henshaw Hayward, 12 December 1874, JHHFP; she later described Florence as 'spoiled' (Francesca Alexander to Fanny Talbot, 7 July 1889, LFT).

17 *The Complete Letters of Constance Fenimore Woolson*, ed. Sharon L. Dean (Gainesville, FL: University Press of Florida, 2021), p.134.

18 *The Letters of Margaret Fuller*, ed. Robert N. Hudspeth (Ithaca, NY: Cornell University Press, 1987), vol.4, p.291.

19 Henry James, *William Wetmore Story and His Friends* (Boston, MA: Houghton, Mifflin & Co., 1904), vol.1, p.245.

20 Lucia Alexander to John Lowell Gardner, 20 May 1863, ISGMC.

21 14 June 1866, SGPD.

22 [William Blundell Spence], *The Lions of Florence and its Environs* (Florence: Felix Le Monnier, 1847), pp 62–3; and James Jackson Jarves, 'Bric-a-Brac at Florence', *The Art Journal* 2 (1876): pp 216–17 and 253–5.

23 Richard P. Wunder, *Hiram Powers. A Life* (Newark, DE: University of Delaware Press, 1991), vol.1, p.95.

24 On the geography of this community, see Daniela Lamberini, 'Residenti anglo-americani e *genius loci*: ricostruzioni e restauri delle dimore fiorentine', in Marcello Fantoni, ed., *Gli Anglo-Americani a Firenze. Idea e costruzione del Rinascimento* (Rome: Bulzoni, 2000), pp 125–41.

25 Giuliana Artom-Treves, 'Come Firenze divento Florence', in *Inghilterra e Italia nell' 900* (Florence: La Nuova Italia, 1973), p.12.

26 For an overview of contemporary newspapers, see Isabelle Richet, 'English-Language Periodicals and Reading Rooms in Nineteenth-Century Italy as Spaces of Intercultural Contact and Exchange', *Cultural History* 10, no.2 (2021): pp 226–42, and 'Standing on the Edge of Two Cultural Worlds. The English-Language Press in Nineteenth-Century Italy', *Media History* (2022): pp 1–17.

27 Laura Desideri, 'Cronologia del Gabinetto Vieusseux, 1819–1995', *Antologia Vieusseux* 2, nos 3–4 (1996): pp 17–155.

28 William D. Howells, *Indian Summer* (Boston, MA: Houghton Mifflin Company, 1886), p.85.

29 They subscribed at least 11 times: on 12 November 1853, 6 July 1865, 30 June 1866, 18 June 1867, 19 May and 20 June 1870, 3 June 1871, 13 May 1878, 22 July 1879, 27 April 1882 and 28 November 1884, LDS.

30 *Memoirs of Margaret Fuller Ossoli* (Boston, MA: Phillips, Sampson and Company, 1852), vol.2, p.227.

31 Jacqueline Marie Musacchio, 'Jane M. Healey Jackson, a Sculptor's Wife Abroad', in Lynn Catterson, ed., *Florence, Berlin & Beyond: Late Nineteenth-Century Art Markets and their Social Networks* (Boston, MA: Brill, 2020), pp 377–9.

32 Henry Greenough Huntington, *Florentine Notes* (London: Remington & Co., 1884), p.8.

33 Scrapbook no.121, FAS.

34 On these women, see Alison Chapman, *Networking the Nation. British and American Women's Poetry and Italy, 1840–1870* (Oxford: Oxford University Press, 2015).

35 Although I have not been able to find extensive evidence about a relationship between the Alexanders and the Brownings, there certainly was one; allegedly Lucia 'never forgave her friend Robert Browning for espousing the cause of the South' ('Miss Alexander', *Manchester Guardian*, 31 January 1917).

36 Lucia Alexander to Catherine Peabody Gardner, 17 February 1865, ISGMC.

37 Francesca Alexander to Gino Capponi, 30 June and 19 July 1867, CAR.

38 Scrapbook no.1, PAF.

39   Ettore Leopardi to Francesca and Lucia Alexander, March 1904, AF (this was removed from one of Lucia's scrapbooks); and Scrapbook no.120, FAS.

40   Scrapbook no.120, FAS.

41   Scrapbook no.5, PAF.

42   Scrapbook no.122 (1 and 2), FAS. For a summary of most of Castromediano's letters to the Alexanders, see Fabio D'Astore, *'Mi scriva, mi scriva sempre…' Regesto delle lettere edite ed inedite di Sigismondo Castromediano* (Lecce: Pensa Multimedia, 1998).

43   Cinzia Polato, 'Caterina Percoto scrittrice e protagonista del suo tempo', Ph.D. dissertation, Università Ca'Foscari, Venice, 2014, pp 131–68; and Caterina Percoto, *Raccontini*, ed. Edoardo Colombaro (Udine: Biblioteca Civica V. Joppi, 2020), p.206.

44   Fabiana Savorgnan Cergneu di Brazzà, 'La corrispondenza di Caterina Percoto con Giovanni Lotti', *Aevum* 91, no.3 (2017): pp 798–801, 808.

45   Ornella Pittarello, ed., *Lettere d'Amicizia a Marina Sprea Baroni Semitecolo (1881–1909)* (Bologna: Casa editrice nuova, 2009), p.81 ('che ottime e sante creature!').

46   For letters from Alishan to the Alexanders, dated between 1870 and 1895, see Scrapbooks nos 1, 4, 6 and 7, PAF.

47   Scrapbooks nos 120 and 121, FAS, and no.3, PAF; see also 'Versi di Giuseppe Barellai', *La Gioventù. Rivista dell'istruzione pubblica in Italia* 1 (1870): pp 96–8; and *Nozze Fasolo-Antonibon* (Bassano: Tipo-calcegrafia Sante Pozzato, 1867).

48   Scrapbook no.1, PAF; see also *Versi di Erminia Fuà-Fusinato* (Florence: Le Monnier, 1874), p.245.

49   Scrapbook no.121, FAS.

50   Francesca Alexander to Lilly Cleveland, 26 October 1861, JRC.

51   Scrapbook no.4, PAF; and CA 1358, CRSCND. For the ticketing process, see Mahnaz Yousefzadeh, *City and Nation in the Italian Unification* (Basingstoke: Palgrave Macmillan, 2011), pp 95–127.

52   For their exchange, see Lucia Alexander to Henry Wadsworth Longfellow, 29 June 1865, LHWL; *The Letters of Henry Wadsworth Longfellow*, ed. Andrew Hilen (Cambridge, MA: Harvard University Press, 1982), vol.5, pp 51–2; and Lucia Alexander to Henry Wadsworth Longfellow, 29 June 1866, LHWL.

53   Francesca Alexander to Lilly Cleveland, 11 September 1860, JRC

54   Francesca Alexander to Lilly Cleveland, 3 January 1866, JRC.

55   James Jackson Jarves, *Italian Sights and Papal Principles Seen Through American Spectacles* (New York: Harper & Brothers, 1856), p.107.

56   Thomas Ball, *My Threescore Years and Ten* (Boston, MA: Roberts Brothers, 1891), pp 173–4.

57   Swett, 1931, p.231.

58   Francesca Alexander to Lilly Cleveland, 1 December 1883, JRC; on Francesca as a collector, see also Lilian Whiting, *The Golden Road* (Boston, MA: Little, Brown, and Company, 1918), p.112.

59   For some of these paintings, see Mojmír S. Frinta, 'The Quest for a Restorer's Shop of Beguiling Invention. Restorations and Forgeries in Italian Panel Painting', *Art Bulletin* 60, no.1 (March 1978): pp 7–23; Christie's (London), *Old Master Pictures*, 7 July 2000, lot 193; and Sonia Chiodo, *A Corpus of Florentine Painting. Painters in Florence after the 'Black Death'. The Master of the Misericordia and Matteo di Pacino*, ed. Miklós Boskovits (Florence: Giunti, 2011), pp 323 and 473. According to Frinta, a number of these paintings were restored in the same workshop, perhaps that of the forger Icilio Federico Joni; if Francis was instead responsible, it may indicate that he owned the entire group.

60   C.G. Alexander, pp 72–5; and Lilly Cleveland, Diary, 20 and 21 July 1859, CPFP.

61   C.G. Alexander, pp 83 and 74.

62   Matilda Lucas, *'Every Body Comes Back to Rome.' The Complete Letters of Matilda Lucas, 1871–1902*, ed. Robert Sénécal (London: Gatehouse Editions, 2013), vol.2, p.621; and C.G. Alexander, pp 71–7; on Bastianini and his contemporary reputation, see Jeremy Warren, 'From Florence to Paris: New Evidence for Giovanni Bastianini and his Work', *Burlington Magazine* 163 (March 2023): pp 222–35.

63   See, for example, Francesca Baldry, 'Rooms of Taste', in Lucia Mannini, ed., *The Treasure Rooms. Collectors and Antique Dealers in Florence between the 19th and 20th Centuries* (Florence: Polistampa, 2011), pp 45–64.

64   I[sa].B[lagden]., 'Felicie de Fauveau', *The English Woman's Journal* 2, no.8 (October 1858): p.84.

65 Kate Field, 'English Authors in Florence', *The Atlantic Monthly* (December 1884): p.663.

66 H. Buxton Forman, 'An American Studio in Florence', *The Manhattan* 3, no.6 (June 1884): pp 538–9.

67 Annie Adams Fields, Diary, 22 January 1860, AAFP; and Annie Adams Fields, ed., *Life and Letters of Harriet Beecher Stowe* (Cambridge, MA: Riverside Press, 1897), p.255.

68 Lucia Alexander to John Greenleaf Whittier, 26 August 1871 and 24 April 1872, PWP.

69 'The Old Masters of Boston', *Boston Evening Journal*, 26 December 1878.

70 19 May and 7 June 1866, SGPD; Francis Boott, *Recollections of Francis Boott for His Grandson F.B.D.* (Boston, MA: The Southgate Press, 1912), p.78; and Jacqueline Marie Musacchio, 'Finding Florence Freeman', *Nineteenth-Century Art Worldwide* 21, no.1 (Spring 2022). In 1895, a group of unidentified female artists rented a villa for the summer and hired instructors (Willard Fiske to his mother, 21 June 1895, DWFP).

71 Anne Whitney to Addy Manning, 23 May 1875, AWP; and Florence Intaglio Donlevy Grey to the Ladies' Art Association, 8 March and 16 May 1872, ADP.

72 Lilly Cleveland, Diary, May 1861, CPFP.

73 Francesca Alexander to Lilly Cleveland, 11 September and 8 October 1860, and 27 December 1861, JRC.

74 She also painted landscapes while summering near Vallombrosa; see Lucia Alexander to John Greenleaf Whittier, 26 August 1871, PWP.

75 Sheila Barker, 'Complete Transcriptions of All American Artists' Letters in the Historical Archive of the Uffizi Museum in Florence, 1763–1860', unpublished manuscript, 2008.

76 Lucia and Francesca Alexander, Notebook, fols 23r–23v, LGSANP.

77 The Magdalene drawing is at Columbus Museum in Georgia; the Dante was part of the cache sold by Childs Gallery in Boston.

78 Ball, p.173. The Balls and Alexanders remained close and both Francis and Francesca later signed the guestbook kept at Villa Ball, Francesca with a drawing of a *contadina*; see TBG, unpaginated.

79 Francesca Alexander to Lizzie Boott, 25 June [1865], FDEBDP; and Francesca Alexander to Lilly Cleveland, begun 2 September 1865, JRC; on the Misses Forbes, see Lady Mary Meynell, *Sunshine and Shadows Over a Long Life* (London: John Murray, 1933), pp 224–7. As much as Francesca was thrilled by the art, she was distressed by the state of the cloistered nuns (Alexander, fol.96 ½, LGSANP).

80 Francesca Alexander to Lilly Cleveland, October 1862, JRC; see also Francesca Alexander to Lilly Cleveland, 11 September 1860, JRC.

81 Francesca Alexander to Lilly Cleveland, 11 May 1875, JRC.

82 Ball, p.173.

83 *Catalogue of Paintings at the Artist's Exhibition, in Harding's Gallery, School Street, Boston. May, 1834* (Boston, MA: J.H. Eastburn, 1834), pp 4–6.

84 Scrapbook no.7, PAF.

85 Francesca Alexander to Lilly Cleveland, begun 18 February 1861, JRC.

86 Francesca Alexander to Lilly Cleveland, 13 August 1861, JRC.

87 Elizabeth Kinney, Journal, 19, 23 and 26 June 1855, ECSP.

88 Sarah Freeman Clarke to Rebecca Hull Clarke, 28 October 1855, PCA.

89 Francesca Alexander to Lilly Cleveland, begun 28 May 1868, JRC.

90 *The Complete Letters of Constance Fenimore Woolson*, ed. Sharon L. Dean (Gainesville, FL: University Press of Florida, 2021), p.119.

91 Elizabeth Barrett Browning, *Aurora Leigh* (New York: C.S. Francis & Co., 1857), pp 265–6.

92 Francesca Alexander to Lilly Cleveland, begun 27 December 1860, JRC; and Scrapbook no.3, PAF.

93 Francesca Alexander to Lilly Cleveland, 28 July 1860, JRC; *The Brownings' Correspondence*, ed. Philip Kelley, Edward Hagan and Linda M. Lewis (Winfield, KS: Wedgestone Press, 2022), vol.28, pp 165–74; and Elizabeth Kinney, Journal, 13 January 1858, ECSP.

94 Francesca Alexander to Lizzie Boott, 9 March [between 1865–8], and Francesca Alexander to Lizzie Boott, 25 June [early 1860s], FDEBDP; for Lizzie, see Carol M. Osborne, 'Lizzie Boott at Bellosguardo', in Irma B. Jaffe, ed., *The Italian*

Presence in American Art, 1860–1920 (New York: Fordham University Press, 1992), pp 188–99; and Anna Mazzanti, 'Lizzie come Ilaria. La breve vita di Elizabeth Boott Duveneck e il realismo Macchiaiolo', *Imagines* 5 (July 2021): pp 191–223.

95 Henry James, *Notes of a Son and Brother* (New York: Charles Scribner's Sons, 1914), pp 475–500.

96 Henry James, 'Recent Florence', *The Atlantic Monthly* (May 1878): p.588.

97 James T. Fields, *Hawthorne* (Boston, MA: Houghton, Mifflin and Company, 1881), p.68; for a similar quote, see 'What It Costs to Live at Florence', *The Living Age* 65, no.827 (7 April 1860): p.44; and, for a much lower and probably exaggerated quote, see Francis Boott, *Recollections of Francis Boott for His Grandson F.B.D.* (Boston, MA: The Southgate Press, 1912), pp 77–8.

98 Frances Power Cobbe, *Life of Frances Power Cobbe as Told by Herself* (London: Swan Sonnenschein & Co., 1904), p.376.

99 Anson Howe Smith, 'Some Early Flower Holders', *Antiques* 57, no.4 (April 1950): p.282.

100 Richard P. Wunder, *Hiram Powers: A Life* (Newark, DE: University of Delaware Press, 1991), vol.1, pp 337–8; and Anne Brewster, 'American Artists in Rome', *The Lippincott's Magazine of Literature, Science and Education* (February 1869): p.196; for examples of seed sharing, see Francesca Alexander to Lilly Cleveland, 25 August 1888, JRC; and Lucia Alexander to Joan Severn, 13 November 1889, CLLAJS.

101 Francesca Alexander to Annie Adams Fields, 29 March 1862, JTFC. She later shared seeds from her columbines; see Francesca Alexander to Joan Severn, 21 November 1885, CLFAJS.

102 Roberto Lunardi and Maria Emirena Tozzi Bellini, *Il Giardino Sapiente* (Florence: Polistampa, 2021), pp 13, 15–16.

103 Francis Alexander to Mary Crowninshield Sparks, 7 November 1857, JSL.

104 See, for example, Francesca Alexander to Annie Adams Fields, 29 March 1862, JTFC; Francesca Alexander to Lilly Cleveland, 21 March 1862, JRC; Lucia Alexander to Henry Wadsworth Longfellow, 29 June 1865, LHWL; and Lucia Alexander to John Greenleaf Whittier, 23 March 1865, PWP.

105 Scrapbooks nos 2 and 3, PAF.

106 Scrapbook no.121, FAS; and *Trustees of the Museum of Fine Arts. Eighth Annual Report* (Boston, MA: Alfred Mudge & Son, 1884), p.25.

107 Address Books, GPMC.

108 Francesca Alexander to Caroline Crane Marsh, 23 March 1868, CFP.

109 Sarah A. Hayward Dorr, Diary, 19 April 1859, JHHFP.

110 10 June 1866, SGPD.

111 Florence Freeman to family, 13 and 26 April 1862, FFL.

112 Florence Freeman to family, 26 April 1862, FFL.

113 For Lucia's condolences following the death of Florence Powers, see Lucia Alexander to Elisabeth Gibson Powers, 6 August 1863, HPP; and for their attendance at the wedding of Preston Powers, see Lucia Alexander to John Greenleaf Whittier, 24 April 1872, PWP.

114 Richard P. Wunder, *Hiram Powers: A Life* (Newark, DE: University of Delaware Press, 1991), vol.1, pp 306–7, 315.

115 Francesca Alexander to Lilly Cleveland, 5 and 8 June 1860, and 15 June 1861, JRC; on Eckley, see Alison Chapman, *Networking the Nation. British and American Women's Poetry and Italy, 1840–1870* (Oxford: Oxford University Press, 2015), pp 198–223.

116 Francesca Alexander to Lilly Cleveland, October 1862, JRC; and Charles Callahan Perkins, *Tuscan Sculptors. Their Lives, Works, and Times* (London: Longman, Green, Longman, Roberts & Green, 1864), vol.1, pp 194–5.

117 Lilly Cleveland, Diary, 11/12 November 1858, CPFP.

118 Joseph Pennell, *The Adventures of an Illustrator* (Boston, MA: Little, Brown, and Company, 1925), p.117.

119 This etching was donated to the Museum of Fine Arts in Boston by George Washington Wales, who claimed Lucia made it after a drawing by Francesca, but that seems unlikely; see *Trustees of the Museum of Fine Arts. Twelfth Annual Report* (Boston, MA: Alfred Mudge & Son, 1888), p.23. Lucia's scrapbooks include a second copy of this etching (Scrapbook no.3, PAF), as well as one of a stone bridge with a tabernacle near Pistoia and two of *contadine* (Scrapbook no.3 and Folder 10, PAF).

120 Lilly Cleveland, Diary, 24 June 1859, CPFP.

121 'American Citizens Abroad. The Outrage at Perugia. Message and Documents', *New York Times*, 3 February 1860.

122 *The Brownings' Correspondence*, ed. Philip Kelley, Edward Hagan and Linda M. Lewis (Winfield, KS: Wedgestone Press, 2022), vol.26 (2019), p.200; see also pp 199, 204–5.

123 Theodosia Garrow, *Social Aspects of the Italian Revolution* (London: Chapman and Hall, 1861), p.43.

124 Lilly Cleveland, Diary, 24 February 1860, CPFP.

125 Francesca Alexander to Lilly Cleveland, 13 August 1861, JRC. Francesca later described how Niccolò Tommaseo composed the text on the plaque that city officials placed on the Casa Guidi after the poet's death; see Francesca Alexander to Lilly Cleveland, begun October 1862, JRC.

3 FANNY AND HER POOR

1 Annie Adams Fields, Diary, 28 January 1860, AAFP.

2 Francesca Alexander to Lilly Cleveland, begun 2 August 1862, JRC; on Abetone, see Emilio Bertini, *Le dimore estive dell'Appennino Toscano* (Florence: Luigi Niccolai Editore, 1896).

3 Francesca Alexander to Gino Capponi, 19 July 1867, CAR.

4 Francesca Alexander to Lilly Cleveland, begun 2 August 1862, JRC.

5 Florence Freeman to her family, 8 September 1862, FFL.

6 For example, see 5 October 1879, WH; for a counterpoint, see 'Charity in Tuscany', *Florence Gazette*, 12 November 1892.

7 Zeffiro Ciuffoletti and Maria Grazia Proli, 'Popular Life in the Streets of Florence', in Monika Poettinger and Piero Roggi, eds, *Florence. Capital of the Kingdom of Italy, 1865–71* (London: Bloomsbury Academic, 2018), pp 113–20; and Francesco Ammannati, 'Food Availability and Consumption Patterns in Florence and Tuscany after Italy's Unification', in Poettinger and Roggi, pp 230–32.

8 Nathaniel Hawthorne, *The Marble Faun* (Leipzig: Tauchnitz, 1860), vol.2, p.63.

9 Van Wyck Brooks, *The Dream of Arcadia* (New York: Dutton, 1958), p.182.

10 For these books, see Jacqueline Marie Musacchio, 'Carrying Home Renaissance Florence in Extra-Illustrated Editions of George Eliot's *Romola* (1863)', in Lynn Catterson and Denise Budd, eds, *Italy for Sale. Alternative Objects, Alternative Markets* (Leiden: Brill, 2023), pp 169–203.

11 Monica Pacini, 'Straw Hats: The Invisible Work of Women Behind the International Image of Florence', in Poettinger and Roggi, pp 263–74.

12 Francesca Alexander to Lilly Cleveland, 20 April 1861 and 16 May 1862, JRC.

13 On the Evangelical church in Italy, see Alessandra Pecchioli, ed., *La Chiesa 'degli italiani'. All'origine dell'Evangelismo risvegliato in Italia* (Rome: Edizioni GBU, 2010).

14 Pietro Guicciardini to Francesca Alexander, 23 July 1873, Folder 9, PAF.

15 On this sympathy, see Candido Greco, 'Ester [*sic*] Frances (Francesca) Alexander. Il suo epistolario con Giannina Milli', *Bullettino della deputazione abruzzese di storia patria* III (2020): pp 175–8.

16 See, for example, Francesca Alexander to Lilly Cleveland, 11 September and 8 October 1860, JRC; Alexander, fols 74r–75v, LGSANP; and Francesca Alexander to John Ruskin, [summer 1890], CLFAJS.

17 Francesca Alexander to Lizzie Boott, 9 March [between 1865–8], FDEBDP.

18 Alexander, fols 10r–v, LGSANP; Matilda Lucas, *'Every Body Comes Back to Rome.' The Complete Letters of Matilda Lucas, 1871–1902*, ed. Robert Sénécal (London: Gatehouse Editions, 2013), vol.2, p.621; Constance Grosvenor Alexander, *Francesca Alexander. A 'Hidden Servant'* (Cambridge, MA: Harvard University Press, 1927), p.31; and Francesca Alexander to Charles Warren Stoddard, 21 May 1889, SSCL.

19 Francesca Alexander to Lilly Cleveland, 23 February [1882], JRC.

20 Alexander, fols 70r–81v, LGSANP.

21 Lucia Alexander to John Greenleaf Whittier, 24 April 1872, PWP.

22 Francesca Alexander to Lilly Cleveland, 18 February 1861, JRC.

23 Francesca Alexander to Lilly Cleveland, 31 December 1863, JRC.

24 Francesca Alexander to Lilly Cleveland, 11 September 1860, JRC.

25 Francesca Alexander to Lilly Cleveland, 8 October 1860, JRC.

26 Francesca Alexander to Lilly Cleveland, 27 March 1863, JRC.

27 For a copy of the letter, see Lucia Alexander to unknown, 2 April 1863, and Alexander, fols 135r–136r, LGSANP.

28 Alexander, fols 81v–82r, LGSANP.

29 *Florence Gazette*, 31 January 1891.

30 Francesca Alexander to Lilly Cleveland, 8 October 1860 and 27 March 1863, JRC; and Francesca Alexander to Fanny Talbot, 21 January 1887, LFT.

31 She also shared remedies she learned from them to help others, too; see Francesca Alexander to Caterina Tommaseo, 16 July [1875], CAR.

32 Francesca Alexander to Lilly Cleveland, 27 March and 16 June 1863, JRC.

33 Francesca Alexander to Lilly Cleveland, 23 April 1908, JRC; she also described the pain caused by conscription in Francesca Alexander, *Roadside Songs of Tuscany*, ed. John Ruskin (Sunnyside, Kent: George Allen, 1885), pp 230–41.

34 Lilly Cleveland, Diary, 14 and 16 September 1859, CPFP.

35 Francesca Alexander to Lilly Cleveland, 8 October 1860, JRC. The American sculptor Moses Ezekiel installed a Christmas tree in his Roman studio; see Moses Ezekiel, *Memoirs from the Baths of Diocletian* (Detroit, MI: Wayne State University Press, 1975), pp 211–12.

36 Francesca Alexander to Lilly Cleveland, [21 December 1859], JRC; for other lists, see Francesca Alexander to Lilly Cleveland, 27 December 1860, 26 December 1861, 2 January and 31 December 1863, 4 February 1865, 3 January 1866, 1 January 1867 and 28 May 1868, JRC.

37 Francesca Alexander to Lilly Cleveland, 5 June, 11 September and 8 October 1860, JRC; her description of one of her Cinderella paintings is similar to the drawing in fig.30. For Motley's observations, see Chapter 2 above and Scrapbook no.7, PAF.

38 Francesca Alexander to Lilly Cleveland, begun 28 July 1860, JRC.

39 Francesca Alexander to Annie Adams Fields, 29 March 1862, JTFC. She continued painting while in the Apennines that summer; see Florence Freeman to family, 8 September 1862, FFL.

40 Francesca Alexander to Lizzie Boott, 9 March [between 1865–8], FDEBDP.

41 Francesca Alexander to Lilly Cleveland, 29 April 1864, JRC.

42 Bayard Taylor, 'Letters. American Sculptors in Florence', *New-York Tribune*, 23 April 1868.

43 Francesca Alexander to Lilly Cleveland, 29 April 1864, JRC.

44 A later printed copy of this is in JRC; see also C.G. Alexander, p.20.

45 Catherine W. Pierce, 'Further Notes on Francis Alexander', *Old-Time New England* 56, no.2 (October–December 1965): pp 35–44.

46 Francesca Alexander to Sally Hayward, 11 June [1869], JHHFP.

47 Francesca Alexander to Lilly Cleveland, 26 October 1861, JRC.

48 Roswell Park, *A Hand-Book for American Travellers in Europe* (New York: G.P. Putnam, 1853), p.20.

49 Francesca Alexander to Lilly Cleveland, 21 March 1862, JRC.

50 FAH, fol.1.

51 FAH, fol.47.

52 Francesca Alexander to Fanny Talbot, 11 February 1889, LFT.

53 Lucia mentioned a manuscript for a Mrs Mason, likely Sarah Ellen Francis Mason, in her letter to Catherine Peabody Gardner, 17 February 1865, ISGMC. The Mason home in Newport and most of its contents, presumably including this manuscript, was destroyed by fire in 1899; see Bertram Lippincott, 'The Mason Sisters of Newport and their Rhode Island Avenue Mansion', *Newport History* 75, no.254 (Spring 2006): p.34.

54 Lucia Alexander to Elizabeth Russell Lyman, 7 February 1905, LGSANP.

55 Lucia Alexander to John Lowell Gardner, 20 May 1863, ISGMC.

56 Lucia Alexander to John Lowell Gardner, 20 May 1863, ISGMC.

57 Francesca Alexander to Lilly Cleveland, 1 November 1864, JRC.

58 Francesca Alexander to Catherine Peabody Gardner, 10 November 1864, ISGMC.

59 Francesca Alexander to Catherine Peabody Gardner, 10 November 1864, ISGMC.

60 Lucia Alexander to Catherine Peabody Gardner, 17 January 1865, ISGMC.

61 Lucia Alexander to Catherine Peabody Gardner, 17 February 1865, ISGMC.

62 Lucia Alexander to Catherine Peabody Gardner, 25 April 1865, ISGMC.

63 Lucia mentioned Florence's 1865 Dante celebrations in Lucia Alexander to Catherine Peabody Gardner, 25 April 1865, ISGMC. Isabella and Jack also appreciated Francesca's later publications. Isabella gave Jack a copy of *Roadside Songs* for Christmas 1884, and she had copies of *The Story of Ida* and *Christ's Folk*; Fanny gave Isabella a copy of *Hidden Servants* in 1901 and Lucia sent her a copy of her *Libro d'Oro* at an unknown date.

64 Lucia Alexander to Catherine Peabody Gardner, 27 January 1866, ISGMC.

65 Francesca Alexander to Lilly Cleveland, begun 2 September 1865, JRC.

66 Francesca Alexander to Sarah Cleveland, 23 January [1864], JRC; and Francesca Alexander to Lilly Cleveland, begun 11 February 1864, JRC. The painting is visible in a photograph of the library at Nutwood, the Cleveland home in Jamaica Plain (Historic New England, Domestic Interiors Photographic Collection 168259).

67 Francesca Alexander to Lilly Cleveland, begun 2 September 1865, JRC.

68 Lawrence Park, *Gilbert Stuart. An Illustrated Descriptive List of His Works* (New York: William Edwin Rudge, 1926), pp 733–4; Richard H. Saunders, *John Smibert. Colonial America's First Portrait Painter* (New Haven, CT: Yale University Press, 1995), pp 185–6; and David B. Warren et al., *American Decorative Arts and Paintings in the Bayou Bend Collection* (Princeton, NJ: Princeton University Press, 1998), pp 177–9. Lucia also inherited a mahogany cellarette attributed to Boston cabinetmakers John and Thomas Seymour

which was sold through New York's Levy Galleries in 2020.

69 Francesca Alexander to Lilly Cleveland, begun 28 May 1868, JRC.

70 22 May 1868, VB.

71 James Freeman Clarke to Lillian Freeman Clarke, 15 July 1869, PCA.

72 Francesca Alexander to Sarah Smith Bryant Fay, [before 21 August 1869], FMFP; and Francesca Alexander to Lilly Cleveland, [July 1869], JRC.

73 W.J. Stillman, 'Francesca's Country', *The Critic* 9, no.234 (23 June 1888): p.302; and Ruth Faure, 'Frances Alexander', *The Christian Advocate* 74, no.3 (2 February 1899): p.174.

74 Robert F. Perkins Jr and William J. Gavin III, eds, *The Boston Athenaeum. Art Exhibition Index 1827–1874* (Boston, MA: The Library, 1980), p.9; and Scrapbook no.121, FAS.

75 Francesca Alexander to Lilly Cleveland, [July 1869], JRC.

76 Francesca Alexander to Diamante Tommaseo, 4 March 1869, CAR ('non possono distorre il mio cuore da quelli che ho lasciati, e che mi stanno a tutte l'ore nel cuore').

77 Francesca Alexander to Caroline Crane Marsh, 23 March 1868, CFP; and Francesca Alexander to Mrs Ripka, [before 20 August 1869], FMFP; on Castorani, see Candido Greco, 'Severino Castorani, scultore di Teramo', *Rivista Abruzzese* 69, no.1 (2016): pp 76–9.

78 Francesca Alexander to Henry Wadsworth Longfellow, 7 March 1869, LHWL.

79 Francesca Alexander to Lilly Cleveland, 28 May 1868, JRC.

80 Francesca Alexander to Niccolò Tommaseo, 18 September [1869], CAR ('Io, da parte mia, ho promesso, tanto a lei tanto al Babbo, di tenermi pronta a ripartire per l'America la prossima primavera; e sono cert anche, dopo d'avermi rinfrescati gli occhi ed il cuore colla vista della patria della mia affezione, e delle mie persone care, potrò poi, coll'aiuto di Dio, vivere contenta anch nella lontananza, perchè vedo che l'America è troppo necessaria a Babbo e Mamma'); similarly, see Francesca Alexander to Caterina Tommaseo, [September 1869], CAR; and Francesca

Alexander to Sarah Smith Bryant Fay, [before 21 August 1869], FMFP.

81 Scrapbook no.1, PAF. The wood samples are still in the museum, identified as an Alexander donation; Anna Svensson, '"Specimens of Woods": A Natural History of the Pianoforte', unpublished paper.

82 Scrapbook no.1, PAF.

83 Scrapbook no.122 (1), FAS.

84 Sigismondo Castromediano, *Carceri e galere politiche. Memorie del Duca Sigismondo Castromediano* (Lecce: Il Tipografia Editrice Salentina, 1895), vol.2, p.164 ('son note per gran cuore e beneficenza; tanto esse amano l'Italia!').

85 Esther Frances Alexander, 12 August 1869, USPA.

86 Alessandro Carraresi, ed., *Lettere di Gino Capponi e di altri a lui* (Florence: Le Monnier, 1885), vol.4, p.235.

87 Francesca Alexander to Caterina Tommaseo, [September 1869], CAR.

88 *Northern Italy. Handbook for Travellers* (Coblenz: Karl Baedeker, 1868), p.341.

89 Francesca Alexander to Lilly Cleveland, 9 December 1882, JRC; Francesca Alexander to Caterina Tommaseo, [September 1869], CAR; and, for the studios, Lucia Alexander to John Greenleaf Whittier, 24 April 1872 and 16 March 1875, PWP.

90 Francesca Alexander to Lilly Cleveland, 11 September 1860, JRC.

91 Francesca Alexander to Fanny Talbot, 8 March 1892, LFT; see also Francesca Alexander to Joan Severn, 16 October 1885, CLFAJS.

92 Francesca Alexander to Lilly Cleveland, [winter 1870], JRC; and Lucia Alexander to John Greenleaf Whittier, 26 August 1871, PWP.

93 Lucia Alexander to John Greenleaf Whittier, 18 March 1870, PWP.

94 Lucia Alexander to John Greenleaf Whittier, 26 August 1871 and 24 April 1872, PWP; see also Francesca Alexander to Sarah Henshaw Hayward, 28 February and 31 August 1871, JHHFP.

95 Lucia Alexander to John Greenleaf Whittier, 26 June 1882, PWP; and Lucia Alexander to Mary Rice Bowditch, [1901], BLFP.

96 Lucia Alexander to John Greenleaf Whittier, 24 April 1872, PWP.

97 Scrapbook no.122 (1), FAS.

98 Francesca Alexander to Lilly Cleveland, [winter 1870], JRC; for other examples of these gatherings, see Frances Macbeth Glessner and John Jacob Glessner, Journal, 29 March 1890, GFP; and Eunice Farley Felton, 'Mrs. Alexander and Her Daughter Francesca', *Cambridge Historical Society Publications XIV. Proceedings for the Year 1919* (Cambridge, MA: The Society, 1926), p.107.

99 Francesca Alexander to Fanny Talbot, 8 January and 10 June 1889, and 12 February 1890, LFT.

100 Francesca Alexander to Caterina Tommaseo, 10 July [1875], CAR; and Lucas, vol.2, p.620.

101 Francesca Alexander to Lilly Cleveland, 6 June 1871, JRC.

102 Francesca Alexander to Mrs Ripka, [before 21 August 1869], and Francesca Alexander to Sarah Smith Bryant Fay, [before 21 August 1869], FMFP.

103 Francesca Alexander to Lilly Cleveland, 6 June 1871, JRC.

104 Lydia Maria Child to Francis Alexander, 1 July 1877, ALC.

105 James Russell Lowell, 'To F.A.', *The Atlantic Monthly* (May 1875): p.560; see also Scrapbook no.6, PAF; and Thomas Wortham, 'Lowell's "Agassiz" and Mrs. Alexander', *The Yale University Library Gazette* 45, no.3 (January 1971): pp 118–22.

106 Francesca Alexander to Sally Hayward, 31 August 1871, JHHFP.

107 *United States Centennial Commission. International Exhibition. 1876 Official Catalogue Part II. Art Gallery, Annexes, and Outdoors Works of Art* (Philadelphia, PA: John R. Nagle and Company, 1876), pp 41 (n.912), 48 (n.1125), 49 (n.1129) and 54 (n.1270); for the Madonna, see note 34 to Chapter 5, below.

108 Francesca Alexander to Lilly Cleveland, 31 May 1878, JRC.

109 Francesca Alexander to Lilly Cleveland, 28 July 1860, [November 1877], 31 May 1878 and 25 June 1879, JRC.

110 William H. Gerdts, *American Neo-Classic Sculpture. The Marble Resurrection* (New York: Studio, 1973), p.69; Lizzie Boott also made a drawing of Ruth in one of her early sketchbooks, now at the Museum of Fine Arts Boston.

111 Florentia, 'A Walk Through the Studios of Rome', *Art Journal* 1 (June 1854): p.186.

112 Leo M. Alishan, trans., *Armenian Popular Songs* (Venice: S. Lazarus, 1852).

113 Francesca Alexander to Lilly Cleveland, begun 8 October 1860, JRC; see also Lucia Alexander to Joan Severn, 11 May [1889], CLLAJS.

114 Francesca Alexander to Sally Hayward, 31 August 1871, JHHFP.

115 Francesca Alexander to Lilly Cleveland, 31 May 1872, JRC.

116 Francesca Alexander to Lilly Cleveland, 11 May 1875, JRC; for her description of an earlier *giostra*, see Florence Freeman to her family, 8 September 1862, FFL.

117 Scrapbook no.6, PAF.

118 Lucia and Francesca Alexander to Lilly Cleveland, 2 August 1875, JRC.

119 Alexander, LGSANP. Additional stories copied out on lined paper by an unknown hand, now missing some pages and titled 'Miss Alexander's Letters', are in Folder 10, PAF.

120 Leader Scott, *A Nook in the Apennines* (London: C. Kegan Paul & Co., 1879), pp 228–33.

121 Francesca's manuscript is transcribed in C.G. Alexander, pp 193–220.

122 Francesca Alexander to Caterina Tommaseo, 4 September 1875, CAR ('perchè sono a lavorare tante fissa, a fare i disegni per un libro, e questi disegni devono essere terminati prima d'andar via, ed il tempo è molto ristretto. Avrò tanto piacere poi a farti vedere i miei designi, quando ti vedrò a Firenze, che credo ti piaceranno, che sono per una leggenda che ho voluto imparare quassù da una ragazza del paese, e l'è molto curiosa ed originale. Tra l'altre cose ho dovuto far il disegno di molti di questi delicatissimi fiori del paese, per farne le bordiere alle pagine').

123 Francesca Alexander to Sally Hayward, 11 June [1869], JHHFP.

124 Francesca Alexander to Caterina Tommaseo, 13 October [1876], CAR ('sono stata occupatissimava far i disegni per quel libro, il quale, mi pare, tu hai visto principiato, e che manca ancora un pezzo a terminarsi, sebbene è stato venduto da più di sei mesi').

125 Scrapbook no.7, PAF.

126 Francesca Alexander to Lilly Cleveland, [early September 1877], JRC.

127 Francesca Alexander to Lilly Cleveland, begun 3 January 1866, JRC.

128 Scrapbook no.7, PAF; see also Francesca Alexander to Lilly Cleveland, begun 2 August 1875, JRC.

129 Scrapbooks nos 6 and 7, PAF.

130 Scrapbook no.6, PAF.

131 Elizabeth Cabot Cary Agassiz, Diary, 17 February 1895, PECCA; for additional references to their interactions, see her entries on 20 and 21 February, 9, 10, 25, 26 and 28 March, and 2, 3, 8, 13 and 14 April, as well as letters from Elizabeth Agassiz to Sarah Cary, 22 February, 5 and 13 March, and 9 and 14 April 1895, PECCA; and Louise Hall Tharp, *Adventurous Alliance. The Story of the Agassiz Family of Boston* (Boston, MA: Little, Brown, 1959), pp 284–5.

132 Elizabeth Agassiz to Sarah Cary, 14 April 1895, PECCA.

133 'Francesca's Book', *Worcester Daily Spy*, 25 December 1883; *Trustees of the Museum of Fine Arts. Eighth Annual Report* (Boston, MA: Alfred Mudge & Son, 1884), p.34; and *Monthly Bulletin of Books Added to the Public Library of the City of Boston* 7, no.11 (November 1902): p.449.

134 Lucia Alexander to Cornelia Rockwell Bowditch, 9 July 1899, BCBFP. One of these copies was displayed at the Cambridge Historical Society in 1919; see Felton, p.113. The Boston Public Library now has three copies and the Boston Athenaeum and Wellesley College have one each.

135 Niccolò Tommaseo, 'Gita nel Pistojese', *Antologia. Giornale di Scienze, Lettere, Arti* 48 (1832): pp 12–33, and *Canti popolari toscani* (Venice: Tasso, 1841).

136 Louise Winsor Brooks, Diary, 4 May 1854, WFP; see also 26, 28 and 29 April, and 1 and 3 May 1854.

137 Scrapbook no.7, PAF.

138 Giuseppe Tigri, *Canti popolari toscani* (Florence: Barbèra, Bianchi e Comp., 1860), vol.1, pp 146 and 315; and Isa Blagden, *The Cost of a Secret* (London: Chapman & Hall, 1863), pp 200–201.

139 Elizabeth Barrett Browning, *Casa Guidi Windows* (London: Chapman & Hall, 1851), pp 1, 2 and 12; Elizabeth C. Kinney, *Poems* (New York: Hurd and Houghton, 1867), pp 3–6 and 10–12; and Alison

Chapman, *Networking the Nation. British and American Women's Poetry and Italy, 1840–1870* (Oxford: Oxford University Press, 2015), pp 61–2. For Kinney's poems, see Elizabeth Kinney, Journal, 25 and 30 November 1854, ECSP.

140 Janet Ross, 'Popular Songs of Tuscany', *Fraser's Magazine*, April 1877, pp 707–21, and *The Fourth Generation* (New York: Charles Scribner's Sons, 1912), pp 184–5; see also Claudia Capancioni, 'Janet Ross's "Love of Italian Peasant Songs": Tuscan Folk Songs and the Victorians', in Fausto Ciompi et al., eds, *Interconnecting Music and the Literary World* (Cambridge: Cambridge University Press, 2018), pp 110–23.

141 8 December 1880, MEEL.

142 On Beatrice, see C. Schubert, 'La pastorella poetessa', *L'Illustrazione italiana* 31 (1888): pp 51–2; 32: pp 71, 74; and 34: pp 108–9, 112; A. Chiappelli, *Una pastora poetessa. Beatrice di Pian degli Ontani* (Florence: Seeber, 1902); and more recently Paolo Bellucci, *Poetessa pastora. La storia e i canti di Beatrice di Pian degli Ontani, scoperta dal Tommaseo e amata dal Ruskin* (Florence: Medicea, 1986); and Arthur Whellens, '"A Tuscan Sibyl": A Note on Beatrice di Pian degli Ontani', in Jeanne Clegg and Paul Tucker, eds, *The Dominion of Daedalus* (St Albans: Bretham Press, 1994), pp 50–57.

143 Francesca Alexander to Lilly Cleveland, 2 August and October 1862, JRC.

144 Felice Bernabei, 'Giannina Milli e Francesca Alexander', *Nuova antologia. Rivista di lettere, scienze ed arti* 205, no.1152 (16 March 1920): pp 178–85; and Greco, 'Ester', pp 186–219.

145 Francesca Alexander to Lilly Cleveland, begun 8 July 1864, JRC.

146 Francesca Alexander, *Christ's Folk in the Apennine*, ed. John Ruskin (Sunnyside, Kent: George Allen, 1887), vol.2, pp 36–44.

147 Scrapbook no.121, FAS.

148 Francesca Alexander to Joan Severn, 4 December 1890, CLFAJS; and Lucia Alexander to Charles P. Bowditch, 24 January 1893, BCBFP.

149 FASA, fol.104.

150 For the songs, see Giuseppe Tigri, *Canti popolari toscani* (Florence: Barbèra, Bianchi e Comp., 1860), vol.1, pp 82 and 143.

151 Francesca Alexander to Lilly Cleveland, 28 July 1860, JRC.

152 Lucia Alexander to Charles P. Bowditch, 24 January 1893, BCBFP.

153 Lucia Alexander to Charles P. Bowditch, 24 January 1893, BCBFP.

154 Those in the Anglo-American community knew of it, too. In 1883, Constance Fenimore Woolson reminded fellow writer John Hay that he had seen Fanny's 'book of sketches & translations'; see *The Complete Letters of Constance Fenimore Woolson*, ed. Sharon L. Dean (Gainesville, FL: University Press of Florida, 2021), p.264.

155 On his time in Abetone, see Frederic Leighton to William Cornwallis Cartwright, [after August 1879], WCCC; and Lucia Alexander to Charles P. Bowditch, 24 January 1893, BCBFP.

156 Scrapbook no.6, PAF. The resulting lithograph may be one of a bust-length young woman wearing a gauzy veil, now in the Massachusetts Historical Society.

157 Sarah Perkins Cleveland to Mary Dwight Parkman, 24 April [1879], JRC.

158 Lucia Alexander to Charles P. Bowditch, 24 January 1893, BCBFP.

159 Francesca Alexander to Lilly Cleveland, 26 May 1880, JRC; on Magrini, see Grazia Gobbi Sica, *In Loving Memory. Il cimitero agli Allori di Firenze* (Florence: Leo S. Olschki, 2016), p.119.

160 Lucia Alexander to Sarah P. Cleveland, 26 May 1880, JRC.

4 FRANCESCA

1 Newman used this address for his subscriptions at the Gabinetto Vieusseux on 4, 12, 21 and 28 November 1870, LDS.

2 Francesca Alexander to Lilly Cleveland, 9 December 1882, JRC; see also William G. Collingwood, *Ruskin Relics* (London: Isbister & Company Limited, 1903), p.102.

3 Royal Leith, *A Quiet Devotion. The Life and Work of Henry Roderick Newman* (New York: Jordan-Volpe Gallery, 1996), pp 24–5.

4   Lucia Alexander to James Russell Lowell, 4 January [1884], JRLAP.

5   John Ruskin to Lucia Alexander, 9 October 1882, ALSWC.

6   *The Diaries of John Ruskin 1874–1889*, ed. Joan Evans and John Howard Whitehouse (Oxford: Clarendon Press, 1959), vol.3, p.1031.

7   John Ruskin to Lucia Alexander, 9 October 1882, ALSWC; see also *The Diaries of John Ruskin*, vol.3, p.1032.

8   John Ruskin, 'The Editor's Preface', in Francesca Alexander, *Roadside Songs of Tuscany*, ed. John Ruskin (Sunnyside, Kent: George Allen, 1885), pp 10–11.

9   *The Works of John Ruskin*, ed. E.T. Cook and Alexander Wedderburn (London: George Allen, 1907), vol.32, pp xviii–xxxv.

10   'Letter from Florence', *The Roman News*, 28 March 1883.

11   'Literary Notes', *The American Register*, 26 May 1883.

12   Others did the same, perhaps because of her innocent demeanor; for an example, see *The Complete Letters of Constance Fenimore Woolson*, ed. Sharon L. Dean (Gainesville, FL: University Press of Florida, 2021), pp 264–5.

13   Jeanne Clegg and Paul Tucker, *Ruskin and Tuscany* (London: Lund Humphries, 1992), p.120.

14   *The Correspondence of John Ruskin and Charles Eliot Norton*, ed. John Lewis Bradley and Ian Ousby (Cambridge: Cambridge University Press, 1987), p.453.

15   Clegg and Tucker, p.68; and John Ruskin to Francesca Alexander, 22 October 1882, JRCLFA.

16   Clegg and Tucker, p.68.

17   Rachel Dickinson, *John Ruskin's Correspondence with Joan Severn* (London: Legenda, 2009); and James L. Spates, 'Ruskin's Life: A Radical Revision', www.whyruskin.wordpress.com (2020).

18   John Ruskin to Francesca Alexander, 23 September 1888, JRCLFA.

19   Pamela Gerrish Nunn, 'Ruskin's Patronage of Women Artists', *Woman's Art Journal* 2, no.2 (Autumn 1981–Winter 1982): pp 8–13; and Jennifer M. Lloyd, 'Raising Lilies: Ruskin and Women', *Journal of British Studies* 34, no.3 (July 1995): pp 345–8.

20   Anna Lloyd, *A Memoir. With Extracts from Her Letters* (London: The Cayme Press Limited, 1928), pp 97–8; for similar sentiments in an 1894 talk to female students at the Royal Academy, see also *The Works of John Ruskin*, vol.24, p.641.

21   Francesca Alexander to Lilly Cleveland, 9 December 1882, JRC.

22   Francesca Alexander to Lilly Cleveland, 9 December 1882, JRC.

23   John Ruskin to Lucia Alexander, 9 December 1882, JRCLFA; for Ruskin's drawing, see Robert Hewison, *Ruskin, Turner and the Pre-Raphaelites* (London: Tate Gallery, 2000), p.261.

24   John Ruskin to Francesca Alexander, 26 October 1885, JRCLFA.

25   John Ruskin to Francesca Alexander, 21 and 31 January 1883, JRCLFA.

26   His mysterious reference did result in some speculation; see 'London Letter', *Cincinnati Commercial Tribune*, 13 April 1883.

27   *The Works of John Ruskin*, vol.33, pp 282–3.

28   *The Works of John Ruskin*, vol.33, pp 324–5.

29   John Greenleaf Whittier to Lucia Alexander, 2 August 1869, PWP; and Francesca Alexander to Lilly Cleveland, July 1866, JRC.

30   Francesca Alexander, *Ricordi d'Ida*, trans. Attilio Guadagni (Florence: George A. Cole, 1884); see Francesca Alexander to Constance Oldham, 21 March 1887, CLFAJS.

31   Scrapbook no.6, PAF.

32   John Ruskin to Francesca Alexander, 1 June 1888, JRCLFA.

33   Francesca Alexander to Lilly Cleveland, December [1883], JRC; and Scrapbook no.6, PAF; see also A. Lloyd, p.132. Francesca later sent installments of her third book, *Christ's Folk in the Apennine*, to Herrick (now in the Schlesinger Library) and inscribed one of them, 'in grateful remembrance of the honour paid by him to Ida's memory'.

34   Benjamin Goluboff, '"If Madonna Be": Emily Dickinson and Roman Catholicism', *The New England Quarterly* 73, no.3 (September 2000): p.372.

35   Scrapbook no.6, PAF; on Manning, see Emma Sdegno, 'Edited by Ruskin: Francesca Alexander's Roadside Songs of Tuscany', in Emma Sdegno et al., eds, *John Ruskin's Europe. A Collection of*

Cross-Cultural Essays (Venice: Edizioni Ca' Foscari, 2020), pp 322–6.

36 Scrapbook no.6, PAF.

37 Francesca Alexander to Fanny Talbot, 10 June 1889, LFT. Francesca later included Alishan's niece, the 'Armenian Ida', in her *Christ's Folk in the Apennine* (Sunnyside, Kent: George Allen, 1887), pp 201–7; for his reaction, see Scrapbook no.7, PAF.

38 Scrapbook no.6, PAF.

39 [Maria Trench?], 'A Conversation on Books', *The Monthly Packet of Evening Readings for Members of the English Church*, March 1884, pp 156–8.

40 Scrapbook no.6, PAF.

41 John Greenleaf Whittier to Annie Adams Fields, 23 July 1883, JTFPA.

42 Scrapbook no.6, PAF.

43 John Greenleaf Whittier, *The Bay of Seven Islands, and Other Poems* (Boston, MA: Houghton, Mifflin and Co., 1883), p.81.

44 Francesca Alexander to Lilly Cleveland, December [1883], JRC.

45 'A Drawing-Room Lecture', *The Spectator*, 9 June 1883; see also *St James Gazette*, 7 June 1883; and 'Notes', *The Tablet*, 9 June 1883. Maria La Touche, Rose's mother, noted Ruskin's enthusiasm for Francesca at this time; see Margaret Ferrier Young, ed., *The Letters of a Noble Woman* (London: George Allen & Sons, 1908), pp 93–4.

46 Eunice Farley Felton, 'Mrs. Alexander and Her Daughter Francesca', *Cambridge Historical Society Publications XIV. Proceedings for the Year 1919* (Cambridge, MA: The Society, 1926), pp 106–13, on p.107.

47 Joseph Pennell, *The Adventures of an Illustrator* (Boston, MA: Little, Brown, and Company, 1925), p.117.

48 W.J. Stillman, 'Francesca's Country', *The Critic* 9, no.234 (23 June 1888): pp 301–2.

49 Willard Fiske to his mother, 26 August 1883, and to Charles [Warner?], 8 September 1883, DWFP.

50 Willard Fiske to Charles [Warner?], 8 September 1883, DWFP.

51 Willard Fiske to Charles [Warner?], 8 September 1883, DWFP.

52 Willard Fiske to his mother, 15 October 1883, DWFP.

53 Willard Fiske to his mother, 15 January 1884, DWFP; and Scrapbook no.2, PAF; neither Fiske's documentation of his collection nor Cornell's records identify this title.

54 Alexander, fols 97r–101v and 120r–123r, LGSANP; and Lucia Alexander to John Greenleaf Whittier, 26 August 1871, PWP.

55 *The Italian Gazette*, 3 November 1894.

56 Francesca Alexander to Sally Hayward, 28 February 1871, JHHFP.

57 Frances Macbeth Glessner and John Jacob Glessner, Journal, 29 March 1890, GFP.

58 Matilda Lucas, *'Every Body Comes Back to Rome.' The Complete Letters of Matilda Lucas, 1871–1902*, ed. Robert Sénécal (London: Gatehouse Editions, 2013), vol.2, p.620.

59 Joseph Lindon Smith, Diary, 5 May 1894, SFPDHS; and Isa Carrington Cabell, 'The Author of "The Story of Ida"', *The Critic*, 30 April 1887, p.213.

60 Felton, p.107; 'Notes and Queries', *The Journal of the Friends Historical Society* 26 (1929): pp 80–81; and Lucas, vol.2, p.621.

61 John Ruskin to Francesca Alexander, 18 September 1883, JRCLFA; and Scrapbook no.6, PAF.

62 John Ruskin to Lucia Alexander, 9 December 1883, JRCLFA.

63 Francesca Alexander to Lilly Cleveland, 1 December 1883, JRC.

64 John Ruskin to Francesca Alexander, 15 August 1883 and 10 March 1884, JRCLFA.

65 On his pedagogical interests – which also incorporated color, something Francesca's drawings did not – see Colin Harrison, 'Color in Ruskin's Teachings', in Charlotte Ribeyrol et al., eds, *Colour Revolution. Victorian Art, Fashion & Design* (Oxford: Ashmolean Museum, 2023), pp 31–5.

66 *John Hay-Howells Letters*, ed. George Monteiro and Brenda Murphy (Boston, MA: Twayne Publishers, 1980), p.71.

67 Francesca Alexander to Lilly Cleveland, 5 May 1883, JRC.

68 Will of John C. Gray, 28 March 1881, MWPR; and 'The Will of Samuel W. Swett', *Boston Daily Journal*, 4 June 1884. Lucia and Francesca had earlier inherited $9000 from Lucia's uncle Frances Calley

Gray; see Will of Frances C. Gray, 10 October 1856, MWPR.

69 Constance Grosvenor Alexander, *Francesca Alexander. A 'Hidden Servant'* (Cambridge, MA: Harvard University Press, 1927), pp 30–31. This may be where she got the 'cranberry sauce made in Boston' that she served at Thanksgiving in 1889 (Lucia Alexander to Joan Severn, 27 November 1889, CLLAJS).

70 A. Lloyd, pp 131–2; see also Francesca Alexander to Lilly Cleveland, 1 December 1883, JRC.

71 Lucas, vol.2, pp 620–21.

72 Francesca Alexander to Lilly Cleveland, 1 December 1883, JRC; and Lucia Alexander to Joan Severn, 1 December 1892, CLLAJS.

73 Augustus Thorndike Perkins, 'Sketch of Some of the Losses to the Departments of Literature and the Fine Arts Occasioned by the Great Fire in Boston of 1872', *The New-England Historical and Genealogical Register and Antiquarian Journal* 27 (October 1873): p.369; and 'Art and the Boston Fire', *Hartford Daily Courant*, 17 May 1873.

74 'November Meeting, 1884', *Proceedings of the Massachusetts Historical Society* 1 (Cambridge: John Wilson and Son, 1885), p.298. These samplers cannot be traced.

75 Scrapbook no.6, PAF.

76 Scrapbook no.4, PAF.

77 Leonard & Co.; see also 'The Alexander Collection', *Boston Daily Advertiser*, 22 April 1884.

78 The inscription on a sixth, a portrait of Lucrezia Guicciardini, was not by 'Magludi Oddo Gaetani' as stated in the catalogue; that inscription instead names the sitter as the wife of ('moglie di' in Italian) Oddo Gaetani.

79 Joseph Lindon Smith, Diary, 9 May 1894, SFPDHS; a few years later another visitor affirmed that 'Their rooms are filled with good pictures' (Charles L. Peirson, Diary, 27 April 1898, RFP).

80 Scrapbook no.7, PAF; I believe this article is by Charles Warren Stoddard but I have been unable to find the source for it. For Lucia's objections, see Lucia Alexander to Fanny Talbot, 31 July 1889, LFT.

81 Lucia Alexander to Joan Severn, 1 July 1889, CLLAJS.

82 Alexander, 1885, pp 1 and 6.

83 Robert Flynn Johnson and Joseph R. Goldyne, *Judging by Appearance. Master Drawings from the Collection of Joseph and Deborah Goldyne* (San Francisco, CA: Fine Arts Museum, 2006), pp 192–5.

84 H. Buxton Forman, 'An American Studio in Florence', *The Manhattan* 3, no.6 (June 1884): p.530; and John Ruskin to Lucia Alexander, 22 June 1883, JRCLFA.

85 Francesca Alexander to Lilly Cleveland, 5 May 1883, JRC; see also John Ruskin to Lucia Alexander, 9 October 1882, ALSWC; and *The Diaries of John Ruskin*, vol.3, p.1032.

86 FASA, fols 192–3.

87 For these arrangements, see A. Lloyd, pp 129–30; John Ruskin to Francesca Alexander, 13 April and 13 May 1883, JRCLFA; and Lilly Cleveland, Diary, 10 November 1883, CPFP.

88 A. Lloyd, pp 126–7.

89 John Ruskin to Francesca Alexander, 13 May 1883, JRCLFA.

90 A. Lloyd, p.132; see also Francesca Alexander to Lilly Cleveland, [late 1883], JRC.

91 Francesca Alexander to John Ruskin, [after 5 April 1885], ABL.

92 For the location of the folios in 1907, see *The Works of John Ruskin*, vol.32, pp 44–7. Many of Ruskin's folios appeared on the art market beginning in 1981; see *Francesca Alexander. Drawings for the Roadside Songs of Tuscany* (Woodside, CA: Sven H.A. Bruntjen Fine Arts, 1981); and *Francesca Alexander 1837–1917. A Special Exhibition. Pen and Ink Drawings* (New York: Jeffrey Alan Gallery, 1983).

93 Robert Sewell to Lilly Cleveland, [before December 1883], JRC (with a copy in Scrapbook no.6, PAF); see also Francesca Alexander to Lilly Cleveland, [1 December 1883], JRC.

94 Clegg and Tucker, p.131.

95 Ruskin, 'Editor's Preface', in Alexander, 1885, pp 7–8.

96 On Ruskin's intervention, see also Jessica R. Feldman, *Victorian Modernism* (Cambridge: Cambridge University Press, 2009), pp 43–55.

97 Francesca Alexander to Lilly Cleveland, 2 August 1862, JRC.

98 FASA, fols 114–59; an earlier version of Edwige's biography is in Alexander, fols 54r and 60r–63v, LGSANP.

99 Lucia Gray Swett, *John Ruskin's Letters to Francesca and Memoirs of the Alexanders* (Boston, MA: Lothrop, Lee & Shepard Co., 1931), p.155; she was referencing Cabell, pp 213–14.

100 Scrapbook no.6, PAF.

101 Constance Oldham to Francesca Alexander, 9 August 1885, ALSML.

102 Clara Benedict, *Constance Fenimore Woolson* (London: Ellis, 1930), p.304.

103 Scrapbook no.7, PAF.

104 *The Diaries of John Ruskin*, vol.3, p.1092; see also Mrs Russell Barrington, *G.F. Watts. Reminiscences* (New York: The Macmillan Company, 1905), p.15; and Lucia Alexander to Charles Bowditch, 24 January 1893, BCBFP.

105 Francesca Alexander to Fanny Talbot, 22 April 1885, LFT.

106 Scrapbook no.7, PAF.

107 Francesca Alexander to John Ruskin, [after 5 April 1885], ABL; John Ruskin to Lucia Alexander, 22 June 1883, JRCLFA; and Lucia Alexander to Joan Severn, 24 May 1889, CLLAJS.

108 John Ruskin to Francesca Alexander, 13 November 1885, JRCLFA. These sketches are now split between the Museum of Fine Arts Boston and Wellesley College Special Collections, both with a note from Francesca stating 'These drawings are all by Mr. Ruskin, and were given by him to me, in 1885.'

109 John Ruskin to Francesca Alexander, 10 June, 31 July and 13 October 1883, JRCLFA.

110 Francesca later described owning many works by Ruskin, including what she believed were studies for *Proserpina*; see Ray Haslam, 'A Letter from Francesca Alexander', *The Ruskin Review and Bulletin* 4, no.2 (Lent 2008): p.54.

111 John Ruskin, 'Preface', in Alexander, 1887, p.vi.

112 Francesca Alexander to Lilly Cleveland, 25 August 1888, JRC.

113 Ruskin, 'Preface', in Alexander, 1887, p.vii.

114 John Ruskin to Francesca Alexander, 21 July and 2 October 1885, JRCLFA.

115 William G. Collingwood to Lucia Alexander, 12 January 1892, ALSWC.

116 *The Diaries of John Ruskin*, vol.3, p.1150; see also Ornella Pittarello, ed., *Lettere d'Amicizia a Marina Sprea Baroni Semitecolo (1881–1909)* (Bologna: Casa editrice nuova, 2009), p.17.

117 Francesca Alexander to Fanny Talbot, 1 December 1888, LFT.

5 'A MEDIEAVAL SAINT'

1 Francesca Alexander to Joan Severn, 16 July 1887, CLFAJS.

2 John Ruskin to Francesca Alexander, 26 October 1885, JRCLFA.

3 Constance Grosvenor Alexander, *Francesca Alexander. A 'Hidden Servant'* (Cambridge, MA: Harvard University Press, 1927), p.128; and John Ruskin to Francesca Alexander, 10 October 1887, JRCLFA.

4 Francesca Alexander to Joan Severn, 25 December 1890 and 18 February 1891, CLFAJS; and Francesca Alexander to Fanny Talbot, 19 February 1891, LFT.

5 Francesca Alexander to Lilly Cleveland, 25 August 1888, JRC.

6 Lucia Alexander to Katherine Hay Cobb Hayward, 7 July 1896, JHHFP.

7 For the wills and other estate information, see D173709 and D176380.

8 Eunice Farley Felton, 'Mrs. Alexander and Her Daughter Francesca', *Cambridge Historical Society Publications XIV. Proceedings for the Year 1919* (Cambridge, MA: The Society, 1926), p.112.

9 Francesca Alexander to unknown, 20 June 1891, and unknown to Francesca Alexander, 3 August 1891, ACCVV.

10 Francesca Alexander to John Ruskin, 8 October 1884, 20 March 1886 and 9 February 1888, JRCLFA; and Francesca Alexander to Constance Oldham, 18 June 1885, ALSML.

11 Thomas Ball, *My Threescore Years and Ten* (Boston, MA: Roberts Brothers, 1891), p.173.

12 Lucia Alexander to Joan Severn, 7, 13, 18 and 30 August 1887, CLLAJS; and Francesca Alexander to Lilly Cleveland, 25 August 1888, JRC.

13 Lucia Alexander to Sara Anderson, 12 July 1889, CLFAJS; John Ruskin to Francesca Alexander, 1 June 1884, JRCLFA; and Francesca Alexander to John Ruskin, 27 June 1889, CLFAJS.

14 Anna Lloyd, *A Memoir. With Extracts from Her Letters* (London: The Cayme Press Limited, 1928), pp 187–8.

15 Antonio Messeri, ed., *Da un carteggio inedito di Giosue Carducci* (Bologna: Zanichella, 1907), p.158 ('l'americana famosa che parla e scrive così bene l'italiano').

16 See note 35 to Chapter 4, above.

17 Francesca Alexander to Horace Scudder, 17 July 1890, HESC.

18 Giuseppe Tigri, *Canti popolari toscani* (Florence: Barbèra, Bianchi e Comp., 1860), vol.1, p.331.

19 Scrapbook no.7, PAF.

20 Charles Warren Stoddard, *The Lepers of Molokai* (Notre Dame, IN: Ave Maria Press, 1908), pp 127–8; and Francesca Alexander to Charles Warren Stoddard, 21 May 1889, SSCL.

21 Francesca Alexander to Charles Warren Stoddard, 21 May 1889, SSCL.

22 Charles Warren Stoddard to Daniel E. Hudson, 10 June 1889, UNDA.

23 Theodore Stanton, 'Artists in Florence', *Daily Inter Ocean*, 13 July 1890.

24 Georgina Forbes to Lilly Cleveland, 26 August 1893, JRC.

25 Francesca Alexander to Lilly Cleveland, 31 May 1872, JRC.

26 Francesca Alexander to Joan Severn, 25 June 1889, CLFAJS; Francesca Alexander to John Ruskin, 27 June 1889, CLFAJS; and [Lucia Alexander] to Sarah Orne Jewett, 7 July 1894, JFP.

27 FMGEA, unpaginated.

28 Frances Macbeth Glessner and John Jacob Glessner, Journal, 29 March 1890, GFP.

29 Frances Macbeth Glessner and John Jacob Glessner, Journal, 29 March 1890, GFP.

30 Grace Warrack, ed. and trans., *Florilegio di canti toscani. Folk Songs of the Tuscan Hills* (London: Alexander Moring Ltd, 1914), facing p.lxxiv.

31 Francesca Alexander to Frances Glessner, November 1892, in Frances Macbeth Glessner and John Jacob Glessner, Journal, GFP.

32 Francesca Alexander to Frances Glessner, 19 May 1892, SLFMGJJG.

33 Francesca Alexander to Frances Glessner, 7 January [1893], in Frances Macbeth Glessner and John Jacob Glessner, Journal, GFP; Lucia's scrapbook, however, is now lost.

34 *Trustees of the Museum of Fine Arts. Tenth Annual Report* (Boston, MA: Alfred Mudge & Son, 1886), p.23; 'New Paintings in the Fourth Gallery, Museum of Fine Arts', *Boston Evening Transcript*, 29 December 1894; and *Trustees of the Museum of Fine Arts. Nineteenth Annual Report for the Year Ending Dec. 31, 1894* (Boston, MA: Alfred Mudge & Son, 1895), pp 58–9. The Madonna was later described as 'by Fanny Alexander, after Italian School' and valued at $100 (Inventory of Elizabeth Brooks Wheelwright, 14 January 1920, WFP); a painting matching this description appears in a photograph of the Wheelwright home in 1902 (WFPH).

35 See, for example, Ruth Faure, 'Frances Alexander', *The Christian Advocate*, 74, no.3 (2 February 1899): p.174; and M.R.F.G., 'Two Cities of Eastern Italy', *Springfield Daily Republican*, 4 September 1901.

36 Olivia Cushing Andersen, Diary, 16 October 1892, HCAP.

37 A. Lloyd, pp 144–8.

38 Elinor Mead Howells, *If Not Literature. Letters of Elinor Mead Howells*, ed. Ginette de B. Merrill and George Arms (Columbus, OH: Ohio State University Press, 1988), p.255.

39 Lilian Whiting, *The Golden Road* (Boston, MA: Little, Brown, and Company, 1918), p.112.

40 Lucia Gray Swett, *Sisters of Reparatrice* (Boston, MA: Lee and Shepard, 1902), p.39.

41 Eugenia Brooks Frothingham, *Youth and I* (Boston, MA: Houghton Mifflin Company, 1938), p.87.

42 Margaret Cabot to Marian Cabot Putnam, 21 June 1892, JLP.

43 Margaret Cabot to Louisa Higginson Cabot, 27 June 1892, JLP.

44 Joseph Lindon Smith to his parents, 8 May 1889, SFPDHS.

45 Joseph Lindon Smith to his parents, 11 June 1889, SFPDHS. Smith's description of Lucia's head-covering corresponds with a description of her use of what were known as 'Japanese napkins', or a sort of doily, as noted by other visitors; see Cora Bowditch to 'Ingles', 21 June [1898], BCBFP; and fig.116.

46 Joseph Lindon Smith to his parents, 21 and 23 June 1889, SFPDHS; and Benjamin Lillard, *Practical Hints and Formulas for Busy Druggists* (New York: J.H. Vail & Co., 1884), vol.1, p.20.

47 Joseph Lindon Smith to his parents, 6 May 1894, JLSP.

48 Joseph Lindon Smith, Diary, 5 May 1894, SFPDHS.

49 Charles L. Peirson, Diary, 27 April 1898, RFP; for further references to Francesca as medieval, see Edward A. Silsbee to Miss Hooker, [undated], and Edward A. Silsbee to 'Hill', [c.1869–71], SFPPEM.

50 C.G. Alexander, p.4.

51 Katharine Putnam Bowditch, Diary, 11, 16, 21, 22 and 24 June 1898, CPBFP; Cora Bowditch to 'Ingles', 21 June [1898], BCBFP; and Cora Bowditch, Diary, 26, 28 and 31 May, and 7, 11, 21, 22 and 24 June 1898, BCBFP; for an earlier visit, see Lucy Bowditch, Travel Diary, 9, 10, 14, 17, 23 and 28 May, and 1 June 1893, BCBFP

52 Cora Bowditch, Diary, 26 May 1898, BCBFP; see also her sister's account in Katharine Putnam Bowditch, Diary, 26 and 31 May 1898, CPBFP.

53 Cora Bowditch, Diary, 22 June 1898, BCBFP.

54 Cora Bowditch to 'Nellie', 1 August 1898, BCBFP.

55 Cora Bowditch, Diary, 21 and 24 June 1898, BCBFP.

56 Anna Fuller, 'Introduction', in Francesca Alexander, *The Hidden Servants and Other Very Old Stories* (Boston, MA: Little, Brown, & Co., 1900), p.ix; and Alexander, fol.116r, LGSANP.

57 Ornella Pittarello, ed., *Lettere d'Amicizia a Marina Sprea Baroni Semitecolo (1881–1909)* (Bologna: Casa editrice nuova, 2009), p.61; Vittoria Aganoor, *Lettere a Domenico Gnoli*, ed. Biagia Marniti (Rome: Salvatore Sciascia Editore, 1967), p.14; for her translations, see *Il Buon Cuore* 4, no.52 (25 December 1905), and Victoria Aganoor, *To My Father*, trans. Francesca Alexander (Venice: Ferd. Ongania, 1894).

58 J.-A. George, 'Translating Tuscany: Francesca Alexander's *Roadside Songs* (1888)', *Forum for Modern Language Studies* 39, no.2 (April 2003): p.235.

59 Lucia Alexander to Cornelia Rockwell Bowditch, 9 July 1899, BCBFP.

60 Alexander, 1900, pp xi–xv.

61 Francesca Alexander to Sally Hayward, 28 February 1871, JHHFP; she also described the origin of the story, and her plan to draw it, in the collection of letter excerpts in Folder 10, PAF.

62 Lilly Cleveland, Diary, 10 November 1883, CPFP.

63 See, for example, 'Talk About New Books', *The Catholic World* 72, no.429 (December 1901): p.410.

64 Lucia Alexander to Mary Rice Bowditch, 15 July 1902, BLFP.

65 Little, Brown, & Company to Francesca Alexander, 9 April 1906, and Edward E. Allen to N.P. Hallowell, 25 February 1910, LGSANP. A Braille edition was issued several years later.

66 Lucia Alexander to Joan Severn, 11 May [1889], CLLAJS.

67 Lucia Alexander to Charles Bowditch, 24 January 1893, BCBFP.

68 Lucia Alexander to Joan Severn, 31 January 1890, CLLAJS; see also Francesca Alexander to Constance Oldham, [1890], ALSML.

69 Francesca Alexander to Joan Severn, 29–30 November 1890, CLFAJS.

70 William G. Collingwood to Lucia Alexander, 8 October 1891, ALSWC.

71 William G. Collingwood to Lucia Alexander, 21 January and 7 March 1892, ALSWC.

72 William G. Collingwood to Lucia Alexander, 19 and 26 November 1892, ALSWC; see *The Academy*, 26 November and 3, 10 and 17 December 1892; *The Athenaeum*, 19 and 26 November and 3 December 1892; *The Daily Graphic*, 17 and 24 November and 1 December 1892; and 'Notabilia', *The Magazine of Art*, January 1893, p.xvi.

73 'Notabilia', *The Magazine of Art*, December 1894, p.xii. Although at least one more folio was located later, another one, representing the young Saint Anthony, was still missing in 1903; see Lucia Alexander to Joan Severn, 10 August 1903, CLLAJS; and Francesca Alexander to Joan Severn, [1903], CLFAJS.

74 W.G. Collingwood to Joan Severn, 24 September 1891 ALSWC; and Lucia Alexander to Charles Bowditch, 24 January 1893, BCBFP.

75 Lucia G. Alexander, Roadside Songs of Tuscany by Francesca Alexander, HMCC; and Louise Hall Tharp, *Adventurous Alliance. The Story of the Agassiz Family of Boston* (Boston, MA: Little, Brown, 1959), pp 235–6.

76 For the differences between *Roadside Songs* and *Tuscan Songs*, see *The Works of John Ruskin*, ed. E.T. Cook and Alexander Wedderburn (London: George Allen, 1907), vol.32, pp 42–8.

77 M.H. Spielmann, 'Francesca Alexander, and "The Roadside Songs of Tuscany"', *Magazine of Art* 18 (June 1895): p.299; and John C. Van Dyke, 'An Exponent of Pre-Raphaelism', *The Dial*, 16 March 1898.

78 *Trustees of the Museum of Fine Arts. Twenty-Seventh Annual Report for the Year 1902* (Cambridge: The University Press, 1903), p.138.

79 Francesca Alexander to Sydney Cockerell, 16 November 1897, SCCAL.

80 Francesca Alexander to Fanny Talbot, 15 May 1885, LFT.

81 Francesca Alexander to Joan Severn, 21 January 1900 and 5 February 1900, CLFAJS.

82 Francesca Alexander to Joan Severn, 29 June [1900], CLFAJS; see also Joan Severn to Charles Eliot Norton, 3 July 1900, CENP.

83 Ray Haslam, 'A Letter from Francesca Alexander', *The Ruskin Review and Bulletin* 4, no.2 (Lent 2008): pp 53–5; and Francesca Alexander to George Allen, 24 March 1905, ALSML.

84 Pittarello, p.147.

85 Whiting, 1918, p.112.

86 Francesca Alexander to Lady Walburga Paget, [1890s?], PP.

87 Lucia Alexander to Alfred Bowditch, 19 October 1906, and Francesca Alexander to Alfred Bowditch, 22 January 1907, BLFP; and Lucia Alexander to Charles P. Bowditch, December 1906, CPBFP.

88 A. Lloyd, p.148.

89 Lucia Alexander to [Katherine Hay Cobb Hayward?], 10 February 1911, SCSC; see also Lucia Alexander to Charles Bowditch, 22 August 1910, BCBFP.

90 Lucia Alexander to Cornelia Rockwell Bowditch, 25 July 1905, BCBFP; and Francesca Alexander to Lilly Cleveland, 1 December 1902, JRC.

91 Lucia Alexander to William G. Collingwood, 29 April 1892, ALSWC; and Scrapbook no.3, PAF.

92 See, for example, 'About Authors', *The Bookseller, Newsdealer and Stationer*, 1 December 1906, p.577;

John Patrick Ryan, 'Il Libro d'Oro', *American Catholic Quarterly Review* 31, no.122 (April 1906): p.412; and Lilian Whiting, 'A Truly Remarkable Woman', *Duluth News-Tribune*, 7 June 1910.

93 Scrapbook no.7, PAF.

94 Warrack, 1914, pp lxxi–lxxiv; see also Grace Warrack, ed. and trans., *Dal cor gentil d'Italia: Canti dal Veneto alla Sardegna. Out of the Heart of Italy: Folk Songs from Venetia to Sardinia* (Oxford: Basil Blackwell, 1925), pp xxv–xxvi and lv–lvii.

95 Lucia Alexander to Charles P. Bowditch, December 1906, CPBFP.

96 Lucia Alexander to Joan Severn, 26 February 1893, CLLAJS; Edith Longfellow Dana to Anne Allegra Longfellow Thorp, 15 and 21 April 1899, HWLFP; and Alice Longfellow to Edith Longfellow Dana, 3 June [1899], HWLFP.

97 Erica Thorp to her family, 21 November 1913, HWLFP.

98 Alice Longfellow to Edith Longfellow Dana, 27 November 1913, AMLP.

99 A. Lloyd, pp 149–50; and 'Mrs. Alexander is 100', *New York Times*, 3 April 1914.

100 Francesca Alexander to Sydney Cockerell, 16 November 1897, SCCAL.

101 'An Appeal from "Francesca"', *Boston Evening Transcript*, 14 November 1905.

102 'An Appeal from "Francesca"', *Boston Evening Transcript*, 22 November 1905; for the acknowledgment of the donation, see Hettore Capialbi to Alfred Bowditch, 5 December 1905, and Francesca Alexander to Alfred Bowditch, 16 December 1905, BLFP.

103 Francesca Alexander to Lilly Cleveland, 9 May 1907, JRC.

104 Lucia Alexander to Cornelia Rockwell Bowditch, 22 July 1906, BCBFP. She also provided a goat for a newborn in Bassano whose mother died; see Lucia Alexander to Charles Bowditch, 27 August 1906, BCBFP.

105 Lucia Alexander to Charles Bowditch, 4 September 1912, BCBFP; and Alfred Bowditch to Charles H. Tyler, 10 March 1914, ABP.

106 Lucia Alexander to [Katherine Hay Cobb Hayward?], 10 February 1911, SCSC.

107 Eva Madden, 'Ruskin's Francesca', *The Christian Register*, 23 November 1916, p.1113.

108 Lucia Alexander to Cornelia Rockwell Bowditch, 22 July 1906, BCBFP.

109 Harold Acton, *Memoirs of an Aesthete 1939–1969* (New York: Viking Press, 1971), p.207.

110 F.T.F. Dumont to the Secretary of State, 23 May 1916 and 23 January 1917, RDACA.

111 A. Lloyd, pp 148–9.

112 Lilly made bequests to various institutions, friends and relatives, but her will did not mention art or books specifically by Francesca (16 May 1905 and July 1908, MWPR).

113 Charles H. Tyler to Alfred Bowditch, 14 February 1914, ABP.

114 For Dumont's statements, see F.T.F. Dumont to the Secretary of State, 23 May 1916 and 23 January 1917, RDACA.

115 F.T.F. Dumont to the Secretary of State, 23 January 1917, RDACA.

116 Statement of Dr Ugo Milli, 19 May 1916, RDACA.

117 A. Lloyd, p.150.

118 Elenco Generale dei Membri dell'Adunanza dei Fratelli in Firenze, ACCVV; and Gaspare Pult, *Il Cristiano*, July 1916.

119 'Woman Dies at Age of 105', *Washington Post*, 22 May 1916; 'Mother of Artist Dies', *Times-Picayune* (New Orleans), 23 May 1916; and Madden, p.1111.

120 Information in this paragraph comes from F.T.F. Dumont to the Secretary of State, 23 January 1917, RDACA.

121 Francesca Alexander to Constance Oldham, 21 March 1887, ALSML.

122 A. Lloyd, p.150.

123 *La Nazione*, 21 and 23 January 1917.

124 N. 3467, MACEA; Elenco Generale dei Membri dell'Adunanza dei Fratelli in Firenze, ACCVV; and 'Miss Alexander', *Manchester Guardian*, 31 January 1917.

125 *The Florence Herald and Italian Herald*, 27 January 1917.

126 *The Florence Herald and Italian Herald*, 3 February 1917.

127 'Death Notices', *Boston Journal*, 24 January 1917.

128 *New York Sun*, 30 January 1917.

129 'Miss Alexander'.

130 Information in this paragraph comes from D173709; and F.T.F. Dumont to the Secretary of State, 23 January 1917, RDACA.

131 Vice Consul Leoni to Secretary of State, 9 July 1919, RDACA; and D176380.

132 D176380. According to Goodspeed, he acquired some objects 'Through the disposal in Boston of the effects of Miss Francesca Alexander after her death' (Charles E. Goodspeed, *Yankee Bookseller* (Boston, MA: Houghton Mifflin Company, 1937), p.265). I can find no record of a public sale but he may have purchased items the heirs did not want directly from them; he later donated much Ruskin- and Francesca-related material to Wellesley College.

133 Secretary of State to F.T.F. Dumont, 3 June 1916, RDACA.

134 Christie's (New York), *Storied Treasures: Antiquities from the Toledo Museum of Art*, 19–26 October 2016, lot 35; and Harlan J. Berk, Ltd (Chicago, IL), *201st Buy or Bid Sale*, 13 July 2017, lots 633–43. Lucia planned to donate at least some of the vases to the museum that held Castromediano's collections, where she also donated an ancient coin and textiles; see P. Chiesa, 'Nel Museo Provinciale Castromediano', *Rivista storica salentina* 8, nos 5–6 (May–June 1913): p.169, and 'Nel Museo Provinciale – Visitatori illustri e doni', *Rivista storica salentina* 9, nos 7–8 (July–August 1914): p.211.

135 There is no evidence that the Alexanders visited La Pietra; there are no visitor books from this period, and a reference in R. Terry Schnadelbach, *Hidden Lives/Secret Gardens* (New York: iUniverse, Inc., 2009), p.143, is otherwise undocumented.

136 For conflicting information on the sale of the Alexander collection see Harold Acton, *Memoirs of an Aesthete 1939–1969* (New York: Viking Press, 1971), pp 206–7; and Dialta Alliata-Lensi Orlandi, *My Mother, My Father, and His Wife Hortense. Provenance: Villa La Pietra* (self-pub., 2013), pp 237–8.

137 According to Schnadelbach, p.91, a 'distress sale' was held in 1917, citing a 16 July 1921 letter from Bernard Berenson to Isabella Stewart Gardner (ISGMC) as evidence, but that letter has no reference to a sale or the Alexanders.

138 For a reference to the archive, see Sonia Chiodo, *A*

Corpus of Florentine Painting. Painters in Florence after the 'Black Death'. The Master of the Misericordia and Matteo di Pacino, ed. Miklós Boskovits (Florence: Giunti, 2011), p.323.

EPILOGUE

1   Francesca Alexander to Lilly Cleveland, October 1862, JRC; Francesca Alexander to Annie Adam Fields, 29 March 1862, JTFC; and notes 32 and 33 to Chapter 3, above.

2   See, for example, Richard M. Dunn, 'Villadom: The Florence of Mary Berenson, Mabel Dodge, and Mina Loy', *Italian History & Culture* 7 (2001): pp 41–55; Martha Banta, 'Henry James and the New Woman', in John Carlos Rowe and Eric Haralson, eds, *A Historical Guide to Henry James* (Oxford: Oxford University Press, 2012), pp 55–93; and Frances Fowle, 'The New Woman', in Erica E. Hirshler, et al., *Fashioned by Sargent* (Boston, MA: Museum of Fine Arts, 2023), pp 41–51.

3   Helen Zimmern, 'Ruskin's Florentine Francesca', *Daily Inter Ocean*, 30 March 1890; see also Helen Zimmern, 'Old Florentine Villas. Medieval Palaces with Wonderful Stories of Tradition and Legend', *Daily Inter Ocean,* 18 January 1891.

4   Mary Berenson, Diary, 21 April 1894, BMBP.

5   Mary Berenson, Diary, 30 November 1903, BMBP. Interestingly, given these comments, Francesca's relative Charlotte Bartlett Hallowell brought the Berensons to the Alexander home, and Constance Grosvenor Alexander was a frequent visitor to the Berensons' Villa I Tatti.

6   Mabel Dodge Luhan, 'The Story of Francesca', *The Arts* 8, no.1 (July 1925): pp 24–7; see also her *Lorenzo in Taos* (London: Martin Secker, 1933), p.122, and *European Experiences* (New York: Harcourt, Brace and Company, 1935), pp 411–19. Luhan's version of Francesca's biography is often cited as fact; see Lois Palken Rudnick, *Mabel Dodge Luhan: New Woman, New Worlds* (Albuquerque, NM: University of New Mexico Press, 1984), pp 36–7.

7   For one exception, see Eugenia Brooks Frothingham, *Youth and I* (Boston, MA: Houghton Mifflin Company, 1938), pp 86–7.

Archival Source Abbreviations

AAFP   Annie Adams Fields Papers, Massachusetts Historical Society, Boston, MA

ABL   Armstrong Browning Library, Waco, TX

ABP   Alfred Bowditch Papers, Massachusetts Historical Society, Boston, MA

ACCVV   Archivio Carte della Chiesa di Vigna Vecchia, Chiesa Cristiana Evangelica dei Fratelli, Florence, Italy

ADP   Alice Donlevy Papers, New York Public Library, New York, NY

AF   Autograph File, Houghton Library, Harvard University, Cambridge, MA

ALC   Alma Lutz Collection, Schlesinger Library, Harvard University, Cambridge, MA

ALSML   Autograph Letters Signed, Morgan Library Department of Literary and Historical Manuscripts, New York, NY

ALSWC   Autograph Letters Signed, Special Collections, Wellesley College, Wellesley, MA

AMLP   Alice Mary Longfellow Papers (LONG 16173), Longfellow House-Washington's Headquarters National Historic Site, Cambridge, MA

ASC   Anti-Slavery Collection, Boston Public Library, Boston, MA

AWP   Anne Whitney Papers, Archives, Wellesley College, Wellesley, MA

BCBFP   Bowditch-Codman-Balch Family Papers, Massachusetts Historical Society, Boston, MA

BLFP   Bowditch-Loring Family Papers, Massachusetts Historical Society, Boston, MA

BMBP   Bernard and Mary Berenson Papers, Villa I Tatti, Florence, Italy

CAR   Carteggi, Biblioteca Nazionale Centrale, Florence, Italy

CDC   Charles Dickens Collection, Free Library, Philadelphia, PA

CENP   Charles Eliot Norton Papers, Houghton Library, Harvard University, Cambridge, MA

CFP   Crane Family Papers, New York Public Library, New York, NY

CLFAJS   Collection of Letters from Francesca Alexander to Joan Severn, Morgan Library Department of Literary and Historical Manuscripts, New York, NY

CLLAJS   Collection of Letters from Lucia Alexander to Joan Severn, Morgan Library Department of Literary and Historical Manuscripts, New York, NY

CPBFP   Charles P. Bowditch Family Papers, Massachusetts Historical Society, Boston, MA

CPFP Cleveland-Perkins Family Papers, New York Public Library, New York, NY

CRSCND Carteggio relative al sesto centenario della nascita di Dante, Archivio Storico del Comune di Firenze, Florence, Italy

D173709 Docket 173709, Suffolk County Probate and Family Court, Boston, MA

D176380 Docket 176380, Suffolk County Probate and Family Court, Boston, MA

DTPP David Thomas Pottinger Papers, Houghton Library, Harvard University, Cambridge, MA

DWFP Daniel Willard Fiske Papers, Cornell University Library, Ithaca, NY

ECSP Edmond Clarence Stedman Papers, Rare Book & Manuscript Library, Columbia University, New York, NY

FAH Francesca Alexander. 'History of Fifty Francesconi Given to the Poor.' c.1862, Boston Athenaeum, Boston, MA

FAS Francesca Alexander Scrapbooks, Houghton Library, Harvard University, Cambridge, MA

FASA Francesca Alexander. 'Some Account of the People Whose Portraits are Given in the Roadside Songs.' 1883, private collection

FDEBDP Frank Duveneck and Elizabeth Boott Duveneck Papers, Archives of American Art, Smithsonian Institution, Washington, DC

FFL Florence Freeman Letters, Boston Athenaeum, Boston, MA

FMFP Fay-Mixter Family Papers, Massachusetts Historical Society, Boston, MA

FMGEA Frances Macbeth Glessner, European Addresses, Glessner House Archives, Chicago, IL

GFP Glessner Family Papers, Chicago History Museum, Chicago, IL

GPMC George Perkins Marsh Collection, University of Vermont Library, Burlington, VT

HCAP Hendrik Christian Andersen Papers, Library of Congress, USA

HESC Horace Elisha Scudder Correspondence, Houghton Library, Harvard University, Cambridge, MA

HFP Howells Family Papers, Houghton Library, Harvard University, Cambridge, MA

HMCC Houghton Mifflin Company Contracts, Houghton Library, Harvard University, Cambridge, MA

HPP Hiram Powers Papers, Archives of American Art, Smithsonian Institution, Washington, DC

HWLFP Henry Wadsworth Longfellow Family Papers (LONG 27930), Longfellow House-Washington's Headquarters National Historic Site, Cambridge, MA

IMC Individual Manuscripts Collection, University of Rochester Rare Books, Special Collections, and Preservation, Rochester, NY

ISGMC Correspondence, Isabella Stewart Gardner Museum Archives, Boston, MA

JFCAP James Freeman Clarke Additional Papers, Houghton Library, Harvard University, Cambridge, MA

JFP Jewett Family Papers, Historic New England, Boston, MA

JHHFP Joseph H. Hayward Family Papers, Massachusetts Historical Society, Boston, MA

JLP Joseph Lee Papers, Massachusetts Historical Society, Boston, MA

JLSP Joseph Lindon Smith Papers, Archives of American Art, Smithsonian Institution, Washington, DC

JRC John Ruskin Collection of Papers, New York Public Library, New York, NY

JRCLFA John Ruskin Correspondence with Lucia and Francesca Alexander, Boston Public Library, Boston, MA

JRLAP James Russell Lowell Additional Papers, Houghton Library, Harvard University, Cambridge, MA

JSCDLB John S. Cogdell Diaries and Letter Books, Winterthur Museum, Garden, and Library, Winterthur, DE

JSL Jared Sparks Letterbooks, Houghton Library,

	Harvard University, Cambridge, MA
JTFC	James Thomas Fields Collection of Autographs and Portraits of Distinguished Women, Houghton Library, Harvard University, Cambridge, MA
JTFPA	James T. Fields Papers and Addenda, Huntington Library, San Marino, CA
LDS	Libro di soci, Gabinetto Vieusseux, Florence, Italy
LFT	Letters to Fanny Talbot, John Rylands University Library, University of Manchester, Manchester, England
LGSANP	Lucia Gray Swett Alexander Notebook and Papers, Boston Athenaeum, Boston, MA
LHWL	Letters to Henry Wadsworth Longfellow, Houghton Library, Harvard University, Cambridge, MA
MACEA	Mandato, Archivio del Cimitero Evangelico agli Allori, Florence, Italy
MEEL	Mary Enid Evelyn Layard, Journals, British Library, London, England
MWPR	Massachusetts Wills and Probate Records, ancestry.com
NYAPCL	New York Arriving Passengers and Crew Lists, ancestry.com
PAF	Papers of the Alexander Family, Schlesinger Library, Harvard University, Cambridge, MA
PCA	Perry Clarke Additions, Massachusetts Historical Society, Boston, MA
PECCA	Papers of Elizabeth Cabot Cary Agassiz, Schlesinger Library, Harvard University, Cambridge, MA
PP	Paget Papers (2nd series), British Library, London, England
PWP	Packard-Whittier Papers, Houghton Library, Harvard University, Cambridge, MA
RDACA	Reports of Deaths of American Citizens Abroad, ancestry.com
RFP	Ropes Family Papers, Massachusetts Historical Society, Boston, MA
SCCAL	Sydney Cockerell Collection of Autograph Letters, National Art Library, Victoria & Albert Museum, London, England
SCSC	Smith College Special Collections, Northampton, MA
SFPDHS	Smith Family Papers, Dublin Historical Society, Dublin, NH
SFPPEM	Silsbee Family Papers, Peabody Essex Museum Phillips Library, Rowley, MA
SGPD	Sarah Gooll Putnam Diaries, Massachusetts Historical Society, Boston, MA
SLFMGJJG	Scrapbook of Letters to Frances Macbeth Glessner and John Jacob Glessner, 1880–1904, Glessner House, Chicago, IL
SSCL	Small Special Collections Library, University of Virginia, Charlottesville, VA
TBG	Thomas Ball Guestbook, Archives of American Art, Smithsonian Institution, Washington, DC
UNDA	University of Notre Dame Archives, Notre Dame, IN
USPA	United States Passport Applications, ancestry.com
VB	Visitor Books, Sir John Soane Museum Archives, London, England
WCCC	William Cornwallis Cartwright Correspondence, Northamptonshire Archives, Northamptonshire, England
WFM	Winslow Family Memorial, Massachusetts Historical Society, Boston, MA
WFP	Wheelwright Family Papers, Massachusetts Historical Society, Boston, MA
WFPH	Wheelwright Family Photographs, Massachusetts Historical Society, Boston, MA
WH	W. Hearn, Diary of a Tour to Italy, British Library, London, England

Books by Francesca Alexander

The following are first editions of each book by Francesca Alexander in English and Italian published during her lifetime:

The Story of Ida, ed. John Ruskin. Sunnyside, Kent: George Allen, 1883.

Ricordi d'Ida, trans. Attilio Guadagni. Florence: George A. Cole, 1884.

Roadside Songs of Tuscany, ed. John Ruskin. Sunnyside, Kent: George Allen, 1885.

Christ's Folk in the Apennine, ed. John Ruskin. Sunnyside, Kent: George Allen, 1887.

Tuscan Songs. Cambridge, MA: Houghton Mifflin & Co., 1897.

The Hidden Servants and Other Very Old Stories. Boston, MA: Little, Brown & Co., 1900.
Ten of the chapters in this book were published individually in Italian translation as:
Il crocifisso della provvidenza, trans. Helen L. Merrick. Venice: Ditta Rizzi, 1908.
Le croci sul muro, trans. Pasquale Lefons. Florence: Tipografia Galileiana, 1909.
I servi occulti, trans. Pasquale Lefons. Florence: Tipografia Galileiana, 1909.
Il vescovo Troilo, trans. Pasquale Lefons. Florence: Tipografia Galileiana, 1909.
Angeli nel cimiterio, trans. Pasquale Lefons. Florence: Tipografia Galileiana, 1910.

La croce d'argento, trans. Pasquale Lefons. Florence: Tipografia Galileiana, 1910
La figlia primogenita del re, trans. Pasquale Lefons. Florence: Tipografia Galileiana, 1910.
Le lacrime della penitenza. Florence: Tipografia Galileiana, 1910.
I lupini, trans. Pasquale Lefons. Florence: Tipografia Galileiana, 1910.
L'origine del granturco, trans. Pasquale Lefons. Florence: Tipografia Galileiana, 1910.

Select Bibliography

Alexander, Constance Grosvenor. *Francesca Alexander. A 'Hidden Servant'*. Cambridge, MA: Harvard University Press, 1927.

B[ale]., E[dwin]. '"Madonina" [*sic*] by "Francesca" Alexander.' *The Magazine of Art* 12 (September 1889): p.392.

Ball, Thomas. *My Threescore Years and Ten*. Boston, MA: Roberts Brothers, 1891.

Bellucci, Paolo. *Poetessa pastora. La storia e i canti di Beatrice di Pian degli Ontani, scoperta dal Tommaseo e amata dal Ruskin*. Florence: Edizioni Medicea, 1986.

Bernabei, Felice. 'Giannina Milli e Francesca Alexander.' *Nuova antologia. Rivista di lettere, scienze ed arti* 205, no.1152 (16 March 1920): pp 178–85.

Brooks, Van Wyck. *The Dream of Arcadia*. New York: Dutton, 1858.

Cabell, Isa Carrington. 'The Author of "The Story of Ida".' *The Critic*. 30 April 1887.

Chiappelli, A. *Una pastora poetessa. Beatrice di Pian degli Ontani*. Florence: Seeber, 1902.

Clegg, Jeanne and Paul Tucker. *Ruskin and Tuscany*. London: Lund Humphries, 1992.

Collingwood, William G. *Ruskin Relics*. London: Isbister & Company Limited, 1903.

D'Astore, Fabio. *'Mi scriva, mi scriva sempre . . .' Regesto delle lettere edite ed inedite di Sigismondo Castromediano*. Lecce: Pensa Multimedia, 1998.

Dickinson, Rachel. *John Ruskin's Correspondence with Joan Severn*. London: Legenda, 2009.

'A Drawing-Room Lecture.' *The Spectator*. 19 June 1883.

Faure, Ruth. 'Frances Alexander.' *The Christian Advocate* 74, no.3 (2 February 1899): p.174.

Feldman, Jessica R. *Victorian Modernism*. Cambridge: Cambridge University Press, 2009.

Felton, Eunice Farley. 'Mrs. Alexander and Her Daughter Francesca.' *Cambridge Historical Society Publications XIV. Proceedings for the Year 1919*. Cambridge, MA: The Society, 1926, pp 106–13.

Francesca Alexander. Boston, MA: Childs Gallery, 1977.

Francesca Alexander. Drawings for the Roadside Songs of Tuscany. Woodside, CA: Sven H.A. Bruntjen Fine Arts, 1981.

Francesca Alexander 1837–1917. A Special Exhibition. Pen and Ink Drawings. New York: Jeffrey Alan Gallery, 1983.

'Francesca's Book.' *Worcester Daily Spy*. 25 December 1883.

G., M.R.F. 'Two Cities of Eastern Italy.' *Springfield Daily Republican*. 4 September 1901.

George, J.-A. 'Translating Tuscany: Francesca Alexander's *Roadside Songs* (1888).' *Forum for Modern Language Studies* 39, no.2 (April 2003): pp 227–38.

Greco, Candido, 'Severino Castorani, scultore di Teramo.' *Rivista Abruzzese* 69, no.1 (2016): pp 76–9.

— 'Ester [*sic*] Frances (Francesca) Alexander. Il suo epistolario con Giannina Milli.' *Bullettino della deputazione abruzzese di storia patria* III (2020): pp 171–219.

Haslam, Ray. 'A Letter from Francesca Alexander.' *The Ruskin Review and Bulletin* 4, no.2 (Lent 2008): pp 52–5.

Johnson, Robert Flynn and Joseph R. Goldyne. *Judging by Appearance. Master Drawings from the Collection of Joseph and Deborah Goldyne.* San Francisco, CA: Fine Arts Museum, 2006.

Leith, Royal. *A Quiet Devotion. The Life and Work of Henry Roderick Newman.* New York: Jordan-Volpe Gallery, 1996.

Leonard & Co. (Boston, MA). *A Large Portion of the Private Collection of Paintings of the Late Francis Alexander.* 24–5 April 1884.

'Letter from Florence.' *The Roman News.* 28 March 1883.

'Literary Notes.' *The American Register.* 26 May 1883.

Lloyd, Anna. *A Memoir. With Extracts from Her Letters.* London: The Cayme Press Limited, 1928.

Lloyd, Jennifer M. 'Raising Lilies: Ruskin and Women.' *Journal of British Studies* 34, no.3 (July 1995): pp 325–50.

'London Letter.' *Cincinnati Commercial Tribune.* 13 April 1883.

Longfellow, Henry Wadsworth. *The Letters of Henry Wadsworth Longfellow*, ed. Andrew Hilen. Cambridge, MA: Harvard University Press, 1966–82.

Lowell, James Russell. 'To F.A.' *The Atlantic Monthly* (May 1875).

Lucas, Matilda. *'Every Body Comes Back to Rome.' The Complete Letters of Matilda Lucas, 1871–1902*, ed. Robert Sénécal. London: Gatehouse Editions, 2013.

Luhan, Mabel Dodge. 'The Story of Francesca.' *The Arts* 8, no.1 (July 1925): pp 24–7.

Madden, Eva. 'Ruskin's Francesca.' *The Christian Register.* 23 November 1916.

'Miss Alexander.' *Manchester Guardian.* 31 January 1917.

'Notes.' *The Tablet.* 9 June 1883.

Nunn, Pamela Gerrish. 'Ruskin's Patronage of Women Artists.' *Woman's Art Journal* 2, no.2 (Autumn 1981–Winter 1982): pp 8–13.

Perkins, Robert F. Jr and William J. Gavin III, eds. *The Boston Athenaeum. Art Exhibition Index 1827–1874.* Boston, MA: The Library, 1980.

Pierce, Catherine W. 'Francis Alexander.' *Old-Time New England* 44, no.2 (October–December 1953): pp 29–46.

— 'Further Notes on Francis Alexander.' *Old-Time New England* 56, no.2 (October–December 1965): pp 35–44.

Pittarello, Ornella, ed. *Lettere d'Amicizia a Marina Sprea Baroni Semitecolo (1881–1909).* Bologna: Casa editrice nuova, 2009.

Polato, Cinzia. 'Caterina Percoto scrittrice e protagonista del suo tempo.' Ph.D. dissertation, Università Ca'Foscari, Venice, 2014.

Ruskin, John. *The Works of John Ruskin*, ed. E.T. Cook and Alexander Wedderburn. London: George Allen, 1903–12.

— *The Diaries of John Ruskin 1874–1889*, ed. Joan Evans and John Howard Whitehouse. Oxford: Clarendon Press, 1959.

Sdegno, Emma. 'Edited by Ruskin: Francesca Alexander's Roadside Songs of Tuscany.' In Emma Sdegno et al., eds. *John Ruskin's Europe. A Collection of Cross-Cultural Essays*, pp 317–34. Venice: Edizioni Ca' Foscari, 2020.

Sica, Grazia Gobbi. *In Loving Memory. Il cimitero agli Allori di Firenze.* Florence: Leo S. Olschki, 2016.

Spates, James. L. 'Ruskin's Life: A Radical Revision.' www.whyruskin.wordpress.com. 2020.

Spielmann, M.H. 'Francesca Alexander, and "The Roadside Songs of Tuscany".' *Magazine of Art* 18 (June 1895): pp 295–9.

Stanton, Theodore. 'Artists in Florence.' *Daily Inter Ocean.* 13 July 1890.

Stillman, W.J. 'Francesca's Country.' *The Critic* 9, no.234 (23 June 1888): pp 301–2.

Swett, Lucia Gray. *Sisters of Reparatrice.* Boston, MA: Lee and Shepard, 1902.

— *John Ruskin's Letters to Francesca and Memoirs of the Alexanders.* Boston, MA: Lothrop, Lee & Shepard Co., 1931.

Taylor, Bayard. 'Letters. American Sculptors in Florence.' *New-York Tribune.* 23 April 1868.

Van Dyke, John C. 'An Exponent of Pre-Raphaelism.' *The Dial.* 16 March 1898.

Warrack, Grace, ed. and trans. *Florilegio di canti toscani: Folk Songs of the Tuscan Hills.* London: Alexander Moring Ltd, 1914.

— *Dal cor gentil d'Italia: Canti dal Veneto alla Sardegna. Out of the Heart of Italy: Folk Songs from Venetia to Sardinia.* Oxford: Basil Blackwell, 1925.

Whellens, Arthur. "A Tuscan Sibyl": A Note on Beatrice di Pian degli Ontani.' In Jeanne Clegg and Paul

Tucker, eds. *The Dominion of Daedalus*, pp 50–57. St Albans: Bretham Press, 1994.

Whiting, Lilian. 'A Truly Remarkable Woman.' *Duluth News-Tribune.* 7 June 1910.

— *The Golden Road.* Boston, MA: Little, Brown, and Company, 1918.

Whittier, John Greenleaf. *The Bay of Seven Islands, and Other Poems.* Boston, MA: Houghton, Mifflin and Co., 1883.

Wortham, Thomas. 'Lowell's "Agassiz" and Mrs. Alexander.' *The Yale University Library Gazette* 45, no.3 (January 1971): pp 118–22.

Zimmern, Helen. 'Ruskin's Florentine Francesca.' *Daily Inter Ocean.* 30 March 1890.

— 'Old Florentine Villas. Medieval Palaces with Wonderful Stories of Tradition and Legend.' *Daily Inter Ocean.* 18 January 1891.

Acknowledgements

This book has been on my mind for many years. It began as a chapter in a larger, and still in progress, book about American women artists in nineteenth-century Italy. But that chapter never seemed to fit; unlike the other women I examine, Francesca was largely unconcerned with achieving success as an artist, and she lived in Florence rather than Rome. While I mulled over what to do – because I couldn't imagine *not* doing something – I was grateful to Lynn Catterson for including my talk on Francesca in a panel at the College Art Association conference in 2015, to Gillian Malpass for discussing Francesca's life with me in 2017, and to Nigel Farrow for reaching out enthusiastically in 2021; they helped me decide to turn that chapter into this book.

The challenges of researching and writing a book during a global pandemic were daunting. Friends and colleagues have assisted with enthusiasm, references and photographs; and curators, librarians and archivists have been incredibly patient with remote queries and visits. I should single out Judy Acs at Weschler's Auctioneers and Appraisers; Albert & Shirley Small Special Collections Library at the University of Virginia; Antiquariat Clemens Paulusch; Berg Collection at the New York Public Library; Bienecke Library at Yale; Margarita Blanco; Marisa Bourgoin at the Archives of American Art; Norma Broude and Mary Garrard; Andrew Brown at Royal Collection Trust; Danielle Carrabino at Smith College Museum of Art; Community of the Sisters of St Anne-Bethany; Congregazione Armena Mechitarista at San Lazzaro, Venice; Flora Dennis and Alexander Masters; Will Evans, Lauren Graves and Christina Michelon at the Boston Athenaeum; Laurent Ferri at Cornell University; Antonella Fumo at the Procuratoria di San Marco; Michael M. Gorman; Kate Hanson-Plass at Longfellow House-Washington's Headquarters; Erica Hirshler and Patrick Murphy at the Museum of Fine Arts Boston; Hobart and William Smith Library; Zaixin Hong; Jessie Hopper at the Concord Free Public Library; Diana Larsen at Boston College's McMullen Museum of Art; Heping Liu; Hannah Lund at Leighton House; Elizabeth Mann at Sotheby's; John and Mary McGuigan; Paolo Moretti at *Il Cristiano*; Peta Motture and Alistair McFarlane; Samantha Nicolas at Suffolk County Probate and Family Court; Mick O'Malley; Sue Palmer at Sir John Soane's Museum; Roberto Pecchioli at Chiesa di Vigna Vecchia; Debra Pincus; Francis Plowden; Princeton University Library Special Collections; Katherine Rabogliatti; Mary Ross; Kerry Schauber at the Memorial Art Gallery at the University of Rochester; Sheffield Museums Trust; Grazia Gobbi Sica; Nathaniel Silver at the Isabella Stewart Gardner Museum; Carl Brandon Strehlke; Anna Svensson; University of Notre Dame Archives; and Jeremy Warren. Staff in Archives & Special Collections at the Boston Public Library, knowing I was desperate to examine their Alexander material following a multi-year closure for renovations, invited me in at the first possible moment and were unfailingly helpful. At Wellesley College, Ruth Rogers and Mariana Oller always provided access and critical assistance in Special Collections, while Marci Hahn-Fabris and

Abi Stark in Library and Technology Services expertly photographed whatever I needed. Alice T. Friedman, Jack Jarzavek, Martha McNamara and Nancy Siegel read my manuscript in multiple iterations, and offered endless advice and encouragement. And, of course, Erika Gaffney and the team at Lund Humphries turned my manuscript into the book you now hold.

Although I could not find many of the manuscripts, drawings and paintings mentioned in her early biographies, I did find a community of people interested in Francesca and her art. Francesca Baldry's work on the Acton Photographic Archive at Villa La Pietra confirmed my hypotheses about the Alexander collection. William Tyre at Glessner House tirelessly sought out the connections between Francesca and the Glessners. Royal and Mary Joan Leith shared otherwise impossible-to-find references. Paul Worman's enthusiasm and great generosity transformed my understanding of her early work. Sven Bruntjen helped me track drawings that passed through Childs Gallery in Boston in the late 1970s, and he put me in contact with Joseph Goldyne, whose trust in me was remarkable and so very appreciated.

My research was funded in part by Wellesley College as well as an Eccles Fellowship at the British Library, an Andrew Oliver Short-Term Fellowship at the Massachusetts Historical Society, an Ailsa Mellon Bruce Visiting Senior Fellowship at the Center for Advanced Study in the Visual Arts, National Gallery of Art, a Short-Term Fellowship at the Winterthur Museum, Garden & Library, and the Tavolozza Foundation. Tavolozza also provided for the purchase of many of my illustrations, and Tavolozza and the Estelle Trust contributed to the costs associated with book production; Andrew Shennan at Wellesley College stepped in at the last minute to provide further, much-needed help. As this is the first monograph on Francesca Alexander, I was eager to provide a thorough understanding of her art and life. But an ongoing struggle in art history publishing remains the costs associated with both procuring illustrations and reproducing them, and those costs are shouldered increasingly by authors. I am grateful to the institutions and private collectors who provided scans and allowed me to publish them at no or nominal cost in the interest of scholarship and the promotion of their collections. But I also had to make hard choices; when institutions insisted on monetizing their collections, I was forced to either not illustrate their objects or forego illustrating other objects because of budget constraints. I very reluctantly paid for new photography or high fees if I had no alternative; Francesca's art, beyond some of the folios in *Tuscan Songs*, is rarely reproduced and this meant new photography was often necessary. The shocking costs levied by some institutions and organizations infringe on scholarship and they need to be addressed by the discipline at large.

Tony Ratyna, and Primo and Secondo, lived with this book for much longer than I promised (which seems to be true of all of my projects), yet they never failed to encourage and sustain me; I dedicate this book to them.

Image Credits

The publisher would like to thank the copyright holders for granting permission to reproduce the images illustrated. Every attempt has been made to trace accurate ownership of copyrighted images in this book. Any errors or omissions will be corrected in subsequent editions provided notification is sent to the publisher. The copyright for reproduction of photos is listed below.

Index

Note: Italic page numbers indicate figures and Francesca Alexander is abbreviated to FA in headings. Because much of the book is about the Alexander family and Florence, specific page numbers for those topics have not been provided.